HAROLD
AND
JACK

HAROLD
AND
JACK

THE REMARKABLE FRIENDSHIP OF
PRIME MINISTER MACMILLAN
AND PRESIDENT KENNEDY

CHRISTOPHER SANDFORD

Prometheus Books

59 John Glenn Drive
Amherst, New York 14228

Published 2014 by Prometheus Books

Cover image © gettyimages
Jacket design by Nicole Sommer-Lecht

Inquiries should be addressed to
Prometheus Books
59 John Glenn Drive
Amherst, New York 14228
VOICE: 716–691–0133
FAX: 716–691–0137
WWW.PROMETHEUSBOOKS.COM

18 17 16 15 14   5 4 3 2 1

Library of Congress Cataloging-in-Publication Data

Sandford, Christopher, 1956–
    Harold and Jack : the remarkable friendship of prime minister Macmillan and President Kennedy / by Christopher Sandford.
        pages cm
    Includes bibliographical references and index.
    ISBN 978-1-61614-935-2 (hardcover) — ISBN 978-1-61614-936-9 (ebook)
    1. Kennedy, John F. (John Fitzgerald), 1917–1963. 2. Macmillan, Harold, 1894–1986.
3. United States—Foreign relations—Great Britain. 4. Great Britain—Foreign relations—United States. 5. United States—Foreign relations—1961–1963—Decision making. 6. Great Britain—Foreign relations—1945–1964—Decision making. 7. Presidents—United States—Biography.
8. Prime ministers—Great Britain—Biography. I. Title.

E183.8.G7S26 2014
327.7304109'046—dc23
                                                                                2014009989

Printed in the United States of America

For Ted Stanley
(1927–2013)

"We need first of all to be thoroughly frightened."
> —Harold Urey, winner of the Nobel Prize in
> Chemistry, in a speech on the atom bomb,
> December 1945

"Mr. Kennedy and Mr. Macmillan are the wickedest people in the story of man."
> —Bertrand Russell, winner of the Nobel Prize
> in Literature, September 1961

"I have just finished watching you on television. There is nothing in all these last long years that has moved me so much, or made me so proud."
> —Jacqueline Kennedy Onassis, writing to Macmillan,
> November 1972

CONTENTS

ACKNOWLEDGMENTS

This is not a book in any way authorized by the estates of John F. Kennedy or Harold Macmillan, nor is it a biography of either man. Anyone interested in reading more about one or both of them will find some suggestions in the bibliography at the end of the book. Instead, I've tried to write a comparative study of the two men, in some ways the odd couple of the Atlantic alliance, whose brief shared time in office (just thirty-three months) saw some of the great set-piece dramas of the postwar era, including the Berlin Wall, the Bay of Pigs, nuclear proliferation, the Cuban missile crisis, a whole host of regional clashes from British Guiana to the Congo, and the start of the long American ordeal in Vietnam. Many historians have touched on the special relationship between Kennedy and Macmillan, but no one, so far as I know, has attempted to place their lives, and the lives of their friends and family, alongside each other and to follow them together in those uniquely charged days. Other than the sweep of the story itself, I can offer only the modest credential of sharing with Macmillan the distinction of an American mother and a British father and of having gone on to divide my life almost equally between the two countries. As a child in Washington, DC, I can remember the excitement of Kennedy's inauguration on a day of truly Siberian cold, and, back in the hot English summer of 1963, like millions of others, I thrilled to the long run of sex-and-spy scandals that seemed to engulf Macmillan's government on a daily basis, and which, along with the coming of the Beatles and one or two other factors, was surely among the birth cries of what we now think of as "the Sixties." More than this, I have tried to pursue the story in a spirit of honest inquiry. Some of the individuals or organizations who helped in the research are shown here, and a fuller list of sources appears at the end of the book. I only wish I could blame any of those named for the shortcomings of the text. They are mine alone.

For archive material, interviews, or advice, I should thank the following: Abacus; the *American Conservative*; the Avon Papers at Birmingham University, United Kingdom; Andrew Baird; the Bodleian Library, Oxford; Bookfinder; the British Library; British Newspaper Library; Kia Campbell; *Chronicles*; the CIA;

Companies House, London; the Devonshire Collection at Chatsworth House; Patrick Dowdall; the Dwight D. Eisenhower Presidential Library, Abilene, Kansas; Paul Elgood; the FBI—Freedom of Information Division; General Register Office, London; Tess Hines; the John F. Kennedy Presidential Library and Museum, Boston; *Hansard*; Barbara Levy; Antony Lewis; the Library of Congress; the Massachusetts Historical Society; Millbanksystems.com; the *Missoulian*; Steven L. Mitchell; Mariel Bard; National Security Archives; Renton Public Library; Jill Rolfe; the Salisbury Papers at Hatfield House; Sam Satchell; Seaside Library; the *Seattle Times*; the Seeley Library, Cambridge; the *Spectator*; Andrew Stuart; UK National Archives; the US National Archives and Records Administration; the University Library, Cambridge; University of Montana, Missoula; University of Puget Sound, Tacoma, Washington; Vital Records; James Waters; Emily Watlington; and Peter Wigan.

And on a personal basis: Rev. Maynard Atik; Pete Barnes; Hilary and Robert Bruce; Jane Camillin; Paul Camillin; Don Carson; Common Ground; Tim Cox; Celia Culpan; the Davenport; Monty Dennison; the Dowdall family; John and Barbara Dungee; Explorer West; Malcolm Galfe; the Gay Hussar; Gethsemane Lutheran Church; James Graham; Tom Graveney; Grumbles; Masood Halim; the late Judy Hentz; Alastair Hignell; Charles Hillman; Alex Holmes; Hotel Vancouver; Jo Jacobius; Lincoln Kamell; the late Tom Keylock; Terry Lambert; Belinda Lawson; Todd Linse; the Lorimers; Les McBride; the Macris; Lee Mattson; Jim and Rana Meyersahm; Sheila Mohn; the Morgans; John and Colleen Murray; Chuck Ogmund; Phil Oppenheim; Valya Page; Robin Parish; Peter Perchard; Greg Phillips; Chris Pickrell; Roman Polanski; the Prins family; the late Robert Relyea; Scott P. Richert; Ailsa Rushbrooke; Debbie Saks; Sam; the late Sefton Sandford; Sue Sandford; Peter Scaramanga; Seattle C. C.; Fred and Cindy Smith; Rev. and Mrs. Harry Smith; the Spaldings; the Stanley family; Thaddeus Stuart; Jack Surendranath; Diana Turner; Ben and Mary Tyvand; Diana Villar; Lisbeth Vogl; the late Chris West; the Willis Fleming family; Heng and Lange Woon.

And a low bow, as always, to Karen and Nicholas Sandford.

C. S.

1

MENDING FENCES

The weather in southern England was warming up; the sky above rural Sussex was cloudless. The British and American flags fluttered over the prime minister's country house, Birch Grove, which had seen a riot of activity over the previous days. Rooms had been hurriedly painted, the lawn re-turfed, and banks of flowers laid out in mutually patriotic shades of red, white, and blue. Workmen had descended from London to assemble a huge canopied bed built to the visiting president's specifications and to help ease his chronic back pain, a special rocking chair was found for his use during the talks. Caterers had followed, bearing trays of cakes with colored sugar, and a butler was commandeered from Government Hospitality in Whitehall. Upstairs in his childhood bedroom, the sixty-nine-year-old premier, Harold Macmillan, awoke each morning that week to the sound of hammers and saws, the shouted orders and grumbles of builders, and all the animation that marked the refurbishment of his family home into the setting of a great transatlantic summit. It was a peculiarly British affair, with many last-minute improvisations. On the morning of the visit, the butler—already in full regalia— and a party of gardeners, chauffeurs, and junior civil servants were still hard at work erecting a marquee on the back lawn. Restaurants and pubs in the neighboring villages had been requisitioned to house and feed the president's 120-strong retinue, while large crowds of the curious or the obsessed began to form outside the estate's front gates, some with flags, others with banners protesting the visit. Macmillan himself wrote of the "fantastic, even romantic atmosphere that prevailed during these thrilling hours. . . . Inside the house it seemed more like a play or rather the mad rehearsal for a play, than a grave international conference."[1] Shortly before six on a then-overcast Saturday evening, amid new frenzies of excitement, an enormous olive-green helicopter descended onto the nearby park. Macmillan's memory of the event was rhapsodic:

I can see [the president] now, stepping from the machine, this splendid, young, gay figure, followed by his team of devoted adherents. Never has a man been so well or so loyally served. Until he left, the whole of our little world was dominated by the sudden arrival and equally sudden departure of leading figures in the drama.[2]

It was June 29, 1963, and the seventh meeting between Macmillan and his American counterpart, forty-six-year-old John F. Kennedy, since the president's inauguration twenty-nine months earlier. Between them they had rescued the transatlantic Special Relationship after the rupture of the Suez Crisis, and done so at a time of uniquely high tensions around the world. Among other political or military challenges, their brief shared time in office had seen the coming of the Berlin Wall, the apparent risk to world peace posed by the Soviet Union and its territorial ambitions everywhere from Laos to British Guiana, the very real threat of the Cuban missile crisis, and a bitter internecine dispute about Britain's possession of an independent nuclear deterrent. These were just the set-piece dramas. Through it all, the two leaders had exchanged not only formal messages but also a steady flow of handwritten notes, Christmas and birthday cards, personal gifts, congratulations, and, on occasion, condolences—Macmillan felt a "genuine personal warmth" for his younger colleague and sent what the First Lady later wrote back to and described as "the most tender of letters" when the president and his wife lost their newborn son in August 1963. The premier's decision to address his boyish-looking counterpart as "Friend" or "Dear Friend" seems to have been a conscious step in the gradual assumption of a more human "special relationship," something like that between an Oxford don and an exceptionally gifted undergraduate. At Birch Grove, Macmillan wrote, "There was none of the solemnity which usually characterises such meetings. After all, we were all friends; and the whole atmosphere was that of a country house party, to which had been added a garden party and a dance. . . . The President seemed in the highest spirits and was particularly charming to [my wife] and the children. None of [his] disabilities seemed to have the slightest effect upon his temperament. Of our party, as doubtless of many others, he was what is called 'the life and soul.'"[3]

Just twenty-four hours later, the Secret Service having reconnoitered, the president left as he came, by helicopter. "Before he said goodbye," wrote Macmillan, "we discussed once more our plans for frequent communication, by telegram or telephone; with another meeting before Christmas or, at the latest, in the New Year. Hatless, with his brisk step, and combining that indescribable look of a boy on a holiday with the dignity of a President and Commander-in-Chief, he walked across the garden to the machine. We stood and waved. I can see the helicopter now, sailing across the valley above the heavily laden, lush foliage of oaks and beech at the end of June."[4]

After more than six years in office, Macmillan found himself just then governing Britain in as turbulent a period as the nation had known outside of wartime. The early part of 1963 had seen a series of security scandals, culminating in the defection to Moscow of Kim Philby, formerly the head of the branch of MI6 specifically charged with investigating communist activity. Meanwhile, Britain's long-running application for membership of the European Economic Community had been summarily vetoed by President de Gaulle of France. At around the same time, some seventy thousand antinuclear protesters had taken to the streets of London, demanding a change of government. To cap it all, thick, Dickensian fog had regularly settled on southern England, leaving spectacular rime deposits on streets and houses, followed by the coldest, and certainly most protracted, winter in two hundred years. There was no desolation more complete than Britain in the grip of repeated winter storms prior to the arrival of widespread domestic central heating. One way or another, these were trying times for the apparently decrepit prime minister known for his shuffling gait and capacious plus-four trousers. Speaking in the House of Commons earlier in the week of Kennedy's visit, Macmillan had been asked by the Labour MP Marcus Lipton whether "he does not feel that the President should be given the opportunity of exchanging views with a new Prime Minister, and not one who is under notice to quit, and whose political status at home and abroad is inevitably impaired?" Macmillan replied that no, he didn't think so.[5] In the wake of the sex scandal involving John Profumo, the British war minister, and certain other difficulties that summer, much of the country as a whole had begun to wonder if the PM might not finally resign or at least test his popularity in a general election. A Gallup poll brought to Kennedy's notice shortly before he arrived for his meeting at Birch Grove showed 71 percent of the British public favoring a change of leadership. To no avail: A month after the president's visit, Macmillan faced a meeting of his party parliamentary colleagues where "I was received with great applause and banging of desks. I spoke for 40 minutes, on broad policy, home and abroad. . . . When I sat down, after simply saying about myself that my sole purpose was to serve the Party and the Nation and to secure a victory at the Election, there was great applause. . . . Altogether it was a triumphant vote of confidence."[6] From a public approval rating of minus seventeen in July, Macmillan rebounded to the relative prosperity of minus five in August. The worst of the Profumo business was already behind him, he told Kennedy, and he once again "confidently looked forward" to their next meeting, and to many more after that.

For once, the subtle Macmillan touch failed him. The Western world's two most powerful leaders would not meet again. Well before Christmas, the prime minister had left office, and the president had been cut down by an assassin's bullet.

═══

In what Macmillan called "my responsible and rather lonely position," he was sustained by a particularly close—if not untested—friendship with two successive American presidents. There is almost always a human factor in a politician's relations with other politicians. In Macmillan's case, this was especially true. What often seems to have been overlooked in the analysis of policy, economics, and shared cultural values that constituted the Atlantic alliance of the day was that the strongest and most enduring link between the two countries was a warmly personal one. For each leader, appearing on the other's home stage was a badge of honor, a pilgrimage back to the scene of his most character-forming family history. For Kennedy, there was the seminal year he spent at the age of eighteen studying under Harold Laski, the firebrand political theorist at the London School of Economics, where he developed not only a taste for high-born British society, and more particularly for her young women, but also a clearer understanding of the part played in a public figure's life by social and religious inequality. "In speaking of Boston, he [Laski] said, 'Boston is a state of mind'—and as a Jew, he could understand what it is to be an Irishman in Boston," Kennedy wrote in his diary. "That last remark reveals the fundamental, activating force of Mr. Laski's life—a powerful spirit doomed to an inferior position because of race—a position that all of his economic and intellectual superiority cannot raise him out of."[7] These words would resonate a generation later, when Kennedy sought to be the first Roman Catholic to occupy the White House. In May 1959, a quarter of all respondents said that they would not vote for a Catholic as US president, no matter how well qualified he might otherwise be for the job.

Two years after leaving Harold Laski's tutelage, Kennedy was back in London to spend the summer working at the US embassy. He returned once more in the spring of 1939, "having a great time," he wrote, as Europe drifted into war. Although notionally researching a thesis about international law and diplomacy, he admitted he was not "doing much work, but have been sporting around in my morning coat, my 'Anthony Eden' black Homburg and white gardenia." Kennedy was thrilled to have met the king "at a Court Levee. It takes place in the morning and you wear tails. The King stands and you go up and bow. Met Queen Mary and was at tea with the Princess Elizabeth with whom I made a great deal of time. Thursday night—am going to Court in my new silk breeches, which are cut to my crotch tightly, and in which I look mighty attractive."[8] Six months after he wrote this, the twenty-two-year-old Kennedy was with his parents and his sister Kathleen in the strangers' gallery of the House of Commons to hear the British prime minister Neville Chamberlain explain his country's decision to declare war on Nazi Germany. Immediately following this, he had his first taste of practical diplomacy when he was sent to Scotland to help console the distressed American survivors of the SS *Athenia*, which had been sunk by a German submarine while on her way from Glasgow to Montreal, with the loss of 117 lives. These were not, perhaps, the standard experiences of a young man who was yet to graduate from Harvard. The twin results of Kennedy's early adventures in Britain were a lifelong fascination with that country's social and cultural elite and, more immediately, his publication of a thesis on Chamberlain's appeasement policy, titled *Why England Slept*. The author Paul Johnson suggests in his book *A History of the American People* that "Old Joe [Kennedy's father] and his men turned *Why England Slept* into a bestseller, partly by using influence with publishers, [and] partly by buying 30,000–40,000 copies, which were secretly stored at the family compound at Hyannis Port." Adding to this intellectual and emotional connection, there was also a personal Kennedy connection to the old country. In May 1944, John's younger sister Kathleen, or "Kick," married William Cavendish, heir apparent to the tenth Duke of Devonshire, who as a captain in the British army died in action in Belgium only three months later. Since Harold Macmillan's wife was herself the daughter of the ninth duke, this made him Kathleen's uncle by marriage. The living relationship was to be tragically short-lived. Just four years after her husband's death, Kathleen was killed in a plane crash while on her way from Paris to the French Riviera. She was twenty-eight. In the perhaps fanciful pop-psychological account of one Kennedy biographer, Macmillan thus became "the alternate father whom in death Kick had bestowed on her brother Jack."

Macmillan also had profound personal links underpinning the political Special Relationship. He was very proud of his ancestry, which he could trace back for dozens of generations and frequently did. Although often portrayed as the model of an English gentleman, not least by himself, Macmillan was actually part of a colorful Scots-Canadian tapestry. American blood, too, flowed in his veins. His mother, Helen Artemisia Tarleton Belles, was born in Indianapolis in the middle of 1856 (precise local records weren't kept at the time), and Nellie, as she preferred to call herself, grew up there and in the nearby hamlet of Spencer, a community of some 1,500 souls nestled on the banks of the White River. In January 1876, at the age of nineteen, she sailed to France in order to study music and pursue an understandable wish to see something of the world beyond rural southern Indiana. On November 22, 1884, Nellie married a thirty-one-year-old publisher named Maurice Macmillan, whose people came from the remote regions of Kintyre in Argyle, an area settled almost entirely by sheep. Their third son, Harold, born in February 1894, was later to skillfully portray himself for public consumption as the product of generations of simple Scottish crofters. In fact, Maurice had led a slightly more cosmopolitan life than the legend of a bonneted, claymore-wielding highland laddy insists: after taking a first-class degree in Classics at Cambridge, he had taught at St. Paul's School in London and then joined the family publishing firm, for whom he traveled on extended book-buying tours of Europe. It was while on a visit to Paris that he met Nellie Belles, whom he described in a note to his brother as "a dark-eyed beauty who wore exquisitely made shoes on her tiny feet, and spoke exuberant French in a gay American accent."

There was to be a moving scene in September 1956, when the sixty-two-year-old British chancellor of the exchequer traveled to Spencer to read the lesson in his mother's Methodist church and talk about her life. "I owe her everything," Harold Macmillan said, in a stirring speech that was full of family pathos. "I found it rather difficult to get through, without breaking down," the normally unflappable politician later wrote in his diary. "I really felt that my mother was there watching us and enjoying the satisfaction of so many of her hopes and ambitions for me. When I remember all that I owe to her, it's difficult to express what she did for me."[9] It did not go unnoticed that Macmillan selected as his text Matthew 25:14–30, the Parable of the Talents, traditionally seen as an exhortation to Christians to use their God-given gifts wisely. Accompanied by the British ambassador, Macmillan later attended a number of local events to celebrate the centenary year of Nellie's birth. She had passed onto her children a "rudimentary culture," he went on to tell a political colleague, and, far more than the diffident Maurice, she had been "the motivating force . . . the dynamo whose ambition [for] me never stopped ticking" in his early life. The dictum that "a man who has been the indisputable favorite of his mother keeps forever the feeling of a conqueror" was undoubtedly true here. Following the church service in Spencer, Macmillan laid a wreath on the grave of his grandfather, Dr. Joshua Belles, "an overwhelming rite" during which he wept openly.

Adding further poignancy to these events, they came as a sentimental prelude to the gravest crisis in Anglo-American relations since the Second World War. From Indiana, Macmillan flew through a somehow appropriate thunderstorm into Washington, DC. According to his diary, on the morning of September 25, he was smuggled into the White House by "an ordinary car (not the Rolls), and taken to a little used and private entrance," so as not to alert the press, for a meeting with President Eisenhower. The crucial issue at stake was what action to take against the Egyptian dictator Colonel Gamal Nasser following his nationalization of the Suez Canal Company, which was not only in apparent breach of the 1888 Treaty of Constantinople but also, of more practical concern, a serious threat to Britain's oil supplies. Macmillan wrote that Eisenhower's manner "could not have been more cordial," and he came away convinced that the United States would not oppose—in fact, would discreetly support—the use of force against Nasser. This was a serious misapprehension. Five weeks later, when Anglo-French bombing raids all but destroyed the Egyptian air force, Eisenhower's anger was sufficient for William Clark, Prime Minister Eden's press secretary, to recall picking up the transatlantic phone and hearing a flow of presidential language at the other end "so furious I had to hold the instrument away from my ear." Nor was this just personal rancor: the US administration was soon moved to join with the Soviet Union in tabling a UN Security Council resolution calling on all fellow members to refrain from the use of force in Egypt. Following that, the Americans convened an emergency meeting of the UN General Assembly to secure an immediate ceasefire in the region. The motion was passed by sixty-four votes to five. Only Britain, France, Israel, Australia, and New Zealand opposed it. Somewhat disarmingly, Macmillan was to acknowledge, "We certainly made a profound miscalculation as to the likely reaction in Washington to the Franco-British intervention. . . . We altogether failed to appreciate the force of the resentment. . . . For this I carry a heavy responsibility. I knew Eisenhower well. . . . I believed the Americans would issue a protest [in] public, but that they would in their hearts be glad to see the matter brought to a conclusion."[10]

It's worth dwelling on the tragicomic humbling of the British government at Suez a moment longer, if only to show that it was not a foregone conclusion the Special Relationship would even still exist in the 1960s. The details of the fiasco are a reminder of how volatile the whole alliance was during Eisenhower's second term in office and Macmillan's first. In July 1955, the United States and the United Kingdom had cohosted a summit in Geneva that saw the first major public appearance as Soviet head of state of Nikita Khrushchev. Macmillan was not initially impressed. "How can this fat, vulgar man, with his pig eyes and his ceaseless flow of talk, really be the head—the aspirant Tsar—of all these millions of people and this vast country?" he asked in his diary.[11] Confronted by the simultaneously ludicrous and terrifying Khrushchev, the Western delegations had come together in like-minded alliance. Britain would always find the United States "like family" and "sympathetic," Eisenhower had assured Macmillan and Eden, even if their joint discussions with the Russians in Geneva on matters such as German reunification and nuclear-arms inspections yielded little of substance. All parties had at least agreed on "the futility of armed confrontation in the atomic age," since any nation that used its new weapons of mass destruction faced the certainty of being destroyed itself. Translating these remarks for the press on his return to London, Macmillan made headlines by announcing, "There ain't gonna be no war."[12]

This core conviction was enough, Macmillan felt, to "sustain and fortify" the Anglo-American alliance into the nuclear era. Put more bluntly, Britain could no longer afford to deviate significantly from American positions. But only fifteen months later, the "family" began to tear itself apart, and Eisenhower went on to make a series of blistering attacks on the British and French "idiocy" in Suez. In the measured words of Winthrop Aldrich, the US ambassador in London, the administration was "not pleased" with her principal allies, "not only [for] not letting us know, but actually deceiving us as to what would happen . . . the President just went off the deep end."[13] In a sign of how the grass roots of friendship had suddenly withered, Macmillan complained that there was now a conspiracy by the American authorities to undermine the British economy. In his memoirs he wrote of the United States resorting to a form of financial blackmail by "selling of sterling by the Federal Reserve Bank." Attempting to draw on British gold reserves with the International Monetary Fund, Macmillan "received the reply that the American Government would not agree to the technical procedure until we had agreed to a ceasefire [in Suez]." One large nation had effectively frozen the bank account of a friendly, smaller nation. On November 6, it was left for Macmillan to bitterly tell his cabinet colleagues, "There [has] been a serious run on the pound, viciously orchestrated in Washington."[14] It was all a long way from the communal goodwill and family spirit of just a few weeks earlier in Spencer, Indiana.

On October 30, as the clock ticked down toward the use of force in Egypt, the British cabinet had "proposed to send notes [to Nasser] in order to guarantee freedom of transit through the Canal. . . . It was proposed that if, at the expiration of 12 hours from the delivery of these notes, [he] had failed to undertake to comply with the requirements stated in them, British and French forces should intervene in order to enforce compliance."[15] (With the collusion of the British and French, Israel had attacked the Egyptian army in Sinai the day before, quickly occupying the whole peninsula up to the eastern edge of the canal.) Even then, it was recognized that such action might not be well received by an American president who was just a week away from a closely contested national election. "We should do our utmost to reduce the offence to US public opinion which [is] liable to be caused by our notes," it was recorded by the British cabinet. "Our reserves of gold and dollars [are] still falling at a dangerously rapid rate; and in view of the extent to which we might have to rely on American economic assistance, we [can]not afford to alienate the US Government more than absolutely necessary."[16]

Since some thirty-five books—not to mention fifty-eight years' worth of scholarly articles, self-serving memoirs and interviews, and a continuing lively Internet exchange—are all available on the subject, it's perhaps best to be brief on the specific events that followed in November and December 1956 and that led directly to the resignation of Anthony Eden and to his replacement by Harold Macmillan.

On November 3, in a rare Saturday session, the House of Commons broke up amid what the Speaker called "the worst uproar in modern parliamentary history" while debating Suez. At first light on the fifth, British and French paratroopers landed at Port Said and swiftly advanced on the Canal area, amid Soviet threats to launch retaliatory attacks on Western Europe. On the sixth, Eisenhower was duly reelected by a popular majority of 58 percent to 42 percent. This was by no means to effect a sudden new alignment of interests in the Middle East. Nor was it the end of the personal and political fallout from the Suez escapade. At the height of the crisis, Eisenhower's secretary of state, John Foster Dulles, a stereotypical 1950s public official to look at and listen to, with some of the same general demeanor of an Old Testament prophet (and cordially loathed by the British), had been rushed to the hospital for emergency cancer surgery. In London, Anthony Eden was running a fever of 105° and living on a diet of stimulants and tranquillizers. Within twenty-four hours of the decision to invade Suez, Macmillan was warning his colleagues that "in view of the financial and economic pressures we must stop"[17] the action, a U-turn characterized as "first in, first out" in the caustic words of Labour's Harold Wilson in the House of Commons. On the seventh, Eisenhower acknowledged that recent tensions in the alliance had been "a family spat,"[18] and that it would likely be poor judgment for the British to seek an early summit with him. In the week of November 12, the United Kingdom lost a further $80 million in gold reserves, and Macmillan told the cabinet it "might shortly face the grave choice of deciding whether to mobilise all our financial resources in order to maintain the sterling/dollar rate, [or] let it find its level."[19] On the twenty-second, Anglo-French troops began to pull back from the canal zone in a phased withdrawal continuing through December. Since control of the canal then reverted to Nasser, who soon refused passage to most Western ships, which led in turn to fuel rationing in Britain, the operation could not be called a strategic success. Grotesque though it is to use the word *only* in relation to casualties, it might be applied on a relative basis here. The British and French lost sixteen and ten men, with ninety-six and thirty-three wounded, respectively. There were approximately 330 Israeli deaths. The Egyptians suffered roughly three thousand casualties and won a considerable propaganda victory. Among other lessons of Suez, it seemed to Macmillan, was that Britain should ideally "not again be allowed to find [itself] on the wrong side of a major policy dispute" with Washington.[20]

As the recriminations continued in London, Anthony Eden took his doctor's advice and flew to Jamaica for a rest cure. The British gold reserves continued to plummet. Shortly after Eden's departure, George Humphrey, the US secretary of the treasury, placed a call to the caretaker prime minister "Rab" Butler. To do so, he "had shut himself with the telephone in the meat safe so as to avoid the intrusions of my family." Humphrey's essential message was that Washington was now prepared to support the pound and "supply the 'fig leaf' which the British say they need to cover their nakedness in withdrawing from Suez . . . providing they [get] out of the area at once."[21] On December 12, Humphrey and a convalescing Dulles visited London and Paris for fence-mending meetings with the allies. Macmillan told them that "he, personally, was very unhappy with the way in which the matter was handled, [but] that he had had no real choice but to back Eden. . . . He said the British action was the last gasp of a declining power and that perhaps in 200 years the United States 'would know how we felt.'"[22] Two days later, Eden returned to England from his tropical retreat. He struggled on for a further three weeks, but on January 8, 1957, told colleagues "that he had had a bad report on his health . . . [His doctors] had advised that it was no use his trying to go on. . . . While the pain continued he could only sleep under dope." Eden resigned his office the following day. During this same febrile time in international affairs, the Soviet Union had threatened Britain with atomic weapons unless she cease and desist in Egypt, and within twenty-four hours of that crushed the Hungarian revolution at the cost of some twenty-two thousand casualties. Between January 8 and 9, the fifth Marquess of Salisbury ("Bobbety"), as Lord President of the Council, interviewed the cabinet one by one and, with his much-parodied speech impediment, asked each one whether he was for "Wab" or "Hawold." (There was thought to have been only one vote for Wab, and two abstentions.) In the early afternoon of the tenth, Salisbury and Winston Churchill went to Buckingham Palace to advise the queen on her choice of Eden's successor. The matter was quickly concluded. "The next event," Salisbury wrote, "so far as I at 2.45 was concerned, was a message from Harold asking me to go and see him. . . . I walked along the passage and found him in very good spirits."[23] At his moment of supreme triumph, Macmillan himself wrote in his diary, "I thought chiefly of my poor mother."

———

In the late summer of 1956, as tensions came to the boil in Egypt, Jack Kennedy was a thirty-nine-year-old first-term senator with ambitions to higher office. He made a significant impression that August at the Democratic National Convention in Chicago, where the *New York Times* became the first but not last of the major dailies to compare his appearance to that of a "movie star," with an "instant appeal." Although Kennedy was proposed for vice president on a ticket with his party's nominee, Adlai Stevenson, the honor eventually went to Estes Kefauver of Tennessee by a vote of 755½ to 589. Given the scale of Stevenson's subsequent defeat by Eisenhower, this was one of those political losses that was in fact a net gain. Kennedy campaigned tirelessly on behalf of the ticket, giving 152 speeches in twenty-six states over the course of the next twelve weeks. At a women's college in Louisville, a crowd of some two hundred screaming students, many wearing T-shirts customized with slogans indicating how positively they would react to any overture Kennedy might make to them, attempted to block his car as he left their campus, informing him that he was "a doll" and "better than Elvis Presley."[24] These were not the stock accolades of a 1950s presidential election. Appraising the orgy of upside-down faces mouthing endearments through his windshield as they drove off, Kennedy calmly turned to an associate and informed him that, while this was good, it would be even better next time. (Another colleague would remember him remarking that fall, "If I work hard for four years, I ought to be able to pick up all the marbles."[25]) Kennedy had little to say on either Suez or any other substantive policy issues, but audiences found plenty to admire in his charm, his compulsive need for fun and action, and his finely tuned ear for a joke, often at his own expense. "Socrates," he told an initially puzzled audience in Twin Falls, Idaho, "once said that it was the duty of a man of real principle to avoid high national office, and evidently the delegates at Chicago recognized my principles even before I did."[26] In both public and private life, he was clearly a man in a hurry. Kennedy fell in love, as he did most things, with amazing speed, announcing his intention to marry the attractive, baby-voiced Jacqueline Bouvier shortly after he met her at a dinner party in the summer of 1951. Even so, the intending bride was to remark on the "spasmodic courtship"[27] that then intervened before their wedding two years later. It is a matter of record that Kennedy fell some way short of the traditional monogamous ideal. In the run-up to the Chicago convention in August 1956, the aspiring vice president managed to slip away on a sailing trip in the Mediterranean, where he enjoyed "a bacchanal, with several young women getting on and off the boat at its ports of call. . . . [Notably] a stunning but not particularly intelligent blonde who . . . referred to herself as 'Pooh.'"[28] At that time, Kennedy's wife was in Boston, in the final stages of a pregnancy that ended in a miscarriage.

The newly reelected president Eisenhower lost no time in welcoming Macmillan—colleagues since their mutual wartime service in North Africa—to high office.

> I assure you that the new [problems] will be to the old like a broken leg is to a scratched finger. The only real fun you will have is to see just how far you can keep on going with everybody chopping at you with every conceivable kind of weapon. . . . Remember the old adage, "Now abideth faith, hope, and charity—and greater than these is a sense of humor."
>
> As ever,
> D. E.[29]

It would be many years before the full story of Britain's shotgun wedding to the French and Israelis at Suez, and of Eisenhower's fury at the issue, was made public. In retrospect, it seems clear it was the end of an era. The crisis is often said to have marked the moment when the British political establishment fatally overreached itself, in the process handing its foreign and domestic critics an unprecedented propaganda gift. One short-term result was a postmortem debate in the House of Commons on May 15–16, 1957, which went better than Macmillan had feared—an opposition motion of censure, supported by Lord Salisbury (who, adding a personal layer of complexity, was also related to Macmillan by marriage), lost by a majority of forty-nine. The PM wrote in his diary, "How odd the English are! They rather like a gallant failure. Suez has become a sort of Mons Retreat." Perhaps unsurprisingly, Salisbury would not again hold public office. The longer-term consequences of Suez included the bitter realization that Britain no longer had the military and economic resources to maintain a global presence, a fact borne out in 1968 when the Labour government of Harold Wilson announced the dismantling of all British Middle Eastern bases and ports. Foreign policy, under Macmillan and his successors, would henceforth largely be a matter of decline management.

As we'll see, the seven years from Suez up until Macmillan's abrupt resignation from office saw periods of coolness in the Special Relationship, which was frequently tested by conflicting views on Berlin and the correct response to Soviet nuclear arms rattling, among a host of other fast-changing and constantly replenished regional crises, some of them slow-burning and others that erupted with blowpipe fury. But the essential through line of the Atlantic alliance between 1957 and 1963 was that Britain would in future adhere to US policy, even at its most exasperating. There would be no more unilateral colonial adventures or furtive tactical alliances struck behind America's back. Macmillan was not speaking purely for himself or narrowly of the particular issue of Laos when he wrote of events in March 1961, "Intervention [in Southeast Asia] was not an easy choice; there was a grave danger of provoking Russian or Chinese intervention. . . . On the other hand, it would be tragic to separate ourselves from the Americans. We had suffered enough in a previous crisis from an Anglo-American schism. At all costs, we must try and work with the new President and the new Administration."[30]

Macmillan's charm offensive to win back American friendship and support began in a meeting with Eisenhower in Bermuda in March 1957. The new prime minister perhaps didn't realize the full depth of the president's resentment about Suez until the two heads of government and their foreign ministers met alone after dinner on the first night. When Macmillan used the occasion to launch a spirited attack on Nasser, Eisenhower interjected that the British "could not at the same time seek his co-operation and combat him."[31] A heavy silence had followed this rebuke. When the discussion continued the next morning, Eisenhower "rather sharply" noted that American policy in the region had at least been consistent, before he complained about "particularly vicious and coordinated attacks" made on him in the British press. Clearly the transatlantic love affair was not about to be rekindled overnight. The following October, Macmillan and his officials appeared for talks in Washington. This time, the visitors' chief goal was the repeal of the 1946 Atomic Energy—or "McMahon"—Act, which prevented American administrations from sharing atomic information with even friendly foreign regimes. During the discussions, Eisenhower remarked that he "personally felt ashamed" of the law as it applied to countries like Britain, and he went on to hand his guests a document titled "A Declaration of Common Purpose."[32] Among other steps, this modified the McMahon Act so that the allies could again freely exchange scientific intelligence. Macmillan's confidential account of this breakthrough was euphoric. The American proposal was "in effect, a declaration of inter-dependence," he reported to the cabinet on October 28. "The government and people of the United States had been greatly impressed by recent Soviet successes and above all by the spectacular success, in their launching of an earth satellite, of Soviet achievements in science and technology. They now recognised that no single country, however powerful, could alone withstand the Soviet threat. . . . The prevailing mood in Washington had therefore been favourable to proposals for closer Anglo-American cooperation, and [this] had been achieved."[33]

In June 1958, Macmillan survived the failure of one of his Royal Air Force Britannia's engines two hours out over the Atlantic to eventually land safely for further goodwill discussions in Washington. (While the plane doubled back to London for repairs, shaking violently and pouring clouds of smoke from its stricken left side, the sixty-four-year-old PM lay serenely on his bunk reading Walter Scott's 1822 novel *The Fortunes of Nigel*.) The talks began the practical process of a renewed exchange of scientific, and specifically nuclear, data. Prior to the meeting, the premier had sent the president a "Dear Friend" letter, discussing the urgent need to coordinate arrangements for a Western nuclear response to any Soviet attack. "Dear Harold," Eisenhower replied. "I have read your note. I quite agree with your suggestion that our two governments study how to concert actions under the circumstances that you envision."[34] Seeming to personalize the Special Relationship, Macmillan again took the opportunity to travel to Indiana, where he received an honorary degree from his grandfather's university. The following day he was back in Washington, where he addressed a session of the US Senate. The PM winningly announced in his speech that his mother had once impressed on him that to be an American senator was the pinnacle of human achievement. He was loudly applauded. About the only discordant note came at a formal dinner presided over by Vice President Richard Nixon. Although characteristically tactful in public, Macmillan was more candid in the privacy of his diary. Nixon, he wrote, "poured out a monologue which extinguished any spark of conversation from whatever quarter it might arise. . . . This spate of banalities lasted for three to four hours. . . . I felt sorry for the Americans, who were clearly hurt and ashamed."[35]

Like a family feud patched up for the holidays, in the normal course of events the Special Relationship was still sometimes liable to tear apart at the seams. Macmillan's proposal that he fly to Moscow for bilateral talks in February 1959 reduced Eisenhower to a frenzy. The president did "not give much of a shit," he told John Dulles. "Let him go if he is that good . . . they will come back with their tail between their legs."[36] Dulles relayed the message in more diplomatic terms, allowing Macmillan to note with satisfaction the "friendly" American reply. "They say," he wrote in his diary, "that they have complete confidence in me and I must do what I think best."[37] On another trip to Washington a month later, Macmillan had the melancholy job of visiting the now terminally ill Dulles in hospital; it was their last meeting. Both then and in days to come, virtues were discovered in the voluble—some felt Anglophobic—secretary of state that had previously failed to surface. In a series of public and private remarks, Macmillan treated Dulles—who died that May—with a respect that was as exaggerated as, a month earlier, it would have been astonishing. After the reverence of the hospital room, there was more soldierly language from Eisenhower back in the White House. "With all his crudity, and lack of elegance of expression, he has some very reasonable ideas," Macmillan wrote in his diary on March 22, 1959.

The tables were turned in August 1959, when, having rebuffed British proposals for a three-way summit, Eisenhower announced that he had invited Khrushchev to the United States, a visit he hoped would "break the logjam" over Berlin and certain other pressing issues. Macmillan was not pleased. The president "has caused me great annoyance—alarm—and even anger," he wrote. "It is not (as some of my colleagues seem to feel) the result of American bad faith, but rather of their stupidity, naiveté and incompetence. . . . Everyone will assume that the two Great Powers—Russia and USA—are going to fix up a deal over our heads and behind our backs."[38] Macmillan was at least able to persuade Eisenhower to visit London prior to his talks with Khrushchev. In a largely symbolic program, the two Western leaders played golf, walked around Oxford University, and toured the English countryside in a white Rolls-Royce convertible borrowed from Douglas Fairbanks Jr. Back in Downing Street, the soon-to-be-campaigning prime minister and his guest engaged in an apparently unscripted fireside chat for the television cameras— not quite evincing the folksy charm of today's politicians (both men wore dinner suits), but still something of a forerunner of modern election broadcasts.

In the early weeks of 1960, Macmillan, returned to office with a healthy parliamentary majority of one hundred, sought to act as a broker between the United States and the Soviet Union. "We now [have] an opportunity to conclude an agreement which might be a turning point in the history of international negotiations on disarmament," he told the cabinet on March 22. "The United States . . . must be brought to appreciate the significance of this opportunity." A further visit to Ike in Washington appeared to satisfy both Britain's wishes to restrict future nuclear tests and her ambitions to own a missile system distinct from the Americans'. "We have got out of them," Macmillan wrote in his diary, "a very valuable exchange of notes about Skybolt and Polaris. . . . This allows us to abandon Bluestreak (rocket) without damage to our prospects of maintaining—in the late 60s and early 70s—our *independent nuclear deterrent*." (Macmillan's emphasis) Regrettably, a subsequent Paris summit between the Western powers and the USSR ended in some disarray amid Khrushchev's heated protests about an American U-2 spy plane that had been shot down over Soviet soil. Those who witnessed the Russian's fury would long marvel at the scene, speaking of it like old salts recalling a historic hurricane. Macmillan was sufficiently distressed at the collapse of the talks to contemplate resignation. "It was a terrible performance, reminiscent of Hitler at his worst," he wrote in his diary on May 18, 1960. "[Khrushchev] threatens, rants, uses filthy words of abuse . . ." Four months later, when Macmillan blandly told the General Assembly of the United Nations that he regretted the failure of the summit, a crimson-faced Khrushchev leapt to his feet to shout, "You sent your planes over our territory, you are guilty of aggression!" and started banging his fists on the table. (The prime minister bided his time and then with exquisite courtesy asked the president of the assembly if he might please have a translation.) Immediately on his return to London, Macmillan entered the hospital for treatment of an old war wound to his leg and quite possibly also exhaustion. He would not meet Eisenhower again while in office. Macmillan was generous in a letter to the outgoing president, recalling their "deep unity of purpose and, I like to feel, a frank and honest appreciation of each other's good faith," but the fact remained that between them they had broken with the Soviet Union, sparred over regional issues from Berlin to Central Africa, and, whatever Macmillan's impressions to the contrary, signally failed to achieve a long-term agreement on the matter of Britain's independent nuclear capability. This was an only mixed report card for the Special Relationship as it existed on President Kennedy's inauguration in January 1961.

Although Macmillan had never met Kennedy, the personal omens for the relationship could scarcely have been less promising. Apart from their twenty-three-year age gap, there was a certain bedrock difference of character—the one bluff and self-confident; the other languid, formal, and capable of mandarin inscrutability. Although Kennedy and Macmillan were collaterally related by marriage, this was offset by the premier's view of the president's father, Joe Kennedy, while he

was US ambassador in London before the war. "We regarded him with some contempt," Macmillan told his official biographer. "It was generally thought he was
unfriendly, and defeatist. . . . I had no particular reason to have any affection for the
president."[39] In November 1960, Macmillan entertained Kennedy's vice president–
elect, Lyndon Johnson, to dinner in London. He made an even worse impression
than his predecessor had. "A Texan, an acute and ruthless 'politician', but not (I
would judge) a man of any intellectual power," Macmillan concluded.[40]

=====

By January 1961 it was already late in the day for the sixty-six-year-old Macmillan
to significantly adapt his personal or political style to Kennedy's with much hope
of success. Born under Queen Victoria, wounded in the trenches of the Somme ("I
felt no inconvenience until later," he remarked of his injury[41]), the prime minister
often seemed ludicrously archaic next to a president who confidently promised
to put men on the moon. One spoke in a collegiate Boston accent ("yee-ahs" for
years, "Cu-ber" for *Cuba*), the other in upper-crust Edwardian tones modified by age
into a world-weary drawl, in which *off* became "orff" and *girl*, "gelle." Kennedy's
sense of humor tended to be both sharp and facile—"We'd rather be Ted than Ed,"
he quipped of Ted Kennedy's 1962 senatorial race against Eddie McCormack, the
Speaker's nephew—while Macmillan preferred the comedy of understatement and
irony. The same was true of their views on art, architecture, theater, and music,
subjects in which neither man showed much affinity for the other's taste, although
they shared an almost promiscuous love of books and reading—with a penchant,
in Kennedy's case, for James Bond spy novels that some saw reflected in his more
exotic foreign-policy initiatives. When it came to sex, one of them quickly discovered and developed a lifelong talent for charming women, and the other sustained a
forty-six-year marriage characterized more by mutual affection and shared experience than any grand passion, retiring into a long and celibate old age when his wife
predeceased him. Macmillan seemed to be the stereotypical English "toff," brought
up in the old tradition of great houses, nannies, governesses, and noblesse oblige,
and Kennedy the embodiment of the thrusting, 1960s New Frontiersman.

Both men were creatures of their time and upbringing. Macmillan never quite
reconciled to the television, always referred to "the wireless" and not "the radio,"
and thought the telephone an intrusive and on the whole vulgar contraption best

left to butlers and secretaries. Although he had been occasionally seen at the wheel of a jeep during the war, he never acquired a driver's license. He did take some lessons with his wife in their family car but drove it into a wall of a garage. Set against this was a keen sense of political ambition that showed the steel beneath the Edwardian-clubman façade. Speaking of Macmillan's achievements as minister of housing, the *Economist* wrote in December 1955, "No one who sets about building 360,000 homes a year with such gusto and success, fully knowing . . . what harm he was doing to the national economy, can be regarded as quite the ideal man to do the unpopular thing just because it is right." In fact, throughout his twelve years in high office, Macmillan displayed an often direct, sometimes brutal, and always results-based management style sharply at odds with the English ideal of gentlemanly diffidence and amateurish bumbling. As minister of defence in the winter of 1954–55, he took the unsentimental view that Winston Churchill, though a considerable wartime prime minister, was simply too old to lead the Conservative Party into another election. Churchill's doctor Lord Moran wrote, "Plainly there is a growing feeling among Winston's friends that the time has come for him to go, but only Harold Macmillan has had the guts to say so."[42] As Churchill had brought Macmillan out of the political wilderness with his first government job in 1940, this showed a sense of mission on the younger man's part that apparently insulated him from any feelings of compassion or guilt at undermining his benefactor. Anthony Eden later invited Macmillan to become chancellor of the exchequer as successor to Rab Butler, who was to step sideways to Lord Privy Seal. The move came both as a shock to the political pundits and as an unwelcome surprise to the two men most closely affected by it. Macmillan characterized the reshuffle as a "shattering blow" to his ambitions. Although mutual declarations of "warm goodwill" and "continuing collective responsibility" prevailed in public, this was not the case behind the scenes. In a letter to Eden, Macmillan made it clear that there were limits to his capacity for self-denial on behalf of the party. "If Rab becomes Leader of the House . . . that will be fine. But I could not agree that he should be Deputy Prime Minister."[43] It's been said that Macmillan particularly "despised Butler for not having fought in the First World War, sneered at [the Labour leader] Hugh Gaitskell for not having any medals to wear on Remembrance Day, and loathed Herbert Morrison, his first boss in the [1940–45] coalition, for having been a conscientious objector in the First War, calling him 'a dirty little cockney guttersnipe.'"[44] These were not wholly isolated cases of Macmillan's political wolfishness slipping out from behind a cloak of carefully feigned girlish probity. The surprising thing is the frankness with which he treated his colleagues, and his unerring ability, as prime minister, to swiftly dispose of them if circumstances dictated—most famously in July 1962, when he sacked a third of his cabinet, an act of carnage unprecedented in British domestic politics. According to one biographer, when his son, Maurice, an MP, once asked him why his own political career had fallen short, Macmillan said simply, "Because you weren't ruthless enough."

Where Macmillan was able to benefit from his rivals' misreading of him, in Kennedy's case the drive and ambition were plain for all to see. His keen powers of perception were married with an almost pathological need for personal success. "Competition—that's what makes them go," Joe Kennedy once remarked of his nine children. According to a Kennedy biographer, Joe's second son was "hell-bent on becoming the first Catholic president" from the moment he launched his political career as a twenty-nine-year-old US representative in January 1947. (Although Kennedy displayed tactical skills of a high order almost from the moment he entered Congress, it did not hurt the cause that Joe was able to throw money around during the various campaigns like King Farouk at a casino.) Adlai Stevenson spoke for many in the Democratic establishment when, in July 1960, he asked Kennedy why he had chosen the boorish Johnson as his running mate. The candidate replied that it was simply because he wanted to win. Six years earlier, Kennedy had recuperated from critical spinal surgery by lying on his back strapped to a board, with another board on top of him, writing what became the Pulitzer Prize–winning *Profiles in Courage*.

Macmillan was the ultimate self-made man, or so it seemed; a middle-class boy whose people were "in trade," who not only held three of the great offices of state, which might have been enough for another politician, but was also a war hero, viceroy, publisher, thinker, writer, and statesman whose peculiar fate was to lead his party in the dismal wake of Suez, and his nation at a time of irreversible economic and military decline. Like Kennedy, he grew up aware of the high expectations his family had for him. In the 1920s, Macmillan's ambitious mother rebuilt the family home into a sprawling, neo-Georgian compound she thought fit for a future prime minister and once loudly reprimanded a visitor to the house for kicking a door that belonged to "the most important politician in Britain"—a notable feat of prediction about a then-obscure backbench Tory MP whose speaking voice at the time was described as "a high-pitched drone."[45] The great-grandson of a crofter who became the son-in-law of a duke, Macmillan would eventually be accused of assuming "presidential" airs and graces in office. Kennedy, in turn, was sometimes damned by critics as "regal," especially when the Hoover Commission revealed that the nation's chief executive was now responsible for "nine major departments, 104 bureaus, twelve sections, 108 services, 51 branches, 631 divisions, nineteen administrations, six agencies, four boards, six commands, twenty commissions, 19 corporations, 10 headquarters, three authorities, and 263 miscellaneous organizations"—and that was before the office multiplied under President Johnson.[46] In broad terms, Kennedy was an Anglophile, with extensive British mannerisms and connections but with the virtues most prized in 1960s American culture: innovation, energy, daring. In October 1960, while in New York to address the United Nations, Macmillan happened to turn on the television in his hotel suite and watched a few minutes of the first Nixon-Kennedy presidential debate. He may have been out of a lost social era, when politicians in black tie occasionally deigned to utter a few words to the public over the wireless, but he was also perceptive enough to recognize the wind of change when he saw it. "Your chap's beat," Macmillan told a startled President Eisenhower later that same night. "One of them looked like a convicted criminal and the other looked like a rather engaging young undergraduate. . . . Well, you know, Nixon [has] that curious sort of dark, furtive face."[47]

Kennedy was the first American president to treat the television cameras as an ally. In conversation he was first brisk, and, second, warm or combative, as the situation demanded. As one biographer said, "The President thinks of words as the shortest distance between two points. A man who puts things in a nutshell wins his respect. A rambler loses. In private Kennedy will talk for hours, 'but only', as a Harvard adviser puts it, 'if there is real Ping-pong in the conversation.'"[48] Macmillan may have had more of the dowager style, but under the mask, he was thought to be a surprisingly approachable supremo who enjoyed the difficult, irreverent question. He was also recognizably "modern" in some of his personal approach to power. The atmosphere at 10 Downing Street underwent a dramatic change when the Macmillans replaced the childless Edens, with "bicycles, tricycles, scooters, as well as an occasional perambulator" appearing in the marble hallways. The PM himself issued orders to his grandchildren that they were at liberty to play games with the duty policemen, with the proviso that these "not obstruct the arrival of ambassadors or Cabinet ministers." Macmillan's most frequently used word to describe his time in office, whatever the domestic and global challenges, was that it was "fun."[49] In his later years, he liked to ramble around the grouse moors with a volume of Livy in his pocket or to entertain guests during the early 1980s by reminiscing about the funeral of Queen Victoria. It was a gentle twilight to a life of extraordinary achievement.

As we've seen, Kennedy shared Macmillan's bibliophilia, even if his love of the printed word didn't always extend to the daily press. (Irritated by its coverage, the president once had his spokesman formally announce that the White House had canceled all twenty-two copies of its subscription to the *New York Herald Tribune*.) In April 1961, Richard Nixon called on President Kennedy, who not only seemed to his visitor to take more pride in his extensive library than any other aspect of his new office but also added that every public man should write a book "both for the mental discipline, and because it tends to elevate him in popular esteem to the respected status of an 'intellectual.'"[50] (Nixon responded with his 1962 bestseller, *Six Crises*.) Such a man would have instinctively warmed to a British counterpart who was a third-generation publisher. Over the years, both Kennedy and Macmillan would become painfully aware that grand strategic policy was often lost to the expediency of crisis management. An associate justice of the Supreme Court with the striking name of Felix Frankfurter once informed the president that, as chief executive, his job was to "direct funds, goods, and people to concerns that relate to the human welfare," and to be a "molder of American life."[51] Kennedy's desk diary of his time in office reveals a preoccupation with rather more specific, and often narrowly pragmatic, tasks. Asked what he most feared as prime minister, Macmillan allegedly replied, "Events, dear boy, events"—a quotation no one seems able to authenticate, but which has taken its place alongside other imperishable lines like "A week is a long time in politics," or "It's the economy, stupid."

━━━━━

Politicians can broadly be divided into two categories: those whose public face is different from their private face, and those for whom they're the same; put another way, those who feel it necessary in public appearances to put on an act of inner composure and outer geniality, and those whose hearty, electioneering self is the real man. Generally speaking, Macmillan was in the former category, and Kennedy in the latter.

One of the reasons for the president's serene self-assurance was surely the sense of security that came both from personal wealth and from a loving wife who tolerated his frequent explorations of the limits of his wedding vows. "There was something almost madcap about Kennedy's behavior," his otherwise admiring biographer Robert Dallek has written. While in office, his womanizing included affairs with Pamela Turnure, his wife's press secretary; Judith Campbell Exner, who happened to also be the mistress of the mob boss Sam Giancana; Mimi Beardsley, a nineteen-year-old White House intern; Mary Meyer, the sister-in-law of his friend (and Washington bureau chief of *Newsweek*) Ben Bradlee; Marilyn Monroe; and two West Wing secretaries not conspicuous for their typing or filing skills and known locally as Fiddle and Faddle.[52] The above list is far from exhaustive. So far as is known, Jacqueline Kennedy not once gave her husband anything but her undivided love nor was anything but a charming and considerate (if profligate) hostess on official occasions. No wonder, perhaps, that when *Newsweek*'s James Cannon interviewed the president in April 1963—at a time when the administration was embroiled in issues including civil rights, healthcare reform, and nuclear-arms testing—he "was struck first by the serenity of the [Oval Office] surroundings, and the self-possession of the principal." Cannon wrote in his notes of the meeting: "In this man, at this moment, there was no evidence that he was worn with the cares of office. He was casual. He was affable. He was unhurried, unbadgered . . . 'How are you doing?' I said. 'I must say you *look* fine. From all appearances, the job seems to be agreeing with you.' 'Well,' he said, with a big smile, 'I think it's going well.'"[53] Kennedy's assistant (and, on occasion, sexual procurer) Dave Powers echoed Cannon's observation: "John F. Kennedy enjoyed being president. He loved being where the action was. He was always at his best under pressure."[54]

Macmillan, by contrast, put up a brilliantly constructed front of Edwardian hauteur and a sublime mastery of events while, he later admitted, "never show[ing] how nervous and awful the whole business is. . . . I think I did seem to have what was called unflappability—if only they knew how one's inside was flapping all the time, they wouldn't have said that."[55] It was perhaps this same dissembling ability the Tory MP Enoch Powell had in mind when he dubbed his chief the "old actor-manager." Born into the respectable middle classes, Macmillan did not immediately seem to be a candidate to rise through the upper ranks of the Conservative Party of the 1920s. His health was precarious from his war wounds, and he had a full-scale physical and nervous breakdown, which sent him to recuperate in a German clinic for several weeks in 1931. Two years earlier, his wife, Dorothy, had begun an affair with Robert Boothby, a mercurially talented, reckless, and sexually undiscriminating Scot who also happened to be a parliamentary ally of Macmillan's for the next thirty-five years. The affair ended only with Dorothy's death in 1966. It never became public but was brought painfully home to Macmillan himself, whom his friend David Cecil once saw "banging his head against the wall of a railway compartment in sheer despair."[56] Years later, a family employee hinted at how desperate things had been by alluding to a suicide attempt. In 1933, Boothby wrote about Dorothy to a friend: "The most formidable thing in the world—a possessive, single-track woman. She wants me completely, and she wants my children, and she wants practically nothing else. . . . I am grandly, passionately in love with her. But if I take her, it's goodbye to everything else."[57] This grand passion survived even Boothby's marriage, in 1935, to one of Dorothy's cousins. Macmillan behaved immaculately throughout the long affair, evidently seeing it as a sort of chronic illness on his wife's part, and gave his name to Sarah, Dorothy's daughter born in 1930, reputedly fathered by Boothby. It was a tribute to a certain British resilience—as well as to the docility and decorum of the press—that these arrangements worked as well as they did, but they can only have papered over what was surely an emotional life of continuing disappointment and heartbreak. "If your wife is a great anxiety to you, it is pretty grim," Dorothy's sister remarked of the Macmillans' marriage.[58] Rab Butler, who knew both men well, considered that "Harold *did* suffer greatly, [but] he would never admit it. The extraordinary thing about him was that he had such inner strength. . . . Boothby did have a depressing effect, but not on his moral character, which was so strong."[59]

Perhaps the key difference between the libidinous president and the monogamous and, later, by all accounts, celibate prime minister was best expressed by the moment when Kennedy turned to Macmillan at the end of a lengthy meeting ostensibly arranged to discuss nuclear arms and mildly asked, "I wonder how it is with you, Harold? If I don't have a woman for three days, I get a terrible headache."[60]

It's tempting to see Macmillan as a period character within a period piece. He came of age in that early part of the twentieth century that was still effectively Victorian. His only relaxations were shooting, golf, and reading. He presented an image of a tweedy, shuffling country grandee out of the pages of P. G. Wodehouse. It was not undeserved that in June 1961 the Labour leader Hugh Gaitskell witheringly accused him of "Edwardian nonchalance" during a heated parliamentary debate on the economy. (The barb evidently stung, because Macmillan drafted—but never used—a reply that ran, "If Mr. Gaitskell had a little more experience of life, he would know that sometimes in dangerous moments it is advisable [to] cultivate an outward show of confidence. I learned that in early youth under fire on the battle-field. Unfortunately, for reasons which I wholly understand, this experience was not vouchsafed to Gaitskell."[61]) By the summer of 1963, it struck many commenta-tors, including some on the political right, as verging on farcical that the Britain of the Beatles and the Rolling Stones should still be governed by an apparently tired and effete relic out of the twilight of the nineteenth century.

Of course, this was the same Macmillan who enjoyed the company of the more raffish elements of academic and literary society—who, as a junior minister, had been one of the so-called Glamour Boys, a politically free-thinking, bohemian set who met over well-lubricated dinners at the Café Royal—and whose own family arrangements were far from conventional. In December 1961, David Bruce, US ambassador to Britain, had assessed Macmillan in a cable to the State Department. "I am neither an intimate nor a friend of the PM," he wrote. "Few apparently are. His play, to use a gambling expression, is close; and his inmost thoughts are seldom open to penetration. He is a political animal, shrewd, subtle in maneuver, undisputed master in his Cabinet house. . . . This is no mean man. He has charm, politeness, dry humor, self-assurance, a vivid sense of history, dignity of character. To what extent he would bend conviction to comport with expediency one cannot say."[62]

In much the same way Kennedy's rhetoric defined the American New Fron-tier of the 1960s, Macmillan's major speeches long dwelled on the need for more progressive domestic policies and the futility of party-political ideological disputes, as suggested in the title of his 1938 book, *The Middle Way*. In a speech in 1946 he had even toyed with the prospect of a "New Democratic Party." Macmillan, who represented the depressed northern industrial constituency of Stockton-on-Tees for nineteen of his thirty-eight years in parliament, summarized his political philos-ophy in a document printed and distributed by the Conservative Party in May 1947 titled *The Industrial Charter* as being "to maintain full employment, to sustain and improve the social services, and to continue the strategic control of the economy in the hands of the Government, while preserving wherever possible the tactical function of private enterprise." He later advocated a form of electoral proportional representation favorable to the Liberal Party sixty years before this was put to a referendum. Macmillan's combination of the pragmatic and the speculative was not exactly unique in a politician, but it rather jars with his classic fuddy-duddy image. A *Sunday Times* profile from January 1950 called him "a political philosopher as well as a practical statesman . . . he talks convincingly in the language of an intellectual, yet an intellectual with much practical experience of national and international affairs, of public and private commerce, and a sympathetic understanding of the life and difficulties of the ordinary man."

Kennedy, too, was distinctive in refusing to accommodate his presidency to narrow ideological goals. Asked once whether he was a liberal or a conservative, he quoted Lincoln: "There are few things wholly evil or wholly good. Almost everything, especially of Government policy, is an inseparable compound of the two, so that our best judgment of the preponderance between them is continually demanded." Further pressed to say what executive ambitions he harbored, Kennedy replied, "I hope to be responsible." His wife described him approvingly as an "idealist without illusions."[63] "Kennedy was temperamentally closer to most British Conservatives than to Labour," his biographer Herbert Parmet has written. The man who got him right was his friend, and future Speaker of the House, Tip O'Neill. "Looking back on his Congressional campaign, and on his later campaigns, I'd have to say that Jack was only nominally a Democrat. He was a Kennedy, which was more than a family affiliation. It quickly developed into an entire political party, with its own people, its own approach, and its own strategies."[64] The presidency has quite often been called "the loneliest job in the world." Without descending too far into the briar patch of psychiatry, it seems fair to assume that Kennedy might have felt a need—almost a compulsion—to periodically talk shop with the other ranking political master of the Western world. Speaking of the allies' first summit, in March 1961, Parmet writes, "No foreign country was less foreign to Jack Kennedy [than Britain]. There was the additional, and obvious, point that Macmillan had also gotten his own fill of the seamier side of politics. Not much ice remained to be broken." Even so, there was still some initial wariness between the two democratic-superpower chiefs. "It is curious," Macmillan wrote later, "how all American statesmen begin by trying to treat Britain as just one of the many foreign or NATO countries. They soon find themselves relying on our advice and experience." Within twenty-four hours of their first meeting, Kennedy had privately dispensed with the formal address of "Mr. Prime Minister" in favor of "Mr. Prime" or "Harold," while Macmillan opted to call the president simply "My Friend."

Kennedy and Macmillan helped shape the world in which we now live. The decisions they took, often in personal exchanges, occasionally through more formal state apparatus, preserved a fragile peace in Berlin that would survive until eventual German reunification, rolled back the immediate threat of nuclear weapons aimed at the United States from within her hemisphere, and resolved other strategic uncertainties by means that included the signing of the Nuclear Test Ban Treaty, down to the establishment of a first transatlantic hotline. The real issue, however, as both leaders recognized, was the need for the urgent repair of the post–Suez Crisis Special Relationship in order to present a united front against Soviet, or, more broadly, communist territorial ambitions around the world—what Kennedy called the "touchstone" of his whole presidency. It was not always a perfect arrangement. Only a year or two later, differences in national strategy over Vietnam, for example, illustrated in hindsight just what Macmillan had meant when he complained about "not so much the duplicity as the duality of American policy." He based his concern largely on his "great friend's" need to reach decisions not, like himself, alone or with one or two trusted advisers, but "through the strange complex of power that is distributed between the White House, the State Department and the Pentagon."[65] (Macmillan had been singularly unimpressed when, only three weeks after their first "full and frank" talks, Kennedy had ordered the covert invasion of Cuba without so much as mentioning it either to him or anyone else in the British government.[66]) Relations between Washington and London would be tested more than once in the years ahead, but the like-minded alliance forged by Kennedy and Macmillan proved strong enough to meet its most basic Cold War challenges while dispelling any illusions about the world being conspicuously safer as a result. In that and in other ways, their joint leadership of the West has a particular resonance today.

2

ANCIENT AND MODERN

When Harold Macmillan addressed the United Nations General Assembly in New York on September 29, 1960, he did so at a time, in the guarded words of his memoir *Pointing the Way*, of "not a little global unpleasantness in a variety of spheres, some great, some small." Among the major issues of the day were the continued Allied concerns over the security of Berlin; nuclear tests; the recent installation of US Polaris bases in Scotland's Holy Loch (a decision Macmillan admitted in his diary "turns on whether we are just to give our allies facilities, more or less as a satellite, or whether we can make it a joint enterprise"); and the Congo, where the horrors of colonial rule had been recounted as long ago as Joseph Conrad's 1899 novella, *Heart of Darkness*, and which had now fallen into anarchy following the Belgian decision to abruptly grant the area independence. With President Eisenhower's term in office about to expire and Nikita Khrushchev, according, respectively, to his son and foreign-policy assistant, "determined to take revenge for what had happened at [the] Paris summit" by "humiliating the Prince of Darkness [Eisenhower] by appearing uninvited at the UN,"[1] the world stage was set for a certain degree of drama. After discussing it with the queen and the Commonwealth leaders, Macmillan made the decision to personally go to New York and "do something to counteract Khrushchev and his ilk—if only to rally the West."[2]

The subsequent 902nd plenary meeting of the UN General Assembly delivered in full on its theatrical potential. Khrushchev made an impassioned three-hour speech in which he demanded immediate "freedom" for all colonial territories, called for the abolition of the office of the post of UN secretary-general, and proposed that the assembly itself be relocated from New York to Vienna or Moscow. The formal address was merely the start of Khrushchev's remarks, and over the course of the next few days he took the opportunity to frequently jump to his feet to protest speeches by Western delegates and to give several chaotically ad hoc press conferences around New York, at one point embracing Fidel Castro in the lobby of his transients' hotel in Harlem and later standing on a balcony outside the Soviet Mission to serenade the crowds below with "The Internationale."

Macmillan, by contrast, gave what could be called a classically "British" performance when his turn came to address the assembly, delivering a quietly controlled speech that accentuated the Soviet histrionics. Standing erect, hands clasped in a soldierly manner behind his back, the PM cut directly to Khrushchev when he said: "Gentlemen, where are the representatives of our former British territories? Here they are, sitting in this Hall. . . . Here are the representatives of India, Pakistan, Ceylon, Ghana, Malaya. Here, here in this Hall. In a few days' time, Nigeria will join us. . . . Who dares to say that this is anything but a story of steady and liberal progress?"[3]

At this point, Khrushchev intervened. The details of precisely what followed are unclear due to conflicting testimony, but it seems fairly certain that the Soviet chairman rose to his feet to shout some unappreciative remarks at Macmillan, which were possibly emphasized by banging on the desk with his shoe, and that Macmillan patiently waited for the storm to subside before turning around and saying in a level voice, "Mr. President, perhaps we could have a translation. I could not quite follow."[4] A purple-faced Khrushchev was then obliged to endure the boisterously loud laughter that followed. As Macmillan allowed in his memoirs, "For some reason [I] was thought very witty and effective. Naturally the world Press took up this episode, and British phlegm was contrasted with Russian excitability. . . . The effect of the speech was good both at home, in the United States, and throughout the world."[5] Six months later, it would be the first thing on which the new US president admiringly remarked when the two Western leaders met over a hamburger lunch at a navy base in Florida. Recalling that ice-breaking meeting in his memoirs, Macmillan wrote, "Before our conversation had gone on for many minutes I felt a deep sense of relief. Although we had never met and belonged to such different generations . . . we seemed immediately to talk as old friends."[6] Macmillan was particularly struck by the way Kennedy listened intently during an elaborate Joint Chiefs of Staff presentation that followed lunch and discussed the possibility of Western intervention in the simmering civil war in Laos, sitting politely "while bridges were flung across rivers, troops deployed on a great scale, and all the rest."

Although Macmillan professed relief at the outcome of his first meeting with Kennedy, he had gone in to it with some misgivings on the state of the Atlantic alliance. On December 14, 1960, in Paris, Sir Frederick Millar, permanent under-secretary at the British Foreign Office, met with Livingston T. Merchant, his opposite number at the State Department. Merchant wired the following back to Washington:

> Sir Frederick was anxious to see me. . . . He said that the Prime Minister was concerned as to how best to assure reaffirmation by the new President of assur-ances given to the British Government during the past eight years concerning the use of nuclear weapons. He said that for obvious reasons these assurances were of great importance to the British. . . . [Macmillan] was anxious to send Pres. Eisenhower a private message referring to specific agreements and assurances with the request that prior to leaving office the President inform the President-elect of these engagements. The PM then would send a message to Mr. Kennedy shortly after his inauguration referring to these engagements, and in effect asking for confirmation that they remain in force.[7]

Kennedy, for his part, was even then reading the voluminous State Depart-ment briefing book that gave Macmillan, his UN speech notwithstanding, only a fair report card for his dealings with the Soviet leadership to date. In particular, the late John Dulles had thought the prime minister's visit to Moscow of February 1959 "ill-advised. . . . I had considerable reservations about the wisdom of it."[8] Although Macmillan smoothly told the British press that he was "representing the Western interest" in Moscow, what Dulles actually said was that the PM was "campaigning," and that while in the Soviet Union he spoke only for himself.[9] In May of the fol-lowing year, Macmillan—reportedly with tears in his eyes—begged Eisenhower and de Gaulle to let him make one final effort to win Khrushchev around as the Paris summit neared its meltdown point. An interview with the Soviet delegation was hurriedly agreed to, but for once Macmillan's carefully honed and emollient words failed to carry the day. "Khrushchev was polite, but quite immovable," Rodion Malinovsky "hardly even blinking," and Andrei Gromyko "also silent."[10] After leaving the meeting, the immaculately clad Macmillan could remark only that "the Soviets may know how to make Sputniks, but they certainly don't know how to make trou-sers."[11] (A subsequent unanimous vote by the Central Committee of the Communist Party of the USSR, as quoted by its assistant chief of the Propaganda Department, Comrade I. A. Iakovlev, reaffirming its intention "to make use of concrete facts to expose capitalist reality, political and ideological diversions of imperialism, the totalitarian character of a bourgeois state, [and] the reactionary thought in bourgeois capitalist society," seemed only to underscore the gulf between the Western and Eastern Blocs.) At dinner the next night, Macmillan was sufficiently depressed at his failure to bring the Russians to the negotiating table to consider his own position as prime minister. "I rang the Chief Whip," he recalled, "and asked him if I should resign now [that] my policy is in ruins around me. . . . He told me to hang on."[12]

In the event, Macmillan wrote to Kennedy to share some of his hopes and anxieties about the state of world affairs even before the inauguration. "There is indeed plenty to talk about," he cabled the president-elect on December 19, 1960, before lavishing praise on Kennedy's collection of speeches *The Strategy of Peace*. In something of a role reversal, the sixty-six-year-old British Tory then spoke to the forty-three-year-old American Democrat about the need to "properly adjust [the] Western Alliance to the realities" of the new decade. As a priority, he cited, "what is going to happen to us unless we can show that our modern free society—the new form of capitalism—can run in a way that makes the fullest use of our resources and results in a steady expansion of our economic strength[?] . . . If we fail in this, communism will triumph, not by war, or even subversion, but by seeming to be a better way of bringing people material comforts."

This concern about what Macmillan called "the problem of money" coming as his first order of business when writing to Kennedy (and the assurance that the economic wellbeing of people at all levels of society should be secure) was perhaps another sign that there was more to the British prime minister than his satirical image of an upper-class buffoon dining with earls, quaffing port, and oppressing the proletariat. With a few rare exceptions, over the years, Kennedy would find little to disagree with in Eisenhower's parting words to him at their December 1960 foreign-policy handover briefing: "You'll find Macmillan a good friend whose counsel you should listen to."[13]

═══

Macmillan was not the originator of the postwar Atlantic alliance, but at least he was its philosopher. In public he spoke intently about the need for the English-speaking peoples to act together, while in private he fretted about the equally compelling need for Britain to be more than just an offshore fifty-first state and subordinate vassal to American interests. "[Robert] McNamara's foolish speech about nuclear arms has enraged the French and put us in a difficulty," Macmillan told his diary at one moment of particular cross-Atlantic tension in June 1962. "I shall have a chance to tell [Dean] Rusk on Sunday what terrible damage the Americans are doing in every field. . . . All the allies are angry with the US proposal that we should buy rockets to the tune of umpteen million dollars, the warheads to be under American control. This is not a European rocket. It's a racket of the American industry.[14]

=====

It would be unwise to limit our knowledge of Macmillan, or of his upbringing, purely to his memoirs. His family home at 52 Cadogan Place, a short walk from London's perennially fashionable Sloane Square, was part of a row of tall, white-washed houses facing onto a gated and immaculately trimmed residents' garden and thus somewhat removed from the "poor Highland stock" the rising politician later liked to claim for himself. As we've seen, his father, Maurice, was a teacher, a pub-lisher, and an occasional poet who, in his time, turned eminently respectable with the purchase of Birch Grove House, a seventeen-bedroom country estate set in 108 acres of land on the edge of Ashdown Forest (the "100 Acre Wood" of the Winnie-the-Pooh stories) and boasting two working tenant farms and nine cottages on its grounds. Macmillan's mother was a socially ambitious émigré with some artistic and musical pretensions who lost no opportunity to help advance her youngest son's career. Harold studied Latin and Greek from the age of six; at nine he was sent off to prep school; at twelve to Eton College, where he began his lifelong love of the classics but left prematurely due to either a near-fatal case of pneumonia or an indiscreet homosexual affair, according to which account you read. After a period of home tuition, he went to Balliol College, Oxford, where he spoke in the Union in support of the motion that "this house approves the main principles of socialism" and took a first-class degree in Honour Moderations—"Mods"—in May 1914. Tall, slim, and languid, with a clipped, high-pitched voice said to be like the "noise of coins ringing onto a counter-top,"[15] Macmillan seemed the epitome of what former prime minister Herbert Asquith called "the tranquil consciousness of effortless superiority which is the mark of the Balliol man."[16]

In the early hours of June 29, 1914, Macmillan emerged in his tails and stiff-collar shirt from a society London ballroom to hear a paperboy shouting that morning's news headline: "Archduke and Wife Murdered in Bosnia." It was all faintly absurd, with its cast of ostrich-plumed Habsburg nobility and teenaged Slav anarchists, but in little more than a month Europe's interlocking alliances had pitched her armies against one another in a line of mud and blood that remained all but static for the next four years. In August 1915, Macmillan went to the western front as a twenty-one-year-old officer with the Grenadier Guards and fought there gallantly: successively shot in the head, hand, and leg (after the last of which he lay prone in no-man's-land, calmly reading *Prometheus* in the Greek, a copy of which he happened to have in his battle dress), the cumulative effect of his wounds was the limp handshake and shuffling gait that proved such a satirical gift to his later political opponents. Evacuated to England, he spent much of the next two years undergoing a series of operations. In April 1919, Macmillan's mother arranged for him to become an aide-de-camp to the Duke of Devonshire, then governor-general of Canada, an appointment that brought him in close contact with that richly privileged and whimsical family. By the mid-nineteenth century, the Devonshires had accumulated enough houses to open a chain of luxury hotels and among them exercised a sort of benign despotism on England's social and political life. One eighteenth-century Devonshire agreed to become prime minister on condition that if he didn't like it, he could stop. A Victorian descendant was asked to be PM on three separate occasions, but declined each time. A third relative was asked if he wished to be viceroy of India but decided on the whole that it would be too hot.

While in Ottawa, Macmillan met and fell in love with Lady Dorothy Cavendish, the nineteen-year-old daughter of the ninth duke: she was slim and elegant rather than classically beautiful, vivacious and earthy, and perhaps more accomplished as a horsewoman than as a formally schooled intellectual: a sort of Diana Spencer figure of her day. Macmillan was thought to have been sexually innocent up to that point in his life, preferring to relax in the trenches by playing chess with his valet rather than carousing with the local French girls. The young couple returned to England and were married at St. Margaret's, Westminster, in April 1920. Macmillan spent the next three years in the family publishing business. Encouraged again by his mother and political father-in-law, he stood and narrowly lost as a Conservative parliamentary candidate in the general election of December 1923. Seated a year later for the northern constituency of Stockton, Macmillan, with his piping voice and newly grown walrus mustache—and whose sole knowledge of industry consisted of visits to the printer in the course of publishing the likes of Thomas Hardy and Rudyard Kipling—must have seemed an unlikely representative of a depressed coal-mining town with an unemployment rate of 40 percent among its male workforce. By all accounts, Dorothy had a popular appeal rating higher than her husband's. Where she beamed and hugged, he had an aversion to making physical contact with a stranger. While on the campaign trail, Dorothy knocked on doors, remembered peoples' faces and names, and listened with genuine sympathy while they talked about themselves, their lives, their children, and their often bitterly disappointed economic hopes. Her enjoyment of good gossip matched his disdain for it. In her first year as an MP's wife, Dorothy shook the hands of more than twenty thousand men, women, and children in every corner of the constituency. Returning to the area in 1979 for a tour of his old constituency, Macmillan graciously acknowledged "my dear wife, who was so much more responsible than I for winning the hearts, if not the votes, of Stockton."

For all that, Macmillan had a fitful political career between the wars and often stood at a remove from his own Conservative Party hierarchy. In 1932 he published a pamphlet, *The State and Industry*, calling for increased government intervention in the market, a theme he returned to in a series of books and papers over the next seven years. All Macmillan's speeches of the period were laden with a strong Keynesian argument in favor of a "joined-up" national policy integrating politics, trade, and finance. It's not too much to call him a lifelong disciple of Keynes (a lover, incidentally, of Daniel Macmillan, Harold's elder brother), as well as of Disraeli's "One Nation" Conservatism. In 1938, Macmillan published his manifesto, *The MiddleWay*, which, among other steps, called for the introduction of a minimum wage, "lifting up to a tolerable human standard the unfortunate families now living in conditions that are a disgrace to the community."[17] He became a figure sometimes more respected by his ordinary constituents and by public intellectuals like Keynes than by his parliamentary colleagues. Anyone familiar with the reputation of MP Enoch Powell in the Britain of the 1970s and 1980s needs only to think of him, but with a policy of social inclusiveness, to get some of the flavor.

In other ways, Macmillan was wretchedly unlucky in life. He and Dorothy had a son, Maurice, and three daughters, Carol, Catherine, and Sarah, all of whose lives were touched to some degree or another by alcoholism. His marriage survived even as, with Harold's tacit consent, Dorothy became the mistress of the flamboyant and able Robert Boothby, a fellow MP, and not a man immune to the charms of either sex. The Second World War finally brought Macmillan, who was forty-six, onto the fringes of government as parliamentary secretary to the Ministry of Supply. (Yet to acquire his later reputation for unflappability, at one stage in June 1940 he joined several of his Tory colleagues in proposing that the threat posed to the United Kingdom by Hitler be met by a committee of public safety that would have established martial law, introduced blanket press censorship, and suspended normal sittings of parliament for the duration of the war. It was briskly dismissed as "gibberish" by the prime minister, Winston Churchill.) This was neither a glamorous nor a precocious start to Macmillan's time in office, but from then on he enjoyed a steady series of ministerial appointments: undersecretary of state for the colonies (1942), minister-resident in the Mediterranean (1942–45), air secretary (1945), minister of housing and local government (1951–54), and minister of defence (1954–55). In May 1945, while based in Athens, Macmillan was party to the decision to repatriate to the Soviet Union some forty thousand Cossacks and White Russians, as agreed between the Allied heads of state at the Yalta Conference. He fully recognized that by doing so he was "condemning them to slavery, torture and probably death. . . . It was a great grief to me that there was no other course open."[18] The inevitable fate of those wretched souls commands a very wide literature and was to be the cause of several high-profile lawsuits over the next fifty years. As Macmillan feared, the repatriated Russians were summarily hung, shot, or deported to Siberian labor camps. Following his 1956 secret speech denouncing Stalin, Khrushchev quietly permitted the only fifteen survivors from the original forty thousand to emigrate to Austria. Their subsequent plea for financial assistance was refused by a British government then led by Harold Macmillan, thus arguably making a terrible double blemish on his record.

Macmillan spent eight months in 1955 as Foreign Secretary, the fulfillment of a longtime ambition held for him by his mother. He is remembered for having remarked of that office in the House of Commons: "Nothing he can say can do very much good, and almost anything he may say may do a great deal of harm. He is forever poised between the cliché and the indiscretion." Macmillan's brokering of the Baghdad Pact between Britain, Iran, Iraq, Pakistan, and Turkey into a "northern-tier" defensive axis against Soviet aggression was undermined by the at best tepid support offered by John Dulles and the Eisenhower administration in general. The *Spectator* wasn't alone in complaining that British diplomacy in the region had "failed lamentably for all the hopes pinned to the Pact." Macmillan put it even more bluntly in his diary: "If we lose out in the Middle East, we lose the oil. If we lose the oil, we cannot live . . ." Here were the seeds of the catastrophic Allied breach that came a year later at Suez.

As chancellor of the exchequer from December 1955 to January 1957, Macmillan's inheritance appeared to be a reasonably good one: unemployment had fallen to 1.1 percent, and his predecessor, Rab Butler, had felt able to promise a reduction in the standard rate of income tax. Macmillan gave a typically wry budget speech in April 1956, commenting that even the best-researched economic forecasts were "more like astrology than astronomy" and introducing a new type of savings—or "Premium"—bond which proved wildly popular as the precursor of today's UK National Lottery. Although widely acclaimed at the Treasury when compared to his modern counterparts in the job, like them, Macmillan was faced with the perennial challenge of balancing the books and, in particular, of pleading with both sides of industry for restraint on prices and income—an appeal that was only fitfully successful in the case of the trade unions. As chancellor, he was obliged to make cuts in the subsidies on bread and milk, a political gift to the opposition Labour Party. These relatively minor adjustments to national expenditure of course paled by comparison to the economic consequences of Suez. Whereas previous chancellors had managed to lose as much as £100 million of Britain's gold reserves in a year, Macmillan achieved this in the single week of October 29, 1956.

There is no need to dwell at any length on Macmillan's subsequent record as prime minister from January 1957 until President Kennedy's inauguration four years later. The folk memory remains one of a fusty Edwardian clubman pottering about with his plus-four trousers and tongue-in-cheek humor, a byword for aristocratic *sangfroid*, assuring the nation that "most of us have never had it so good," while absentmindedly presiding over a period of gentle but inexorable decline at home and abroad that climaxed in a spate of sexually charged security scandals. It's a caricature, if one that has a grain of truth. In particular, the successful test of Britain's H-bomb, in April 1957, ushered in a long-running debate about the proper role, if any, of an independent nuclear deterrent, which itself formed part of Macmillan's post-Suez campaign to win back American friendship. Meanwhile, the short-lived economic boom of 1958–59 was followed by the bust of 1960–61, with precipitously falling trade figures, a run on sterling, and that unique combination of a static economy and rising prices that the press dubbed "stagflation." The government's response was the July 1961 "pay pause," the starting point for those cyclical trials of strength between the Treasury on the one hand with the likes of the electrical trades union and the coal miners and railwaymen on the other, that remained a staple feature of national life in the years ahead. As a further direct consequence of both Suez and Britain's diminished economic and military assets, Macmillan continued and accelerated the postwar dissolution of the empire. His February 1960 speech in Cape Town, acknowledging that "the wind of change is blowing through this continent, and whether we like it or not, this growth of national consciousness is a political fact" provided another of the iconic moments of his premiership. So unflappable on the campaign trail or in the House of Commons, which over the years became his personal theater, Macmillan was perhaps less able at the art of man management. His decision on July 12, 1962, to sack seven senior ministers—a third of the total—seemed to suggest that the PM had panicked, or at least conspicuously failed to offer any new energetic or imaginative policy initiatives to meet the needs of what the *Times* called, in its following morning's review, "the dynamic young generation who will soon be the mainstream in Britain." (As it happened, it was the same day the Rolling Stones first took to the stage.) There was to be some critical comment on various other official appointments between the years of 1957 and 1963. Although Macmillan perhaps wisely never promoted his MP son, Maurice, he gave his son-in-law Julian Amery his old job as air minister and his wife's nephew, the eleventh Duke of Devonshire, was drafted in as undersecretary at the Commonwealth Office, in what the duke himself later described as "the greatest act of nepotism ever."[19] As a whole, Macmillan's premiership falls broadly into a first half, when he appeared to be in charge of events, and a second half, which was increasingly devoted to dealing with domestic and foreign emergencies. Coming to office at a time when deference still predominated in all walks of society, and leaving it amid a satirical firestorm that lampooned the PM as a broken-down figure presiding over an inept and sexually incontinent regime, his seven-year tenure was the trigger point for Britain's 1960s modernization crisis.

Contrary to cynical legend, John F. Kennedy was a full-time chief executive of the United States. History, especially of the post-Watergate, revisionist school impatient with traditional limits when discussing a president's private life, mainly remembers him as a photogenic but morally dissolute swinger who was so busy womanizing that he had little time for anything else. In practice, however, Kennedy was an energetic commander in chief and a consistently astute politician who was fond of academic debate, a voracious reader, a master of fine print, and, like Macmillan, one who overcame a certain personal reserve to develop a speaking style that the (admittedly partisan) historian Arthur Schlesinger characterized in his memoir as "offer[ing] a showcase for a number of [Kennedy's] most characteristic qualities—the intellectual speed and vivacity, the remarkable mastery of the data of government, the terse, self-mocking style, and the exhilarating personal command." Writing to the queen in April 1961, Macmillan described his new Atlantic ally as an engaging mix of New World optimism and an ironic, lacerating wit more familiar to the ancient debating chambers of Europe. "He listened well, both to our side and to his own. He was very quick to take every point. . . . The president, apart from his intelligence, has great charm. He is gay and has a light touch. Since so many Americans are so ponderous, this is a welcome change."[20] In later years, following Kennedy's assassination, Macmillan was sometimes seen to discuss him in quasi-spiritual terms. "It is not given to many men to feel that they have made a contribution on anything like an apostolic scale," he wrote to the president's widow in February 1964. "But I like to think that Jack did something in his country (my dear mother's country) of this order. He altered its way of thinking. . . . He brought it faith."[21]

The salient facts are that John Fitzgerald Kennedy was born in the family home in Brookline, Massachusetts, in May 1917, just as the United States was mobilizing her armies to join in the climactic year of the First World War. He was the second son of Joseph Kennedy, a third-generation Irish immigrant who made a fortune on the stock market and later by reorganizing several Hollywood studios, and the grandson on his mother's side of John "Honey Fitz" Fitzgerald, a prominent Boston political fixer who was the city's mayor and a three-time member of Congress. Where the young Macmillan was comfortably off, John Kennedy was privileged on an epic scale: he spent his summers at the family compound in Hyannis Port and his Christmas vacations at their winter home in Palm Beach, Florida. He was described as "creditable" rather than intellectually dazzling at school and eventually graduated cum laude with a bachelor of science in international affairs at Harvard, where he produced a thesis called "Appeasement at Munich" with the somewhat ponderous subtitle, "The Inevitable Result of the Slowness of Conversion of the British Democracy to Change from a Disarmament Policy to a Rearmament Policy." Along the way, as we've seen, he was to study in London and travel extensively through Europe. These years also saw the beginning of a lifelong series of health problems, among them almost constant back pain, and an equally chronic sexual appetite—in October 1936, Kennedy told his friend Lem Billings that he "went down to the Cape with five guys from school—EM [Edward Moore] got us some girls—four of us had dates and one guy got fucked three times, another guy three times (the girl was a virgin!) & myself twice."[22] In December 1941, Kennedy went to war as an ensign in the US Navy, rising to lieutenant a year later. It's possible that his swift appointment to the command of a patrol torpedo (PT) vessel in the Pacific, one of the service's more glamorous commissions, owed something to his father's influence. On the night of August 2, 1943, Kennedy's boat was rammed by a Japanese destroyer near New Georgia in the Solomon Islands. Two of the crew members were killed outright, and the other eleven cast adrift. Despite reinjuring his back in the collision, Kennedy famously swam for five hours, towing a badly hurt shipmate with a life jacket strap clenched between his teeth. He eventually landed on a small island, where, exhausted and half-mad with dehydration, he carved an SOS message on a coconut with a jackknife. The natives agreed to carry this to a nearby US base. Kennedy received the Navy and Marine Corps Medal for his action, to which he later added the Purple Heart, three Bronze Stars, and the World War II Victory Medal. Despite their differences on strategic-policy matters, both he and Macmillan knew full well what it was like to be in the front line of a battle.

War service remained a strong political card in 1946 and likely contributed to Kennedy's crushing defeat of his Republican opponent in that November's race for a seat in the US House of Representatives. At first he showed no particular aptitude for international affairs but later became a vocal critic of the Truman administration's strategy in the Korean War—arguing not that the United States should swiftly leave the region but that more military resources were required. In October 1950, Kennedy voted for the McCarran Act, which mandated the registration of Communists and Communist front organizations during a national emergency. Two years later, he defeated the incumbent Republican Henry Cabot Lodge for a place in the US Senate. In 1954, Kennedy was the only seated Democrat to vote not to censure the anticommunist crusader Joseph McCarthy partly, he later rationalized, because "my brother [Bobby] was working for Joe. . . . It wasn't so much a thing of political liability as it was a personal problem."[23] This was not a position that conspicuously endeared him to the liberal community. During 1956 and 1957, with his eye now on the White House, Kennedy set out a nuanced strategy on civil rights that sought to curb the "odious and malign" abuses of segregation while still appeasing the more traditional-minded Southern voters. His generally forgiving biographer Robert Dallek has written that at this time, "Jack's interest in civil rights was more political than moral. The only blacks he knew were chauffeurs, valets, or domestics, with whom he had minimal contact." Kennedy did, however, come to embrace a series of specific measures designed to enforce equal-employment laws and to end such practices as racial discrimination in bus, train, and plane travel. These arguably advanced African American rights more than any soaring rhetoric. A number of think pieces signed by Kennedy that appeared in the likes of *Look*, *Life*, and the *Progressive* around this time were in fact the product of ghosts, such as Arthur Krock of the *New York Times*. Many of these convincingly portrayed Dwight Eisenhower as an old man asleep at the wheel, under whose watch the communists had opened up an ominous "missile gap" over the United States. Kennedy won the 1960 presidential race against Richard Nixon by 303 electoral votes to 219 but by only 118,574 (or 0.17 percent) out of 68,837,000 ballots cast. (Doubts remain about the integrity of some of the polling arrangements in Illinois and Texas.) The election result was clearly tainted in one respect. During the campaign, Kennedy forcefully pushed his "missile gap" argument, whereas, as Khrushchev himself later admitted,[24] the Soviet Union's arsenal of intercontinental ballistic missiles (ICBMs) at the time—a grand total of four of them—"represented only a symbolic counterthreat to the United States." In due course, Kennedy proposed his brother Bobby, who was thirty-five, as US Attorney General, a defensible choice but also an act of nepotism that rivaled Macmillan's promotion that same winter of his wife's nephew, the eleventh Duke of Devonshire.

———

In later days, Macmillan sometimes liked to think of himself as the shrewd Athenian statesman offering his counsel to Kennedy's dynamic Roman commander. But in its early stages, the relationship was more that of a persistent elderly suitor pursuing an elusive, younger quarry. Hard on the heels of his eager first letter to Kennedy of December 1960, Macmillan mapped out for the president-elect what he half-jokingly called his "Grand Design." This was a scholarly tour d'horizon whose essential thesis was that the "great forces of the Free World—USA, Britain, and Europe [should organize] in a coherent effort to withstand the Communist tide all over the world." Quite apart from the need for a mutual defense policy, Macmillan, the ex-chancellor, held out the hope of a more flexible Western monetary system, "including the expansion of credit by whatever means, orthodox or novel." It was a commendable effort at what amounted to a capitalist manifesto for the incoming administration, but Kennedy was characteristically charming and noncommittal in his reply. "Dear Mr. Macmillan," he wrote on January 13, 1961, "Thank you for the suggestions in your letter. A meeting between us during the week of April 2 seems to me to be a good basis for planning. Would it be difficult for you to delay your [travel arrangements] until our Inauguration? It could be expected that your plans would become known quite soon thereafter and both of us would be faced with questions about a possible trip to Washington. It would be preferable for me not to confirm such plans before Jan 20 and we could handle the matter much more simply after that date."[25] It was all friendly enough, even if, in setting out the president's terms and conditions for the visit, it recalled an old French proverb: "In love there is always one who kisses, and one who offers the cheek." The economist John Kenneth Galbraith later insisted that he had been summoned to the White House to discuss the "Grand Design," and that a flustered president, after ransacking his office, was forced to admit that the document had been "misfiled." It was eventually found stuffed under a crib in three-year-old Caroline Kennedy's nursery.

Macmillan, showing an acute cautious streak of his own, later wrote of his "alarm" at the state of the Special Relationship as it stood on New Year's Day 1961. "[Eisenhower] has sent a strangely hysterical reply to my message about Laos. . . . This is a most dangerous situation for us. If SEATO [Southeast Asia Treaty Organization] intervenes (Thais, U.S. and ourselves) it will cause trouble in India, Malaya and Singapore. If we keep out and let U.S. do a 'Suez' on their own, we split the alliance."[26]

For all that, Presidents Eisenhower and Kennedy would prove as one in their determination to roll back the recent communist incursion in Laos, even while Kennedy complained to his aide Ken O'Donnell, "I don't think there are probably

25 people [in the United States] other than us in the room who know where it is." What was more, "for me to explain how in my first month in office I'm embarked on a military venture" would, the president said, be political suicide. In the end, Kennedy deployed five hundred marines to the Thai–Lao border, a limited response that Macmillan still felt extreme. It would be a poor idea to "become involved in an open-ended commitment on this dangerous and unprofitable terrain," he told Eisenhower in a cable from April 9, 1961. "So I would hope that in anything which you felt it necessary to say about Laos, you could not encourage those who think that a military solution [is] the only way." It was the first practical demonstration of Macmillan gently seeking to apply the brake on American adventuring and, in hindsight, the precursor to future US policy elsewhere in Southeast Asia.

"For several weeks, the [Allies'] telegraphic battle raged," Macmillan wrote in his memoir of the first months of 1961. Apart from specific geopolitical concerns, the premier was "somewhat depressed" to hear that the new president's cabinet appointments were "conservative" and thus, perhaps, more prone to military intervention in a "tiny, distant and miserably impoverished" country like Laos than they were in the sort of fundamental review of the Western economic system laid out in the "Grand Design." Macmillan wasn't alone in his initial misgivings about what he privately called the "cocky young Irishman" now occupying the White House.[27] The British Foreign Secretary, the tough and able Lord (Alec) Home, whose misfortune it was in the television age to resemble a prematurely hatched bird, whose Adam's apple danced up and down his narrow neck, later admitted to qualms about the way Kennedy had conducted himself in the first half of 1961. "The great test was clearly going to be his handling of the international scene. I confess I was disquieted when, instead of giving himself time to play himself in, he launched into a meeting with Mr. Khrushchev. I did not think he would have overestimated himself or underestimated his opponent. He never did either again, but on that occasion [Kennedy] made a very bad mistake from which it took a lot of time to recover."[28]

On January 20, 1961, a sunny but bitterly cold day, Kennedy announced himself in his inaugural address as of that "new generation of Americans—born in this century, tempered by war, disciplined by a hard and bitter peace, proud of our ancient heritage." Like millions of others around the world, Macmillan was particularly struck by the president's call to a renewed sense of national duty and sacrifice. He later presented Kennedy with an elaborately framed inscription of the phrase,

"And so, my fellow Americans: ask not what your country can do for you—ask what you can do for your country" and its lesser-known sequel, "My fellow citizens of the world: ask not what America will do for you, but what together we can do for the freedom of man." Macmillan's nephew and ministerial colleague Andrew Devonshire was invited into the presidential box for the day and reported back that there might be grounds for continued optimism after all. Three days later, the PM wrote his new Atlantic partner an effusive letter. However long and perilous the road ahead might be, he assured him, "we are your enthusiastic allies."[29]

Macmillan was right to point out the obstacles facing the Western super-powers. Nikita Khrushchev's ultimatum to the United States, Britain, and France on West Berlin of November 27, 1958, marked the decisive shift from his policy of peaceful coexistence. The divided city had become "a sort of malignant tumor," Khrushchev announced at a rare Kremlin press conference. Therefore, the Soviet Union had "decided to do some surgery," as outlined in an accompanying twenty-eight-page note. Since then, several deadlines for Allied withdrawal from Berlin had passed and the four-power standoff continued, with Macmillan coming to see himself as the honest broker who could do business with both Washington and Moscow. (After one set of Kremlin talks, even so, Khrushchev had remarked of his distinguished British guest, "I fucked him with a telephone pole."[30]) Apart from the set pieces of the Cold War, there was also a wide array of regional concerns ranging from the increasingly isolated state of South Africa, whose policy of apartheid was clearly inimical to most of the black Commonwealth countries, among others; the continued political upheavals in Laos, Ghana, and the Congo; the status of Red China; and, not least, the distinct prospect of a Marxist regime coming to power in British Guiana, soon to be the cause of a US covert program to work "against pro-Communist developments by building up anti-Communist clandestine capabilities" in the area, in the words of the CIA. It was a full agenda for anyone. "We still feel," Macmillan told the House of Commons on January 31, 1961, "that the first thing to do, if possible, is to restore peace. That does not, of course, preclude other steps."[31] He was speaking specifically of Laos, but it could have served as an overview of half a dozen other flashpoints around the world.

If Macmillan had ever been in any doubt that he could expect to be com-pared, often unfavorably, to the dynamic new presence in Washington, he would have been enlightened just four days after the inauguration by an exchange in the

House of Commons. "In view of the uncertainty of the right hon. Gentleman's plans," Desmond Donnelly (of the Labour Party) inquired, "will he consider consulting with the Leader of the Opposition to get a report on the competence of the Kennedy administration, as compared with the staleness and mediocrity of his own?"[32] (Macmillan replied merely that he had enjoyed watching the president on television.) A week later, the MP Woodrow Wyatt wondered if the PM had "read Mr. Kennedy's State of the Union message yesterday, in which he indicated a number of measures for reactivating the American economy, and will he take a leaf out of his book and not simply rely on the precept that exports are fun?"[33] (Macmillan: "I have read the most interesting address of the president.") Meanwhile, the Foreign Office had cabled Sir Harold Caccia, Britain's ambassador in Washington, on January 26, 1961, instructing him to extract "firm commitments" from Kennedy "concerning Allied consultation before the use of nuclear weapons and the use of bases in the United Kingdom." Despite several more such requests, there were to be no immediate American assurances on the subject. A hitherto unpublished paper from Livingston Merchant to the new secretary of state, Dean Rusk, dated January 27, 1961, suggested only that the British note "be reviewed by Mr. Kohler, Mr. Farley, and the Acting Legal Adviser, who thereafter could prepare a draft reply by the President to Mr. Macmillan for you to consider and, if you approved, to discuss with the President."[34]

Whether swayed by the legal niceties or some deeper sense of commitment to the Atlantic axis, Kennedy finally replied to Macmillan on February 6, 1961. "Dear Mr. Prime Minister: You will recall that you sent me a message through your Ambassador concerning the continuance of Anglo-United States Understandings. . . . I am writing now to tell you that the three points of clarification [you] make are entirely acceptable to me and reflect our own interpretation of these Understandings. I am happy, therefore, to confirm to you that these Understandings reflect the agreements in force between our two Governments. . . . Needless to say, I welcome this continuing evidence of the intimacy with which our countries work together in all matters." Attached to these warm thoughts on the wider canvas of the alliance were some of the more specific details Macmillan had requested; before launching any US nuclear weapons from bases in the United Kingdom, "the President and Prime Minister will reach a joint decision by speaking personally with each other," Kennedy assured him, although in the case of a possible launch from sites located within the United States or from submarines positioned anywhere outside British waters, the president undertook only to "take every possible step to consult with the UK and our other allies."[35] Washington, in other words, would do its best to exchange views with London in the event of an imminent nuclear strike, but there were no promises.

Macmillan didn't mention the president's measured response when he met with his cabinet colleagues on the morning of February 7. He may have been reminded of it, however, when his defence secretary, Harold Watkinson, informed the meeting that the West German government "has now submitted a request for facilities in the UK for the storage of ammunition [and] general supplies for their army and navy; for maintenance facilities for naval vessels; and for exercises with armed aircraft."[36] Macmillan told his minister that he should press the Germans for more details "and obtain a report on [likely] French reaction" before a final decision was made.

Macmillan himself then went to Paris in order to sell the "Grand Design" to President de Gaulle. He found his host "relaxed, friendly, and seem[ingly] genuinely attracted by my themes. . . . Europe to be united, politically and economically; but France and Great Britain to be something more, and to be so recognized by the U.S."[37] For tactical reasons largely to do with Britain's application to join the European Common Market, the PM wanted to help de Gaulle develop an independent nuclear weapon and thus to give the French "a sense of importance which they have done little to deserve," as he confided in his diary. Macmillan's good mood was deflated when a "somewhat discouraging" message then arrived from Kennedy. "While agreeing with our views on most other questions, it was clear that the new President was no great admirer of de Gaulle's general political philosophy, as well as distrustful of French security methods." After that it was left for Macmillan to write formally to the queen, asking her permission for him to travel to the West Indies at the end of March and then on to the United States. "I am sure that the sooner I can meet Mr. Kennedy and discuss our affairs frankly with him, the better," he told her. "I cannot hope to re-establish at once the same close personal relations as I had with Eisenhower, but it is difficult to form any very strong impression about the new Administration until I have established some personal contact with the President."[38] The queen agreed.

The news that Macmillan was to go to Washington was met by a renewed barrage of questions, often hostile, in the House of Commons. There were demands for him to "raise the effect of the economic situation in the USA on the problem of unemployment in Great Britain," to "suggest to President Kennedy that however grave is his fiscal crisis in America, we will not be pleased if he exports it here," "to draw to the attention of the President the desirability of adopting a common policy [among] the major trading countries of the world," and to address a raft of other issues from the balance of nuclear power to a possible import quota on American canned fruit.[39] Macmillan's old adversary Desmond Donnelly drew his notice to unspecified "investigations" then taking place in Britain, noted the "certain humorous irony" of their timing, and wondered, "Will the Prime Minister raise the matter with President Kennedy?"[40]

The reference was to the recent rounding up of the so-called Portland Spy Ring, a cabal of two Englishmen, two Poles, and a Russian that for several years had used an impeccably respectable address in the London suburbs to supply Soviet intelligence with secret information from Britain's Underwater Weapons Establishment. It was the first of what proved to be a long series of embarrassing national-security breaches. Even before the Portland Ring came to trial, there was the case of George Blake, who held the seemingly contradictory roles of being a senior officer of MI6 and an openly practicing Marxist. Blake had been taken prisoner by advancing North Korean troops when serving at Seoul in June 1950 and later had been "turned" by his captors. He spied for the KGB for nine years, most famously blowing the Anglo-American Berlin tunnel, an operation against Soviet communications in that city. Blake's subsequent sentence of forty-two years' imprisonment was thought to represent one year for each of the Western agents killed when he betrayed them. There was then a public inquiry, which reported that, while there was no clear-cut negligence on the part of Macmillan's government, a number of British civil service trade unions had been "too freely susceptible" to infiltration by communists. As luck would have it, Blake was arrested on the very day that Macmillan flew to Washington, an early forewarning of the security crises that would dog the prime minister through much of his remaining time in office. Macmillan's report to Kennedy that "at least we've put the man away" also proved premature. Five years later, Blake escaped from prison with the help of some antinuclear campaigners who admired him. He later resurfaced, to some fanfare, in Moscow and as of mid-2014 is still living there, aged ninety-one, on a KGB pension.

In early 1961, it seemed to many British commentators that Kennedy represented an invigorating new spirit on the world stage. He enjoyed an almost religious adulation among most of the twenty thousand or so ordinary Britons who
felt moved to write to him. "You are like a meteor before our tired eyes," one
woman gushed in a long letter addressed to "Esteemed Mr. President." Another
correspondent believed Kennedy personified "hope and enlightenment in a world
of scepticism and despair. . . . We are your servants in the struggle for the mastery
of the future." The firebrand Labour MP Anthony Wedgwood Benn, who was then
thirty-five, wrote: "Though I am a few years younger than you, I feel myself to be of
your generation, and am very conscious that you have been speaking for us in recent
months. . . . I might add that you would receive a tremendous welcome here if you
were able to come over on a visit."[41]

Kennedy seems to have been interested to discover whether such comments
reflected his standing in Britain as a whole, because in late February 1961 he had
the US Information Agency conduct a poll on the subject. The results proved the
point. "Among those (61 per cent) who had heard your speeches in whole or in
part," the agency reported, "the reactions were overwhelmingly favorable, with 80
per cent voicing [a] good to very good opinion and only 2 per cent [an] adverse
opinion. . . . The aspects of your presentations which look to have most favorably
impressed British auditors were the elements of challenge and inspiration, and the
candor about current problems and the difficult times ahead."[42]

Kennedy appears to have rapidly taken the view that as much of his time as president would be spent in arbitrating a series of bitter but often arcane disputes as in
imposing any coherent "grand design." Within a week of his soaring inaugural address,
he was embroiled in a fierce battle to expand the House Rules Committee from twelve
to fifteen members; his plans for an early civil rights bill were swiftly bogged down in
Congress; and, surveying an economy he characterized as "in trouble,"[43] he was forced
to warn against expecting "to make good in a day or even a year the accumulated deficiencies of several years."[44] (When, six weeks later, the economy was reported to be
getting weaker rather than stronger, Kennedy quipped to the press, "The Secretary of
Treasury [told] me that the worst of the recession was not yet spent—but everything
else was."[45]) Just as the prime minister had his "events," so the president ruefully noted
of his office, "All you do is choose between the bad and the worse."

Foreign affairs would also prove an early test both of Kennedy's political skills and of his patience. Awaiting the new president on his desk when he returned to the Oval Office after his swearing in was a detailed paper by the RAND Corporation on the true state of the "missile gap" and the only moderate prospects for a global nuclear-test ban. In February, after reading this same document, the secretary of defense, Robert McNamara, told reporters that the United States in fact had "more operational stock" than the Soviets, thus undermining what Kennedy had confi-dently said on the campaign trail. We shall meet McNamara again. Aged forty-four at the time of his appointment, a former titan of industry, he looked steely eyed and supremely rational behind his wire-rim glasses, his center-parted, crisp brown hair and brusque, unambiguous manner giving one observer the impression of "a human computing machine." McNamara was not a theoretician, nor a politician philosopher. He was a systems man, concerned chiefly with the balance sheet of national assets and liabilities. There was an unsentimental precision to his nature, and his robotic concentration on the job at hand became the stuff of transatlantic legend. Men injured in combat were "spoiled assets," McNamara once observed in the course of a White House meeting to decide whether or not to commit US troops to an invasion of Cuba. "Bob could always sit down to dinner with twenty other people, and three hours later, when the bill came, remember exactly who had the soup and who had the house salad," a colleague remembered.[46]

McNamara's counterpart at the State Department, Dean Rusk, was a balding, compact figure whose air of scholarly detachment from events emphasized the aptness of his forename. Behind his back, Macmillan, among others, some-times referred to him as "Buddha." The secretary's closely argued and sometimes-convoluted way of speech was only to be expected, another British official reasoned, "in one who has his office in Foggy Bottom." Born in 1909, Rusk had served with the US Army in Burma during the Second World War and apparently formed a poor impression of British colonial rule as a result. Neither instinct nor experi-ence had equipped him to be a natural cheerleader on behalf of the Atlantic alli-ance. But against this, it could be said that in the truest sense Kennedy acted as his own foreign minister, establishing broad policy and leaving merely the fine detail to others. "There were bureaucratic jobs to be done which neither the president, nor anyone else, particularly wanted, and which Rusk was willing to take on," the same official observed. "He wasn't a remotely political person, despite being surrounded by political struggles. He spoke in a soft voice. Nothing was likely to shock him."

Kennedy's other foreign-policy concerns on taking office ranged from a report by the Atomic Energy Commission that worried that current NATO command procedures were "flawed" and "might trigger a nuclear war" down to the need to reassure even the least of America's allies that the new administration truly valued them. A cable of March 1, 1961, from Rusk to the US embassy in Accra read: "The President is anxious not to give [Ghanaian strongman Kwame] Nkrumah any reasonable grounds to feel snubbed in connection with his reception here. Therefore if Nkrumah's reaction to suggestion that [the] President receive him after his return from London is in any way hurt or resentful you may indicate that in your opinion you believe it might be possible to arrange meeting before he proceeds to Britain."[47]

By the middle of March, Kennedy was spending much of the daily seven or eight hours he typically devoted to foreign policy in preparing for his first meeting with Macmillan. A fat briefing book from presidential aide Fred Holborn included the note: "Here is one of the most perceptive and well-written articles I have read on the PM. Though I do not think he is quite as clever as Fairlie makes him out (he only *seems* that clever in his surroundings), it does catch quite well the flavor of the man." Four days later, Undersecretary of State Chester Bowles followed up with a thirty-five-page file on Macmillan, who, Bowles noted, particularly wanted to "touch on nuclear matters . . . [and] relations with de Gaulle." On March 29, Kennedy's already-extensive library on the subject was further enhanced by a memo dealing chiefly with the Anglo-American position on Berlin. It began: "Mr. Macmillan's visit may provide an opportunity to deal with one of the weaknesses in the Western reaction to the last Berlin crisis: the real split within the Alliance, which was at times obscured and never fully resolved. More specifically, Great Britain has tended to advocate concessions which are . . . extremely dangerous . . . and which the Soviets are bound to interpret as extreme reluctance to face a show-down." Concluding that "the West should do everything it honorably can to avoid war," but decrying as counterproductive "traditional British 'reasonableness' and 'willingness to compromise,'" the paper reflected the core academic duality of its author, a then-obscure thirty-eight-year-old Harvard professor and part-time White House consultant named Henry Kissinger.[48]

On March 7, Macmillan answered a question in the Commons about the state of Anglo-American relations by assuring the House: "Of course, there are close consultations through diplomatic channels at various levels on [nuclear] matters. I am also hoping to discuss them personally with the President in a very few weeks' time."[49] The opportunity to do so came sooner than that. On the morning of March 24, Macmillan and his five-strong team flew to Trinidad, looking forward to a "not particularly testing time" in the West Indies prior to talks in Washington scheduled to begin eleven days later. However, despite the meticulous planning that had been underway on both sides of the Atlantic since even before the inauguration, it was to be another case of what Macmillan characterized as "Events, dear boy, events." On March 23, Kennedy gave a perhaps unintentionally dramatic press conference about the situation in Southeast Asia. "Laos is far away from America," he announced, in an early foreshadowing of what became the "domino theory," "but the world is small. . . . The security of all [the region] will be endangered if Laos loses its neutral independence. Its own safety runs with the safety of us all," Kennedy added, before going on to privately tell the *Washington Post* that "If he had to [invade] and if it meant he would be around only one term, nonetheless he would do it."[50]

In the predawn hours of the 25th, a Saturday, Macmillan was awoken by a cable from Kennedy asking to meet him at the naval base in Key West for "urgent" talks the following day. This was the way the president's highly personal—and occasionally impulsive—style of leadership worked. Kennedy apparently didn't consider the possible difficulties the sixty-seven-year-old premier might face in making an unscheduled, five-hour flight on such short notice. But Macmillan at least came prepared. For some months, he, too, had been doing his homework on his opposite number, on whom "there was plenty of advice, not to say gossip."[51] Nor can the politician in Macmillan have failed to grasp the irony that this was a rare case of the president of the United States soliciting a meeting with his principal ally, and not vice versa. After hurriedly consulting his colleagues, the PM phoned the number he had been given in Washington to confirm that he would be in Florida on the 26th, "in time for Sunday lunch."[52]

The scene that followed "was at the same time one of the strangest and one of the most interesting among my experiences," Macmillan later wrote.[53] The British plane touched down in Key West a few minutes after the president had arrived on Air Force One. Kennedy and Macmillan strode across the tarmac to greet one another as a marine band struck up the national anthems, after which a military detail provided a nineteen-gun salute. The handshake, the sight of the two beaming leaders, and their departure side by side in the back of an open-top car, which then bore them down palm-fringed streets crowded with saluting sailors and cheering men, women, and children—these news images instantly transformed the Special Relationship, in the minds of millions of mainly American television viewers, from a valued but somewhat abstract alliance into a living and breathing partnership. Macmillan himself lingered over the scene in his memoirs, adding the detail that "a large number of spectators, in a great variety of costume or no costume, lined the route and applauded enthusiastically."

Recalling his first impression of Kennedy, Macmillan told his diary of "a curious mix of qualities—courteous, quiet, quick, decisive—and tough." On arrival at the naval administration headquarters where the talks were to be held, there was another poignant reminder of the relative strength of the two leaders as measured by each one's entourage. "On the one side," wrote Macmillan, "was the President of the United States and Commander in Chief of all American forces, surrounded by officers of every rank and degree in a great naval fortress, and receiving all the honour due to a head of state; on the other, [his private secretary] Tim Bligh and I, with Harold Caccia in support."[54] Following a detailed presentation on Anglo-American options in Laos, the two principals then adjourned to a private room for lunch, which consisted of what Macmillan fastidiously called "meat sandwiches"— or hamburgers, a dish with which he was not familiar.

Meanwhile, the primary cause of their meal together, Laos, was disposed of in a scribbled note that used terms such as *monitoring* and *vigilance*, and conspicuously retreated from the threat of an imminent US invasion. Macmillan thought that Kennedy "did not want to 'go it alone' in any action. He definitely wanted it to be a SEATO exercise. . . . I rather objected to anything on the scale of [his] present SEATO plans."[55] This was a notable paraphrase. What Macmillan actually said was that the recurrent civil warfare in Laos was an "almighty mess," and that his one-word advice for any Western leader thinking of intervening there was *Don't*.[56] In the end, Kennedy agreed to stay his hand, and Macmillan agreed to continue to urge Eisenhower, whose public opinion of them obsessed the new administration, to press home the point that Southeast Asia was far from the ideal place to commit US troops. The former supreme allied commander was happy to oblige, if in more military language than Kennedy might have wished. "That boy doesn't know what the hell he's doing," Ike told Earl Mazo of the *New York Herald Tribune*. "He doesn't even know where Laos is. You mean have Americans fight in that goddamned place?"[57]

While Macmillan's secretary hurriedly typed up a minute of their talks, which Kennedy accepted, the two leaders were able to exchange views on various other matters of mutual concern. Berlin, and the Soviet sword that had hung over it since November 1958, was the most pressing topic. There were thirteen mentions of this threat or of some possible future "interdiction" on the free movement of Berlin's citizens. Macmillan told Kennedy that, to his mind, Khrushchev genuinely wanted a peaceful resolution of the problem but was under pressure from the politburo to look tough. Kennedy responded by pointing out that he had a domestic audience of his own to consider. There was no mention in the record of any possibility of regime change in Cuba, though it was known that Kennedy's views on Fidel Castro had undergone a sea change since the time, only two years earlier, when he had supported Castro's overthrow of the corrupt Batista government. Elsewhere, the two men disposed of whole theaters of the world in an almost-magisterial overview— "Africa's quiet," Macmillan observed at one point. There was no time for any more detailed analysis, and it was left to the civil servants to bring order to what was effectively a getting-acquainted chat between new business partners in the form of a suitably bland communiqué. Macmillan was impressed that the young president with such an equivocal reputation was able to match wits with him on a basis of immediately accepted trust and confidence. "He carries the weight of his great office with simplicity and dignity," he said.[58] Kennedy in turn remarked to aides on the plane returning to Washington that he thought the old boy and his few advisers "kind of slow" compared to the frenetic pace set by the Americans, but he appreciated Macmillan's obvious acumen and dry turn of phrase. "I'm lucky to have a man to deal with with whom I have such a close understanding," the president later told Henry Brandon of the *Sunday Times*. Going to see the prime minister was like his being "in the bosom of the family," he added.[59]

So far, so good for the human face of the Special Relationship. But Kennedy was under pressure from many of his advisers to take a harder line on Berlin when Macmillan returned for the previously scheduled talks in Washington due to begin on April 5. The president prepared for these with a lengthy Easter vacation at his family home in Palm Beach. In the breaks between his golf games and sailing trips, he continued to read voraciously on the issues, among them a CIA-backed proposal for an amphibious invasion of Cuba spearheaded by a band of fanatical (but, it transpired, woefully inadequate) anti-Castro guerillas that went under the fitting code name "Bumpy Road." It was left to his press secretary, Pierre Salinger, to assure reporters that the president remained focused on the business of government during his prolonged absences from Washington. He went so frequently to his father's oceanfront mansion not to have fun but because he needed to do his duty—it was the place for "big picture" thinking, Salinger told them.

On April 4, Kennedy turned to a report on Berlin prepared by Dean Acheson, the former secretary of state, now the emeritus figure of US foreign policy and the man who stung Macmillan with his later remark that "Great Britain has lost an empire and not yet found a role." The cover note on the paper handed to Kennedy read: "Here's a first-rate interim memorandum. It sharpens the issues and offers a base from which you may wish to make one or two comments to Macmillan. Acheson argues: Berlin is of first importance; a crisis is likely this year. . . . His major conclusion is that we must be ready to use force in substantial amounts. He leaves open the question of a possible recourse to nuclear weapons."[60]

A second eyes-only presidential paper, prepared by the State Department, rightly pointed to British "misgivings . . . at both the strategic and tactical level" on any possible armed confrontation in Berlin. In the stark words of the author: "Mr. Macmillan recognizes the UK is no longer a great military power and is able to exert only a marginal effect on the military balance between the US and USSR. He is concerned that by the acts of others the UK may be drawn into a conflict which could result in its annihilation." There was an only-qualified bureaucratic endorsement of the merits of the personal factor in the Atlantic alliance. "We attach high importance to a close private relationship with Mr. Macmillan, but we do not believe he should be encouraged to overburden this channel to the exclusion of more normal diplomatic practices."[61]

Kennedy's national security adviser, McGeorge Bundy, was on hand in Florida to take note of any executive preferences that might emerge. Bundy summarized the key presidential position on Berlin as "Planning—yes. But do we mean no commitment[?] . . . How should we regard a new Berlin Blockade? Unless we look very determined about it, we'll get one."[62]

On April 5, Macmillan and his now modestly large party of nine arrived in Washington, where he received a "nice handshake" and "endless flowers," but no official proclamation of welcome. Since it was the queen, not him, who was British head of state, he qualified only for the "friendly foreign dignitaries" protocol of a "few

State Department chaps, shuffling about, nodding inanely at one," he remembered in later discussion with a political adviser. From there Macmillan was driven away to be entertained at a formal White House lunch. This restored the more convivial mood of the previous visit. During a break in the first morning's talks, Kennedy took Macmillan upstairs into a private room to meet his wife, Jackie, which became the unofficial beginning of an unlikely twenty-five-year-long affectionate friendship. The next day, the two leaders and their staffs were taken on a cruise down the Potomac River on board the presidential yacht *Honey Fitz*. Seated in wicker chairs on the aft deck and fortified by "dynamite-strength" cocktails, they discussed matters ranging from Berlin and nuclear tests to the continuing enigma of Southeast Asia. Peering out onto a ramshackle flotilla of pleasure boats floundering away on the opposite side of the river, Macmillan deadpanned, "Looks like the Laotian Navy." It cracked everyone up. James Reston of the *New York Times* thought that:

> In the past the visit of a British Prime Minister to Washington was usually a solemn procession, full of hands-across-the-sea clichés, formal meetings and dinners and vapid communiqués. Harold Macmillan's visit here this time, in contrast, was like a house party and at times almost like a spree.[63]

Macmillan himself drew a sharp distinction between the set-piece discussions when the president was surrounded by his full court of advisers, principally Dean Acheson talking about high noon in Berlin, and the precious hour he enjoyed alone with Kennedy. "It was really *most* satisfactory—far better than I could have hoped," the PM wrote.[64] "He seemed to understand and sympathise with most of the plans which form what I call the 'Grand Design'. How far he will be able to go with de Gaulle to help me, I do not know. But he will try."

Clearly, the Kennedy-Macmillan axis was still in its honeymoon phase. On April 8, a long communiqué was issued, confirming that the alliance was as strong as ever and that its two principals were "committed to maintain the close co-operation they have established." It *was* all really most satisfactory. At the end of the talks, Macmillan presented Kennedy with an effusively signed framed photograph, which hung on the wall of his White House West Wing office for the remainder of his presidency. Kennedy repeatedly used the word *happy* when briefing reporters on the trip. For all that, the premier was left to wonder if there was much inner resolve behind the gleaming surface charm. Although Kennedy listened politely to a long exposition of the "Grand Design," with particular stress on the need for European unity and the advantages it would present for cross-Atlantic trade, he did so "in a rather detached way," Macmillan was forced to admit. "Perhaps because it is his character to be ready to listen to anything. What he decides, is another matter," he wrote in his memoirs. This caution appeared to be well founded when, only a month later, Kennedy sent a "Dear Harold" letter, clarifying some of the points they had discussed, and seemingly agreed upon, in Washington. "After a careful review of the problem," he wrote, "I have come to the conclusion that it would be undesirable to assist France's effort to create a nuclear weapons capability. I am most anxious that no erroneous impressions get abroad regarding future US policy in this respect."[65] In hindsight, it seems reasonable to conclude that what the president had extended to his British visitor was not so much friendship as friendliness.

Meanwhile, Macmillan cabled Kennedy on April 10, 1961, to tell him, "I was much heartened by our talks. It is fun knowing you and I look forward to going on working with you." This same high-spirited quality was possibly what the PM had in mind when he remarked of the president that there was "something very 18th Century about this young man. . . . He is always on his toes during our discussions. But in the evening, there will be music and wine and pretty women."[66] Macmillan's seven-thousand-word report to cabinet on the Washington talks also drew the distinction between Kennedy's private position on some of the issues and that of his retinue. Of these, Dean Acheson gave the British most cause for concern. Macmillan had been taken aback when, on the first morning of their White House talks, Kennedy nodded toward the gravely formal Acheson, who had first adjusted his bow tie and then proceeded to explain to the room why, in his opinion, an armed confrontation with the Soviets in Berlin was more likely than reaching a compromise solution. Revisiting the thorny matter of a nuclear launch protocol, Acheson had gone on to tell the gathering that the current arrangements were "unsatisfactory. . . . It seemed desirable that in the case of ground missiles and water-borne missiles the President should say that, until the Allies had worked out some better system, if one could be found, he would undertake to use the nuclear warheads at present under American lock and key in Europe if Western forces were subjected to a nuclear attack, or to a conventional attack which could not be contained." Macmillan contented himself by replying that "tinkering" with the existing command structures was not enough, and what was needed was a more integrated continental policy on both this and other issues. "The pride of General de Gaulle and of other determined men in Europe demands that they should have some fuller share of control over the nuclear strength of the West. . . . They could not tolerate a position in which their future was decided by others."[67]

While sitting alone with Macmillan in the White House, Kennedy had casually mentioned the "problem of the Cuban freedom-fighters who were in Miami."[68] This was a somewhat motley collection of anti-Castro exiles who had initially sought refuge in Guatemala before undergoing CIA training to prepare for a possible covert return to their homeland. The plan for their moonlight invasion of the island shared some of the broad characteristics of the James Bond novels Kennedy admired, and Macmillan seems not quite to have known what to make of it. After considering the matter, he half-facetiously remarked that, on the whole, he imagined the exiles would be "more nuisance in America than they would be in Cuba." This witticism seemed to find favor with his host. That was the last Macmillan heard of the matter until twelve days later, when his Foreign Secretary rang to tell him, in a voice quivering with alarm, that some 1,400 paramilitaries were apparently engaged in fighting the revolutionary militia on a beach named Playa Giron, located on Cuba's Bay of Pigs, that American B-26 bombers had previously "softened up" the area, that there were reports of the invaders' supply ship having been sunk, and that God only knew what the outcome might be. It was a shattering demonstration of Kennedy's ability to be both supremely affable and "rather detached," as Macmillan put it in his memoirs, when it came to debating specific policy issues with even his closest ally. The subsequent military fiasco was "an hour of bitter truth," wrote Kennedy biographer William Manchester. "The implications of the tragedy were vast—and among them was the realization that men thought to be infallible had proved to be highly fallible. . . . Certainly Washington's mood changed sharply. The football disappeared from Bobby's desk; his brother became more difficult to see. Their first-stage rocket had burned out." In the newly chastened climate that had come over the Kennedy administration in late April 1961, there was no longer any stomach for imminent military adventuring in Southeast Asia. "I don't see how we can make any move in Laos, which is thousands of miles away," Kennedy reflected, "if we don't make a move in Cuba, which is only ninety miles away."[69] Robert Kennedy later said, "I think we would have sent troops into Laos—large numbers of American troops in Laos—if it hadn't been for Cuba."[70]

The president's reluctance to tax Macmillan with the fine details of Operation "Bumpy Road" continued even after the fact. On April 22, four days after Castro's forces had comprehensively routed the insurgents and scored a knockout propaganda blow in the process, Kennedy sent his ally a long cable on a matter of "high strategic importance" to them both. This turned out to be the question of whether or not to subsidize India's latest five-year plan for economic growth. Macmillan offered only guarded support. "I have every sympathy with the view that the Indian Government should be given an indication of financial assistance for a period of years ahead, on which to base their arrangements," he wrote. "As to the amount of aid that we can promise, we will do our best, but you know our difficulties and our other commitments."[71] A nearly constant theme of all Macmillan's dealings with Kennedy was that to follow American foreign policy wherever it led was to risk bankrupting the home economy.

All in all, Macmillan took the Cuban blunder commendably in his stride, apparently seeing it as the kind of thing a favored but headstrong young nephew was bound to get up to from time to time. His principal worry was that this "unhappy story," as he called it, might be poorly received by some of the Commonwealth countries in the West Indies—particularly Jamaica, where the ruling Labour Party of Alexander Bustamante was pressing for full independence from Britain. On May 3, a minister of state at the Foreign Office named David Ormsby-Gore sent Macmillan what amounted to a damage-assessment report on the affair. "Mr. Arthur Schlesinger, one of President Kennedy's men, came to see me yesterday. . . . He was in London on a rather curious assignment. He had come at the president's request to make contact with leaders of the Labour party in order to explain to them the considerations which had led up to the Cuban invasion, and to try and reassure them that the US administration was not composed of blood-thirsty imperialists."[72] Gore concluded that there were no immediately obvious repercussions of the affair for the British government and her possessions, though the same was not true at home in Washington. "The President evidently took the debacle with extraordinary calm," Gore wrote. "He immediately decided to take full responsibility. . . . However, already a number of others are making attempts to escape their share of the blame for the failure. . . . The President has certainly lost confidence in the CIA, and although he has no wish to sack people hurriedly and make them appear scapegoats, Mr. Allen Dulles would have to leave his job earlier than planned, Mr. Schlesinger thought about July." (In the end, Dulles survived as CIA director until November 1961.)

For Britons of a certain age, it must sometimes feel that their entire life has been spent in the shadow of sterile, unresolved arguments about their place in Europe. The foundation of the European Coal and Steel Community in 1951, followed by that of the European Economic Community—or "Common Market"—in 1958, through to its more recent incarnation as the European Union, has provided one of the most long-running and, at times, circular debates of the post-Second World War era. Should Britain be in or out, and, if in, on what terms? In early 1961, Macmillan was preparing to apply for admission to what was then a group of six states. If the price for entry was to help the French develop nuclear weapons, as General de Gaulle was pressing him to, it was one the prime minister was apparently willing to pay. "We're going to join Europe," Macmillan told George Ball, Kennedy's undersecretary of state for economic affairs, in a personal comment during his April trip to Washington. "We'll need your help, since we have trouble with de Gaulle, but we're going to do it."

Ball was especially persuaded by the arguments Macmillan made about a united Europe being able to prevent forever a recurrence of a continental war and, more specifically, about it being able to better withstand the communist tide. "In my view, it would be in our political and security interest for Britain to join the Market fully and wholeheartedly," Ball said in a note to the president on May 10. Kennedy had then made it known that he would be traveling to Europe later in the month to meet with de Gaulle in Paris and with Khrushchev in Vienna. On May 15, Macmillan sent the president a cable dealing with the former part of the itinerary. "I quite agree that the nuclear question is the most difficult part of the French problem," he wrote. "As I see it the object of your talks with de Gaulle will be to persuade the General to modify his rather insular policies and to act more as a good Free World European."[73]

George Ball was more pragmatic in his advice. Among other notes of caution about Kennedy's European trip, he summarized a "central British paradox" about the Common Market that still lingers some fifty years later. "They feel the compulsion to join the Market, and have moved far in accepting the necessary economic compromises," he told Kennedy. "But they are still reluctant to take the final step— to accept the far-reaching political implications of throwing in their lot with the

Continent. The Prime Minister's [cable] is, in effect, a plea for you to help evade the final political decision."

In the House of Commons, Anglo-American relations, and the Cuban fiasco in particular, brought the following exchanges on May 16:

> *Mr. Healey (Labour):* Is the right hon. Gentleman aware that many of us read with great approval his remarks about the importance of not "going it alone"? Does he not agree that it is most important for the solidarity of the Western alliance that none of its members should take action anywhere in the world which is likely to have grave international repercussions without consulting its allies, and that this applies particularly in the case of Britain and the Cuban affair, in view of Britain's great responsibilities in the Caribbean area?
>
> *The Prime Minister:* I think that as a general proposition that is unexceptionable.
>
> *Mr. Hughes (Labour):* In view of the importance of events in Cuba, will the right hon. Gentleman visit Cuba in order to gain first-hand information about the position there?
>
> *The Prime Minister:* No, sir. I have full confidence in our man in Havana.
>
> *Mr. Hughes:* Is he aware that, even in America, there is not complete confidence now in the "man in the White House"? Is he aware that there is strong criticism of the United States action in Cuba in Canada, India, and many other countries of the Commonwealth? Does not he think it would be a good thing if he went and had a look himself?
>
> *The Prime Minister:* No, sir. I cannot answer for the occupant of the White House.[74]

When Macmillan's cabinet met on the morning of May 30, it was to discuss a series of bitter if sometimes obscure domestic and international issues, from the status of Iran to an arcane dispute on the scale of English regional teachers' salaries. There was no mention of Cuba. However, later that afternoon, Macmillan did have the "distasteful task" of answering questions in the House on the Portland spy affair and its possible implications for the alliance. Richard Marsh (of the Labour Party) wanted to know if the premier agreed with him that it was "a rather frightening situation that documents loaned to the United Kingdom by America could vanish. . . . Unless he can remedy the situation in the near future, would it not be in the national interest that he should consider his resignation?" Macmillan was able only to reply, with a hint of Edwardian archaism, "I think the hon. Gentleman very much underestimates the difficulties as well as the dangers of all these security questions. . . . It is a strange paradox of modern espionage in which I fear there is much more danger of a document being copied—so easy is it now to do—for improper reasons, than of its being actually removed."[75]

On a happier note for the alliance, Macmillan went on to send Kennedy a cable (marked "Top Secret") congratulating him on his forty-fourth birthday. "I had always imagined that you were born on March 17," he quipped. "But the boys in my back room tell me that it is not so and that it is May 29. This letter comes with every good wish for the future to you and yours. I value our friendship and rejoice that relations between the US and my country are close and 'happy'. Harold." In Washington later that week, Kennedy took the opportunity of a speech before a joint session of Congress to talk about matters such as the need to keep the world free from the spread of communism; to extend aid programs in Southeast Asia, Latin America, and Africa; and to surpass the Soviets in space exploration. He also asked for an additional $2 billion tacked onto the current defense budget of $2.34 billion, some of which would go to more troops and weapons and the rest to creating bomb shelters.

During their brief encounter over hamburgers in Key West, Macmillan had asked Kennedy if he had any particular feelings about his choice of a new British ambassador to follow Harold Caccia in Washington. The president had immediately given that "dazzling smile of his, like a boy in a toothpaste advertisement," and said, "I'd like David." It was an appointment that was to significantly strengthen, and humanize, the Special Relationship in the years immediately ahead. David Ormsby-Gore, then forty-three, was a suavely debonair and well-connected man-about-town who had been an MP and a rising star at the Foreign Office since the time of the Suez Crisis. He was also related by marriage to both Macmillan and Kennedy and had known the future president during his prewar days as a libidinous young student in London. Some have speculated that he represented an idealized, smooth Englishman—a sort of James Bond figure with extra diplomatic training—to the Anglophiles in the new administration. Lean and sharp-nosed, with a silk scarf often tied nonchalantly around his long neck, Gore gave one admirer the impression of an "animated ferret." Although his personal tastes ran more to jazz and sports cars than to fast women, he was within hailing distance of being a sort of anglicized version of Kennedy in his fundamental outlook on life. On May 18, Gore signaled that a new era in Atlantic relations had begun when he sent the president a five-page handwritten letter. "Dear Jack," it began, "I have been meaning for some time to write to you privately—ever since the PM told me that you had received with admirable fortitude the news that he and Alec Home wanted me to come over as Ambassador."[76]

On May 31, the presidential party arrived in Paris. Kennedy flattered the seventy-year-old general de Gaulle, remarking, "You've studied being a head of state for 50 years—have you found out anything I should know?"[77] The First Lady dazzled her host and the French people as a whole with her beauty and charm. But otherwise the visit failed to achieve any of its more tangible objectives. Reporting on what Kennedy had told him of the talks, Macmillan briefed his cabinet on June 6: "The president made little progress towards his aim of knitting France more closely into the Western Alliance. . . . On the question whether the United Kingdom could join the Common Market, [de Gaulle] once again expressed doubt whether we could do so consistently with our economic relations with other Commonwealth countries. But he laid even more emphasis on the political difficulties which we should find in acceding to the Treaty of Rome. From this the president had deduced that de Gaulle had no particular wish to see the United Kingdom join the Six."[78]

To Kennedy, Paris must have seemed idyllic compared to what followed in Vienna. Although he had briefly met Nikita Khrushchev during the latter's 1959 visit to Washington, this was his first experience of the earthy, sixty-seven-year-old Soviet chairman and first secretary up close. Kennedy summarized it to *New York Times* columnist James Reston as "the roughest thing in my life." The president later told Macmillan that Khrushchev had "maintained a stubborn and unyielding attitude on almost all the questions discussed. . . . On Berlin he had been insistent that a solution must be found before the end of the year along the lines which he had previously advocated. On nuclear tests, he had shown no readiness to reach an agreement. . . . The president felt that the members of the Western Alliance would have to consider very carefully what their response should be to this increasingly intransigent attitude of the Soviet Union."[79]

A flavor of Khrushchev's preferred debating style when confronted with American leaders had come two years earlier, during Vice President Nixon's visit to Moscow. Khrushchev had marked his displeasure at a recent anticommunist resolution of the US Congress by announcing that "it stinks like fresh horse shit, and nothing smells worse than that." Unfazed, Nixon had replied: "I am afraid that the

Chairman is mistaken. There is something that smells worse than horse shit, and that is pig shit."[80] Evidently, the vice president had found a talking point. A sort of "grudging respect" ensued between the two men, Nixon recalled.[81] Khrushchev avoided such narrowly agricultural language when speaking with Kennedy, but there is no doubt it was a bruising encounter for the young commander in chief. "He treated me like a little boy, like a little boy!" the president complained, restlessly pacing the floor of his Vienna bedroom, following the first day's talks.[82] As in Paris, Jacqueline Kennedy gave perhaps the more compelling performance. When Khrushchev, at a formal dinner, attempted to lecture her on the quota of teachers currently available in the Ukraine as compared to the figures fifty years earlier, the First Lady chided him, "'Oh, Mr. Chairman, don't bore me with statistics'—and he suddenly laughed and became for a moment almost cozy."[83]

After his experience with de Gaulle and Khrushchev and, before them, with Canadian prime minister John Diefenbaker (whom he thought an "S. O. B." and "a jerk"[84]), Kennedy must have welcomed the chance to decompress during a thirty-six-hour visit to London. Macmillan drove out to the airport to meet his guest, whom he found "impressed and shocked" by his mauling in Vienna. "It was rather like somebody meeting Napoleon (at the height of his power) for the first time," the PM reflected.[85] The next morning, Macmillan put his arm around Kennedy's shoulder and offered him a stiff drink, which was accepted, on their way in to two and a half hours of private talks at Admiralty House. (The Macmillans had moved into this nearby building when it was discovered that the premier's official residence at 10 Downing Street was not so much in need of repair as in imminent danger of collapse; on his last visit to number 10, President Eisenhower had seriously worried that the floor in the Cabinet Room might give way under the weight of his entourage.) It's not known if either Macmillan or Kennedy took note of the large billboard above the Whitehall Theatre, immediately next door to their meeting place, which read: "Now in Its 4th Year—The Classic British Farce, *Simple Spymen*."

Following the talks, which touched on Berlin, the Common Market, and the latest round of British security leaks, there was a lunch that proved "almost a family affair" for Kennedy, crowded as it was with his Cavendish cousins and in-laws and a fair sprinkling of other dukes and duchesses. Writing to the queen about the visit, Macmillan reported that he had found "the President completely overwhelmed by the ruthlessness and barbarity of the Russian Premier, [who had been] completely impervious to his charm." Kennedy had evidently now joined in a political poker game where the other players thought themselves his elders and betters, hardened professionals who were more than a match for his mixture of youthful good looks and collegiate wit. Nonetheless, Macmillan was impressed by the way the president readily acknowledged his errors, took the responsibility for them, and moved on. After their third meeting, something recognizably like a father-son relationship was starting to take shape. When Macmillan and his wife posed for photographs with the president and First Lady before they were driven back to the airport in their limousine, it struck one observer that they "looked rather like two fresh-faced American kids taking leave of their chaperones."[86] (A "generation gap," as embodied by the United States and the United Kingdom more generally, also surfaced from time to time. Three days after the president returned to Washington, he was handed an elaborately sealed letter from the queen that contained details of a new Commonwealth ambassador she wished to appoint. The exact phrasing of the document caused some mirth in the Kennedy White House. It read: "Elizabeth the Second, By the Grace of God of the United Kingdom of Great Britain and Northern Ireland and of her other Realms and Territories Queen, Head of the Commonwealth, Defender of the Faith, To the President of the United States of America Sendeth Greeting! Our Good Friend! BEING desirous of making provision for the representation in the United States of America of the interests of Sierra Leone We have made choice of our Trusty and Well-beloved Doctor Richard Edmond Kelfa-Caulker to reside with You in the character of Our Minister Extraordinary and Plenipotentiary.")

It can't be said that the first half of 1961 fulfilled the highest hopes of either Kennedy or Macmillan. In London, it had become apparent that much of the "Grand Design" had come up against the intransigence of de Gaulle on the Common Market and of Khrushchev on almost all other matters. The Soviet Union was now openly threatening to sign a treaty with East Germany, ending all Western access to Berlin. There had been no appreciable progress on nuclear-arms testing, let alone disarmament. Regional tensions were still simmering everywhere from Laos to the Congo, to Angola, on top of which the United Nations had now exhausted its working capital of $25 million and urgently needed another $10 million merely to stay in business. No sooner was the loan agreed than the UN's secretary-general Dag Hammarskjöld was killed in a plane crash, leaving the organization without effective leadership for several months. Macmillan was left to put the best face he could on this period of "wild oscillation," remarking in his memoirs that, during all these crises, "at least it could not be held against the British government that they had not done their best."

Kennedy, too, had been tested by events during his first six months in office. In particular, it had been "a very sober two days" in Vienna, he told the American people in a television address on his return to Washington. On July 25, he gave a further speech that left no one who saw or heard it in any doubt as to the gravity of the situation. Using a map to illustrate his point, Kennedy called Berlin a "tempting target" for the Soviets. It had "now become, as never before, the great testing place of Western courage and will," he said. "We cannot and will not permit the Communists to drive us out of Berlin, either gradually or by force. We will at all times be ready to talk. . . . But we must also be ready to resist with force, if force is used upon us."[87] To demonstrate his resolve, the president announced that he would ask Congress for a further $3.3 billion military buildup, including an increase of 125,000 in army manpower, a tripling of draft quotas, and an equivalent call-up of reserves.

In the summer of 1961, Kennedy and Macmillan were sailing in uniquely dangerous, and often uncharted, international waters. But for all the challenges and their own differences of temperament and background, there was an affinity between the two men that ran very deep. Nowhere was this better caught than in the letter Kennedy sent Macmillan on June 10, in which he wrote, "I am sorry to see that one or two crabbed minds have suggested that somehow, in trying to get on better with de Gaulle, America is getting on less well with England. It's not so, as we both know, and I'll find the chance to clear the point up soon. Sincerely, JFK." After his signature, he added the handwritten postscript: "Many, many thanks."

Amplifying on his relationship with Macmillan compared to other leaders, Kennedy later told the London *Sunday Times*, "I feel at home with him because I can share my loneliness with him. The others are all foreigners to me."[88]

3

OPERATION ROSE

Shortly after midnight on Sunday, August 13, 1961, Walter Ulbricht, the austere First Secretary of East Germany's Socialist Unity Party and acknowledged national strongman, gave the order to draw a line, literally, marking the new front in the Cold War. In what was euphemistically named "Operation Rose," four thousand soldiers and an army of civilian workers began to seal off all access points between East and West Berlin. The job was initially achieved by a variety of barbed wire, tank traps, breeze blocks, and rough cement. Most of the construction took place in the predawn darkness, although at one or two key points requiring particular technical concentration, such as the ripping up of the east–west axis road passing through the Brandenburg Gate, harsh white arc lights illuminated the scene. As sentries stood guard at six-foot intervals on Berlin's streets, below ground black-uniformed transport police were at work blocking off U-Bahn railway stations at the sector borders. Any passengers hoping to catch the regularly scheduled trains to the west were unceremoniously bundled back upstairs and told that their journeys were no longer possible. Meanwhile, soldiers with dogs were busy patrolling the sewer systems that connected the two halves of the city. State electricians methodically severed phone lines and other forms of communication. By the time most Berliners awoke on a cloudless Sunday morning, sixty-eight of the city's eighty official crossing points had been blocked, and work was proceeding under armed guard at the dozen that remained. Operation Rose had achieved almost total surprise, and there was no significant opposition at either the state or the individual level until it was too late. London and Washington reacted only with statements of regret, and General de Gaulle let it be known through his defense minister, Pierre Messmer, that Frenchmen were "not about to die for Berlin." Five days later, by which time it had become clear there would be no military intervention by the Western allies, work gangs began to build a two-tier, steel-and-concrete blockade some twelve feet high to reinforce the existing barrier at the Brandenburg

Gate, quickly extending it to run only yards away from the Reichstag (national parliament) building and ultimately to form an impenetrable ten-mile-long urban ring, complete with guard towers, floodlights, alarms, landmines, metal spikes, and attack dogs. Ulbricht's "anti-Fascist protection device"—or Berlin Wall, as others preferred to call it—had arrived.

The crisis found President Kennedy relaxing, as he did most summer weekends, at Hyannis Port, where he attended Sunday-morning Mass before setting off on his cabin cruiser, the *Marlin*, for a family picnic. Shortly before noon, word came through from the president's military aide, Major-General Chester Clifton, advising that a "significant" cable had arrived from the White House. Among other things, it included a CIA wire with the news that "on 13 August the East German regime . . . put into effect a series of decrees introducing severe new control measures designed to stop immediately the flow of refugees to West Berlin and West Germany."[1] Although there was no mention of a wall, or even of a physical barrier, being under construction, the cable went on to warn that "the announcement of the new decrees is bound to increase the already high popular tensions in East Germany. If, as seems likely, the new controls are rigorously enforced, the likelihood is sharply increased of spontaneous outbreaks in East Berlin and East Germany of local disturbances such as strikes, riots, and other anti-regime activities."

Kennedy immediately ordered the *Marlin* to return to shore. There he was met by General Clifton in a motorized golf cart and taken to the small, whitewashed oceanfront cottage he used as an office. After briefly calling Dean Rusk and Robert McNamara, the president agreed to an official State Department response insisting that Operation Rose did not affect the "Allied position in West Berlin or access thereto," although it would be subject to "vigorous protests through appropriate channels." It was now some twenty-two hours since the first military and civilian work crews had begun to seal off the two sides of the city.

Macmillan, too, gave a carefully nuanced response to the initial reports of the crisis. As the barbed wire went up in Berlin, he was on holiday, first shooting grouse in the Yorkshire dales, and then playing golf with his wife in Scotland. Despite this "unhappy news" from the Continent, he could see no need to return to London. "A lot of telephoning, morning and evening, to Alec Home about the 'Berlin crisis,'" Macmillan wrote in his diary. "The Foreign Secretary has behaved with admirable sang-froid, and continues to urge the importance of taking at least the preliminary steps to a negotiation."[2] (Some cynical observers remembered that Home had also been one of the leading proponents of appeasement with the Nazis in the 1930s.) "The Americans wanted to issue a great and rather bombastic 'declaration,'" Macmillan continued, "but this has now been shot down. . . . The President sent me a message about sending more troops into Berlin. Militarily, this is nonsense. But I have agreed to send in a few armoured cars, etc., as a gesture." Buttonholed by an insistent reporter on the eighteenth fairway at Gleneagles, Macmillan snapped, "Nobody is going to fight about Berlin," and, "I think it is all got up by the press." For once, it was perhaps too great a show of public insouciance. The US ambassador to London cabled the State Department that, as a result, the "Foreign Office spent a 'ghastly' Saturday trying to explain away . . . the Gleneagles remark. . . . PM . . . sent message to President saying in effect he goofed."[3]

Although nobody in the West was prepared for the reality of a Berlin Wall— there had been no mention of any such thing in Henry Kissinger's scholarly overview of the crisis just four months earlier—Walter Ulbricht had had plans in place for at least a decade to stop the exodus of refugees, or as he termed them, "Counterrevolutionary landowners . . . spies and saboteurs . . . vermin . . . enemies of Socialist power." In January 1953, he'd won Moscow's support for a scheme "to end uncontrolled access to East Berlin for the western sectors" (and vice versa) by a series of armed checkpoints, although Stalin's death and the subsequent modest thaw in the Kremlin seemed to bring about a more measured approach to the problem. Khrushchev later insisted that the preferred way forward was "to try to win the minds of the people by using culture and policies to create better living conditions." Regrettably, this, too, proved unequal to the task of halting the westward flow of East Germany's citizens. In June 1961, slightly fewer than twenty thousand people were able to obtain a twelve-hour pass allowing them to simply walk into Berlin's western zones and, in 92 percent of the cases, to then forgo the return journey. In July, the total had jumped to 30,450. By the first week of August, refugees were leaving East Berlin at the rate of some 1,800 a day. If those figures had kept up, the German Democratic Republic would have been completely empty by 1989.

———

Despite the official caution, the news of Operation Rose rapidly found its way to the top of the cabinet agendas in London and Washington and was greeted with everything from muted relief that it went only as far as it did to the darkest paranoia about the increased prospect of a nuclear war. Kennedy had been receiving advice on what was routinely called the "Berlin Crisis" since his first days in office. Most of it cast the issue as a critical test of Western will and made the case that, strategically speaking, Berlin was a sort of mirror image of Cuba: one was a piece of communist real estate situated within the US sphere of influence; the other, a Western-occupied enclave located provocatively close to the Soviet zone of control. Kennedy understood the relationship between the two territories and how any direct action in one could produce a counterstrike in the other. "The current Russian activities have caused intense feeling in the United States," the British Foreign Secretary told his cabinet colleagues at the outset of the Cuban missile crisis of October 1962. "The President [has] been placed in a difficult position . . . and seems inclined to believe that the Soviet government [is] again deliberately increasing the scale of Russian activity in Cuba in order to provoke an intervention, which [it will] then use as a pretext for the forcible occupation of West Berlin." Kennedy himself put the central question more starkly. A US attack on Cuba would "likely touch off a nuclear war over Berlin," he told the Joint Chiefs of Staff on October 19, 1962.[4] It was a game of "unpleasant consequences."

From early in his presidency, Kennedy was faced with a wealth of material, most of it densely argued and much of it conflicting, pinpointing his dilemma in Berlin: Should Soviet aggression be met in kind, or was there a diplomatic alternative? On April 25, 1961, the CIA sent the White House a detailed National Intelligence Estimate on the subject. It was a relatively rare instance when the agency of that era lined up with the doves on a critical foreign-policy issue. "We believe that in the quite near future the USSR will present a formal demand for a renewal of negotiations on the question of a peace treaty for 'the two Germanys,'" the paper reasoned. "Almost certainly, Khrushchev still prefers to negotiate on this matter than to provoke a crisis by unilateral action. . . . If higher level negotiations do not take place, or if they break down, the USSR might agree to refer the problem to lower level talks. More likely, however, it would move to summon a Bloc-sponsored peace conference. Under this or any other policy, the USSR is likely to continue to offer negotiations."[5]

This was an exceptional case where the CIA strayed out of character to play the "good cop" to the president's "bad cop" on a grave matter of national security. Kennedy's poor response to the paper may have been in part governed by the agency's role in the Bay of Pigs fiasco, which had occurred just eight days earlier.

By early August 1961, a "soft line" of official or semiofficial thought had emerged on Berlin, broadly taking the view that hundreds of thousands of people should ideally not be allowed to perish fighting over a city four thousand miles from the American mainland. Central to this was the desirability of a third course of action that fell between national humiliation and an all-out nuclear war. Wyoming newspaper publisher and White House adviser Robert H. Johnson urged the president on July 12 to "give due consideration to the long-lasting negative, as well as positive, effects of the psychology we are now creating" by increased military deployments in Berlin. Kennedy's special assistant and resident intellectual Arthur Schlesinger lobbied strongly for negotiations with Khrushchev. Alarmed at the direction events seemed to be taking, Schlesinger, Henry Kissinger, and Abram Chayes of the State Department spent one Friday afternoon in July hurriedly typing a five-point paper on Berlin that they were able to slip into Kennedy's briefcase before he left for Hyannis Port for the weekend. On August 11, Kissinger followed this up with a memo urging that the president consider the long-term objectives of American policy in the region. "One way . . . might be to [agree] explicitly just what we are after in Central Europe. What would we envisage Europe to be like in, say, 1965?"[6] It was to be a case of clear-sky academic theorizing being overrun by events. Thirty-six hours after Kissinger sent his memo, Walter Ulbricht gave the orders to seal off access between East and West Berlin.

Kennedy's essential pre-wall position can best be summarized by the minutes, not previously published, of a White House meeting held on July 17, 1961. Defense Secretary McNamara opened by commenting on the "hard and visible" reality of the Cold War—"a declaration of national emergency in the US was not needed before Sept 1st or Oct 1st," he felt, "although there would be a probable need for a call-up of [military] units before the end of the year." The secretary of state, Dean Rusk, agreed that "necessary armed strength should be built up . . . the Department would concur in a budgetary increase of $4.3bn, and a call of National Guard and reserve units [should be made]."[7] Meanwhile, although not physically present, Dean Acheson emphasized in a note tabled at the meeting what could be called the apocalyptical view of Berlin. It reiterated his belief that "Khrushchev wants to bring about a crisis there by the end of 1961. . . . The whole future of the United States is in the balance."

In the face of such a stark consensus, Kennedy preferred to address the problem from the chess player's perspective of looking several moves into the future. The president "made plain his belief that since we shall have to talk with representatives of the GDR at some stage, we should not now take so strong a line that these later talks will look like a defeat," the minutes note. "Our rights in Berlin certainly cannot be discussed, but there can at an appropriate stage be a discussion in which our rights are to be maintained without impairment."

At the National Security meeting of July 19, the president's principal foreign-policy forum unanimously agreed to a "double-barreled" strategy on Berlin. The first "barrel" involved the continuing US military buildup, and the second stressed the need for negotiations. These specifically included the British, who would "almost certainly demand an opening of talks . . . before agreeing to participate fully in [any] military measures." At a news conference that morning at Foggy Bottom, Kennedy spoke in terms that seemed to be led by both popular emotion and calm statesmanship. "Today there is peace in Berlin, in Germany, and in Europe," he began. "If that peace is destroyed by the unilateral action of the USSR, its leaders will bear a heavy responsibility before world opinion and history. . . . The world knows that there is no reason for a crisis over Berlin today . . . and that if one develops, it will be caused by the Soviet Union's and their government's attempt to invade the rights of others and manufacture tensions. It is the objective of our policy that the people of West Berlin continue to [be] free. . . . We again urge the Soviet government to reconsider its course, to return to the path of constructive cooperation it so frequently states it desires, and to work with its World War 2 allies in concluding a just and enduring settlement of issues remaining from that conflict."

———

Meanwhile, Macmillan's tantrum on the golf course gave way to a more characteristic show of serenity as disasters continued to rain down in the summer of 1961. Kennedy spent most of the weekend of August 18–20 trying to agree a strongly worded tripartite communiqué that would explicitly state the Allies' support of West Berlin and their commitment to the ultimate prospect of a reunified Germany. The White House abandoned the struggle because of President Charles de Gaulle's preference for using "uncompromisingly bold" language, a resolve that did not extend to his sending a single extra French soldier to Berlin. Once again,

Macmillan's was the middle way. He was "not minded to reward" Ulbricht and his masters in the Kremlin for their act of "stark brutality," he said to his cabinet. But there were strategic and practical limits to any British response. The nation was again in one of its routine economic crises, and there had been hard talk in the cabinet that summer of defense cuts. On June 23, Macmillan had noted in response to a colleague's concern on the subject: "I still think we are more likely to be bankrupted than blown up."[8] Even after the wall went up, Macmillan's instinct was not to increase the British garrison in West Germany and Berlin but to significantly reduce it. Replying to a cabinet minute of September 12 proposing "a measure of disengagement" of British forces in Europe, he wrote "[I] agree with your thesis" and added, "I think Foreign Secretary is also in sympathy."[9]

It was not that Macmillan lacked only the resources to put up a determined fight in Berlin. He was convinced, too, that there was little of practical use the Allies could do and that, after an initial period of saber rattling on both sides, the wall would come to be seen as what he called in his memoirs a "crude but tolerable . . . material representation of the spiritual gulf that lay across Europe." Khrushchev may have behaved with regrettably bad manners, but, on the whole, the evidence still suggested he was not a criminal psychopath. So long as he was talking, Macmillan reasoned, he would be unlikely to make good on his threats of mutual annihilation. There was also the question, possibly more pronounced in the West than the East, of public opinion: a Gallup poll taken in the week following Operation Rose showed that 71 percent of Americans were "willing to fight" for Berlin, as against 46 percent of Britons, and 9 percent of the French.[10]

On August 18, Kennedy dispatched Vice President Johnson and General Lucius Clay, the architect of the city's lifesaving 1948 airlift, on a goodwill tour of West Berlin. Johnson was not initially happy at his role in this mission. "There'll be a lot of shooting, and I'll be in the middle of it. . . . Why me?" he demanded.[11] On arrival, however, the Americans' motorcade was bombarded with nothing worse than bouquets of red roses, and—Johnson privately noted—several pairs of freshly shed German lingerie. At that, the vice president plunged into the crowd, shaking hands, distributing souvenir ballpoint pens, and later assuring Berliners from the balcony of city hall: "This island does not stand alone."

Kennedy spent that weekend not in Hyannis Port but at the White House, where his military aide reported to him every fifteen minutes on the progress of his delegation. Had Johnson and Clay in fact been dragged from their car or, as once seemed possible, involved in some confrontation with Soviet border guards, a "full response" was promised from Washington. On August 30, Kennedy announced in a press briefing that Clay would remain as his personal representative in Berlin. The president went on to characterize the Soviet decision that week to resume nuclear testing as a demonstration of "utter disregard of the desire of mankind for a decrease in the arms race . . . [and] a threat to the entire world by increasing the danger of a thermo-nuclear holocaust." (His private remarks on the subject betrayed more of his former life in the navy: "Fucked again," Kennedy noted when told of the Soviets' intentions. "That fucking liar," he added of Khrushchev.)[12]

The following week, there were dire warnings that the Russians would attempt to shoot down Allied aircraft on their approach to West Berlin. Kennedy again canceled his scheduled trip to Cape Cod, and US troops went on a state of heightened alert throughout Europe. That same day, Walter Ulbricht issued a secret order that "firearms are to be used against traitors and violators of the border"—the first evidence that a shoot-to-kill policy was in effect at the wall. It had already claimed its first victim on August 22, when middle-aged mother Ida Siekmann fell to her death while attempting to jump from the upper window of a building located between the Soviet and French zones of control. Severely injured but still alive after the initial fall, she suffered greatly while awaiting transportation to hospital. One way or another, it seemed as though an armed clash was more likely than ever. At the height of this drama, with American ground-to-air missiles being rushed up to protect runways, Macmillan was able, in a diary entry from September 9, 1961, to record his feelings about the prospect of a bloody showdown occurring in Berlin. "I rather doubt [it]," he wrote. His repeated calls for patience and calm may have irritated some on his own side, but few of them could have doubted his ability to grasp the more pragmatic nature of Soviet strategy, that "even Khrushchev" wouldn't risk nuclear war over the technicalities of a German air corridor. Nor did he; the deadline passed without a shot being fired.

Still staying in character, Macmillan wrote to the queen on September 15, 1961, telling her that he had "warned President Kennedy that [a hard-line] policy would lead either to a nuclear war or to a great diplomatic defeat. If we continued to be 'tough' there was a risk of war. If we shrank back from a nuclear war at the last moment and made some kind of accommodation . . . the greater would be the loss of dignity when it was clear that some concessions must follow. I think Kennedy has accepted this."[13]

Macmillan may have taken the more stoical approach to the Berlin crisis, but his advance warning of it was no better than Kennedy's. He had told the House of Commons on June 27 only that "Her Majesty's Government, in concert with their allies, have over the years made a number of comprehensive proposals for the just and equitable solution of the problem of Germany, culminating in the Western Peace Plan of 1959. All these proposals have been rejected by the Soviet Government."[14] As well as reiterating his general goodwill for the people of Berlin, Macmillan admitted that "the Chancellor of the Exchequer [is] discussing the question of the cost [of maintaining forces], which is a problem which we have many times raised and which must be solved." Two days later, speaking specifically of Khrushchev's latest ultimatum, the PM observed: "All sorts of things can be settled by negotiation, but not under threat." Asked on July 6 if he proposed to visit Berlin, "in view of the rapidly increasing tension there," Macmillan replied, "no." A lengthy cabinet paper tabled on July 19 noted only that Khrushchev's most recent outbreak of wishful thinking "insists that Russia [will] overtake the United States in total production by 1970, and in *per capita* production soon afterwards," and concluded that "we must expect him to maintain his propaganda line up to the XXIInd Party Congress in October, and to use this as a platform to rally patriotic feeling and endorse his Berlin policy."[15] These calculations were overtaken by the speed and completeness with which Operation Rose went into effect less than a month later. It was the rudest possible shock. Khrushchev and his myrmidons had shown a mastery of direct action, which he knew the Allies, with all their consultative committees, could never match. Now the wall was up. "I still believe that [Khrushchev] does not want to produce a situation which may lead to war," Macmillan wrote. At the same time, he allowed, "Partly because the Americans have got very excited, the situation is tense and may become dangerous."[16]

At one time, virtually every foreign-policy problem the Allies encountered had been referred to the United Nations. Macmillan's predecessor, Anthony Eden, had called it "the one body with the authority and means" to act as an honest broker. It was thought that the UN peacekeeping force, organized along its modern lines between 1953 and 1955, could immunize states from ruinous foreign commitments. Kennedy had gone so far as to call Dag Hammarskjöld, known for his willingness to asset the United Nations' moral and military power, "the greatest statesman of our century." Hammarskjöld's sudden death in September 1961 was particularly ill timed for the purposes of organizing any concerted international response to Operation Rose. Rudderless for several weeks, the United Nations, under its new secretary-general, the Buddhist U Thant, eventually responded to the crisis not with troops on the ground but with platitudinous pro-peace resolutions that Macmillan privately thought "belonged better in a greetings card." By late 1961, even Arthur Schlesinger, a confirmed believer in the collective approach to world affairs, saw the United Nations as merely a "rhetorical aspirin" seeking to treat a more profound international cancer like Berlin. "Not until I began making regular visits to that great glass tower glittering above the East River did I start to grasp the intensity of the UN life," he wrote in his memoir of the Kennedy administration, *A Thousand Days*. "It was a world of its own, self-contained and in chronic crisis, where a dozen unrelated emergencies might explode at once demanding immediate reactions across the government and decisions (or at least speeches) in New York. It had its own Ethos, its own rules, and its own language: delegates would argue interminably over whether to 'note' or to 'reaffirm' a past resolution to 'deplore' or 'regret' or 'condemn' a present action."[17]

By another stroke of ill luck, Operation Rose also happened to coincide with a breakdown in cooperation between the Allies' primary intelligence services. The British would never exactly have a monopoly on traitors and double agents, but at times during the Cold War it must have seemed that way. Hard on the heels of the "Portland ring" and George Blake affairs came the tragicomic case of John Vassall— a vicar's son (like Blake) and a cipher clerk at the British embassy in Moscow—who had been lured into a homosexual trap and blackmailed into becoming a Soviet mole, "though without the least ideological conviction in the matter," he was later at pains to note at his trial. After his posting to Moscow, he had transferred to naval intelligence in London. During the late 1950s and early 1960s, Vassall was able to abstract hundreds of secret military documents and to photograph others, until the CIA eventually began to interest themselves in his activities. He was finally arrested in September 1962 and given a sentence of eighteen years. (Vassall's debriefing revealed, among other facts, that the KGB had been able to plant small, directional microphones hidden in the walls of all the major Western embassies in Moscow.) Well before then, there was a certain cynicism across the Atlantic about the British government's ability to keep a secret. Macmillan's cabinet papers consistently refer to this "regrettable" and "ill-timed" series of security lapses and deplore the fact that Washington's enthusiasm for intelligence sharing had cooled as a result. Even without the subsequent scandals, Kennedy's failure to dwell on the operational detail of the Bay of Pigs expedition when he met Macmillan just nine days beforehand did not bode well for the "full, frank and thorough exchange of confidences" the PM had hoped for with his new ally. At the best of times, the United States could do only so much to anticipate or subvert a state-sponsored event like Operation Rose. Six weeks before the wall went up, Bill Harvey, head of the Berlin Operations Bureau, or CIA station, reported:

> It is unrealistic to believe that we could infiltrate a sleeper net of sufficient size, reliability, and skill to . . . play a part in organizing resistance groups. . . . Our abilities are not equal to this task when balanced against the defensive capability of the [East German] Ministry of State Security.[18]

For all Ulbricht's vocal impatience with what he called in the People's Congress the "traitors and deserters [from] the capital of the workers' and peasants' haven," there were remarkably few advance signs of Operation Rose until the East German construction brigades and their armed escorts actually began work in the early hours of that fateful Sunday morning. West Berlin's mayor, Willy Brandt, would later insist that "not one individual in the West" had predicted the date of the border closure.[19] "No one has the intention of building a wall," Ulbricht himself had assured a press conference on June 15, 1961. Most commentators on either side of the ideological line had taken him at his word. As late as August 7, Khrushchev declared in a televised speech that "nothing precipitous" would happen in Germany, and he appealed for Western leaders to "sit down as honest men around the negotiating table. . . . Let us not create a war psychosis, let us clear the atmosphere, let us rely on reason." Four days later, he warned publicly that "hundreds of millions might perish" in a nuclear war, before turning philosophical: "I appeal to those who have not lost the ability to think calmly and sensibly. . . . Let us not frighten each other, let us not seek out what divides us, let us not deepen the already deep differences. After all, we have common needs and interests since we have to live on the same planet."[20] As Khrushchev spoke, the authorities in East Berlin were in the final stages of assembling nineteen thousand iron stakes and three hundred tons of barbed wire to use as the first installment of the "anti-fascist protection device." Part of the construction cost of the wall was met by a $500 million loan, which came from a Western consortium quietly arranged the previous June by, among others, West Germany's defense minister Franz Josef Strauss, in order to let the GDR stay solvent through the summer. Khrushchev had ordered of Ulbricht that the barrier should go up in stages: first as a "symbolic line," with a wall to follow only if the West acquiesced.

They not only acquiesced, but right up until the dawn of August 13, there was also no concerted Allied strategy about how to counter any significant Soviet move in Berlin. Kennedy's humiliation at the Bay of Pigs had several obvious consequences, in addition to his long-term disenchantment with the CIA. It had led him to forgo much of his initial enthusiasm for armed overseas adventure and to acknowledge generally that "the proper and consistent means of assessing a statesman, temperamentally and technically, is in foreign policy." (Or as Kennedy put it to Richard Nixon: "I mean, who gives a shit if the minimum wage is $1.15 or $1.25 in comparison to something like this?")[21] Reflecting Western irresolution on Berlin, McGeorge Bundy had briefed the president on July 20: "What we hope will scare [Khrushchev], of course, is fear that if a major fracas erupts in Germany, he will be started down a slippery slope which might lead to nuclear war. But conventional preparations, without keeping the nuclear threat alive . . . may actually confirm to him that we dare not use the very weapons which would scare him most. He may well interpret our remarks and preparations as meaning that we are in fact afraid to use nuclears in the clutch. . . . We might even deploy a few more nukes to Europe just to give balance to our public stance."[22]

Seven days later, Bundy circulated a secret memorandum that showed a tentative hardening of US policy. "The Pres[ident] may, at some appropriate point, reach a decision to authorize stand-by preparations for tests of nuclear weapons, such tests to begin not earlier than 1962. Such authorization will be as quiet as possible."[23]

In London, Macmillan held a full cabinet on August 1 that touched on matters ranging from the laws of succession to peerages, to the desirability of controls on the import and use of pig meat, but he failed so much as to mention Germany. A report three days later by the UK Joint Intelligence Committee dwelled at length on the prospect of a future Sino-Soviet war but again offered no coherent strategy in the event of an abrupt change of the status quo in Berlin. The best that British experts could offer were reams of densely typed global analysis, generally meandering off into fuzzy conclusions swathed in murky language and seemingly almost morbidly shy of giving even a simple declarative opinion, let alone a firm recommendation. It was as if the planners were gazing toward the horizon while oblivious to the precipice in front of them. In Washington, a CIA special group meeting on August 10 concluded only that "a small interagency body should be convened to make proposals [for] CIA covert action in connection with Berlin," and that these would be further discussed on August 22—the same day, as it happened, that fifty-eight-year-old Ida Siekmann jumped out of the window of her third-floor apartment that lay immediately on the border of the east and west sectors of the city. Although friends and neighbors had hurriedly laid down blankets on the pavement, these proved tragically inadequate. Siekmann died shortly after her arrival in the hospital, thus becoming the first of 245 known casualties of the Berlin Wall.

It would be wrong, then, to say, as some have, that Kennedy's response to the events of August 1961 was consistently bellicose, and Macmillan's characteristically poised and self-controlled. Particularly later in the crisis, there were frequently moments of role-reversal between the two national extremes. But it seems fair to conclude that it was the American side that reacted more robustly to the initial shock of Operation Rose. In particular, Dean Acheson remained an early and voluble proponent of brinkmanship with that "S. O. B. Khrushchev," arguing that anything less would undermine Western credibility. Dean Rusk remembered his illustrious predecessor in office arriving for White House meetings of the Berlin task force "with a scowl on his face, as if he smelled a dead dog." The éminence grise of US foreign policy had previously called Britain's failure to immediately join the European Coal and Steel Community "the greatest mistake of the post-war period,"[24] a theme he amplified when he later announced that "Great Britain's . . . role based on a 'special relationship' with the United States is about played out." When Macmillan cabled Kennedy advising against any armed response to the events of August 13, Acheson is supposed to have spat in disdain. The former secretary of state grew more indignant with each Western concession. The wall "would have come down in a day if Harry Truman had been president," he noted privately. Kennedy disliked the old cold warrior personally as much as he respected him professionally. The president eventually cooled to Acheson's counsel, remarking of the in-house criticism of his Berlin policy, "Look at this shit. This shit has got to stop." Following a meeting at which Kennedy had made clear his preference for a nuanced approach to the German question as a whole, the former secretary said to a group of friends, "Gentlemen, you might as well face it. This nation is without leadership."[25]

Britain may have played the role of a branch office to its US headquarters, both when it came to Berlin and to other pressing foreign-policy issues. But if so, it was an unusually well-informed and outspoken subordinate. With a firsthand knowledge of Khrushchev's mentality, Macmillan brushed several American proposals aside as unrealistic. "Too much talk of military postures is undesirable because it is likely to frighten people rather than stiffen them, and may easily start a rot among the neutrals," read a paper circulated to the British cabinet on July 26.[26] "However, it is certainly right for the West to strengthen its hand against the eventuality of negotiations in an unprovocative and calm way. The best hope of reaching [this] position is through quiet diplomacy. . . . However, any negotiation on the subject of Germany and Berlin at the present time will be extremely tough, since Mr. Khrushchev's aims are far-reaching, his position strong and his self-confidence vast." The summary of likely future events in Berlin was to prove as good as anything Dean Acheson managed in Washington. "Leaving aside long-term Soviet objectives for Germany and any hope [Khrushchev] may have of inflicting a humiliation on the Western Powers," the paper concluded, "it is probably fair to say his minimum requirement will be a result which stabilizes the GDR to a sufficient degree to lay the spectre of a unified, anti-Communist Germany. The weakness and instability of the GDR is the main driving force behind Soviet insistence upon a change."

"I feel sure you will agree with me," Macmillan cabled Kennedy on August 28, "that the German problem must be settled ultimately by negotiation. The Communists can do great injury to our economies and to the life of our Western peoples by continuing alarms and pressures over a long period. . . . I therefore thoroughly share [the] view as to the importance of stating that we are ready to negotiate at the right time and in the right way."[27] But this was not merely a case of a tired and effete British politician urging a policy of appeasement on a thrusting young American president. Macmillan was also seized by the idea of ending, once and for all, the sixteen years of steadily crumbling East-West relations over Berlin. To him, a wall, "however crude, was preferable to the Soviets turning control of access to the city over to East Germany." Since Walter Ulbricht had promised to use any such power to "throttle the [Allied] presence" in Berlin—and more immediately, to close the city's Tempelhof airport—this would have brought "compelling pressure for a strike—a formal proposition that we might have to resort to a nuclear war." The only way to avoid this, Macmillan felt, was to play Khrushchev at his own game, laying out an at-once detailed and creatively ambiguous response that left both sides free to claim a tactical victory. Some, like Acheson, might have seen the purpose of Allied policy to set forth in clear terms precisely what would happen if the communists took one step too far in a westerly direction. Macmillan saw it differently: when dealing with the "vulgar and ruthless" Soviet leader—"a kind of mixture between Peter the Great and Lord Beaverbrook"—he purposely avoided language that used words like *ultimatum*, *deadline*, or *consequences*. "A peace treaty would be good if it could be concluded with a reunited Germany," Macmillan, seething with reasonableness, told Khrushchev on August 30. Since he knew this was a remote prospect, he went on to speak in reassuringly quasi-socialist terms about the need to protect the dignity and rights of "ordinary working people" in West Berlin. Such people were entitled to their sovereign freedoms, Macmillan wrote, and might reasonably feel themselves uneasy if now integrated into a society that, "if not hostile, [is] at least unfriendly to its way of life." It was the kind of carefully polished and unexceptional phrasing characteristic of a former British foreign minister that could mean one thing to one side and something else to the other. When it became clear that the West would in fact prefer a wall to a war, Khrushchev's son Sergei wrote, "Father sighed with relief. Things had turned out all right."[28]

Among the West's challenges in formulating a cohesive Berlin policy was the familiar Cold War one of collecting up-to-date information about what was actually happening on the ground. As we've seen, the main US intelligence services had been unable to anticipate, let alone subvert, Operation Rose. Thanks chiefly to George Blake, the KGB had eventually shut down the six-hundred-yard-long tunnel the Allies had dug in 1955 thirty feet under the Berlin sector borders (and which had successfully tapped into enemy communications, at one time delivering 150 reel-to-reel tapes of raw data each day). "A venture of extraordinary audacity—the stuff of which thriller films are made," the *New York Herald Tribune* had said. Nothing remotely like it had been attempted since. A CIA situation report of August 15, 1961, two days after the barbed wire went up, concluded only that "the East German regime [has] introduced new measures to give it better control over the [border]. . . . According to the latest information available, telephone service between West Germany and East Germany, West Berlin and East Germany, West Berlin and East Germany, and West Berlin via a third country to East Germany is not possible. Telegram and postal service, however, between these areas is normal." This was to state only what any ordinary citizen of West Berlin already knew.

If Macmillan, broadly speaking, lobbied for a workable accommodation with the Soviets on Berlin, raising 1930s "Munich" analogies from the political Right, Mayor Willy Brandt spoke for those who had more ambitious visions of Allied tanks rumbling up the autobahn to smash the "arbitrary barrier" dividing his city. One State Department official would refer to the "politically rabid" Brandt "yapping at the ankles" of those, unlike him, who "actually [had] the power and resources to wage a war of mutual annihilation with the Reds." Five days after Operation Rose went into effect, the mayor addressed a "personal and informal" letter to President Kennedy. Brandt's list of grievances was long. It began with a complaint of "inactivity and pure defensiveness" on the part of the Allies, and went on from there to get personal. "I cannot think without bitterness," he wrote, "of those declarations that rejected negotiations with the Soviet Union on the grounds that you could not deal under duress. We now have a situation of total blackmail, and already I hear that we shall not be able to refuse to negotiate."[29] Brandt followed up these remarks by a public appeal for reinforcements to the US garrison in Berlin. Kennedy was unimpressed (though he sent 1,500 more troops), apparently believing the rhetoric was part of a political tactic to help Brandt win election to the West German chancellorship. "That bastard from Berlin," he remarked, had turned Operation Rose into a campaign issue, adding that Vice President Johnson would deliver the "blunt" American reply on his forthcoming visit to the city. Johnson did this with his customary finesse. Harold Caccia, the outgoing British ambassador to Washington, cabled Macmillan that "the VP spoke very severely to Brandt, upbraiding him for reacting so impulsively to the East German move and for firing off in public impractical proposals and unwarranted criticisms of the Allies. Brandt was apparently very shamefaced."[30] One source who was present at the meeting later reported that Johnson had seized Brandt by his lapels, stared down at him, and advised, "Don't shit on your own doorstep, son."

On September 5, the vice president delivered his formal report on his visit to Berlin to the president, Secretary Rusk, McGeorge Bundy, and other senior advisers.

Even in its sanitized language, something of Johnson's onslaught on Brandt can be glimpsed in the official record. "The v-p had spoken frankly to the mayor about the importance of firmness in the Berlin leadership, and Brandt in return had indicated his gratitude for the president's prompt and forthright response to the situation"—if true, a notable retreat from his public remarks. "Brandt had been almost apologetic about his letter. . . . The v-p then described in moving terms the character of the reception he had received from the West Berliners, and how deeply affecting it had been to understand how fully the Americans are relied on in that city."

In fact, Kennedy had grasped the "big picture" of Berlin as early as August 14, on his first morning back in the White House following Operation Rose. According to his special counsel Ken O'Donnell, the president had leaned back in his chair, tapped his teeth with his fingers—a sure sign of rapt concentration—and then asked, "Why would Khrushchev put up a wall if he really intended to seize Berlin? There wouldn't be a need of it if he occupied the whole city. This is his way out of his predicament. It's not a very nice solution, but a wall is a hell of a lot better than a war. . . . This is the end of the crisis. We're going to do nothing now because there is no alternative except war. It's all over, they're not going to overrun Berlin."[31]

With Macmillan cabling his support from the grouse moors, the administration set about "rotating press and public opinion in the US 180 degrees" from the Brandt line. On August 16, the New York Times reported: "The government set out today to portray East Germany's closing of the border between East and West Berlin as a dramatic confession of communist failure. . . . As long as Western rights of access to the divided city are respected, officials said, protest and vigorous propaganda will be their primary form of retaliation." Later that week, Kennedy dispatched Allen Dulles of the CIA and Richard Davis of the State Department to confer with General Eisenhower. "I reported on the sudden closing of the Berlin sector boundary . . . the shock of the West Berliners which exceeded our expectation, and the sudden drop in morale as they saw the tanks and barbed wire across the exit points," Dulles later told the president. "The General commented [that] it is hard to negotiate with a man who is coming across your lawn armed with a club and ready to take possession of your house. Khrushchev was asking for a change in the present status, the General said, we were not. [However], he agreed entirely with the action taken."[32] It remains debatable how far Eisenhower himself may have been responsible for the Allied quandary in Berlin in the first place by forfeiting the city to the Red Army in April 1945. Later in the briefing, Ike touched on a certain exasperation with the "like-minded European states" that still remained an issue in the Kennedy-Macmillan era. "He explained that since 1951 he had preached that the European Allies should contribute the major part of the ground forces [in Germany] and that the US contribution should be in the form of the more sophisticated elements, such as airborne troops, air forces, and missiles. The Europeans have not been willing to do this, and so now the US is faced with shouldering a larger part of the ground forces burden than they should have to."

Kennedy and Macmillan may have settled on a containment policy in Berlin, but there were still moments of real anxiety ahead, when either side seemed ready to draw their sword. On August 31, Harold Caccia cabled the Foreign Office that the US administration was sensitive to "criticism, both here and abroad, about the inadequacy and slowness of Allied reactions to recent Communist moves. They are convinced that some move against the Berlin air corridors is planned for this weekend. They are determined not to be caught napping."[33] Robert McNamara recalled of the same period that "when the Soviets put intense pressure on West Berlin . . . we came very, very close to military conflict then." The air-corridor drama passed, but not the mutual marauding at the newly erected wall. On October 27, Soviet and American tanks moved up to Checkpoint Charlie and faced each other, barrel to barrel, in a high-stakes game of chicken, ready to fire if either side encroached on the border. The standoff lasted for sixteen hours. That same week, the Soviets detonated a thirty-megaton nuclear device—nicknamed the "Tsar Bomba"—in the atmosphere above Siberia. It delivered 1,500 times more destructive force than the American bomb that had leveled Hiroshima. Seven days later, they tested an even bigger weapon on a frozen island in the Barents Sea. The flash and mushroom cloud of this latter explosion could be seen over seven hundred miles away, off the coast of Sweden. In one of those sudden temperamental swings that constitute the basic fabric of Khrushchev's personality, the Soviet leader then announced that he no longer saw a "fatal date" for his country signing a treaty with East Germany. A few days later, he added that, "for the time being, it was not good for Russia and the United States to push each other." The wall was a fait accompli, but, as Macmillan observed, it stood as a "permanent rebuke" to a regime whose citizens had otherwise been so reluctant to accept its authority.

That effectively ended the Berlin crisis of 1961, though it remained as a static issue, and a killer of innocent civilians, for many years to come. Kennedy had been right in his pre-wall assessment to NATO commander General Lauris Norstad that a future confrontation "may last for a very considerable period, on an on-again, off-again basis. . . . Your comment on the desirability of arranging our preparations so as to avoid stimulating counterproductive Soviet reactions seems to me very well taken." However, he added, "the US desire to accord priority to conventional forces should not cause any one to doubt our will to use nuclear weapons if need be."[34]

In London, Macmillan accepted the inevitable. Late in November, he reported to Kennedy on recent "discouraging" and "depressing" talks with General de Gaulle. De Gaulle, he said, "agreed that the division of Germany [and] Berlin were facts which could not be altered, at least for the time being." But the French government was firmly against negotiating with the Soviets—the general "would not be prepared for his representatives to take part in [even] exploratory exchanges," the PM admitted. (Macmillan's diary makes a less diplomatic reference to de Gaulle's "inherited hatred of England. . . . Sometimes when I am with him I feel I have overcome it, but he goes back to his distrust and dislike like a dog to his vomit."[35]) Any substantive Allied response to the continuing challenges of Berlin would clearly be down to the Anglo-American partnership. As a symbolic, if not always practical, gesture of the Special Relationship, British engineers now installed a primitive first "hotline" connecting Macmillan's study in Admiralty House to the Oval Office. The apparatus was both unreliable and unwieldy, looking more like a field telephone of Second World War vintage—each party shouted the word *Over* when it was the other man's turn to speak—but still provided a more or less direct access to the president not afforded to any other ally.

———

As configured by November 1961, the Berlin Wall was an uncomfortable fact of life. Kennedy's real concern was not so much this physical icon of the Cold War but the carefully weighed series of "Soviet provocations . . . incremental abuses, and intransigence" that went with it. None of these issues caused him more anguish than Khrushchev's decision to resume nuclear testing after a voluntary three-year moratorium. Following their initial two detonations, the Russians conducted fifty-one further atmospheric tests in two months. Arthur Schlesinger wrote that "Mac [Bundy] told me the President has been harder and harder to restrain on this matter.

Apparently, there was an animated discussion on it. . . . I assume that [Kennedy] did not raise [testing] with me because he had heard my view and was not interested in listening to more liberal guff on the matter."[36] Kennedy was obviously torn on the issue because, later in November, he announced in cabinet only that the United States would prepare nuclear tests "if effective progress were not possible without them," and that even then the fallout from them, both literal and diplomatic, should be restricted "to an absolute minimum." Meanwhile, the Soviet blasts continued on an almost daily basis. By late December, Kennedy was arguing in a Bermuda meeting with Macmillan that the Allies now needed to redress what he called the "balance of terror" by urgently resuming their own series of tests. The premier's distress at this was evident in his impassioned speech arguing that "we should make another effort—in spite of the Russian trickery and bad faith—to put a stop to all this folly." For the first time since he had met him, Macmillan began to wonder if Kennedy was entirely up to the challenge of the more apocalyptical decisions of the day. "There is a marked difference between the President 'in action' on a specific problem . . . and his attitude to larger issues," he wrote in his diary on December 23, 1961. "In the first, he is an extraordinarily quick and effective operator—a born 'politician' (not in a pejorative sense). On the wider issues, he seems rather lost."[37]

Macmillan himself was enough of a politician to know that most British public opinion was skeptical about Khrushchev's future good intentions. "These last Russian tests are rather alarming," he was forced to admit. "We know that they are working very hard on an 'anti-missile' missile. . . . Their 100-megaton is not just a stunt. . . . It would scorch with fire half [of] France or England if dropped. What then should we do?"[38] Macmillan also knew that Kennedy would not ideally wish the American public to see photographs of a mushroom cloud, even under test conditions, eddying up over the Nevada desert. Once again, the PM was in a position to help. In April 1962, the Americans duly began atmospheric testing on Christmas Island, a sparsely inhabited Commonwealth dependency in the Indian Ocean. Although Macmillan felt "morally bound" to support Kennedy, he spoke for many in his fundamental distaste of the nuclear-arms race—"at once so fantastic and retrograde, so sophisticated and so barbarous, as to be almost incredible."[39]

Although the issues involved were "profound . . . sombre in the extreme," the personal relationship between Kennedy and Macmillan flourished following their Bermuda meeting. According to David Ormsby-Gore, the friendship "blossomed very considerably during it, and after that it was almost like a family discussion when we all met."[40] The president's appreciation of Macmillan's obvious intellectual grip on events contrasted sharply with his opinion of his predecessor in the White House. When Kennedy had dinner with Arthur Schlesinger on October 17, 1961, he told him that Eisenhower had been "too stupid to know what was going on."

Meanwhile, there was a long and varied series of other proxy confrontations around the world that threatened to trigger an East-West nuclear event. In the Republic of the Congo, Khrushchev blamed the murder of the Soviet-backed prime minister Patrice Lumumba on "Western colonialists" and promised to retaliate. Some weeks earlier, a CIA operative known only by his cryptonym "QJ/WIN" had been dispatched to the region bearing a syringe, a surgical mask, and rubber gloves in order to introduce poison into the premier's food. But before the plan could be successfully accomplished, Lumumba was captured by his political enemies, who ran him through with a bayonet.[41] In time, the CIA produced a little-known Congolese trade-union leader named Cyrille Adoula, who was installed in office in August 1961. Civil unrest followed, and it was while on his way to mediate between the rival factions that Dag Hammarskjöld was killed when, on September 18, 1961, his plane crashed on its approach to Ndola in Northern Rhodesia. The rumors about a CIA or MI5 involvement in the affair still exercise the press and conspiracy theorists today.

As well as this, there was the troubling matter of the partly Western-funded Volta Dam project in Ghana. Since Khrushchev was also courting the Ghanaian premier Kwame Nkrumah with offers of Soviet gold, and there was then talk of nationalizing the dam, the whole affair had some of the toxic ingredients that had led to the Suez Crisis five years earlier. Neither Kennedy nor Macmillan could have been reassured when Nkrumah announced his intention to visit Moscow in July 1961. Meanwhile, there was no respite for Allied concerns over British Guiana, which several senior officials feared could turn into another Cuba. Although Kennedy received the colony's new prime minister Cheddi Jagan in the White House, the meeting was not a total success. Jagan extracted $5 million in American aid but then gave an ill-judged interview on NBC's *Meet the Press* in which he spoke over-effusively of his country's "ideological friends" in the Kremlin. According to Arthur Schlesinger, while watching the broadcast, the president had "an impression of either wooliness or fellow-traveling," which "instantly diminished his enthusiasm for helping [Jagan's] government." As a result, Kennedy decided to withdraw his $5 million offer and to substitute a covert CIA program aimed at destroying communist influence in British Guiana.

Clearly, though, East Germany's decision to mark its displeasure with its own citizens by erecting a wall to contain them remained the one consistently hot European foreign-policy issue of the Kennedy-Macmillan era. More than anything else, it represented what the president called the "atmosphere of dread" associated with those years of the Cold War. Although it's officially said that 136 individuals died as a direct result of violence at the Berlin Wall, the total is reliably put at nearly double that figure once those who were caught and executed for escape attempts are included.[42] Perhaps the most poignant incident came in August 1962, when eighteen-year-old Peter Fechter was shot by East German guards when attempting to clamber over what was then an eight-foot-high barrier, topped with barbed wire, dividing the Soviet and American sectors at Checkpoint Charlie. Hit in the leg, Fechter fell to the ground in no-man's-land, where, in full view of a watching crowd on both sides of the border, he slowly bled to death. One of the GIs standing on guard at the checkpoint a few yards away is alleged to have shrugged and said, "Not our problem." Walter Ulbricht later personally rewarded the East German patrol commander and two of his men who eventually removed the lifeless teenager to a hospital. They had suffered "significant stress," he said. Some time later, Ulbricht also issued orders that in cases of any future "interdiction of violators" at the border, the victims were "to be recovered *immediately and without delay* and transported to the hinterland for first-aid treatment, so that this is not visible on the enemy side."[43] This sudden outbreak of humanitarianism did not, however, extend to relaxing the East's official shoot-to-kill policy. A seven-page document dated July 1, 1973, found among the papers of a soldier serving in the eastern city of Magdeburg, contains the following instruction: "Do not hesitate with the use of a firearm, including when the border breakouts involve women and children, which the traitors have already frequently taken advantage of."[44] Just a month after this order was issued, Walter Ulbricht, already stripped of most of his power by his masters in the Kremlin, died in his lakeside Berlin villa at the age of eighty. He was given a state funeral.

4

SPECIAL RELATIONSHIPS

During the last days of the 1960 presidential campaign, Jacqueline Kennedy told a friend she felt "so totally inadequate, so totally at a loss, and I'm pregnant; and I don't know how to do anything."[1] Since she also announced during the race that she personally answered all her correspondence (thought to have been up to three hundred letters a day) and cared for her two-year-old daughter Caroline without a nanny, and that the apparently frugal Pat Nixon "certainly spends more than I do on clothes," it's just possible Jackie was being disingenuous. During the campaign, the *New York Times* claimed that she spent $30,000 a year buying French couture. According to her full-time secretary, Mary Gallagher, the true figure for 1961 was more than $40,000, or the equivalent of some $350,000 today. More than one historian has concluded that Jackie's personal expenses as First Lady exceeded the president's annual $102,000 salary. It was a relatively minor matter, except perhaps to her husband and their accountant, but taken as a whole it suggests there was rather more to her than the meek, self-denying ingenue she sometimes portrayed.

In fact, of course, Jacqueline Kennedy was a widely traveled, literate, opinionated young woman, whom a *Look* magazine reporter who knew her well called "very strong-minded and very tough. . . . I think this is one thing that old Joe Kennedy liked about her, that she was a tough babe." Over the years, she proved to be a significant asset to her husband's career, playing a conventional, if notably glamorous, role as spouse to a rising male politician. The First Lady's appearance, clad in a white, silk Givenchy gown at a state dinner given by General de Gaulle, to whom she conversed in fluent French, won her host's approval for her "charm and poise," which was high praise from that particular source. She was also able to rationalize Kennedy's chronic womanizing by saying, "I don't think there are any men who are faithful to their wives. Men are such a combination of good and evil." This exhibited some perception of the way the world worked in the early 1960s. Not many previous First Ladies had shown quite the same combination of youthful vitality, hard-headed wisdom, and public elegance as she did. "Jackie," as one friend privately observed, "often displayed distinct signs of intelligence beneath the coiffure."

Not only that: like both Kennedy and Macmillan, she also enjoyed intellectual company—with a particular weakness for men of letters like France's culture minister André Malraux or aphorists like Gore Vidal—and was herself both a writer and a bibliophile. As First Lady, she read "five or six books a week," she once said, furtively chain smoking while she did so, and later spent eighteen years as a full-time publisher and editor with a list of authors ranging from Michael Jackson to Nobel laureate Naguib Mahfouz, the Egyptian novelist. It was surely a large part of Jackie's appeal that she appeared at once to be regally aloof and girlishly naïve, often punctuating her speech with words like "gosh" and "golly," gasped out in a tiny whisper, while fixing her listener with her fluttering brown eyes and an adoring smile. A significant feature of her early relationships with men is that she immediately assumed the role of the subordinate partner in the dating ritual. If she went out to dinner at a restaurant with someone, she invariably handed him the keys to the car, even if she happened to own it. During the meal, he would be expected to order for both of them. Later in the proceedings, if she wanted a smoke, she would present him with a cigarette lighter. It was all part of an irresistible show of feminine helplessness. It's been said that Jackie "loved men" and "hated women," with the possible exception of her younger sister, Lee—and that even that relationship was a mix of personal competitiveness, shared childhood trauma, and feline humor. As First Lady, she displayed some of her inner strength and mildly overwrought style at the time of the Cuban missile crisis of October 1962. While many administration officials were sending their wives and children away from Washington out of fear of an imminent Soviet nuclear attack, Jackie insisted that she would stay at the White House with her husband:

> Please don't send me away to Camp David. . . . Please don't send me anywhere. If anything happens, we're all going to stay right here with you . . . even if there's not room in the bomb shelter in the White House. . . . I just want to be with you, and I want to die with you.[2]

It was widely said of the period around 1960–62 that American women of a certain age could be divided into two types, the "Marilyn Monroe" or the "Jackie

Kennedy." Broadly speaking, the former was thought to represent the pretty, empty-headed blonde of flexible morals; the latter, the high-born debutante whose dearest wish was the respectability of marriage. Of course, we know now that each of these archetypal female figures shared several, if not most, of the same characteristics. Jacqueline Kennedy may have been charismatic, intelligent, and demure, with an ability to project deference to her husband's office; she was also extravagant, flirtatious, emotional, mawkish, and, on occasion, unapologetically independent. Alluding to the First Lady's love of travel, often unaccompanied by her spouse, one syndicated columnist suggested that the nation's evening news broadcasts should sign off with the words: "Good night, Mrs. Kennedy, wherever you are."

Some of this same characteristic self-indulgence, as well as the very real dignity and moral fiber that helped turn the former First Lady into an American icon, typified the early years of her widowhood. Few people outside the immediate Kennedy family circle knew quite how desolate she was in that first "dark, terrible winter" following the president's assassination. For months after the event, she barely ate or slept, frequently staying up until the early hours to obsessively sort through her husband's papers and to write long, rambling letters to her friends. "I am a living wound," she told one correspondent, journalist Laura Bergquist. "Nearly every religion teaches there's an afterlife, and I cling to that hope."[3]

On January 31, 1964, Jacqueline Kennedy sent Harold Macmillan a deeply personal, eight-page letter on the subject of her husband's life and legacy. Written in her own looping hand, with characteristic punctuation, on black-edged paper, it expressed all the anger, pain, loss, and frustration she experienced in the first months of widowhood. "Dear Prime Minister," she opened, before abandoning the formal tone. "Sometimes I become so bitter—only alone—I don't tell anyone—but I do truly think that any poor school child looking at the record of the 1960s—could only decide that virtue is *unrewarded*. The two greatest men of our time, *you and Jack* . . . And how does it all turn out?" From there she allowed herself some unappreciative remarks on the eighty-eight-year-old Konrad Adenauer, recently retired as West German chancellor, and the apparently irksome General de Gaulle, "with all his plasma." (This might have been a synonym for "bile." Or, equally, it may be a reference to the time in November 1961 when the French head of state had come to stay at the Macmillans' country house in Sussex, bringing with him a large supply of transfusion blood—to be kept in their refrigerator—in the event of an assassination attempt.) The former First Lady was too well-mannered to voice more than her own irritation at these stalwarts of European affairs, but she left Macmillan in no doubt as to her sense of grievance at the way things had turned out. While the ancient German and the unlovable Frenchman were still alive and politically active, others had been cruelly taken from the arena. "The two people who have had to suffer are you and Jack," she concluded.[4]

This was the beginning of a long correspondence, affectionate and sometimes touchingly intimate, that ended only with Macmillan's death in 1986. "Well—I have just read this letter over—and it is so incoherent—but it is also late at night and tomorrow I move my children and all our little possessions—all of them such reminders of Jack—to a new house," Jackie wrote, just before permanently abandoning Washington for an apartment on Fifth Avenue in New York. Her small confidences to Macmillan, with some of the qualities usually associated with an exchange of love letters, had rarely been seen at the upper echelons of government before. "I [wanted] to say to you what I keep saying to myself and what Bobby says to me," she continued, "—our lives are not very happy now—but we have one consolation—that for a few brief years we all worked together for what was the finest . . . I always keep thinking of Camelot—which is overly sentimental—but I know I am right—for one brief shining moment there was Camelot—and it will never be that way again."[5]

Although the widowed First Lady sought to veil the fact under the appearance of modesty, the "Camelot" association and other, similar images would recur both in her private correspondence and her occasional public remarks on the murdered president. They were intended to bolster the cult of Kennedy, and it would be fair to say that for several years following November 22, 1963, he enjoyed something of the status of a latter-day saint of political legend. In the more jaundiced, post-Watergate era, where public reputations were there to be dismantled, the tragic view of JFK appeared to some critics an oversimplification. Over time, a reaction set in that portrayed Kennedy as an ephemeral figure—a telegenic playboy rather than a statesman, whose undoubted charm and engagingly ironic outlook on the absurdities of human existence served in lieu of any more profound worldview. This, too, was an inadequate picture of the man.

Perhaps all that can be said with certainty is that John Kennedy had his full share of humanizing contradictions. There was a degree of both high-minded principle as well as of cold, if not mean, calculation to much of his leadership of the free world. Take just the example of the uniquely volatile period around the late summer and fall of 1962: Kennedy went to some pains at a press conference on September 13 to establish his credentials as being "tough" (a word he used five times) on Cuba. To underline this, he spelled out the specific circumstances in which the United States "would not hesitate to protect its interests" in the region. These included any "extension of Cuban communism" into the United States or the possibility that the island might become "an offensive military base of significant capacity for the Soviet Union." This chimed with the president's assurance to a Republican senator, Alexander Wiley, that any deployment of Cuba's strategic weapons against a neighboring country would trigger an "immediate" US armed response. In the same week, Kennedy released a statement confirming that were the Castro regime to "export its aggressive purposes, by force or the threat of force, [it] will be prevented by whatever means may be necessary." The president also took the opportunity to announce that he was calling 150,000 army reservists to active duty.

But Kennedy balanced his more militant stand on Cuba with several high-profile speeches assuring the American people that the threat of an imminent US invasion was just so much idle talk by Castro himself, largely to divert attention from his crippling economic problems. There was something acrobatic in the way he hedged his positions. Kennedy characterized the complaints of his hawkish opponents in Congress as mere saber rattling by a few right-wing Republican nuts trying to take advantage of the tension in Cuba in the run-up to the 1962 midterm elections. "I recognize that rash talk is cheap, particularly on the part of those who do not have any responsibility," he remarked at one point. As late as October 14, during a campaign trip to support Birch Bayh, the antiwar senatorial candidate from Indiana, Kennedy still insisted that his—and, by extension, the Democratic Party's—was the voice of reason. "These self-appointed generals and admirals who want to send someone else's sons to war, and who consistently voted against the instruments of peace, ought to be kept at home by the voters, and replaced by someone who has some understanding of what this century is all about," he announced, to a response of ecstatic cheers.[6] He had clearly struck the most responsive possible chord with his audience. Kennedy's remarks that day were not too far in tone from the sort of revolutionary ferment that collected around the anti–Vietnam War movement of a few years later.

One can take the view that all this was a farsighted act of statesmanship on the president's part, or that it was a cynical piece of political pandering designed to make him attractive to both sides in the debate. In either case, it seems Kennedy's realism checked and balanced his belief that it was imperative for the United States to continually assert itself in the struggle to halt the tide of world communism. On the campaign trail, he was a consistently reasonable and benign commander in chief who assured his audiences that he would never commit young Americans to battle without the most compelling need to do so. In the War Room, he remained open to the counsel of his military chiefs that bombing Cuba back to the Stone Age was an eminently viable option. Any other course of action would be "almost as bad as the appeasement at Munich," the bluff, cigar-chewing air force chief Curtis LeMay told the president at a closed-door meeting on October 19. "I think that a blockade, and political talk, would be considered by a lot of our friends and neutrals as a pretty weak response to this."[7] When LeMay went on to inform the president that "you're in a pretty bad fix at the present time," Kennedy responded merely: "Well, you're in there with me."

In private, Kennedy combined some of the urbane characteristics of a London clubman with those of a particularly wanton riverboat gambler, and he must rank as among the most libidinous of all twentieth-century presidents. There is no doubt that he enjoyed female society, and that he continued to explore the limits of his wedding vows right to the end of his life. One of his many casual partners later spoke of him fondly as a "wine and roses at night, pat on the ass in the morning" type, who had a "permanent apparatus of self-containment." Kennedy himself seemed to allude to this latter trait when he said, "Once I get a woman, I'm not interested in carrying on. It's the chase I like—not the kill."[8] Several of his companions have said that women lined up—sometimes literally—to make love with him, and that the act itself tended to be brisk. "He didn't even take his shoes off," one date later sighed. According to another informed source, while in office Kennedy was something of a gastronome, whose love of a good meal "rather mirrored his libido." Just as no dinner was complete with less than three courses, so "some of Jack's nights were like a menu, with an entrée, a meat dish, and a dessert" in the form of a blonde, a brunette, and a redhead. Kennedy, in one extreme view, "had a temperament not far from that of a rapist—he didn't seem to care much what his women wanted, and it was beyond their capacity to surprise other than by actually dying on him."

This was perhaps a reference to the president's rumored affair with Marilyn Monroe. Although the actor and Kennedy brother-in-law Peter Lawford dismissed this particular story as "garbage," it was Lawford himself who fulsomely introduced Monroe onstage at New York's Madison Square Garden for a fundraising gala in honor of Kennedy's forty-fifth birthday. For the occasion, she had literally been sewn into a flesh-colored sheath that only accentuated her famous upholstery. A flustered-looking Adlai Stevenson later noted that Monroe had called the dress "skin and beads." "I didn't see the beads," the ambassador added.[9] Watching the proceedings from a box, the president, unaccompanied by Jackie, is reported to have whispered, "What an ass . . . *what* an ass." The columnist Earl Wilson later insisted that Kennedy and Monroe spent the remainder of the evening in his suite at the Carlyle Hotel. There is also the matter of the frequent phone calls listed in the record from Monroe to the president and his brother, the attorney general. Some years earlier, an aide named Peter Summers witnessed the then senator Kennedy and Monroe emerge one morning from the same shower. The actress was heard to refer to him fondly as "Tank." The initiative may have been all on her side, but Kennedy's fondness for the company of nubile young women, whether at the White House or at Peter Lawford's beachfront home in Los Angeles, long proved a release for what Monroe called his "abounding nervous energy."

That energy also made Kennedy a supremely effective public speaker, with the gift of not only arousing the emotions of a mass meeting but also of making each of his listeners believe that he was speaking directly to him or her. It wasn't his only political skill, but it was one in which no other contemporary leader could rival him. Macmillan, by contrast, while capable of the oratorical tour de force, replete with classical allusions, and punctuated by long spells of silence, by and large lacked the same ability to intoxicate his audience. Clichés now, the president's genial public demeanor and lack of pretension showed his originality in the early 1960s. He was everything his predecessor, Eisenhower, wasn't: energetic, informal, and unburdened by any apparent sense of being the head of a firm of undertakers, gravely reading out the minutes of its last meeting. Arthur Schlesinger characterized Kennedy as "urbane, ironic, always in control." In private as well as in public, his conversation was capable of an "easy shift from the light to the serious." Kennedy's visit to Chatsworth House in June 1961 sowed the seeds of many later stories about how he had "devoured the gossip about who was sleeping with whom—or what" in the British aristocracy, before abruptly remarking of his recent summit with the Soviet leader, "God knows where it will end. Khrushchev may blow us all up." Kennedy's seemingly indefatigable high spirits were the other side of his fatalism—the result, perhaps, of seeing both his brother Joe and his sister Kathleen die in air wrecks, quite apart from his own character-forming experience of towing an injured navy shipmate through the shark-infested waters of the South Pacific. His public image as an eternally youthful and engagingly informal chief executive—the first presidential rock star—was all the more striking given his long history of health problems. Kennedy often wore a heavy, cloth back brace, had a shoe fitted with an orthopedic lift, and suffered a variety of other debilitating complaints ranging from Addison's disease to an irritable colon. At one time in the 1940s, he was in the habit of implanting steroid pellets in his leg, which he did by using a pocket knife to cut the surface of the skin and then pushing the "bullet-sized" slug into the soft tissue. After meeting Kennedy in Bermuda in December 1961, Macmillan was sufficiently concerned about his "young friend" to write to the queen: "The President's health was not good. . . . He found it difficult to sit in the same position for any length of time. I noticed the difficulty he had in picking up a piece of paper that had fallen to the floor. We produced a rocking chair, which was of some comfort to him."[10]

Within a few weeks of becoming president, Kennedy's life was settling into a regular pattern. As well as the reasonably full duties of his day-to-day job, he was also persuaded to start a course of exercise sessions, calisthenics, and heat therapy for his back pains, which he did accompanied by blasts of country and western music, as well as show tunes from his adored *Kiss Me, Kate*, on the record player in the White House basement gym. On May 16, 1961, the Kennedys began their first official trip abroad, to Canada. It proved to be ill-fated: not only did the president fail to warm to his host, John Diefenbaker, he managed to further damage his back while wielding a shovel at an Ottawa tree-planting ceremony. The result was an increased reliance on codeine sulfate and procaine injections for pain management, added to the regular cortisone shots for his Addison's, testosterone to counter weight loss, and a variety of other narcotics to help him sleep. Kennedy's biographer Richard Reeves has said, "In a lifetime of medical torment, he was more promiscuous with physicians and drugs than he was with women."[11] To another biographer, Thomas Reeves (no relation), the president's chemical regimen at least allowed him to bond with the First Lady in what fast became a mutual dependency on "happy pills" supplied by Dr. Max Jacobson, a New York practitioner known among his celebrity clients as "Dr. Feelgood." "Soon Jack and Jackie were using the physician's services on a regular basis," Reeves writes.[12] "When the FDA reported that Jacobson's medications contained amphetamines and steroids, [Kennedy] declared, 'I don't care if it's horse piss. It works.'" Some years later, the New York Board of Regents revoked Dr. Jacobson's license, convicting him of administering stimulants "without sound medical judgment."

The Kennedys' marriage also "worked," surely in large part due to Jackie's heroic forbearance in the face of her husband's multiple infidelities. One of her few lapses from this policy of denial and nonconfrontation came during that same trip to Canada in 1961. At one point, the First Couple were working their way down a receiving line of official guests that included a "blonde bimbo," in the words of Kennedy's military aide General Godfrey McHugh. It was too much. According to McHugh, Jackie "wheeled around in fury" and snapped at him in French: "Isn't it bad enough that you solicit this woman for my husband, but then you insult me by asking me to shake her hand!"[13] There is no evidence that the mainstream press ever took up the matter of the president's womanizing. Some reporters, it's true, joked about the precise role of the young Scandinavian masseuses who came to attend to JFK's back spasms. Others archly referred to the White House indoor pool and sauna area as the "nooky room." But by and large, the media treated the commander in chief with a respect that was as exaggerated as, a decade later, it would have been astonishing. It's possibly the case that Jackie's own discretion on the subject followed the pattern of her mother, Janet, and her mother-in-law Rose, both of whom were married to philandering husbands.

If so, we can also speculate that Jack and Jackie bonded in their shared experience of a materially privileged childhood tainted by adultery, drink, and other unspoken issues. Jackie's alcoholic father and emotionally fragile mother had divorced when their elder daughter was eleven. So far as she ever experienced affection as a girl, it was with a series of pet ponies on which she lavished most of her waking hours. "[Kennedy] saw her as kindred spirit," his friend Lem Billings said. "I think he understood that the two of them were alike. They had both taken circumstances that weren't the best in the world when they were younger, and learned to make themselves up as they went along. . . . They were so much alike. Even the names—Jack and Jackie: two halves of a single whole. They were both actors, and I think they appreciated each other's performances."[14] Better, or inner, reasons for the Kennedys' durable love affair aren't available to an author and may not have been even to the parties themselves. He was always true to her in his fashion.

As we've seen, the Macmillans' marriage also faced its challenges. There were elements of real sadness in what was to be a nearly fifty-year-long union that produced four children, two of whom predeceased their father. The couple were publicly devoted to each other, and always remained so, but it wasn't long before Macmillan realized that his wife Dorothy's many sterling qualities did not include faithfulness to her husband. There was a particularly cruel double twist of the knife in 1929. Having lost his parliamentary seat in the election of May 30, a result that led him to break down in tears, later in the year Macmillan realized that Dorothy had fallen in love with his political ally Robert Boothby. It was a blow sufficient to test even the most sanguine of British public figures. In the summer of 1931, after eighteen miserable months of professional failure and private anguish, Macmillan committed himself to a German sanitarium with what would now be called acute depression. On September 20, he wrote to his mother-in-law to report his doctor's opinion that "the organs—heart, digestive, bladder etc—are all free from disease but all are 'tired'. According to him, I have narrowly missed a complete nervous breakdown."[15] As usual with extramarital affairs, there was ample grief to go around. Boothby's biographer Robert Rhodes James quotes a letter he sent from the Hotel Claridge in Paris in September 1932. "She [Dorothy] said to me tragically yesterday, 'Why did you ever wake me? I never want to see any of my family again. And without you, life for me is going to be nothing but one big hurt.'"[16]

In later years, Macmillan's public image, illustrated by his world-weary drawl and his elegant but ancient clothes, was like that of an infinitely accomplished actor-politician whose mind was more on the grouse moors than on the complexities of parliamentary debate. If so, it was a superbly sustained performance. Just six weeks after writing to his mother-in-law from what he called the "booby-farm" in Germany, he was back in the House of Commons as the National Conservative member for Stockton. Macmillan spent much of the next few years before the Second World War writing manifestos and speaking out on behalf of increased welfare provisions—not only financial handouts but also amenities "like scout halls and ping-pong"—for the disadvantaged. In the tangled metaphor of one of his colleagues, Lord Kilmuir, "Harold became a lone independent gun barking on the left of the Conservative party." Taken as a whole, the 1930s confirmed the impression, on which witnesses agree, that after his electoral defeat and private humiliation, Macmillan emerged not only hardened but also with a confidence in his role as a man with a mission that was unshakable, even in these years when he was a back-bencher, consistently overlooked for promotion, who at one point even contemplated joining Oswald Mosley's New Party, before it took its unwise and ill-timed turn toward fascism.

Superficially the British gentleman, Macmillan remained immensely proud throughout his life of the "New World spirit of enterprise" represented by his mother. It was an inspiration that never failed him. Whenever his confidence in himself wavered, it was immediately restored by the magical words she had spoken to him about the need to strive for constant self-improvement, and "to be anything you wish to be." In what way the young Macmillan was to express his genius remained unclear—whether as soldier, writer, publisher, or politician—but there was not a shadow of a doubt in his mother's mind that he was destined for greatness. Readers may again recall Sigmund Freud's words on these occasions. So in later years the elderly British grandee still retained his zeal for the flamboyance and optimism he associated with America, and which he never tired of praising. The Labour minister Hugh Dalton would remember Macmillan telling him in 1950 that "Europe is finished. It is sinking. It is like Greece after the second Peloponnesian war. . . . If I were a younger man, I should emigrate to the United States."[17]

Like Kennedy, Macmillan was a pragmatist. It could fairly be said that his whole premiership was devoted to maintaining the posture of British greatness, and that no one could have worked harder than he did to sugar the pill of national decline. He was vividly aware that an isolated United Kingdom would only continue to lose status in the postwar world. In December 1957, Macmillan wrote a memo expressing concern that "we are reaching a position in which the English people of 50 million, who in material terms are quite unequal to the new giants, will move neither towards Europe nor towards America. It is a stultifying policy." For political, as well as psychological, reasons, he considered that it was "very much so" in Britain's interests to ally more closely with the United States, the still-rising global power, in order to contain, if not actively roll back, the communist tide. By January 1961, the United Kingdom had reduced the size of its military from a combined conscription-and-volunteer force of 692,000 to an all-volunteer one of 373,000. At the same time, the Russians had an estimated 4.5–5.3 million men under arms. Two entire Soviet armies—the 43rd Rocket and the 50th Rocket—were needed just to maintain their nation's land-based nuclear missiles. Simple mathematics, quite apart from the ties of both history and culture, pointed to the wisdom of Britain's nurturing her Atlantic partnership.

Unlike Kennedy, Macmillan never had a particularly easy time with the press. William Haley, the all-powerful editor of the *Times* from 1952 to 1966, apparently felt Macmillan had once insulted him during the war and never quite forgot the perceived snub. According to Harold Evans, Macmillan's press secretary, "Haley hated his guts."[18] In later years, Macmillan found himself out of sorts with the new generation of investigative reporters, muckrakers, and satirists who followed in the wake of the Suez debacle. Perhaps understandably, he was appalled by the more lurid coverage of his daughter Sarah's death in March 1970 at the age of thirty-nine. She had fallen over when drunk and struck her head. It was the same sad story when Macmillan's grandson Joshua died, aged only twenty, by incautiously mixing alcohol and drugs. There were others, but the tabloid headline "'SUPERMAC' BOY CHOKED ON OWN VOMIT—RUMOURS OF FOUL PLAY 'UTTERLY UNFOUNDED'" probably set a benchmark for mendacious innuendo. One of the longer-term, if unintended, consequences of Macmillan's premiership as a whole, and its series of security scandals in particular, was the disinclination of the British public ever to take politicians quite so seriously again. As a result, newspapers were free to abandon any vestiges of deference to the patrician establishment and quickly substituted the cocktail of sexual gossip and topless photographs that readers of many British papers enjoy today.

Like Kennedy, Macmillan was what would now be termed politically incorrect. Speaking in 1982, at the age of eighty-eight, to the BBC interviewer Ludovic Kennedy, Macmillan recalled the forty thousand Cossacks who had gone to their deaths in May 1945 as "rebels against Russia," who were "practically savages." Referring to a Colonial Office proposal for a postwar federation of Kenya, Tanganyika, and Uganda, Macmillan wrote back his concerns: "The Whites cannot afford economically to abandon their supremacy. The Government will be torn between the rights of the settlers and their obligations to the 'natives.'"[19] As prime minister, he once referred to the up-and-coming Conservative politician Keith Joseph—a pioneer of the monetarist economics that became known as Thatcherism—as "the only boring Jew I've met." "Find out what the middle classes want, and put it on a single piece of paper," he magisterially instructed another colleague. Clearly the author of the "Wind of Change" speech was neither an unregenerate racist nor a particularly vocal champion of any of today's other morally disapproved values. He was, however, a product of his times, just as Kennedy was of his.

At home in Birch Grove, Macmillan cultivated his Edwardian music-hall image, padding around in his tweed plus fours or in a pinstripe suit, with an egg-stained cardigan, surrounded by a cast of comic gardeners, cooks, and butlers to act as a backdrop to his starring role in an apparently permanent performance of some bucolic P. G. Wodehouse story. His official biographer, Alistair Horne, has written of the less antic and sometimes wrenchingly lonely aspect of his life there in the 1960s. "Meals were often silent affairs, with Dorothy and Harold sitting at opposite ends of the long table. . . . Apart from sleeping in different bedrooms, they often sat in different rooms—with Harold plunged in the voracious reading in which Dorothy, whose taste ran to Georgette Heyer and gardening books, could never participate. Nor was the family totally at peace within itself. . . . Often, at Birch Grove, there seemed to be more than a slight aroma of sulphur."[20] All four of the Macmillans' children suffered on and off from varying degrees of alcoholism, while Dorothy made no effort to conceal her continuing double life. Over the years, the prime minister's diaries would often note laconically that his wife "remains in Scotland," meaning with Boothby. Beneath the expertly curated image of stoicism and good cheer, Macmillan knew his share of personal misery. His family disappointments very likely strengthened one of his characteristics, recognized by all who came across him even in his early days, his self-sufficiency and reliance on himself alone. Few of those he met socially or politically impressed him, Kennedy being perhaps the one sure exception. Macmillan treated his only son, Maurice, born in 1921, with a sort of exasperated affection, although the relationship improved once the latter controlled his drinking. Even then, there were limits: though an MP continuously from 1955 to 1964, Maurice was never offered a government job. It would be possible to speculate that Macmillan saw in John Kennedy the disciplined, self-confident son he never had.

Just as Macmillan concealed the unhappiness of his domestic life, he went to some pains to present a professional image of himself as a benign but essentially unreachable chief executive whose colleagues regarded him more like a monarch than a friend. Watching him once shuffle down the aisle of a church, Rab Butler muttered: "It's all put on, you know. . . . Harold can be very amusing, but he should really have been a Cardinal archbishop in the middle ages."[21] Even so, Macmillan's famous imperturbability wasn't entirely a pose. There are too many known cases of the cool, phlegmatic way in which he reacted to events to allow any other judgment. To give just a handful of examples: In October 1944, when he was fifty, Macmillan was seen standing serenely on the deck of the cruiser HMS *Orion* as it sailed into the Aegean, with German mines exploding all around it—"a thrilling experience; it really gave one an idea of the problems confronting a navy today," he remarked drily.[22] He was equally undaunted in his role as minister resident in Athens, where his duties were largely carried out in a bright pink embassy building, without heat or light, but under constant siege from snipers. "There was a good deal of firing and shelling," Macmillan allowed. "In the ambassador's study the bullets came through the window, but there was a corner in which one could sit without undue risk."[23] To encourage subsequent negotiations between rival Greek ethnic factions, Macmillan locked the door of his office one evening and announced, "Gentlemen, we will not leave this room until an agreement has been reached"—which it duly was, at 5:30 the following morning. Macmillan's wartime secretary John Wyndham later remarked of this period: "He was Viceroy of the Mediterranean by stealth. [He] managed things modestly and obliquely. . . . He ran the whole show, but he was perfectly content to let the others think that they were doing so. . . . Power for power's sake was what he enjoyed."[24] Thirteen years later, as prime minister, Macmillan accepted the abrupt resignation of his entire team of Treasury officials with legendary insouciance. These were just "little local difficulties," he announced, before flying off with Dorothy on a long-planned tour of the Commonwealth. ("This will annoy a lot of people, but I think it will give them a sense of proportion," he added in his diary.)

Of course, Macmillan worked hard to foster the impression of being an almost horizontally laid-back, gifted amateur. The reality was different. Right to the end of his life, he worried himself sick (often literally so) before giving a major speech. He was a "made," rather than a natural, orator. Everything had to be exhaustively rehearsed, down to the least nuance, far in advance. Macmillan "had absolute mastery," Rab Butler said. "He took the most immense trouble—for example, his speeches had an asterisk marked in, meaning 'careful pause for extempory comment'!"[25] Congratulating Macmillan on his eulogy to the retiring Winston Churchill, a colleague asked, "As you were the sixth person to speak, weren't you afraid that someone else was going to use those [same] words?" He replied, "Ah, yes, . . . but I had five other perorations prepared."[26] Further belying the caricature of a gentleman amateur, Macmillan was acutely sensitive to his majority in even relatively minor parliamentary votes, obsessively noting "Won by 98 . . . won by 94 . . . won by 96" in his diary. The populist image of the office of prime minister enjoyed a vogue in the later 1960s, encouraged by the studied informality of Macmillan's successors and the celebration of this by the tabloid press. Much was made, for example, of the fact that Harold Wilson smoked a pipe (he preferred cigars in private), or that Ted Heath occasionally made himself grilled cheese sandwiches (when not indulging in meals of near-Tudor gluttony). Macmillan had no time for such contrived simplicity. By and large, he enjoyed being prime minister; relished the ceremonial aspects of the job, especially his regular weekly audience with the queen; unashamedly compared himself to his two political heroes, Disraeli and Churchill; and exercised seigneurial authority over his cabinet—"he was definitely a ruler," Butler noted. Macmillan expected a certain deference and was prepared to overlook most political differences if the correct etiquette was maintained. He once commented that Wilson "has beautiful manners, and he has always been very agreeable to me."[27]

Macmillan's specialty when confronted by an enemy was the elegantly phrased putdown, delivered with a showman's timing. Speaking to the Conservative Party conference, he mocked the Labour leader Hugh Gaitskell's ambivalence on the Common Market by, rather improbably, trilling some lines from the 1946 MGM musical film *Till the Clouds Roll By*: "She didn't say 'yes'; she didn't say 'no'; she didn't say 'stay'; she didn't say 'go'; she wanted to climb, but dreaded to fall; so she bided her time and clung to the wall."[28] It brought the house down. Gaitskell never forgave him. Norman Shrapnel, the longtime political correspondent of the *Guardian*, thought Macmillan had "the sort of voice that goes well with disdain. It was a weapon no subsequent PM could hope to use to the same effect. . . . The ambiguity of the total mix had a panache, a lofty grandeur all its own."[29] Macmillan could, and did, exercise his feline wit in the most exalted company. When Geoffrey Fisher retired as archbishop of Canterbury in 1961, he called on the prime minister to ask whether he wished to hear his views on the choice of his successor.

Macmillan replied that he would. Fisher said, "Whoever you pick, under no account must it be Michael Ramsey, the archbishop of York. Dr. Ramsey is a theologian, a scholar, and a man of prayer. Therefore, he is entirely unsuitable as archbishop of Canterbury. I have known him all my life. I was his headmaster at Repton."

Macmillan cleared his throat and replied, "Thank you, your grace, for your kind advice. You may have been Dr. Ramsey's headmaster, but you are not mine."

Ramsey was installed in his new office on June 1, 1961.

No one is likely to remain the quasi-sovereign ruler of one of the world's four or five most powerful nations for nearly seven years without a certain degree of self-will. At every stage, Macmillan was several moves ahead of the other players in the turbulent political game played out in Great Britain in the late 1950s and early 1960s, constantly surprising them by the subtlety of his calculation, the full depth of his ruthlessness, and above all by his unwavering determination to keep Britain seated at the international top table at a time when she was only marginally qualified to be there. One commentator has compared him to the Archie Rice figure in John Osborne's *The Entertainer*—"the old actor manager for whom the moth-eaten show must go on." Macmillan's long-time Labour Party critic Emrys Hughes was one of those who were both repulsed and impressed by the whole performance: "He cultivated [a] style out of the Gladstonian period—to [us] he seemed the political actor and poseur, the cynic, the knock-about artiste of the parliamentary stage."[30] Hughes eventually wrote an entire book about his archrival, which suggests some degree of respect for him. He called Macmillan "flippant, superficial, supercilious and arrogant," but also conceded that he was "clever, hard-hitting, forceful, convincing, eloquent . . . one who knew all the tricks of [the] game."[31]

There's no doubt that Macmillan, like Kennedy, loved the trappings of power. In January 1962, a US State Department official was handed a document summarizing recent British cabinet discussions on the future of Northern Rhodesia. At several key points, the text referred to "HM" having made some binding decision involving not only that colony but also the Commonwealth as a whole. In all innocence, the official reported to the president on the surprising hands-on role Queen Elizabeth was apparently now taking in foreign-policy matters. It was left to Kennedy to genially write back, correcting the misapprehension. "HM" meant not "Her Majesty" but "Harold Macmillan," although he acknowledged that the latter struck him as a "pretty fair alternative" to the former, and, to be honest, "not all that different." Ironically, Macmillan's biographer Charles Williams writes that there was a certain coolness between the monarch and her long-serving premier, largely because he tended to address her as though she were attending one of his public meetings. "The result," Williams says, "was that when Macmillan visited Balmoral [Castle], a junior secretary was detailed to take him for very long walks to get him out of the Queen's way. She was . . . bored at being lectured and not being listened to."[32]

The same Emrys Hughes thought that Macmillan was one of nature's foreign ministers rather than a born leader. "He had presence, deportment, and looked like a Foreign Secretary. He was Eton, Oxford and the Guards, exactly the kind of 'old school tie' idea" of what a British diplomat should be like.[33] It was still then generally assumed, both at home and abroad, that anyone in that particular role carried a social status and a superiority of judgment sufficient to silence his critics. By and large, Macmillan enjoyed his brief tenure at the Foreign Office from April to December 1955. According to his diaries, he took great pleasure in traveling to overseas conferences, where he could generally sum up his counterparts in as few incisive (and necessarily private) words. Macmillan was particularly good on the Soviets: Bulganin, he thought, "looks like a Radical-Socialist mayor of a French industrial town," while Molotov had "a very pale, pasty face; a large forehead. . . . He wore a very respectable black suit and [seemed] rather like a head gardener in his Sunday clothes."[34] Macmillan's own mandarin style of statecraft was much remarked on by his peers. Vice President Nixon thought him a "wonderfully sly" operator, which was surely high praise coming from that quarter. The Atlantic alliance flourished in the months immediately before the Suez Crisis placed an unbearable strain on it. Macmillan was frustrated only that the US administration felt unable to join him in protesting the sale of Soviet arms to Egypt. John Dulles had to patiently explain the practical difficulties involved, which included the fact that President Eisenhower had just suffered a heart attack. Macmillan also had an only moderately good working relationship with the then prime minister, Anthony Eden. Eden himself had been Foreign Secretary, a post he occupied with some charm, on and off, between 1935 and 1955, and it was sometimes hard for colleagues to determine whether he felt he had ever fully left the position.

Although Macmillan and Kennedy both enjoyed the pageantry of high office, neither one was afflicted by what historian Henry Adams called the "almost insane excitement" of possessing great power. Neither appeared to need public validation to impart a sense of self-esteem. Both were superlative talkers, and, in their own ways, masters of the cut and thrust of political debate. If anything, Kennedy's style was more attuned to the comparative irreverence and occasional anarchy of the House of Commons than to the stultifying atmosphere of the US Senate, whose occupants would surely wear togas if they felt they could get away with it. A year into his presidency, Kennedy's biographer William Manchester wrote, "he was still in his inaugural mood. . . . Being in the Oval Office was fun. Some of it was a carryover from three years of incessant barnstorming: He was still behaving like a nominee. And some was a natural consequence of his appetite for work."[35] Both Kennedy and Macmillan generally avoided committees and preferred to do business with one man at a time. Neither was obsessively interested in administration, which didn't correspond with their views of themselves as big-picture thinkers capable of great sweeps of historical analogy, who could safely leave the fine detail to others. Conversely, both had exceptional memories. "Once the attitude of American business was being discussed at a Cabinet meeting," Manchester writes, "and the president casually cited a quarter-page advertisement which, he said, had been published the previous week in the financial pages of the *Times*. He named the date, the page number, and the ad's position on the page. His ministers were skeptical—none of them had noticed it, not even Secretary of the Treasury Dillon—so Kennedy called for the edition, and there it was, just as he had said."[36] Macmillan, at the age of ninety, was still able to hold the floor for over half an hour in the House of Lords, relating, without notes, the exact details of his maiden speech in the Commons sixty years earlier.

Macmillan and, belying his youth, Kennedy were paternalistic figures—both their nations, Khrushchev once observed, needing "a Tsar they can worship." Macmillan held to only a few specifics—the need for Britain's international involvement, the managed decline of her empire, the need to contain the Soviet Union, the Special Relationship, and European free trade. When events clashed with these, he was prepared to be flexible, trusting that he could use his skills to smooth his way through. Macmillan once remarked of a cabinet minister that he was "full of common sense, a sense of history, and very good nerves . . . any government of the nineteenth century would have been full of [such men]—always able to bugger off home to his estates if Parliament no longer wanted him."[37] He was speaking of his colleague Peter Carrington, but the words could have applied just as well to Macmillan himself. The MP Selwyn Lloyd said of him as prime minister both that he saw the "essential absurdity" of the role, and that he possessed "in a high degree the gift of silence, [which] was unique in a profession where everybody talked far too much." In moments of crisis, Macmillan would sit quietly and read his Jane Austen. Kennedy had some of the same patrician detachment from the murky details of politics and the same ability to conceptualize. He once remarked that America's archenemy wasn't so much communism, but "poverty and want," "sickness and disease," "injustice and inequality." The central core of US foreign policy, Kennedy added, should be "not the export of arms or the show of armed might, but the export of ideas, of techniques, and the rebirth of our traditional sympathy for and understanding of the desires of men to be free."[38] (Of course, just in the event the rhetoric failed, by 1963 he also devoted some 58 percent of his national budget to defense, which was about twice that of the British, French, or Germans.[39]) Like Macmillan, Kennedy was an amateur in the best sense of the word and, like him, always able to "bugger off home" should events compel it.

A master both of dissimulation and of acting a part, Macmillan eventually assumed the role of a political tortoise—toothless, slow moving, benign, with an engaging diffidence about his pause-laden public speaking. Always preferring to make a hostile move through others, in the spring of 1962 he let his ambitious party chairman Iain Macleod lead a sustained behind-the-scenes campaign against the supposed deficiencies of the chancellor of the exchequer, Selwyn Lloyd. Only later, when the axe fell on him and six cabinet colleagues, did Lloyd realize the true source of the complaints. "HIS OWN EXECUTIONER" and "MAC THE KNIFE" were two of the following morning's more restrained headlines. Macleod, in turn, was surprised to learn that he was not to be rewarded for his loyalty with Lloyd's job. The maneuvering by which, over a period of nearly seven years, Macmillan continued to dispose of both rivals and opposition was a masterpiece of veiled but, on occasion, brutal Machiavellian politics. Although de Gaulle's intransigence on the Common Market and the fallout of the Profumo scandal eventually combined with Macmillan's illness to bring the performance to a grinding halt, it was mesmerizing while it lasted.

Kennedy was the better strategist, Macmillan the more comfortable with facts and figures. Some people in Britain expected him in July 1962 to become his own chancellor of the exchequer, the job he had held with some success, the Suez affair aside, from 1955 to 1957. Kennedy had a lifelong antagonism to unbalanced budgets but otherwise showed little interest in the mechanics of the economy. During his first year in office, he often remarked that he could best reduce the US trade deficit by keeping his father at home and encouraging his wife to buy American—or, failing that, "the feds" could always print more money. Many well-placed observers believed he was at least half-serious.

Kennedy, of course, was the more imaginatively modern of the two. Committing an estimated $40 billion to put an American on the moon, he remarked that this was "clearly one of the great human adventures," a case where the merits of the "heroic enterprise" far eclipsed the price tag. Not surprisingly, Macmillan, who had learned his politics in the 1920s and personally experienced the Great Depression, tended to have more material concerns. The sheer precariousness of the British economy, and the fragility of her industrial relations, was vividly shown one evening in January 1963, when a wildcat strike by electricity workers plunged a meeting of government officials at Admiralty House into total darkness. Macmillan and his colleagues were obliged to continue their discussions in the freezing cold, by candlelight. "There may be no tribal council in the Upper Andes where such practices still prevail," Macleod remarked sardonically. Somehow, it is hard to imagine the Kennedy White House in quite the same straits.

When Macmillan flew to Washington, he did so in a noisy, turboprop Britannia aircraft and was lucky to be served "stale ham sandwiches, with soup and a swig of tea" en route. Kennedy, by contrast, traveled in imperial style. He had his own 170-seat Boeing 707, a fleet of marine helicopters, limousines, bodyguards, and state-of-the-art communications. After failing to lure away the chef from the French embassy in London in the fall of 1961, Jacqueline Kennedy was able to secure the services of one René Verdon, the thirty-six-year-old culinary genius at New York's La Caravelle restaurant, who enjoyed a reputation for having a way with sweetmeats and truffles. At about the same time, Harold and Dorothy Macmillan were posing lugubriously for their official Christmas card, which showed them standing among the builders' debris at the back of a heavily scaffolded 10 Downing Street. As a snapshot of British austerity compared to the glittering world of Camelot, with its black-tie, candlelit dinners—the "dazzling mixture of 'beautiful people' from New York, jet-setters from Europe, politicians, reporters," at which "the crowd is always young, the women are always gorgeous," recalled by Ben Bradlee of *Newsweek*—it could hardly be bettered. Macmillan's daughter-in-law Katie later told his official biographer of her sitting down for "uneatable" meals at the family table, of which "roast rabbit, with the head still on" lingered longest in the memory.[40] On another occasion, Dorothy prepared a curried lamb for supper, but this, too ended badly. After the first bite, most of her guests could hardly swallow more. She had put in easily twice too much curry powder. As a rule, those at the Macmillans' table ate only to satisfy their basic hunger.

The Kennedys' marriage has naturally attracted the interest of psychiatrists, as have the lives of their family members, and several studies have been published paying particular attention to Macmillan's own mixture of the sincere and the calculating—the way his whole career was, as he privately conceded, all part of a "glorious game."[41] These were all rich characters in their own right. But it's possible the most interesting, and most neglected, case study is still the one tracing the evolution of Dorothy Macmillan from a pampered and aloof young child of the Edwardian era into the Commonwealth's gossipy and humorous First Lady, with no pretension to personal glamour, who came to occupy a public role that largely prefigured that of the queen mother a generation later. As Dorothy's thirty-six years of infidelity attest, hot fires burned barely below the surface, but through it all she remained an endearingly stolid and benign figure to the nation at large—as Macmillan wrote, someone who "treated everybody exactly the same; whatever their rank or station, they were all to be regarded as friends, and as people in whom she took a deep personal interest."[42] Dorothy became, in short, Britain's favorite communal grandmother.

Born in 1900, she was brought up in a British stately-home tradition that may be difficult nowadays to imagine outside a PBS costume drama. Dorothy spent much of her childhood at the 175-room Chatsworth House: the property included twelve thousand acres of parkland, twenty-one kitchens, seventeen staircases, and a full-time staff of between forty-two and fifty. This was only one of a half dozen of the Cavendish family's estates, which they moved around between on their private train. When Dorothy's father was presented with a large tax bill in 1912, he was able to sell twenty-five books printed by William Caxton and four Shakespeare folios, selected from one of his libraries, in order to make good the arrears.

There were obvious attractions here for a young man on the rise, with little money of his own, and the Macmillans, like the Kennedys, could be said to have made an arrangement that was a merger as much as it was a marriage. Perhaps unsurprisingly, none of the ninth duke's five daughters found it necessary to learn to cook or to acquire any other domestic skills, but most of them were proficient on a horse or with a gun. Unlike her future husband, Dorothy was not a top-notch intellectual. She received a largely token education and was "bored rigid" by both books and politics, she once admitted, leaving unsaid the curious fact that she married a publisher who later became the prime minister. Nor was Dorothy a beauty in the classic sense of the word, some would sneer, with her rather plain face, long arms, and somewhat haphazard dress sense. She was, however, warmhearted, sociable, and completely without airs. Like Macmillan, she was also what would now be held politically incorrect. Complaining of the difficulty of entertaining Madame de Gaulle when she and her husband were once visiting Birch Grove, for example, Dorothy sighed that she was "a very difficult woman. . . . Won't go to the hunt, nor the cripples' craft school."[43] Her public support of Macmillan rarely wavered over the course of some forty years. She was said to have been "loud, banal, and relentlessly jolly—on occasion swearing like a sailor" at one Conservative event. As Dorothy aged, and, not to put too fine a point on it, grew matronly, she gradually acquired special status as an officially approved English eccentric. A State Department "biographic information note" given to Kennedy in March 1961 described her as "of a quiet and retiring disposition. . . . She prefers life in the country, and takes a great interest in gardening."[44] The latter part was right, but not the former. Suddenly denied the services of a large staff and unable to drive a car or to balance a checkbook, Macmillan came to depend on his wife in the tragically short interval between his resignation and her own death at the age of sixty-five. "She filled my life," he told biographer Alistair Horne. "She was devoted to me. . . . I had my reward in the end."

In June 1961, Dorothy accompanied her husband in the party standing at the steps of Air Force One to welcome the Kennedys on their visit to London. The contrast between the two First Ladies as they walked side by side down the red carpet could hardly have been more dramatic. While Jacqueline Kennedy glided beside her in a shimmering, blue Oleg Cassini number and eye-catching French high heels, Dorothy, twenty-nine years older, was dressed for the occasion in a full-length floral print dress and a lopsided, matching hat. In one newspaper account, she "could have passed for her guest's slightly dotty maiden aunt"—something like Jackie's real-life relatives, "Big" and "Little" Edie Beale in their dilapidated, cat-ridden home Grey

Gardens. It was another poignant reminder of the way so much of Britain's public façade seemed to be just that bit more threadbare next to the American version. Dorothy and Harold Macmillan could hardly be said to have lived a "normal" life, but it was a solid, bourgeois existence, private, informal, and quiet, not ostentatious or extravagant, and, oddly enough, untouched by public scandal.

It's worth repeating again that Dorothy worked long and hard on behalf of her husband and, in doing so, endeared herself to audiences all over the world. Hours after the mass defection of the Treasury team in January 1958, the Macmillans set off on a month-long tour of the Commonwealth. It was a personal triumph for Dorothy, whose informality and genuine warmth won over large crowds everywhere, from Karachi to Canberra. The cabinet report on the visit as a whole devotes two pages of close-typed print to the "very great contribution played by Lady Dorothy Macmillan," whether attending a myriad of lunch and dinner parties, speaking to women's groups, or lending her name to local charities.[45] At one point in Delhi, a small but vocal mob of anti-British protesters swarmed around the First Lady, shouting and cursing. One man waved a noose close to her head, and there was spitting in her direction. Dorothy remained supremely unruffled, walking unhurriedly ahead in her "sensible wool suit and wearing an expression of utter self-composure. . . . She might have been strolling serenely among the tombola stalls and coconut shies of an English village fete."[46] Of course, when the occasion arose, she was also fiercely protective of her husband's status. It's said that she once expressed displeasure with a foreign visitor at Admiralty House by installing an entire Royal Marine band immediately behind his head at a formal dinner. Whatever their private anguish, Harold and Dorothy Macmillan could (and did) give a dazzling public performance of a couple completely devoted to each other's welfare.

Perhaps little more need be said of Dorothy's long affair with the dark-eyed, saturnine, and velvet-voiced figure of Robert Boothby. Even in those more reticent times, it was quite widely debated among Britain's social and political hierarchy, as opposed to the general public. In certain circles, from the 1930s onward, it was possible to listen to some of the nation's most elite minds argue with all the fury of Lilliput and Blefuscu squaring off on whether to cut the egg at the big end or the small end about the matter of Boothby's precise status: Was he a bounder, a cad, or possibly merely a twister for having stolen a colleague's wife? Was his behavior perhaps more permissible in view of the fact that Dorothy herself had initiated the affair, evidently seeing it as her sole chance, she once said, to be "a woman, [and] not a public statue"? Writing to a mutual friend in September 1932, Boothby confided of an illicit week spent on the Continent: "It was a new world for Dorothy. It was like taking a thrilled child to a play for the first time. She brushed her hair back behind her ears, and actually put lipstick on, and got more radiant every day. . . . And now I have shipped her back to Birch Grove as Mrs. Macmillan."[47]

Though headstrong and promiscuous (he had affairs with at least two of Dorothy's cousins and married one of them), Boothby was not without professional distinction. He was first elected to parliament when he was twenty-four, played a leading role in bringing Churchill to power in 1940, and was consistently ahead of his time on such defining issues as Britain's application to the Common Market, the role of the world gold standard, and the merits of a seafood diet. For a variety of reasons, including his own colorful finances, senior ministerial office eluded him. Boothby was one of the nearly men of British politics, seen by many, including himself, as a future Conservative prime minister. It wasn't to be: Macmillan raised him to the peerage in 1958 as Baron Boothby of Buchan and Rattray Head, which ended any professional ambitions he might have had left. The political tortoise, it could be said, had outrun the hare. Critics still debate the paternity of Dorothy's daughter Sarah, born in August 1930, and left without a name on her birth certificate. In February 1975, Macmillan went to a lunch in London at which Boothby was also a guest. The two old warriors later adjourned to Boothby's flat, where, according to author and historian D. R. Thorpe, they spoke about the whole affair. In a further twist, the conversation was "unwittingly" tape-recorded by Boothby. On the tape, Macmillan is supposed to have described the pain he had endured for forty-five years over the affair and the birth of Sarah, whom he treated as his own until her death in 1970. Boothby denied being Sarah's father, in part because his "roving eye had later taken the girl in," an attraction even he would have denied had they in fact been related. Macmillan in turn described how, following Dorothy's death, he had destroyed Boothby's letters to her. He "piled all of them in an outside incinerator, and the wind got up. Suddenly, the letters were flying all round the garden, and [he] was chasing them."[48]

Macmillan's last words on the tape were: "And so it all ended." Boothby then added: "And so it ended." They died within five months of each other, having outlived Dorothy by twenty years.

5

"THE PROBLEMS WHICH NOW CONFRONT US . . . ARE REALLY TERRIFYING"

"The Prime Minister said that at the end of the debate on the economic situation that had been held in the House of Commons on the two previous days, the Government motion had been carried by a majority of 146. This was a highly satisfactory result, and he wished, on behalf of the cabinet, to congratulate the Chief Whip and his assistants on the efficiency which they had shown in carrying out their contribution towards it."[1]

There was perhaps a hint of overconfidence in Macmillan's report to his ministerial colleagues of July 28, 1961, which also noted the "encouraging vindication" of British policy "in respect of Rhodesia and of Africa generally," and went on to predict that "neither the Western Allies nor the Soviet Union will lightly risk war on the Berlin issue." The premier's equanimity on both these and other matters would be sorely tested in the weeks ahead. A host of professional and personal problems followed one another with "some rapidity," he admitted in his memoirs. There was a protracted government debate about whether to enter into negotiations with the Common Market, and Macmillan's final decision to do so brought some mocking headlines, such as "WHATEVER HAPPENED TO 'YOU'VE NEVER HAD IT SO GOOD'?" and "THE GREAT EUROPEAN GUESSING GAME." Meanwhile, the Iraqis were threatening to invade Kuwait, Laos seethed away, in a perpetual state of on-again, off-again civil war, and there were "unfortunate developments" in Tunisia, where "the French were adopting an intransigent attitude over the port city of Bizerta." Some eight hundred lives were lost in the subsequent armed conflict to determine the area's ownership—"a terrifying example of the result of both sides bluffing and both bluffs being called," Macmillan said, and an example, he now felt, that "easily might be repeated in Berlin."[2] And these were just a selection of the most pressing affairs of state. Macmillan was also reported to be suffering from a range of personal crises running the gamut from cancer (untrue) to gout and insomnia (both true), while a bout of "Black dog," or depression, led him to ask in his diary: "Will 1961 be the end? Who can tell?"[3] Added to this, there were the usual private anxieties over Dorothy. When Macmillan eventually left his prolonged Scottish retreat and flew back to London to deal with the fallout from the Berlin Wall, his wife stayed behind for a further ten days "on her own," which more accurately meant with Robert Boothby. The summer then ended with Nikita Khrushchev goading the leadership of "Britain, France, and Italy [as] nothing but hostages in Russian hands. We will never dare to fight," Macmillan wrote, summarizing the latest "grim tirade" from Moscow. "So I authorised a form of words for the Minister of Defence to use in a speech tonight, reminding Khrushchev that this was just the mistake which had been made about Britain twice in my lifetime."[4]

In time, Macmillan's sour mood even led him to wonder privately about his "staunch new friend" in Washington. "I 'feel in my bones' that President Kennedy is going to fail to produce any real leadership," he told his diary on June 25, shortly after Kennedy's mauling at the Vienna summit. "The American press and public are beginning to feel the same. In a few weeks they may turn to us. We must be ready."[5] At the end of the summer, it was still the same story. "Khrushchev is trying to frighten us and to divide us," Macmillan wrote on September 8. "Unfortunately, the Americans 'get mad' at these tactics. Even President Kennedy, with all his political experience, behaves like a bull being teased by the darts of the picadors."[6]

As the Macmillan-Kennedy star had been waning in the summer of 1961, the roles of their respective satellites—the two Davids, Ormsby-Gore and Bruce—had been rising. Gore, as he was widely known, had finally taken up the reins as British ambassador in Washington that July. Well-connected (Gore's sister was married to Macmillan's son); boyishly enthusiastic; with a glamorous wife, Sylvia, and five children (who eventually came to inhabit a sort of hippy commune on the grounds of their ancestral home); but also abnormally bright, with genuine political instinct and an extraordinary ability to learn, he was clearly on Kennedy's own wavelength. It was said, not always approvingly, that he became more a de facto member of the administration than merely the envoy of a friendly power. In time, Dean Rusk was to complain that the president saw more of Gore than he did of his own secretary of state. At the height of the Cuban missile crisis, Lyndon Johnson similarly observed that "the limey" was seated front and center at a meeting of a steering group in the Cabinet Room, while he, the vice president, was "down in a chair at the end, with the goddamned door banging into my back."

It has been further said of Gore that "he was almost a resident at the White House," where he "supplied Kennedy with a stream of advice, and Cuban cigars via his diplomatic bag." Nor does it seem the First Lady was entirely immune to the Welshman's combination of silky good manners and mild bohemianism, captured in her later admiring phrase calling him an "Edwardian diplomat who had somehow listened to *Sergeant Pepper's*." Publicly, of course, the British ambassador never deviated from the official line, and a significant amount of Gore's time was devoted to conveying Macmillan's messages to the White House or, where necessary, other agencies of the federal government. Privately, he was able to call upon twenty-five years of personal friendship to write to Kennedy as "Dear Jack," to call him on his direct line, and to enjoy summer weekends as his guest at Hyannis Port. Again, this was a degree of access even senior cabinet officials could only dream of. In October 1962, Gore was the first national representative in Washington to learn that Soviet missiles had been discovered in Cuba and to cable his government accordingly. Macmillan thus became the first and, for a time, only foreign head of government to be informed or consulted on the facts as they unfolded during some of the most critical days in modern history.

David Bruce, Washington's man in London, was a similarly happy fit to his host government. Born in 1898 and a combat veteran of the First World War, he shared a number of experiences and characteristics with Macmillan. Both men could be alternately tough and charming: "a man with a nice smile and iron teeth," it was said of Bruce. Both married into great wealth, and both showed a certain courage when it came to overcoming the depression and loneliness of a dead marriage. Each also shared the melancholy distinction of seeing two of their children predecease them. Macmillan's son Maurice and daughter Sarah had both succumbed to an alcohol-related illness, while Bruce's daughter Audrey was lost in an air crash, and her younger half sister, Sasha, was found shot in the head, lying under a tree on the family's estate in Virginia. Sasha died without regaining consciousness, and it remains unclear whether her death was a murder or a suicide.

Like Macmillan, Bruce was also handsome, courtly, and intimidatingly literate—he'd been a Princeton classmate of F. Scott Fitzgerald and became a boon companion of Ernest Hemingway before himself going on to write a bestselling book of biographical essays on American presidents. It was said that he and Macmillan sometimes passed the time while sitting together at Admiralty House, awaiting Kennedy's phone call during the depths of the missile crisis, by taking turns reading aloud from Jane Austen. Bruce's witty reports on the Profumo scandal were later eagerly received in the Oval Office. Among other things, he rightly predicted that "Britain wasn't quite ready for a bachelor PM like Ted Heath" in the immediate wake of all the "Profumo innuendos," but that Heath's turn would come "in about 1970." Like Macmillan, Bruce could play the languid aristocrat superbly well and was a natural part of the circle that journalist Joseph Alsop later termed the "Wasp Ascendancy." Less flatteringly, Richard Nixon once called him typical of the "unelected, decision-making, candyass elite" of Washington life, although he thought sufficiently well of Bruce's diplomatic skills to later appoint him to conduct public peace talks with the North Vietnamese. Above all, Bruce was clearly another one of those men who could "bugger off home to his estates" if the circumstances arose.

====

Shortly after nine on the Friday morning of September 1, 1961, Herbert Scoville, chairman of the US Atomic Energy Commission (AEC), cabled the Department of Defense. "An explosion has been detected as having occurred in the atmosphere at 0700 hours," he reported. "Signals have been read by three acoustic stations. No seismic, nor electromagnetic, signals have yet been received. The preliminary estimate of the yield is 50 to 500 KT, with a best estimate of 150 KT."[7] Coming at a time when the cement was still wet in the Berlin Wall, Khrushchev's decision to resume nuclear testing was clearly part of his continuing, high-stakes campaign to alarm the West. He succeeded to the extent that Kennedy now sought to reopen his own program of tests. Macmillan's deep concerns on the subject did not end American planning for a possible nuclear exchange. It was a classic case of the harsh truth that national self-interest would generally, if not always, triumph over a fuzzy concept such as the "Special Relationship." Macmillan eventually sent Kennedy an eighteen-page, six-thousand-word letter full of "sombre thoughts . . . intended to lead to at least some proposals for finding 'a way out' of the maze in which we are lost."[8] Although he felt "morally bound" to support US policy, he also felt that the West "should repeat our abhorrence of the need for these tests. . . . We should announce our absolute determination to make every effort to pull the world out of this ruck," and specifically that "we should invite [changed by Macmillan from the original "summon"] Mr. Khrushchev to meet us in Stockholm, or Vienna, or Geneva, or Paris. We should inform General de Gaulle of our decision and ask him to join us in the invitation."

According to Kennedy adviser Arthur Schlesinger, Macmillan's latest global cri de coeur received only a "dusty answer" in Washington.[9] In the event, Khrushchev was not interested in meeting in Stockholm or anywhere else, and the US testing program duly resumed in April 1962. "A lot of telegrams; teleprinter messages; telephone calls between Washington and London have gone on all the week," Macmillan told his diary. "The position is really rather sad. . . . The Russians have another test series ready, and [as] soon as the Americans start theirs, the Russians will follow—larger and more alarming! If that is so, there never has been much hope. Yet it may well be that both Mr. K's are similarly placed, and that both have to deal with military and political pressures."[10]

Both sides of the alliance accepted that what Khrushchev was really testing was not only his nuclear weapons but also the West's resolve. But they could not agree on what followed from there. Kennedy described himself as a "great antitester" but took the view that so long as the Soviets were embarked on this "deranged kind of atomic blackmail," a firm response was vital. It was too bad "the Reds had twisted out of their obligations," he added. There were those, such as Glenn Seaborg of the AEC, who wondered if the president might not have gone further than he did to compromise with Khrushchev, but for the pressures on him from members of Congress. Khrushchev himself later echoed this point when he complained to Robert Kennedy that his brother was "putting heat on us." Instead of "accepting risks for peace," he added, the United States demanded Soviet concessions to "suit the bad mood of a senator [Barry Goldwater] from Arizona."[11]

Macmillan was inclined to see Moscow's intransigence on testing as a propaganda gift to the West—a gift, if carefully handled, they could parlay into "a very considerable strategic asset." As the cabinet heard on September 5, "While the Russians' resumption of nuclear tests might be due in part to a desire to improve their military position, it was likely also a deliberate attempt to intimidate neutral Governments in the hope that they would bring pressure on the West to accept a negotiated settlement of the Berlin question on terms favourable to Moscow. The Soviet decision had, however, given us a considerable public relations advantage. . . . It was unlikely that the USSR would accept the proposal made by the US and UK Governments for a cessation of nuclear tests. In that event, further advantage might be derived if those Governments could continue to refrain from making such tests."[12] To Kennedy, this was all wishful thinking, particularly as the Russians had been "brazenly preparing" their latest tests while assuring him that nothing could be further from their minds. "We will not get taken twice," he told Glenn Seaborg.[13]

While the Soviets continued to explode bombs at the rate of one every other day in the fall of 1961, Macmillan fretted not only about the global-strategic ramifications but also about the "very literal fall-out" as it affected Britain. Twenty-seven of the thirty-one major Russian tests were in the atmosphere and of a particularly "dirty" kind. After the tenth or eleventh detonation, the Labour opposition began to make headlines by asking whether the government was in the least concerned about the toxic pollution of the British homeland. The climactic fifty-megaton bomb, released over Siberia on October 30, was enough for Macmillan to summon his minister of agriculture, Christopher Soames, to prepare "a complete scheme for dried milk for infants, if the iodine contamination from fall-out should become serious."[14] Even before this, popular newspapers like the *Daily Express* had begun to warn their readers in the most stark terms of the "poison belt" steadily forming above them, ready to "leak down in an acid rain." To some Britons, this all seemed to have come in the nature of a ringing alarm clock, waking them up to the ghastly realities of the arms race. On September 19, Home Secretary Rab Butler remarked in cabinet on the previous day's "great demonstration [in] London against nuclear armaments. . . . In spite of the scale of the police action which had been taken it was understood that no one had suffered injury," he reported, although any future protest might cause him to "give consent to an [injunction] under the Public Order Act."[15]

Not all of Macmillan's distaste for atmospheric tests was based on his moral abhorrence of the nuclear-arms race as a whole—a race that, if unabated, "would bring us into the contempt of Christian people all over the world," he informed Kennedy in a letter from January 5, 1962. Nor was it primarily about his newly expressed concerns over soil contamination or tainted milk. Those factors were all important, but, as so often in the history of postwar Britain, hard financial facts lay behind the government's thinking not just on strategic-arms proliferation but in general foreign policy, including Anglo-American relations.

In the summer of 1961, Britain's recurrent economic calamity was bad enough to require emergency treatment—a so-called Little Budget, famous for its introduction of a public-sector "pay pause." This particular initiative did not conspicuously add to the smooth running of the nation's industrial relations. Strikes in the mining, railway, and electricity sectors, among others, remained a staple feature of the British landscape in the early 1960s. The "pause" notwithstanding, wages continued to grow by some 8 percent, and production by only 3 percent, annually. Britain's vulnerable currency reserves were at their lowest level since the Suez Crisis, with a loss of £67 million in a single day in April 1961. The *Times* was sufficiently concerned to editorialize that the nation's economic malaise was "beyond any Chancellor of the Exchequer. No matter what [his] measures may be, they will not, on their own, cure the deep-seated ills of the British economy."[16] Macmillan was left to ruefully note in his diary: "The problems which now confront us, internally and externally, are really terrifying. No one seems to realise their complexity."[17] The minutes of the cabinet meeting of September 19, which contain one nine-line paragraph on nuclear tests, devote three full pages to the nation's precarious finances. "There was general agreement that the Government must urgently proceed with its proposal to enlist the co-operation of both sides of industry in a new form of planning," the note concludes. Macmillan was undoubtedly committed to the principle of nuclear disarmament on moral and humanitarian grounds, but the most persuasive argument against his endorsing a program to build and test a new generation of British weapons was simply that he couldn't afford it.

Kennedy may have had the deeper pockets, but he also paid the penalty of the more direct, and emotionally bruising, relationship with Nikita Khrushchev. Throughout 1961, Khrushchev showed a nervous state that found expression in regular outbursts of rage, petulance, even threats of global annihilation. As his gorge rose, he sometimes turned literally red, using what was termed "rural" language and frequently drumming his fists on his desk for emphasis. "Leave politics to us—we're the specialists," he once shouted at the nuclear physicist and future dissident Andrei Sakharov. "We have to conduct our policies from a position of strength—the imperialists don't understand any other language. Look, we helped elect Kennedy last year. Then we met him in Vienna, a meeting that could have been a turning point. But what does he say? 'Don't ask me for too much. Don't put me in a bind. If I make too many concessions, I'll be turned out of office.' Quite a guy!

He comes to a meeting, but can't perform. What the hell do we need a guy like that for?"[18] Paradoxically, Khrushchev also possessed an earthy (often scatological) sense of humor and wasn't above deploying a charm offensive to win over an enemy. His "difficult" nature and tendency to swing rapidly from the psychotic to the jovial and back again, frequently in the same meeting, surfaced one weekend in July 1961, when he summoned the chairman of the US Council on Foreign Relations—and former Chase Bank president—John McCloy to join him at his Black Sea dacha. That Saturday night, Khrushchev was happy to pose for photos in his bathing suit with his arm around the similarly clad capitalist, before going on to play a somewhat erratic game of badminton and then sharing a meal of roast boar and vodka with his guest, all the while loudly protesting that they were part of a "brotherhood of man." It was as if they were "two good old boys from the Ukraine on a summer drunk together," an American observer wrote.

The following morning, however, Khrushchev awoke "really mad" and delivered a long harangue over the breakfast table about Kennedy's supposed intentions in Berlin. These would lead to a "thermonuclear event," he bellowed, in which America's European allies would be "completely destroyed." "We will meet war with war," Khrushchev added, before abruptly concluding the visit. McCloy and others in the US administration were left to speculate quite openly whether the Soviet ruler might be clinically schizophrenic.

On September 8, 1961, the State Department sent the president an eyes-only report on recent US-Soviet relations. Among other things, it quoted the views of Khrushchev's foreign-policy adviser Igor Usatchev. These suggested that the atmosphere in the Kremlin was "heavy . . . with intrigue [and] suspicion," and thus that there were limits on what even a dictator could achieve without the agreement of his subordinates. "Usatchev said there had been great pressures on Khrushchev to resume tests from the military and the scientists, and that the US had assisted these pressures by intensifying world tensions. . . . He also said he couldn't understand why President Kennedy had started out his Administration by increasing the arms budget—he said this had set in train a number of unhappy events, including the resumption of tests. He answered his own speculation by saying he believed Kennedy had made campaign promises to help unemployment, and that the best way of doing this was to increase military expenditures. . . . He said that the Soviets will reject the United States–United Kingdom test ban offer. He repeated that the

Soviet resumption of tests was a reaction to US actions. If it was necessary to continue them, they would be continued."[19]

Later that winter, a reporter asked Kennedy what he considered the biggest disappointment of his first year in office. "Our failure to get an agreement on the cessation of nuclear testing, because . . . that might have been a very important step in easing the tension and preventing a proliferation of [nuclear] weapons," the president replied.[20] A sign of Macmillan's own preoccupation with the issue was his using a protracted absence from government duty while suffering from the flu to draft a new and improved version of his Grand Design. "I pondered and brooded in bed and produced by last night a plan for trying to get a general détente between the West and communism, in which all the questions which seem insoluble by themselves might be subsumed into a new and general approach," he told his diary.[21] Some of his proposals, he admitted to Kennedy in a phrase that may have been specifically devised for him, might "produce a panic in the Capitalist society which, we must remember, is a more delicate young lady, given to fainting and vapours and currency disturbances, than the lustier and coarser Communist wench."[22] Nonetheless, the effort was worth making—"It is not the things one did do in one's life that one regrets, but the opportunities missed. One can only live once," Macmillan said.[23]

It was a line he would repeat, speaking of "the dark clouds cast by nuclear armaments, daily increasing," "the Russian trickery and bad faith" on testing, and "the danger that without some concert[ed] effort on our side we might one day find ourselves at their mercy."[24] Macmillan was under no illusions about the scale of the challenge facing the West. "We have to consider that the Soviet 100-megaton weapon seems not merely to correspond with Mr. Khrushchev's natural instinct for magnitude, but also to have valuable potential military importance and to pose a further quite difficult requirement for a defence system," he wrote Kennedy, characteristically understating the destructive capacity of a device some five thousand times more lethal than the one dropped on Hiroshima. Like many others, Macmillan may have exaggerated Khrushchev's desire to actually deploy such a bomb. But he was adamant that nothing less than a master plan by the West aimed at effecting "some genuine improvement in the underlying malady from which humanity suffers" must be made. Macmillan could offer only a few specifics, among them a meeting of the foreign ministers of the three nuclear powers in tandem with a "private communication of a rather more detailed kind to Khrushchev, urging him to co-operate . . . to save man from the threat and the wastage of a new [nuclear] competition." One can question the practical worth of what amounted to a pro-posal for another round of talks, but it showed again that Macmillan was consis-tently ahead of Kennedy in terms of forward thinking, if not in the taking of hard, strategic decisions. It was the man born in 1894 who was left to point out to his young ally that their policies were "not properly adjusted to the realities of the 1960s."[25] So deep was Macmillan's wish to "turn the nuclear spiral downwards, [to] save mankind from the increasing threat of events of surpassing horror," that the Conservative prime minister came to privately believe that the Democratic presi-dent was dragging his feet in terms of his "moral obligation . . . to protect the most basic rights" of his fellow human beings. "I think that once more I must try to press [Kennedy] on," Macmillan wrote. "He is good, but *very* cautious."[26]

Kennedy reacted to Macmillan's analysis by creating a task force of military and scientific advisers to determine whether the United States should resume nuclear testing. The president thus far had stubbornly resisted the Pentagon's pressure for "urgently . . . and actively improving our strategic-weapons capability," as the note put it, unconvinced that the benefits to America's national defense would outweigh the likely Soviet response elsewhere. At one point, Kennedy told David Ormsby-Gore, with tears in his eyes, of a "terrible image" he had had of London being incin-erated by a Russian bomb. Nonetheless, he was a pragmatist. Kennedy's advisers told him not only that testing was strategically advisable but also that it would make it cheaper to produce more bombs in the future. The price "might go down by a factor as large as ten or a hundred," the panel concluded, "so that it will cost very little to produce nuclear weapons."[27] (Macmillan later remarked in his memoirs that this was a sorry case where the philosophical arguments had lost out to the military ones and that the president had been forced, "very unwillingly, to yield to pressure from the Pentagon.") Before long, Kennedy was pressing ahead with his plans to conduct atmospheric tests on Christmas Island. In return for making these facilities available, Macmillan was to be given his own underground-testing privileges in Nevada. As a partial result of this development, in May 1962, Nikita Khrushchev decided to install some thirty-two thousand troops and a total of forty medium-range and intermediate missile launchers on Cuba "with one purpose—to scare [the United States], to restrain them . . . to give them back some of their own medicine."[28] The initial assessment of the American intelligence community was that the Soviets would be able to deliver nuclear warheads on targets like New York City within six minutes of launch.

═══

On October 17, 1961, the 22nd Congress of the Communist Party convened in Moscow. It marked perhaps the apogee of Soviet postwar power and was followed even more closely than usual by Western observers. Khrushchev's two keynote speeches lasted a total of eleven hours, and contained several robust assertions of the Soviet Union's shining future in general and her unyielding commitment to East Germany and East Berlin in particular. (Less publicly, Khrushchev also took the opportunity to order that Stalin's embalmed body be removed from the Red Square tomb it had shared with Lenin's and buried overnight in a nearby pit, which was then covered over with three tons of cement.) On the same day, a small US party under the leadership of General Maxwell Taylor left for a two-week fact-finding tour of Vietnam. Kennedy described their brief as to "seek ways in which the US can better assist the Government in Saigon in meeting the threat to its independence."[29] Taylor's eventual report stressed the need for continued US economic support of Vietnam but also warned of a destabilizing threat to Southeast Asia posed by "Khrushchev's 'wars of liberation,' or 'para-wars of guerilla aggression.' This is a new and dangerous Communist technique, which bypasses our traditional political and military responses." Taylor concluded that a form of "limited partnership" between the United States and South Vietnam was needed in order to restrain Soviet adventuring in the region. An initial military task force of some seven to eight thousand troops should have been sufficient, he felt. "We have many assets in this part of the world, which, if properly combined and appropriately supported, offer high odds for ultimate success."[30]

While these momentous events were being played out in Washington and Moscow, Macmillan struggled to maintain a convincing British posture of greatness. On the eve of his own party conference in October 1961, he sent the White House the details of some minor shuffling of the London cabinet before stopping to review the troops at an army barracks in Yorkshire on his way home from another shooting holiday in Scotland. It seemed to one observer that "all [the] Edwardian cocked hats and gold braid on display that day look[ed] sadly Ruritanian," when one remembered how few British soldiers, sailors, and airmen actively remained in the field. Macmillan's foreign-policy concerns reflected the same harsh fact that, in every material sense, he was the junior partner in the alliance. Many of his long and frequent messages to Kennedy read like the slightly overeager memos of a clever subordinate seeking to cultivate the patronage of a powerful and elusive boss.

Even while he was denigrating Kennedy behind his back as overcautious, Macmillan was busy praising his "imaginative" and "dauntless" leadership in a series of transatlantic messages.

"Dear Mr. President," he wrote on October 2, 1961, opening another comprehensive review of the situation in Berlin. "I was very glad to have a talk with you on the telephone yesterday, and it seems that we share the same anxieties. I feel that we may have to have either a Three-Power meeting of you, me and de Gaulle, or a Four-Power meeting including Adenauer. . . . But of course as you pointed out on the telephone, this idea has the risk that with all the publicity attached, failure to reach agreement would be serious. If a Heads of Government meeting is not practicable in the immediate future, are we to try for a Four-Power meeting of Foreign Secretaries next week, perhaps in Paris? If it seems hopeless to get [such] a meeting arranged so soon . . . would it help if we got agreement on some Western meeting to be held [later], and indicated to the Russians that we hoped to resume contacts with them soon thereafter? I am frankly puzzled by this. I am only sending you this preliminary picture of the problem as I see it, and will await your thoughts before sending you a further message, or telephoning you again."[31]

Two weeks later, following the party congress in Moscow, David Bruce cabled Kennedy a blunter summary of the Berlin question as he saw it. Bruce parted from Macmillan in the latter's ceaseless desire for talks and instead stressed the hard political realities. "The Western position in Berlin has always been minimal," he wrote, "since as a result of disastrous terms of 1944 wartime agreement, possibility of Berlin enclave (ringed by hostile territory) preserving any real independence, depended on (A) determination of Western powers to preserve position through military force, and (B) forbearance of Soviets. Latter chance never existed. Also, successful closure of Berlin sector border, without Allied military reaction, has now made Western tenancy still more vulnerable, and deterioration in West Berlin and West German morale is already significant. We are left from a trading standpoint with no real assets coveted by the Soviets."[32]

Three days after Kennedy read this message, US and Soviet tanks began their day-long standoff over the barbed wire at Checkpoint Charlie. Kennedy immediately ordered that four of the new *Ethan Allen*–class atomic submarines take up position in the Barents Sea, just outside Soviet territorial waters. They carried a total of sixty-four Polaris missiles, aimed at targets including the military airfield at Nizhniy Tagil, the forward base for Russia's fleet of SU-9 rocket-armed interceptor fighters. Other US and British military assets were put on high alert throughout the world. When the tanks eventually rolled back to their barracks, the East Berlin city authorities decided to erect a steel barrier running across the road, close to the scene of the confrontation, to "forestall [any] future imperialist posturing," as Walter Ulbricht put it to his like-minded colleagues in the Council of Ministers. US border guards responded by shining 100,000-candlepower searchlights during the night at their East German counterparts. The nuclear submarines remained submerged at their war stations. Philip de Zulueta, the prime minister's foreign-affairs secretary, was left to write to him on November 1, "I am afraid that no one knows what the Americans may do."[33] It was all "very disturbing," the premier glumly agreed in cabinet.

Eight days later, Macmillan wrote again to Kennedy. A sign of the gravity of the situation was that he addressed him not as "My friend" or "Jack" but as "Mr. President." "I was very glad to have our talk tonight," Macmillan told him. "I am thinking over what you said, and will send you a considered message in the next few days. Meanwhile, I do hope we can keep the Berlin situation quiet on the ground."[34]

Kennedy's chief proposal was that he attempt to bring eighty-five-year-old Chancellor Adenauer around to the view that "negotiations with the Soviets . . . are a necessary part of our effort to achieve a satisfactory and peaceful solution to the Berlin crisis." Kennedy agreed with Adenauer's poor estimate of Khrushchev's recent behavior but reminded him that the sheer "logic of a thermonuclear war demands that we exhaust every effort to find a peaceful solution consistent with the preservation of our vital interests."[35] Adenauer saw the wisdom of this. Having effectively seduced the German, Kennedy then drew him in to his campaign to win over the Frenchman. Adenauer should join Macmillan, he said, to restrain de Gaulle, who had recently warned in an August 26 letter to Kennedy that any negotiations over Western rights of access "would be considered immediately as a prelude to the abandonment of Berlin—as a sort of notice of our surrender."

Macmillan's reply to Kennedy of November 23 combined his usual emollient and thoughtful tone with a touchingly misplaced attempt to speak in the president's own voice.

"What you say about Adenauer is very encouraging," he gushed. "You seem to have collected a homer. I will now do my best with the General, and will send you an account as soon as I can. On [nuclear] tests, I will give instructions for the reconnaissance party arrangements to be put in hand as soon as you wish. I take it that you will inform us when you are ready for the consultations about a specific test programme?"[36]

Unfortunately, Macmillan struck out in his talks with de Gaulle in late November 1961 at Birch Grove. Even in these relatively informal surroundings, the Frenchman was "determined [and] immovable. . . . He saw no advantage in embarking on negotiations [on Berlin] at the present time," Macmillan reflected. The great contrarian of the Western alliance still declined to commit a single extra French soldier to support his rhetoric. "Even if the West German Government of the day accepted the concessions which would be asked of them," Macmillan continued, summarizing de Gaulle, "the German people would be left with a sense of betrayal. . . . Whatever the United States and the United Kingdom might do, France, although not proposing to fight a war with the Russians on her own, would not be party to such an arrangement."[37] In spite of himself, Macmillan admitted he was "oddly impressed" by the general's arm's-length attitude to his old wartime saviors—whom he called "*les Anglo-saxons*"—if not by his obstinacy. "De Gaulle was a man who was never rude by mistake," he wrote.

Kennedy cabled Macmillan on December 1 to compare notes on their respective attempts at Allied courtship.

> I appreciate very much receiving such a prompt and full report of your weekend conversations with de Gaulle, together with your personal message. The results, I agree, were not very promising, and it does seem that the main burden of trying to bring him around must be Chancellor Adenauer's. . . . I have sent the Chancellor a letter expressing disappointment over de Gaulle's continuing negative attitude on the subject of negotiations, as reported by you. I think it highly important that he be brought to accept that talks with the Soviets . . . are a necessary [step] before we move on to the confrontation which a failure of diplomacy would bring.[38]

While Kennedy and Macmillan moved cautiously forward with repeated assurances of their nations' peaceful intent, pressure grew on both men to combat Khrushchev's role as the latest interpreter of Lenin, as expressed by his country's nuclear-arms buildup. The Soviet leader had come to supreme power in 1958 with promises of peace, land, and social justice to Russia's poor, hungry, and war-weary masses. By late 1961, that vision had been matched by his campaign to intimidate the West. Speaking at a closed meeting of Warsaw Pact leaders in Moscow, Khrushchev announced to his appreciative audience, "I am the commander in chief, and if war begins, I will give the order to the troops." Should Kennedy provoke the issue, he would be the "last president of the United States."[39]

Ironically, Khrushchev shared with Macmillan a fear that what the former called "reactionaries within the imperialist Washington regime" might ultimately prevail over Kennedy's better intentions. The downturn in East-West relations in August 1961 revived the hopes of those in the US administration who thought in terms of matching Soviet aggression in kind. Beginning in 1956, Macmillan had long spoken of the mollifying influence of the State Department as opposed to the "bellicose sorts" in the Pentagon and the Atomic Energy Commission. Khrushchev amplified this view when he later informed the Warsaw Pact leaders that the United States was "barely governed." The American president, he insisted, "exerts very little influence on the direction and development of policy," while Congress resembled some medieval cabal where the representatives "shouted, yelled, and pulled at each other's beards." Reviewing the global situation as a whole, Khrushchev concluded that Kennedy "is too much of a lightweight for both Republicans and Democrats, whereas the US state is so big and so powerful that it poses definite dangers."[40]

Although some of Khrushchev's rhetoric might seem to have applied equally well to the Soviet Union, he was right to identify the fact that certain tensions existed between Kennedy and a number of his senior advisers. In particular, the president's meetings with his gung-ho air force chief, General LeMay, were often lively affairs. According to Deputy Secretary of Defense Roswell Gilpatric, Kennedy regularly "ended up in a fit. I mean he just would be frantic at the end of a session with LeMay because, you know, LeMay couldn't listen or wouldn't take in, and he would make what Kennedy considered . . . outrageous proposals. I saw the president right afterwards. He was just choleric."[41]

If anything, Kennedy was even less at home in the company of Lyman Lemnitzer, the much-decorated army chief of staff and chairman of the five Joint Chiefs.
In a masterful understatement, the president told Gilpatric he doubted that Lemnitzer would "take the lead in effectively bringing the military along to a new doctrine such as flexible response," as opposed to one of all-out retaliation. Kennedy's
national security adviser, McGeorge Bundy, characterized the senior echelons of
the Pentagon as being composed of "nuclear war men." In March 1962, Lemnitzer
and his fellow chiefs put their names to a top-secret paper outlining their recommendations for the "Northwoods Plan." This included a specific proposal to stage
attacks on the American homeland and to blame Cuba in order to create a pretext
for invasion. Among other initiatives, the memo notes, "We could develop a Communist Cuban terror campaign in the Miami area, in other Florida cities, and even
in Washington. . . . We could blow up a US ship in Guantanamo Bay and blame
Cuba. Casualty lists in US newspapers would cause a helpful wave of indignation."[42]
Forty years later, more than one conspiracy theorist would claim that the Northwoods Plan served as a blueprint for the US government to attack its own citizens on 9/11. Perhaps providentially, Kennedy told Lemnitzer that he doubted the
wisdom of "bombing ourselves to shit" in an effort to succeed where the Bay of Pigs
invasion had failed.

On October 25, 1961, a special group of the US nuclear panel, under the
chairmanship of Dr. Ernst Plesset, the German-born head of a scientific-research
firm in Los Angeles, presented Kennedy with their recommendations on "future
directives and plans for atmospheric tests of nuclear warheads." Plesset and his
seven colleagues, among them the theoretical physicist Edward Teller, were in no
doubt as to the way forward. "We strongly endorse the resumption of testing in the
atmosphere," they reported. "Space testing is advocated also, in order to establish
a new capability, and to ensure continued readiness of devices which contribute
considerable amounts of information. . . . Operational wing test with live bomb
appear[s] to us to deserve high priority."[43]

The paperwork coming across Kennedy's desk that week embraced much more
than nuclear rearmament. On the same day as he read the special panel's report,
he was also dealing with the high-noon standoff at the border crossing in Berlin.
Between times, Kennedy, as we've seen, met with and offered an aid grant of $5
million to British Guiana's Cheddi Jagan, the gift that was abruptly withdrawn when

Jagan unwisely went on to criticize the United States in a live television interview before the money was safely in his bank. Although only a subplot in the wider Cold War, it was an event that significantly strained the Anglo-American alliance. On the eve of Macmillan's next meeting with Kennedy, the Colonial Office prepared a brief for him that still seems unusually frank coming from the British civil service. "We believe that if our major aim of policy is to be achieved, which is to keep British Guiana in with the West, it is vital that the Americans should be thinking in much larger terms than $5 million, which they [had] in mind. [They] should concentrate on producing some more aid, and very quickly indeed."[44] Duncan Sandys, the Commonwealth secretary, was even blunter in his response to Kennedy's suggestion that the British continue with direct rule until a suitable alternative could be found to Jagan. "I welcome the proposal to accelerate the independence of Guiana," he wrote to Macmillan on January 11, 1962. "The sooner we get these people out of our hair the better."[45] Dean Rusk went on to send the British a possibly intemperate letter on the subject. "I must tell you that I have come to the conclusion that it is not possible for us to put up with an independent British Guiana under Jagan. The American public and congressional opinion would not tolerate another Castro or Cuba," Rusk pronounced. Macmillan thought the letter "pure Machiavellianism," and his Foreign Secretary, Lord Home, abandoning his normal air of scholarly diffidence when dealing with his American peer, wrote back to ask Rusk: "You say that it is not possible for you 'to put up with an independent Guiana under Jagan'. How would you suggest that this can be done in a democracy?"[46] Kennedy became more acutely aware of the problem when, in February 1962, he entertained the Conservative MP Hugh Fraser—a family friend since the 1930s and another one of those faintly raffish British aristocrats whose company the president enjoyed.

"You're trying to ask us to remain [in British Guiana] forever, which means keeping four or five battalions, maybe, in the place," Fraser briskly told his host. "This isn't on. You must see . . . fundamentally, Guiana is a mudbank, and really hasn't any contact with the rest of Latin America. It's surrounded by forests and mountains with no natural communications, except by air, and after all, Moscow's got good communications by air with Latin America. And I think we're going."[47]

While the Allies continued to debate the future political arrangements of a cricket-playing sugar colony of some six hundred thousand souls, Kennedy and Khrushchev entered into a secret correspondence—archly dubbed the "Pen Pal letters" by Macmillan—on the broader issues of the Cold War. These frequently involved Berlin. On November 9, 1961, Khrushchev seemed to signal that he, too, was a prisoner of his domestic circumstances. "You have to understand," he wrote, "I have no ground to retreat further, there is a precipice behind me." Three weeks later, in one of those characteristically abrupt mood swings that were his trademark, the Soviet leader turned belligerent. Both Kennedy and the United States were guilty of "megalomania," he fumed. "We must conclude a German peace treaty and we will conclude it even if you do not agree."[48]

Kennedy did not favor his closest strategic ally by including him in his back-channel exchanges with the Kremlin. Macmillan was left to rather forlornly announce in parliament only that "our two Governments maintain close co-operation over the problem of Berlin, and the president and I are of course in contact." Even this was perhaps to gloss the true state of affairs, and in later years Macmillan admitted, "The weakest part of our position consisted in the disparity of view, or at least of emphasis, in the Allied camp, as to our best tactical reply to the Russian offensive" in Berlin.[49] As if these differences of emphasis weren't bad enough for Macmillan, he had to face the continuing intransigence of the soon-to-be third member of the Western nuclear club. "On Berlin, the French have not moved at all," he cabled Kennedy in November 1961. "Their position is that at present they see no basis on which a satisfactory negotiation could be conducted; in other words, the minimum Soviet demands are greater than the maximum Western concessions. . . . This is bad, and makes it indispensable for us to try and make sure that the German government fully share the responsibility for our explorations [with Khrushchev]. Otherwise, there will be the beginning of a myth about an Anglo-American sell-out."[50] Taking stock of the German impasse as a whole, he could only ruefully ask the president: "What then do we do?"

At that, Macmillan returned to the other pressing business of government, which included the usual domestic industrial-relations crises, with strikes announced in the post office and in the London Underground, and a "go-slow" threatened by civil servants ("How could they go any slower?" the PM wondered), a heated debate on whether the Immigration Bill applied to citizens of the Irish Republic wishing to settle in Britain, and the emergency provisions for dealing with a fresh outbreak of swine fever.

President Kennedy responded to that week's announcement by Fidel Castro that the latter was a confirmed Marxist-Leninist and would remain one for the rest of his life by instructing his US task force in Cuba to examine ways in which to build "a nucleus of anti-regime feeling" in Havana and to follow it with "a number of collateral supporting actions."[51] The next day, Edward Teller came to meet the president at the White House and told him that Americans needed to dig deeper fallout shelters if the Russians built bigger bombs. In December, Kennedy requested a $695 million budget for civil defense, which was nine times more than the existing appropriation.

Khrushchev continued his mercurial pronouncements on Berlin, telling the Polish communist boss Władysław Gomułka: "There will not be a war, but signing a peace treaty with the GDR might exacerbate the situation. . . . We must continue our game. We are not afraid, but we do not want war."[52]

Macmillan's government continued to spend ruinously more money than it took in, with a record trade deficit in January 1962 of £68 million. In a sobering note to the cabinet, Martin Redmayne, the chief secretary to the Treasury, "recalled that the Chancellor of the Exchequer had undertaken to do his utmost to ensure that the total of the Estimates for 1962–63 would not exceed the total of those for the current year by more than 2½ per cent in real terms." He added: "This would require some major changes of policy." The chancellor himself told the meeting that the United States had proposed that the Western allies "set a collective target for growth in the member countries of at least 50 per cent during the years 1962–70. . . . The US administration, who are anxious to pursue policies of expansion in their own country, thought that this would be attainable. In the United Kingdom, however, the maximum figure that seems likely to be possible is of the order of 30 per cent over the period. It would therefore be unwise for us to endorse the higher figure which the US has in mind."[53] It seemed even a sovereign ally's economic policy now came under American scrutiny. The comedian Peter Cook caught a popular mood when, speaking in Macmillan's voice, he told the audience at a London theater:

> I then went to America, and there I had talks with the young, vigorous president of that great country, and danced with his very lovely lady wife. We talked of many things, including Great Britain's role in the world as an honest broker. I agreed with him when he said that no nation could be more honest. He agreed with me, when I chaffed him, and said that no nation could be broker.[54]

On December 7, 1961, the rumbling Congolese crisis erupted once more when Macmillan and his cabinet reluctantly agreed to provide the United Nations with twenty-four heavy-duty bombs for deployment against Moise Tshombe's breakaway freedom fighters. Although the bombs were never used in anger, the political fallout was extensive. Macmillan faced a parliamentary revolt by Conservative backbenchers and wrote in his diary of "an internal party crisis" that was "both acute and dangerous." Within the Tory ranks as a whole, a kind of ideological brushfire erupted about British colonial policy in central Africa, which for a time threatened the entire Macmillan government. One or two imaginative newspaper commentators went so far as to compare the worsening situation in the Congo to the incremental series of steps that had led up to the outbreak of the First World War. Fortunately, this was a case where the Special Relationship, as embodied by the US president and his family friend the new British ambassador, proved worthy of the name. At a private White House dinner on December 13, David Ormsby-Gore told Kennedy that the government in London was in danger of falling and that to avoid this, Macmillan urgently needed "a request from the United Nations to cease fire—in twelve hours—24 hours at the most." Anything short of that might mean that the Americans would find themselves dealing with a Far Left Labour government in the new year.

Kennedy listened to Gore's summary of events, immediately picked up the telephone at his elbow, and in short order told his representative at the United Nations, Adlai Stevenson, to hold the bombers and instead start negotiations between Tshombe and the Congolese government. Although it could be argued that no vital American national interest was involved (other than continued access to the Congo's vast resources of copper, cobalt, and uranium), and thus that he could afford to be generous, Kennedy was "wonderful," Gore later enthused. "He threw the full weight of his authority behind getting the results that Harold Macmillan required."[55] The British premier then gave a masterful speech in the Commons debate and won the day with a majority of ninety-four. The internal chaos in the Congo continued at intervals until 1965, when the young army officer Joseph Mobutu (later known as the "archetypal African dictator" with a penchant for Concorde-flown shopping trips to Paris) seized power and began the process of turning the state into the latter-day Zaire.

Kennedy and Macmillan saw the necessity of prioritizing foreign policy over domestic political issues, even if the former's abstract of this credo ("Who gives a shit [about] the minimum wage in comparison to [Cuba]?") might not have been to the personal taste of a prime minister born under the reign of Queen Victoria nor necessarily a sentiment shared by all low-income Americans.

In fact, of course, Kennedy was fully alive to a whole raft of home-affairs concerns, most obvious among them the sense of injustice that many African Americans felt about their system of government. On the day after the president's inauguration, a twenty-seven-year-old black US Air Force veteran named James Meredith applied for admission to the all-white "Ole Miss," the University of Mississippi at Oxford. Twice denied by the school authorities, Meredith eventually took his case to the Supreme Court, which ruled that he had been unfairly treated because of the color of his skin. Some five hundred US marshals, supported by combat troops and military police, were subsequently on hand to chaperone the new student on his first day on campus. Amid scenes more like a Latin American revolutionary skirmish than a typical college enrollment, Meredith duly reported for classes on October 1, 1962. (Perhaps wisely, at the last moment he abandoned his plan to celebrate his arrival by driving up to the front door in his new, gold Thunderbird.) The sense of inequity and the system of virtual apartheid in the South highlighted by the Meredith case would come to fully exercise both the president and his brother the attorney general, even as they grappled with geopolitical threats that included the possibility of an estimated seventy million of their fellow citizens being incinerated in a thermonuclear exchange. After Mississippi, as Arthur Schlesinger put it, "the Kennedys began to understand how profoundly the republic had been trapped by its history."[56]

Nonetheless, President Kennedy consistently gave race-related and economic concerns a lower priority than he did the danger of a global conflagration that could jeopardize human survival. Writing in 1962, Kennedy biographer William Manchester reported: "The president estimates that eighty per cent of his first year in office [has been] spent mulling over foreign policy. In the 1960s, foreign policy thoughts are long thoughts. 'Of course he's preoccupied,' a member of the Kennedy family remarks. 'It would be a miracle if he weren't. Saigon, Germany, fifty-megaton bombs—that's why he can't get to sleep until two or three in the morning.'"[57]

Following Allen Dulles's replacement by John McCone as CIA director in November 1961, Kennedy was presented with a new form of daily foreign-intelligence briefing. Instead of a thick document written in sometimes-impenetrable bureaucratese and full of fussily annotated footnotes, McCone prepared an analysis that typically consisted of a few vernacular paragraphs illustrated by colored maps. Kennedy was soon expressing his personal delight with "the checklist." McCone knew he had struck on a winning formula early one morning when he, his assistant, and McGeorge Bundy were huddled in the basement of the West Wing, finalizing that day's briefing, and the president called down asking where they were and when they were going to bring it to him. The normally guarded Dean Rusk later called the checklist "a damned useful document," which qualified as a uniquely ringing endorsement from him.[58]

For Macmillan, it was a more varied and, on the whole, depressing daily regimen. An array of domestic problems not only steadily mounted during the second half of his premiership but also, as he remarked, "came around in a hideous loop." Every few weeks, it seemed, a vital sector of industry, such as the mines or the railways, would go on strike, added to which there were equally cyclical runs on sterling. As a result of these, money continued to flow out of Britain's depleted reserves; the exchequer lost £187 million (or close to a quarter of its total gold and currency holdings) following a single, concerted "bear" attack on the pound in April 1961. In the midst of the crisis management, Macmillan still somehow found the time to set up a number of commissions or inquiries to examine the longer-term needs of Britain's rail networks, roads, and ports; he was also able to order reviews of the country's secondary and higher education, public-health provisions, consumer-protection rights, newspapers and television, company law, and even the state of its littered high streets. Alongside this, Macmillan's frequent proposals for "global monetary reform," specifically the expansion of credit, continued to confound all but the most technically minded experts. It was a full enough agenda for anyone, let alone a man who saw his supreme challenge in life as being to avert a nuclear holocaust. Ironically, the instinctively conservative prime minister was more actively engaged in a program of national modernization than the supposedly reform-minded president. As a young US congressman, Kennedy had consistently opposed "dangerous" Democratic spending plans on social and welfare programs, instead calling for an across-the-board 10 percent cut in appropriations. "Does not the gentleman think that a very important item in the Cold War is the economic stability of the country, so that we shall have resources in case of war?" he asked on the floor of the House in April 1950.[59] Ten years later, the Kennedy agenda remained one of extreme fiscal prudence and sound stewardship of the nation's traditional values, modified just enough to appeal electorally to the constituency Arthur Schlesinger described to him as "the kind of people who provide the spark in Democratic campaigns . . . the liberals, the reformers, the intellectuals. . . . Once the issue-minded Democrats catch fire, then the campaign will gather steam."[60] Schlesinger later remarked privately that Kennedy had "hoped . . . that the civil rights movement would remain low-key, perhaps the subject of an occasional note on page 5 of the *New York Times*, permitting him to deal with what he saw as his top priority: the truly apocalyptical issue of atomic war."[61]

═════

On December 20, 1961, Macmillan, his Foreign Secretary, two political advisers, a scientist, a detective, and a doctor flew to Bermuda to meet Kennedy, who arrived in the tropical British colony with an entourage of 141. One presidential observer thought that, seen from above, the honor guard of multinational troops on hand at the airport, in their polished steel helmets gleaming in the sun, looked like "an army of densely packed ball bearings."[62] Earlier that week, the president's seventy-three-year-old father had suffered a stroke severe enough for both his children and a priest to be summoned to his bedside in Palm Beach. On hearing the news, Macmillan had immediately sent a "Dear Friend" wire, offering to change their meeting place to "Florida or Washington—or any other plan which might suit you." Although the stroke left Joseph Kennedy partially paralyzed for the remaining eight years of his life, in the end the Allies' conference went ahead as scheduled. As well as the ranks of troops, the governor of Bermuda, Major-General Sir Julian Gascoigne, was on parade to meet the presidential party. "Kennedy was at first rather amused by the somewhat antique form of the Governor's military costume, cocked hat, feathers, sword and gold spurs," Macmillan wrote. "But he soon began to realise the real quality of our host."[63] Kennedy was also suffering from an acutely painful back, and Gascoigne would long remember the poignant sight of the president "bound[ing] around at the airport, like a puppy fresh off the leash, and then, a half-hour later, once out of view of the press, slowly shuffling up the stairs at Government House one step at a time."

The ensuing talks did not go that well.

The list of contentious items awaiting discussion was headed by Laos, where the continuing "Phoumi versus Phouma" debate, pitting a moderately pro-American leader against a mildly pro-Russian one—if not without its comic-opera aspects, Macmillan felt—exposed a difference in not only opinion but also in style between the two allies. Kennedy came to the table with a voluminous briefing book that Gascoigne only half-jokingly said reminded him of a "large metropolitan telephone directory, though without its variety." Supported by a team of eight officials at his side, and with literally dozens more waiting in adjacent rooms with additional data, if required, the president, "quite different from the debonair figure of myth," was instead "a grey-faced man, seemingly transfixed by details." While Kennedy gave an almost real-time account of the recent activities of General Nosavan Phoumi, America's preferred client in the fitful civil war between communist and broadly pro-Western forces, Macmillan was left to doodle on the single typed sheet of paper in front of him, which was headed: "South-East Asia: Neutrality Pact." To Gascoigne, it was all "slightly redolent of the British establishment's acknowledged touch of 'amateurism'. The president and his team diligently read off all the facts and figures of recent border skirmishes in this inhospitable region, down to the precise strengths of individual man-militia companies, and the length of available dirt airstrips. . . . In general, the British civil service looked down, at least officially, on such calibrations, regarding them as 'academic', and uninteresting to their heads of government."

Kennedy's recitation can have been only partly reassuring to his British counterpart. He revealed that US paramilitary trainers, the so-called White Star organization, were both operating against the Pathet Lao communist-nationalist group in Laos and harassing North Vietnamese units on the Ho Chi Minh Trail to the east. Phoumi's own military prowess was considered modest: his action against Pathet Lao forces at Nam Tha, near the Thai border, ended in a full-scale rout. The US government was also supplying Phoumi with some $4 million a month in cash and materiel in order to advance its interests in the region. Macmillan could see the clear danger signs in what he called "this foolish internecine war," and had written to the queen shortly before flying to Bermuda of his frustrations with Britain's own client, the centrist Prince Souvanna Phouma, and his apprehensions of a wider conflict:

> Meanwhile, the position in South Vietnam is deteriorating, and the Americans are giving all the support they can, short of actual military operations—which in any case are not suitable to deal with this kind of infiltration.[64]

Macmillan was equally uneasy about continuing American support for the UN hard line on the Congo. Kennedy had, it's true, temporarily saved the day by brokering talks between Moise Tshombe's rebels and the Congolese government of Cyrille Adoula. For the moment, Tshombe retained control of the mineral-rich breakaway province of Katanga. Although discussions between the two groups had reached a fragile agreement on December 20, 1961, this soon broke down and the area degenerated into further chaos, exacerbated by well-documented atrocities committed by UN peacekeepers on the ground, and not helped by the avalanche of resolutions, proposals, and motions emanating from the General Assembly, which Macmillan thought was "driven on by the Afro-Asians and the 'non-aligned', with their bitter 'anti-colonial' complex."[65] The British position was that Katanga was a relatively well-governed enclave within the larger turmoil of the Congo and thus should be left to its own devices. In Bermuda, Kennedy asked Macmillan to cosign a communiqué that called for a formal alliance between Tshombe and Adoula and a reunification of their country. The premier declined to do so, telling the Americans that Tshombe, if not a model democrat, remained the West's best hope of resisting the communist tide in the region. Macmillan went on to propose a compromise, which would have seen Katanga reintegrated into a Congo federation while still retaining a degree of autonomy in its law-making and economic policy. "Thus," he later wrote, "I found myself in the peculiar position of trying to persuade [Kennedy] that the only solution for a country embracing a great area, with many local traditions, was a federal constitution in preference to a unitary state. For some reason, the Americans appeared to regard this as a somewhat rash and even novel proposition."[66]

Kennedy also told Macmillan that he had "had some secret correspondence with Khrushchev. . . . He now showed it to me and Lord Home." This led to a discussion on Berlin, where Macmillan thought the president was moving from a policy of confrontation to one of containment, "although outwardly and publicly he talks big."[67] Soon the prime minister was again speaking of his hopes for a test-ban treaty while graphically evoking the horrors of a nuclear war. We should "not sit in an ordinary little room four days before Christmas and talk about these terrible things without doing something about it," he told Kennedy. Macmillan added that both his firsthand dealings with Khrushchev and his familiarity with Russian literature convinced him that the Soviets could be made to see reason. "I made a tremendous appeal," he reflected in his diary. Kennedy was courteous but insisted that this was not the time for further negotiations. The United States would postpone their plans to explode a bomb over Christmas Island by a few weeks to allow Macmillan to discuss the details with his cabinet, but that was all. The talks then touched on the Common Market and the broader issues of world trade. "At this point, having no financial advisers to hinder me, I tried to expound some of my ideas on monetary reform," Macmillan said. Some in the room wondered if the president had used the opportunity of the lengthy recitation that followed to discreetly take a nap. Macmillan's self-confidence was not, however, impaired. He wrote in his memoirs: "Kennedy sympathised, but I knew that he, too, would be impeded by the spiritual heirs of those who had frustrated the full acceptance of the policies of Maynard Keynes. I was ten years too soon."[68]

Although the Bermuda conference had failed to find agreement on almost every substantive issue, Macmillan "felt that Kennedy and I had become even closer friends than before." Even in the privacy of his diary, he called the president "courteous, amusing . . . and *very* sensitive. He seemed particularly pleased by the present which I brought him (a copy of the William and Mary ink stand on the Cabinet table) and by Debo Devonshire's gift (silver buttons—of the footmen's coats—with ducal coronet and crest)."[69] It was their fourth personal meeting within a year, which was two more than Kennedy had managed with any other world leader and considerably more of his undivided time than he gave to his cabinet in the White House. Both sides agreed that they had enjoyed "two days of valuable discussions surveying the world situation." Macmillan was also touchingly worried about the president's bad back, finding him a rocking chair to sit on and fussing about his health generally. He seems to have watched over him as an anxious employer might do a precocious but frail protégé settling in to an important new job. Kennedy, in turn, thanked the prime minister for his concern, assured him he was fine, and added matter-of-factly the line that if he did not have a woman every three days, he would get a terrible headache.[70]

6

AVOIDING THE ROGUE ELEPHANT

Macmillan returned from Bermuda well disposed toward Kennedy personally but convinced that their two days of talks had led nowhere. The consensus among the British team was that the youthful president, while undoubtedly attractive and charismatic in public, tended to distance himself from individual people and events. While listening to Kennedy's "interminable, rather flat recitations" at Government House, one British participant had thought him "more like a bystander than an active member" of the conference. It seemed he was there primarily "to read out his brief, and then methodically place a tick by each item on the agenda, rather than to engage in debate." Kennedy, in another estimation, was "perfectly friendly, but essentially detached" at Bermuda. "He delivered his position like a highly trained civil servant, but I have to say there was no real sense of personal connection, whether because his mind was on his stricken father, or because it was his style to keep his distance from other politicians."[1]

It was left to Macmillan, in bed over the Christmas holiday with a heavy cold and a case of "black dog" depression, to once again labor over a document that sought to rise above the technicalities and address the broader strategic issues of the thermonuclear age. The premier's six-thousand-word "Dear Mr. President" letter of January 5, 1962, was another bold (perhaps overbold) attempt to provide a scholarly overview of the way the world was tilting in the early 1960s—proof not only of considerable foresight for a man of Macmillan's age, but also that the editor inside him was still alive and at work.

> In our recent talks . . . we touched on a number [of] points of importance. These included Laos and Viet-Nam . . . the confused and always uncertain [changed by Macmillan from the original "dangerous"] situation in the Middle East; Africa . . . and the likely development of the United Nations. . . .

Running all through these discussions there was one common thread. All of these problems . . . are dominated by a single theme, since all of them reflect the results of the great division which has dominated the world since the end of the Second World War. . . . It is the contest [original: "struggle"] between Communism and the free world—each struggling to contain the other, and to attract the somewhat cynical support of the so-called unaligned nations.

The more one reflects over all these problems, the more one is led to the conclusion that none can be satisfactorily dealt with singly.

After a somber account of the "underlying malady" of the global condition under threat of nuclear war, Macmillan was forced to admit:

It may be that there is no way out. It may be that we are condemned, like the heroes of the old Greek tragedies, to an ineluctable fate . . . and that, like those tragic [original: "doomed"] figures, we must put up with it . . . somehow postponing at least for a period a fatal [original: "serious"] crisis. All my life there have been two views about the best way of dealing with this sort of problem. I still remember [original: "vaguely remember"] these arguments before the first War. . . . One line suggests that we should keep patiently at work trying to chisel away the excrescences which deface the body politic of mankind, and hope by this method to remove one by one the major dangers . . . arriving eventually at a point when an effective all-round settlement [original: "détente"] can become practical politics. The other view has been that there are moments in history when it is better to take a bolder choice, and put a larger stake upon a more ambitious throw.[2]

Macmillan favored the bold throw. In practice, this meant bowing to the inevitable and making Christmas Island available to his ally while pleading for another tripartite conference in order to seek a test-ban treaty and, ultimately, a deal on general disarmament. Kennedy repeated his determination to resume testing but agreed to give Khrushchev three months in which to signal his willingness to talk. Khrushchev responded by detonating several more bombs. The Soviet leader told Anatoly Dobrynin, his new ambassador to Washington, that the latest American test program was "arrogant."[3] Since the Russians were thought to have less than ten functioning intercontinental missiles, it had begun to occur to them to relocate some of their stockpile of shorter-range weapons in such a way that they could better menace the American heartland. Siting the missiles in Cuba would allow them to target not only the Eastern Seaboard but also cities as far inland as Dallas, Chicago, and St. Louis. "The Americans . . . would learn just what it feels like to have enemy rockets pointing at you," Khrushchev noted blandly in his memoirs. "We Russians have suffered three wars over the last half-century. America has never had to fight a war on her own soil . . . and made a fortune as a result."[4]

Meanwhile, the Kennedy administration showed their appreciation of the populist government in British Guiana by continuing to insist that the mother country somehow impose its will over that of the elected prime minister. "Jagan and his American wife are very far to the left indeed, and his accession to power cause[s] us acute embarrassments with inevitable irritations to Anglo-American relations," Secretary of State Dean Rusk informed his opposite number, Alec Home.[5] The situation only worsened in February 1962, when anti-Western demonstrations broke out on the streets of Georgetown, with pictures beamed around the world of rioters looting the capital city's few recognizable stores and gleefully burning foreign flags. David Ormsby-Gore cabled back to London of a meeting at the State Department that Rusk "went on to warn the continuation of Jagan in power is leading us to disaster in terms of . . . strains on Anglo-American relations."[6] This was enough for Macmillan, in turn, to begin to seriously doubt the good judgment of Kennedy's hitherto largely innocuous secretary of state. The American position "show[s] a degree of cynicism which I would have thought Dean Rusk could hardly have put his pen to," the PM wrote to Home, adding one of those sardonic character sketches he sometimes allowed himself. "He is after all, not an Irishman, or a politician, nor a millionaire. He has the reputation of being an honourable and somewhat academic figure."[7]

On Laos, meanwhile, the British cabinet could note in January 1962 only that "despite the pressures exercised by the United States, General Phoumi was still unwilling to accept the proposals for a national government" and that all parties "had therefore been summoned to Geneva."[8] The same meeting heard that there had been some easing of tensions in the Congo, though it was hoped the "United Nations authorities refrain from pressing too vigorously the policy of hunting down the mercenaries in Katanga." Apparently persuaded by Macmillan's argument that to do otherwise might drive Ghana—as with Egypt—into the Soviet camp, Kennedy then agreed to contribute to the financing of the Upper Volta dam project with an initial loan of $95 million. It was not a universally popular decision within either the administration or the president's family. "I can feel the Attorney General's hot breath of disapproval on the back of my neck," Kennedy remarked.[9]

From Macmillan's angle, the Volta River dam affair "worked out most satisfactorily." Ghana remained in the Commonwealth and, for the most part, resisted the ongoing Soviet attempts to sour Kwame Nkrumah's government against its Western backers. Even so, it remains doubtful if Kennedy's generosity was moved as much by personal benevolence toward the British premier as it was by broader concerns about "losing" Africa, like China before it, to the communists. Arthur Schlesinger was convinced it was a case of the Allies having "tunneled along their own separate routes to the same end." Macmillan noted drily only that he had dealt with the matter "amid a host of messages, cables, telephones and boxes full of papers, [over] what was called the holidays."[10] Even during his infrequent breaks at his home in Sussex, the PM's working routine varied little. Macmillan would begin his day with a prolonged breakfast in bed over the newspapers, of which he often pretended to read only the *Flook* cartoon in the *Daily Mail*. ("I have a commercial stake in it," he once announced, straight-faced, to the Canadian premier.) His formal schedule began in midmorning, when he would shuffle downstairs for the first of a series of meetings, dressed, according to location, in a funereal black suit or baggy tweeds, in both cases often worn over an ancient pullover offering asylum to various stray bits of food. Whether alone or in committee, Macmillan then typically kept going with few breaks until well after dinner, which was fortified by a glass of port and a cigar. On a relatively "quiet" day, he might then retire around midnight and spend a further two hours going through his red dispatch boxes and writing up his diary before unwinding with a few pages of Trollope. It was a relentlessly full routine for anyone, much less a man approaching his seventieth birthday. In general, Macmillan bore the strain of office remarkably well for his age, even if he was to increasingly remark in his diary how tired he was. "Of course," he admitted there, referring to the Trollope, "it's a sign of old age and mental laziness to re-read books one knows so well. But I *am* ageing, and I do deserve a bit of mental relaxation."[11]

On January 6, 1962, in between dealing with the latest round of public-sector strikes and paying a flying visit to Bonn, Macmillan wrote another "Dear Mr. President" letter on the nuclear situation. Admitting to qualms about the general direction events were taking, he was left to confirm, ultimately, "We . . . feel morally bound to support any decision you might make to carry out this [testing] programme. My colleagues and I therefore agreed that it would be right to make available to you the facilities at Christmas Island which you require, subject, of course, to the conclusion of an agreement on scientific and technical collaboration, as well as about the financial arrangements."[12]

Kennedy promptly wrote back to assure him:

> I find myself in deep agreement with nearly all of what you say about the dangers of the arms race, and the boldness of action required from those who bear primary responsibility in these matters . . .[13]

before noting that the eight-week process of preparing Christmas Island for tests would now begin. Addressing the cabinet on January 18, Macmillan saw the cold realities of the matter: "Much would be lost by declining to make the facilities at Christmas Island available. . . . This would not prevent the United States Government from deciding to resume testing, and the United Kingdom Government would lose what power they had to influence that decision and to be brought into consultation."[14] Even then, Macmillan was moved to ask Kennedy to delay his official announcement, somewhat dramatically telling him it would "shatter the hopes of millions of people across the earth." Despite the appeal, the president appeared as scheduled on national television to inform the American public that the ongoing Soviet threat to their survival demanded that their government prepare and maintain a sufficient nuclear arsenal. "No single decision of this administration has been more thoroughly or more thoughtfully weighed," Kennedy announced. He also regretted that "even one additional individual's health may be risked" by the fallout from any testing.

While an Anglo-American task force mustered to prepare the nuclear detonation on Christmas Island, six thousand miles away in Moscow talks continued on that other defining issue of the Cold War. "Mr. Thompson, the United States ambassador, has now held three discussions with the Soviet foreign minister, Mr. Gromyko, to ascertain whether a basis could be found for negotiations on the future of West Berlin," Lord Home, in his characteristically mandarin language and oddly strangulated voice, told the cabinet on February 6. The Russians were apparently now content to play the long game, he said, "as no progress had been made, but Mr. Gromyko had shown no signs of impatience."[15] Two weeks later, Home reported that there were "disturbing indications" of a rift in the Western camp on

Berlin. "President Kennedy is obviously dissatisfied with the meagre response of his European Allies to the military build-up, which the Americans carried through last autumn in order to make Mr. Khrushchev realise that they meant business. The president seems to doubt whether the extra United States effort can be maintained indefinitely in view of the lack of a matching contribution from Western Europe."[16] Kennedy was frustrated not so much by the response of the British as that of the French and Germans. Home's summary of the resulting impasse allowed his colleagues a fleeting glimpse of the grandee Foreign Secretary's well-concealed sense of humor. "The president tried to make Dr. Adenauer see reason in Washington last November," he reported, "and seemed to have had some temporary success. But, to judge from the current German attitude to the talks in Moscow, alas, the effect has now largely worn off." Home concluded: "We must proceed cautiously, both because our own position on the military build-up is a disappointment to the Americans, and because good relations with our two main European allies matter very much to us for weighty reasons unconnected with Berlin," chiefly the Common Market. "Only President Kennedy is in a position to bring pressure to bear on Dr. Adenauer. The attitude of de Gaulle will also have to be considered," he said.

In the meantime, the diplomatic gavottes continued with a fresh meeting of foreign ministers in Geneva—"the most boring city on earth," as Macmillan called it in emphasizing British commitment to the talks. By now, even the normally calm and undemonstrative Home had begun to betray distinct signs of anxiety on Berlin, telling the cabinet that he had "been struck by the thoroughness with which the Western [sector] has been sealed off. It was now surrounded by something like a permanent frontier. This might mean," Home acknowledged, "that the Soviet Government may be less concerned to negotiate about the status of West Berlin. They might be more ready to accept continuance of the *status quo*. If so, this might explain the unresponsive attitude which Mr. Gromyko has adopted in the opening stages of his conversations with ourselves."

Summarizing the "few and disagreeable" options available to the West, Home told his colleagues:

> Serious study [will] have to be made of the two documents which the Soviet foreign minister has handed over—a draft statute for a free city of Berlin, and a protocol embodying guarantees for West Berlin.

After further cabinet discussion, Home abandoned his customary note of reserve and concluded:

> There are serious dangers in delay. The local situation in Berlin is explosive . . . and there is a continuing risk that some precipitate action might be taken which would provoke a crisis. . . . [Further], there are persistent rumours of a challenge to Mr. Khrushchev's authority within the Soviet Union.[17]

Home was right, at least, when he spoke about the volatile situation on the ground in Berlin. In January 1962, US military police began halting Soviet army vehicles in order to determine the identity of officers entering the American sector. The measures were taken, in part, to ensure that the Russian commandant did not defy an order banning him and his staff from the Western-controlled areas of the city, and several local skirmishes ensued. The following month, a CIA informer named Walter Linse was bundled off the street outside his West Berlin apartment, thrown in the back of a car, and never seen again. Bombs were detonated at locations close to the wall on three consecutive nights in February. President Kennedy and Secretary McNamara then announced that they were sending four thousand more infantry troops to Berlin in a "training drill." The British sent in three hundred extra soldiers, and the French none. Kennedy subsequently summoned General Lucius Clay for talks and announced that he and his point man in Berlin had reached full agreement on handling "any future crises" that might occur there. This followed in the wake of press reports that the general had been disturbed by the restrictions placed by the White House on his freedom to take "full retaliatory steps" against any Soviet provocations, should the circumstances require it. (Clay later recalled that Kennedy, who was seeking to impose price and wage restraints on the US steel industry at about the same time, was as keen to talk about the troubled economy as he was about Berlin. "He was greatly concerned about all that," the general said, "and, of course, he knew that I had been the head of a firm [i.e., Continental Can Company] that was a large user of steel, and he simply asked me whom he could get in touch with in the industry, off the record, and talk quietly to"—another example of Kennedy's intuitive skill in finding problem-solving resources that others might have overlooked.[18]) Clay went back to Berlin and duly "beefed up [our] state of alert" and determination to "stand fast in the face of any Soviet encroachment." The sixty-four-year-old general's own preparations included carrying a loaded gun at all times and placing a thermite bomb atop his office safe, in the event it needed to be swiftly destroyed during a Soviet attack.

The following week, fifteen US tanks lumbered away from their holding position near Checkpoint Charlie, where they had been based since the standoff with the Russians the previous October. Forty-eight hours later, the Soviet army pulled back their own formation of tanks from the heart of East Berlin, half a mile from the sector border. Even so, this was not quite to "normalize" the situation in the city, as claimed in a press release that month by the State Department. In the early weeks of 1962, there were several individual attempts to scale, breach, or attack the Berlin Wall using high explosives. To counter these initiatives, the Soviet authorities announced that anyone wishing to cross the border into East Berlin would require an entry visa stamped into their passport. Anyone returning to the west without such a visa would be regarded as a potential escaper. Before long, the bureaucratic procedures were reinforced by more tangible ones. In February 1962, the wall perimeter was enlarged to include an outer road patrolled by armed guards and attack dogs. In May, sentries in the east shot and wounded a fourteen-year-old schoolboy named Wilfried Tews after he had slipped into a city canal after dark, swum successfully to the far bank, and lay exhausted but apparently safe on western soil. Forty years later, three former East Berlin border guards would go on trial for this incident, but all were found not guilty on the grounds that "no clear intent to murder" could be established. Wilfried Tews remains crippled.

During this same period, Foreign Ministers Rusk, Home, and Gromyko continued to pursue their cyclical round of talks, sometimes held in one or other of their capital cities but often, by default, in Geneva. At one point, Rusk summoned ambassador Dobrynin to a meeting in Washington and told him that, if Moscow agreed to respect Western vital interests in Berlin, other issues, such as nuclear testing, "might fall more easily into place."[19] Dobrynin responded that, even so, the Soviet Union remained firm in its view that all Western "occupying troops" be withdrawn from the city as a prerequisite to any further talks. By the summer of 1962, the overall situation in Berlin had settled into the strategic stalemate, punctuated by individual border outrages and diplomatic crises, that remained largely unchanged for the next twenty-seven years.

In this early period, the Soviet negotiating tactics were simple. They involved "crushing the [Allies] with information and with mind-numbingly profuse complaints and grievances," Clay said, while "exploiting every possible incident" that might put the West in a bad light. Over the course of Wilfried Tews's escape, an East Berlin border guard named Private Peter Goring had somehow been fatally shot. It was never fully established if he had been struck by police deliberately aiming at him from the west or, as many claimed, by friendly fire from his own side. But, whatever the precise means of Private Goring's death, he was immediately made into a martyr to the cause, with a state funeral, several posthumous decorations, and a variety of streets and buildings named after him throughout the German Democratic Republic. It was another example of the East's willingness not only to deter with extreme prejudice any would-be escapers but also to hold out the promise of opportunities and rewards to their own citizens, if they cooperated, not just in their careers and in their social and cultural activities, but even after death.

While the tortuous round of foreign-minister discussions and recriminations continued, so did Khrushchev's own wildly erratic series of public and private remarks on Berlin. In June 1962, the Soviet leader sent a message informing Kennedy of his renewed commitment to a pact with East Germany that would eradicate "war remnants . . . and on this basis, the situation in Berlin would be normalized," by which he meant free of Western troops. Khrushchev went on to tell US secretary of the interior Stewart Udall, who was on a goodwill tour of Russia, that the situation in Germany was "no longer tolerable. . . . Do you need Berlin? Like hell you need it. . . . It's been a long time since you could spank us like a little boy. Now we can swat your ass."[20] Days later, Khrushchev then performed a characteristic about-face and sent a warm personal message to the White House. "Nothing will be undertaken [in Berlin] before your congressional elections that could complicate the international situation, or aggravate tension in the relations between our two countries," he assured Kennedy and his advisers—a tactical appreciation of the niceties of a democratic political campaign that surprised many of them.[21] Kennedy later told Cyrus Sulzberger of the New York Times that Khrushchev reminded him of a sort of Mafia figure who could as easily shoot you in the back of the head as "disarm you with his politeness."

In general, Kennedy was increasingly inclined to back off from a direct conflict with Khrushchev on Berlin and to quietly seek ways to accommodate the Soviets in other areas. In early 1962, for example, he sent two letters to Khrushchev that suggested that the United States and the Soviet Union should find ways in which to cooperate in the exploration of outer space. The first, dated February 21, acknowledged Moscow's congratulations following the orbital flight of Col. John Glenn and concluded, "I am instructing the appropriate officers of this Government to prepare new and concrete proposals for immediate projects of common concern." The second, dated March 7, followed up with specific suggestions where the two ideological foes could pool resources, "including the joint establishment of a weather satellite system, the sharing of other satellite and tracking technology . . . and a mutual exploration of space medicine."[22] It might not quite be fair to say that Kennedy came to follow Macmillan's lead and embrace the cause of economic and technical cooperation—or "appeasement," as some, like Senator Goldwater, called it—over that of confrontation with the Russians. But from the early part of 1962, six months after the initial shock of having East Berlin sealed off through Operation Rose, the two Western leaders were at last as one in their Berlin policy. Essentially, it was a case of Macmillan's "middle way." On the one hand, both de Gaulle in France and Adenauer in West Germany remained disinclined to consider any readjustment of the postwar administrative arrangements in central Europe. On the other, a number of the NATO countries, "with Canada, Italy, and Belgium in the lead," wanted a negotiated settlement of the Berlin crisis "at almost any price."[23] At one point, the NATO secretary general with a name like that of a 1950s action hero, Dirk Stikker, proposed a "parallel peace treaties approach" as the ideal bargaining position, a course that envisaged the phased departure of Western forces from Berlin, a period of peaceful coexistence between the two Germanys, and then that country's full reunification. The Belgian foreign minister, Paul-Henri Spaak, went on to produce a version of the same plan but called for the immediate withdrawal of all Western troops. Finally, there was Khrushchev's own continuing, if constantly adjusted, fixation on Berlin, one that was perhaps based less on fraternal solidarity with Walter Ulbricht and his colleagues and more on a not wholly unjustified fear that the Americans might be planning to arm their West German clients with nuclear weapons, sited only four hundred miles from the Soviet border.

If the big issues facing Kennedy and Macmillan remained unresolved, the personal rapport between the principal Western leaders and their families had grown appreciably over the past year. The First Ladies now exchanged handwritten notes and cards on roughly a monthly basis, sometimes including snapshots of the work in progress at their respective official homes: Jacqueline Kennedy's showing a preponderance of French Empire–style furniture, with walls covered in pale-yellow silk and chairs finished in matching mustard velvet; and Dorothy Macmillan's, a series of small rooms cluttered with workmen's ladders and paint pots, the grimy windows and bare lightbulbs offering a sharp contrast to Jackie's taste for rock-crystal chandeliers. Macmillan's biographer Alistair Horne writes that, while at Admiralty House, the premier slept in a "single bedroom simple as a cell, with a green telephone by the bedside."[24]

Clearly, the great divide between American ostentation and British austerity in the early 1960s was as pronounced at the senior government level as it was elsewhere. But for all that, there was a real warmth both between the Kennedys and the Macmillans, and at least some of their advisers. As we've seen, David Ormsby-Gore served both as an intermediary and a collegiate friend of the American First Family. Robert Kennedy later remarked that "he was one of us, really." "Dear Mr. President," Gore wrote on March 7, 1962, adopting his more formal style of address, "Her Majesty the Queen has heard that Mrs. Kennedy will be in London, [and] I have been asked to convey an invitation from the Queen to Mrs. Kennedy to luncheon at Buckingham Palace on March 27th": a case of two powerful men making social arrangements for two highly influential women.[25]

Speaking in the House of Commons on January 23, 1962, Emrys Hughes had somewhat leadingly "asked the Prime Minister, in view of the horror and indignation he expressed at the Russian atomic tests, [if] he would give a definite assurance that Christmas Island will not be given to the Americans for similar purposes." "No, sir," Macmillan had replied. Six weeks later, the premier, confirming in the House that the tests were to go ahead, denied that this was a case of the "United States us[ing] her nuclear and continental might for the same sort of reason that we used to use the gunboat."[26] Privately, Macmillan continued to harbor doubts up until the formal announcement, writing to Kennedy that while he accepted the scientific need for tests, he hoped his friend "would give a longer period of warning, thus allowing more time to try to achieve an agreement with the Russians." In the end, Kennedy agreed to change the wording of his cabled announcement to Khrushchev from "April 15" to "towards the end of April." This was enough for the Soviet leader to hurriedly agree to another meeting of the three foreign ministers in Geneva. Until Macmillan reminded him, Kennedy forgot to even mention the date of the tests to his other NATO allies, "which [made] me think that the State Department had not been in on this to any extent."[27]

Increasingly, a sure sign of Macmillan's personal feelings about Kennedy and of the success of their partnership was whether he addressed him as "Mr. President," "Friend," "Good Friend," or, ultimately, "Jack." Amid a flurry of eight cables leading up to the first Christmas Island test, there were four "Friends," three "Mr. Presidents," and one that eschewed any salutation. The sheer volume of the traffic was another mark of the new Macmillan-Kennedy axis. "I was most grateful for your message about Tests and Berlin," the premier wrote on March 13. "I have of course kept the paragraphs of your message on the wider issues entirely to myself and Alec Home."[28] The "wider issues" were those concerned with establishing a monitoring system, supported by an international inspection team, to detect any violations of a future test-ban treaty—a protocol Khrushchev deemed "grossly unacceptable" and likened to "a rape" of his country. Kennedy cabled back on April 3 (using the more guarded "Dear Mr. Prime Minister") to talk about the prospects of establishing a Western listening station, which he called by its code name of "International Minus." Macmillan in turn said that the Soviets had agreed with him on the need for inspections during his visit to Moscow in 1959, a fact that appeared to have since slipped Khrushchev's mind. Time was already running out that spring, and the scientists insisted that there was an optimum "blast window" for the first Christmas Island test of between April 23 and 28. Many of the technical papers daily coming across his desk "were to me unintelligible," Macmillan later admitted.[29] But if he was bewildered by the arcana of fissile yields and radiological isotopes, he was convinced more than ever of the need to put up a united front to the Soviets.

"Dear Friend," Macmillan cabled Kennedy early in April. "I am not really concerned with the public opinion of Britain at the present time. In my experience, that always stabilises itself in the long run behind what is right and sensible. But my colleagues are impressed by your thought that there might be advantage [in a mutual statement] from the whole Western point of view."[30] Four days later, a joint communiqué from Macmillan and Kennedy was handed to the Soviet government. The message broke down along national lines with an emollient British first half and a harsher American warning in the tail. After expressing the hope that the Russians might yet accept the principle of international verification, the cable added that, were this not possible, the Western allies would conclude that the current test-ban negotiations were at an end, and the detonation "scheduled for the latter part of this month will have to go forward."[31]

Macmillan was "immensely relieved" that Kennedy at least agreed to continue to present the Soviets with a "thoroughly coordinated" Anglo-American nuclear policy. He had pursued the president "with perhaps unjustifiable obstinacy" on this point, he acknowledged. In his heart, however, Macmillan knew that tactical differences still remained in the Allied camp. As he told his cabinet on April 5, "The outstanding question for decision was whether, before [a] joint UK-US statement was issued to Moscow, a final personal request should be made to Mr. Khrushchev, urging him to accept the principle of international verification by on-site inspection." It was another case of the Allies adopting the good-cop and bad-cop roles when dealing with Moscow. "President Kennedy has said that he would not be prepared to join in making such a request," Macmillan admitted.[32]

If the West differed in some of the detail of policy, signs were also appearing of a secret struggle at the top of the Kremlin hierarchy. Along with the standing ovations to Khrushchev's speeches at the party congress of October 1961, there had been muted dissent on the platform about the "cult of personality," and "the winding up of the Stalin revolution," as the politburo member Otto Kuusinen had put it. Behind the scenes, Stalin's foreign minister Vyacheslav Molotov had sought to defend his old boss's reputation by sending Khrushchev a letter condemning his "appeasement" of the West as "scandalous for Communists."[33] Khrushchev responded by expelling some three thousand malcontents from the party. In a gesture Stalin himself might have recognized, the ringleaders were sent to Siberia. In due course, their family members each received a bill for the cost of transporting their loved ones into long-term exile. Molotov was dispatched as ambassador to Outer Mongolia, following which he served as a delegate to the International Atomic Energy Agency in Vienna but was then brought back to Moscow to be formally denounced, after which his documents and files were removed from the party archives. A nonperson, he survived into the Gorbachev era and died in bed at the age of ninety-six.

A theme running through much of the West's public opinion on the arms race, as expressed by a growing number of newspaper stories and protest marches, was "unease . . . about the inadvertent outbreak of a nuclear spat," as Macmillan had delicately put it in cabinet. Such concerns weren't wholly in the realm of fantasy, given the control structures that existed in the early 1960s. There were at least three known incidents during Kennedy's first year in office in which a subordinate military commander had been sufficiently worried about Soviet air force movements to take the initiative for ordering the preliminary steps toward a missile launch. As Ros Gilpatric, deputy secretary at the Department of Defense, recalled, "We became increasingly horrified over how little positive control the President really had over the use of this great arsenal of nuclear weapons."[34] In a November 1961 episode that could have prefigured the movie *Dr. Strangelove* in showing the almost absurd ease with which a war could be triggered, American nuclear bombers around the world went on high alert following a breakdown of communications between the Pentagon, Strategic Air Command (SAC), and the American air force base at Thule, Greenland. Some reports claimed that the agitated duty officer at Thule had taken the silence that met his first routine, but then increasingly urgent, attempts to raise his command headquarters in Nebraska as evidence that SAC itself was under attack, and that he had been "within three minutes" of initiating a launch sequence. Five months later, when the near crisis became public knowledge, Macmillan found himself "defend[ing] the probity of this nation's greatest friend" in the House of Commons:

> *Mr. Swingler* asked the Prime Minister, in view of the false alarm arising from a double failure of communication, if he will discuss with the President of the United States proposals covering all bases on British soil to end the system of instant readiness to use nuclear weapons, because of the danger of a war by accident or miscalculation[.]
> *The Prime Minister:* The recently publicised incident arose from some disruption of part of the communications system. United States strategic aircraft, including some stationed in this country, were brought to a more advanced state of readiness as part of a standard procedure.
> *Mr. Zilliacus:* Is not it a fact that if there had been a triple instead of a double failure of communication, none of us might have been alive today?[35]

Not long after this, in May 1962, senior Allied ministers and NATO chiefs met in Athens to review the future control and uses of the West's nuclear stockpile. Marked "Cosmic Top Secret," the minutes of the meeting reveal just how much the United States and the United Kingdom relied on intercontinental rockets rather than conventional weapons. "The Soviet Union," Dean Rusk remarked, "should be certain that the alliance would not use nuclear bombs for trivial reasons, but *would* use them to defend vital interests. . . . His country hoped that the cohesion of the

Alliance would be further enhanced by President Kennedy's commitment to consult in the Council prior to the use of nuclear assets anywhere in the world"—"if time permitted," Rusk added. Harold Watkinson, Britain's defence minister, went on to note that he "particularly welcomed the commitment to NATO of Polaris submarines, which would provide a degree of second-strike capability, representing an immense gain to the Alliance. . . . He pointed out that over-reliance on conventional weapons might be interpreted by the Soviet Union as a sign of unwillingness on the part of the West to use nuclear ones."[36]

Rising above the fray, Kennedy took the opportunity of several speeches that spring to address the larger ideological issue about what was at stake in the Cold War. Though respectable opinion in Washington and elsewhere held that the Russians were perfectly reasonable people—"just like us," as Eleanor Roosevelt had observed—the president, thinking years ahead of his time, already realized that the doctrine of Marx, Lenin, and Stalin would ultimately be exposed as a gruesomely failed experiment. "Wisdom requires the long view," he told an audience at the University of California in March 1962. "There used to be much talk a few years ago about the inevitable triumph of communism. We hear such talk much less now. No one who examines the modern world can doubt that the great currents of history are carrying the world away from the monolithic idea, and towards national independence and freedom."[37]

"Our military policies must assist nations to protect the progress of democratic reform," Kennedy said elsewhere that spring. The presence of some four thousand US "advisers" so engaged in Southeast Asia continued to pique the American news media. "We have increased our assistance to the government in Saigon—its logistics," Kennedy told a White House press briefing. "We have not sent combat troops there, although the training missions that we have there have been instructed if they are fired upon, to—they would of course fire back, to protect themselves. But we have not sent combat troops in the generally understood sense of the word."[38] Unconvinced by the president's tap dancing, a reporter stood up at a State Department press conference on April 11 and asked him: "Sir, what are you going to do about the American soldiers getting killed in Vietnam?" "We are attempting to help [Saigon] maintain its independence, and not fall under the domination of the communists," Kennedy replied. "It presents a very hazardous operation. In the same sense that [in] World War 2, World War 1, Korea, a good many thousands, and hundreds of thousands, of Americans died, so these [casualties] are in that long roll. But we cannot desist in Vietnam."[39]

In the predawn hours of Wednesday, April 25, an American B-52 released the first of what eventually became a total of twenty-four high-yield bombs to explode in the air over Christmas Island. Going under the collective name "Operation Dominic," the program included twelve detonations elsewhere in the Pacific and put a variety of nuclear submarines and missile launchers through their paces. The inhabitants of Christmas Island who chose to stay in their homes rather than be evacuated reported seeing a huge, sunlike fiery ball regularly appear in the night sky. Macmillan, preparing to fly to Washington for his next meeting with Kennedy, was sardonically amused by the copious, and often contradictory, flow of technical data that ensued. "The interchange of telegrams and memoranda between British and American scientists continued gaily," he noted in his diary. "Scientists, who are the poets of the 20th Century, seem to be the subject of the most conflicting moods."[40] Uninterested in the fine detail, Macmillan now took the view that the nuclear-arms race was a "rogue elephant" and a "lunatic conceit" that could only end badly for the human race. The weapons would ultimately find their way into the hands of "dictators, reactionaries, revolutionaries, madmen," he fretted in a letter to Kennedy. "Then, sooner or later, and certainly I think by the end of this century, either by error or folly or insanity, the great crime will be committed."[41]

On that note, Macmillan and his small party of eight, which did not contain Lady Dorothy, boarded the plane for New York, where he was to address a convention of American newspaper publishers before flying on to meet Kennedy in Washington. It was another example of the daily "twelve or thirteen hours of variegated work" the PM typically put in. Aside from his concerns about the "rogue elephant," Macmillan was also facing a wide array of domestic political challenges. In March, the Conservatives had managed to lose a previously safe parliamentary seat at a by-election in the London suburb of Orpington. A number of trade unions were chaffing against the government's pay policy, with a fresh round of strikes promised by the teachers and miners. The budget in early April had rashly increased by 15 percent the duty on soft drinks, chocolate, and ice cream, leading to headlines accusing Macmillan of "taxing the kiddies." A Gallup poll taken on the eve of the PM's flight to America showed the Liberal Party ahead with 33.9 percent, Labour second with 33.4 percent, and the Tories trailing in third place. "It is a very extraordinary change in a very few months," Macmillan was left to admit, ruing the "long menu of crises" facing him and rather forlornly promising in an eve-of-departure speech at Stockton: "What I can now do is to hold out to you the Government's hope of success—at the end—in achieving an ever more dynamic influence in the affairs of the future of Western Europe and the Western world."[42] As rhetoric went, this was not quite in the rallying class of Kennedy's "We shall pay any price, bear any burden, meet any hardship, support any friend, oppose any foe to assure the survival and success of liberty." A painfully sore throat only made things worse. Macmillan's doctor, Sir John Richardson, was hurriedly summoned to accompany him on the flight to New York.

In the event, the PM's speech to the newspaper publishers on April 26 was a tour de force. Rising above his bad throat, he told his audience that he had come to speak to them "on the health and outlook of your transatlantic cousin—something which, putting aside any question of sentiment, is perhaps of some significance to you." After telling them about the current state of British politics (carefully avoiding the opinion polls), he went on to a masterly overview of the balance of world strategic power and, in particular, his continuing hopes for a nuclear-test ban. Macmillan received a Soviet-style twelve-minute standing ovation, part of "a greater friendliness to the UK than I remember before, pervading every aspect of our relations," he noted happily in his diary.[43]

In Washington, Kennedy pulled out all the ceremonial stops, with a marine guard of honor, effusive welcoming speeches, and a helicopter ride for Macmillan and himself back to the White House. A mark of the personal warmth of the alliance was that the First Lady then flew home from her extended Easter break in Palm Beach to join the two heads of government at a glittering dinner in the British embassy. The subsequent formal talks, which, in an unusual gesture, took place largely around the president's Cabinet Room table, were equally friendly, if offering little new on either Berlin or test bans. Kennedy spoke in general terms about Laos and Vietnam. In other business, Macmillan told his host that he did not see any "Communist threat to British Guiana," and Kennedy replied that, nonetheless, the United States intended to pursue "a policy of getting rid of Jagan." Following that, words were exchanged on the subject of Britain's possible entry into the Common Market. The president was guardedly enthusiastic although worried that such a move might "accentuate the US balance of payments problem, severely affect agri-

culture, and could cause withdrawal of US forces from around the world."[44] This
was a signal for Macmillan to begin coughing violently. After a short delay, Kennedy
turned over the meeting to his undersecretary of state, George Ball, who lectured
the British about their historical responsibilities to the United States. As Macmillan
listened, his facial expression, according to one observer, passed from "polite and
attentive, to quizzical and uncertain, to annoyed and enraged, with a rapidly rising
flush to his cheeks." The premier later wrote in his diary that he partly blamed
Kennedy for allowing "Mr. Ball . . . to go on with his intrigues against us in Europe
and the Common Market negotiations."[45]

After that, all that remained was for Kennedy and Macmillan to exchange personal best wishes, summer book lists, and political gossip. The president extolled
the merits of James Bond, while the prime minister inclined more toward the likes
of David Copperfield and Obadiah Slope. This wasn't exactly a solution to the
world's ills, but Macmillan was delighted by the prevailing warmth of the occasion. He found Kennedy an altogether more relaxed character than he had been
four months earlier in Bermuda, possibly, in part, a result of the daily cocktail of
painkillers and amphetamines Dr. Jacobson was prescribing him. Before taking his
leave, Macmillan presented his host a gift described in the official catalog as an
"early 19th century crystal punch bowl with base, with alternating panels of dia-
monds and fluting, and 16 fan-shaped lobes on the rim." Kennedy gave his guest a
signed book of photographs in return.

"The President and the Prime Minister conducted a general review of international problems facing their two countries," the communiqué said. "In particular,
they reviewed the problems of disarmament, and of nuclear test control. They reaffirmed their regret that the Soviet government has not been willing to join in an
effective treaty which would end such testing. . . . The prime minister informed the
president of the progress in the Brussels negotiations between Great Britain and the
European Community. The president expressed [his] hopes that these negotiations
would be crowned with success."

When Macmillan returned to London, he might have rested on his laurels and
enjoyed his apparent diplomatic triumph. Instead, he was faced with a Conservative Party in continued freefall, with disastrous results in May's local-government
elections and a threatened strike by dock workers, prompting the PM to dispatch
troops to keep the nation's ports open. Macmillan was sufficiently worried by it

all to ask the party chairman, Iain Macleod, for an analysis of what was behind the recent "alarming reverses." The eventual report can have been only partly comforting to him. "One thing that emerges with absolute clarity," Macleod wrote, "is that the popular reasons, such as pensions, nuclear disarmament and colonial policy, had nothing whatever to do with it. Incomparably the leading factor was the dislike of the pay policy, and general dislike of the Government."[46]

On closer inspection, Macmillan's meeting with Kennedy was also perhaps more of a symbolic, "big picture" performance than one of solid success. The premier himself alluded to this when, on April 29, he wrote to thank the president for his hospitality, before adding: "We may not seem at the time to achieve any definite result, but I believe that this sort of discussion is of incalculable importance in preserving and strengthening that Anglo-American fellowship which I value so highly."[47] In fact, several major areas of concern, notably the now-daily round of "air-burst" nuclear blasts above Christmas Island, remained to be resolved. Pressed in the House of Commons to expand on the "nebulous platitudes" of the communiqué and to assure the House that he would "seek an urgent summit with the Americans and Russians" on nuclear disarmament, Macmillan could blandly reply only that "meetings, whether between two, three, or four Heads of Government, can be useful. Other meetings can be useful. I do not rule out anything, but I do not wish at this moment to make any more precise statement."

Privately comparing it to one of his regular attacks of gout—"apparently cured, only to flare up with renewed vigour"—Macmillan also soon felt compelled to write to Kennedy, advising him that the situation in the Congo was again threatening to erupt, with "bad effects not only in the United Nations and in Africa, but in Anglo-American relations." The PM continued to press the case that the best solution was for the Congo to be a sovereign state under a federal constitution, "leaving the provinces in general, and Tshombe in particular, a considerable degree of local autonomy." Kennedy demurred, cabling back his belief that some more direct form of action might be needed to "convince Tshombe to continue sincere talks with Adoula."[48] The president leaned liberal but consistently defaulted to pragmatism where he considered the American national interest was concerned. After expressing the hope that the Allies could avoid an "open disagreement" on the subject, Kennedy ended with a veiled warning about "the difficulties that we will have to face if the Congo crisis is not abated."[49]

There, for now, it remained. Macmillan was rapidly coming to see the whole saga of the Congo as one of those slightly ludicrous international scrapes that defied a logical solution. "These particular Africans seem really impossible to deal with—Tshombe and Adoula are equally difficult," he wrote in his diary.[50] Both he and Kennedy "adamantly agreed" that they wanted to keep the Soviets out of the region. But where Macmillan favored a two-tiered Congolese government, balancing central and provincial power, the Americans (perhaps impressed as much by Katanga's significant copper deposits as by any ideological consideration) wanted a "thoroughly integrated and unified" state under their friend Adoula. Tripartite talks on the subject between the United States, Britain, and Belgium proved to be one of those rare events in inter-Allied diplomatic negotiations—that is, a total disaster. In time, Kennedy wrote to inform Macmillan that, should their efforts to stabilize the Congo "fail through Tshombe's fault, Adoula would no longer heed, or be free to follow, the counsels of restraint . . . the Chief of the Congolese Government w[ould] be obliged to reassert his authority."[51] This was an only thinly coded expression of the president's view that British policy in the area lacked grip and that the Americans might have to intervene. When Macmillan's aide Philip de Zulueta brought him his daily batch of foreign-affairs correspondence, he generally attached a cover note to each cable, giving his opinion as to whether or not it was broadly helpful to the British cause. After reading Kennedy's latest broadside on the Congo, de Zulueta wrote across the top, "This is *not* a good reply."[52]

Before long, Macmillan was also forced to admit that the Allies were similarly deadlocked on the subject of British Guiana. The Washington talks on this issue had been very pleasant, the PM wrote in his diary, but "all very vague. And when it came down to brass tacks, we don't make much headway." Once again, the British and Americans were agreed on the need to keep the Russians out but divided as to how precisely to do so. On May 30, Macmillan wrote a "Dear Mr. President" letter that acknowledged that "developments in Guiana—and, for that matter, in British Honduras—are of special concern to the United States government. When these territories become independent, as they must before very long, they may well be of more direct concern to you than to us."[53] While Macmillan was once again left to offer the prospect of talks, Kennedy, under pressure from Senator Goldwater and others, wanted the British to commit to delay any decision about withdrawing from Guiana until at least mid-1963. Meanwhile, the CIA would continue its opera-

The solid and eminently respectable home where Harold Macmillan grew up in Cadogan Place, London. In later years, he made some play of the fact that he came from "simple crofter stock" in the west of Scotland. *Photo by C. Sandford.*

John Kennedy's birthplace, a seven-room house on a tree-lined street in Brookline, Massachusetts, was modest compared to his later homes. *Photo courtesy of Patrick Dowdall.*

Macmillan's wedding to the nineteen-year-old Lady Dorothy Cavendish was the social event of the 1920 London season. *Photo used by permission of the Mary Evans Picture Library.*

President-elect Kennedy enjoys the plaudits of the crowd in Los Angeles, November 1960. Macmillan never quite aspired to the same level of public frenzy. *Photo used by permission of the Mary Evans Picture Library.*

Kennedy and Macmillan at their first meeting, Key West, March 1961. *Photo by Don Pinder.*

Pointing the way: Kennedy and Macmillan at their first Washington talks, April 1961. *Photo by Abbie Rowe, White House Photographs. Courtesy of the John F. Kennedy Presidential Library and Museum, Boston.*

British and American officials pose for a group photograph, April 1961. *Front row, left to right:* US Representative to the United Nations Adlai Stevenson, Secretary of State Dean Rusk, Kennedy, Macmillan, British Foreign Secretary Alec (Lord) Home, and British Ambassador to the United States Harold Caccia. Averell Harriman and David Bruce, dark and light tie, respectively, stand behind Stevenson and Rusk. *Photo by Abbie Rowe, White House Photographs. Courtesy of the John F. Kennedy Presidential Library and Museum, Boston.*

The two First Families meet in London, June 1961. *Photo used by permission of the Mary Evans Picture Library.*

Former secretary of state and later Kennedy adviser Dean Acheson. Following Acheson's remarks about Britain's lack of a postwar "role," Macmillan wrote in his diary, "He was always a conceited ass." *Photo from the LBJ Presidential Library, by Yoichi Okamoto.*

Robert Kennedy at a desegregation rally in Washington. At times he seemed to the British (and others) almost to hold a copresidency with his brother. *Photo by Warren K. Leffler, Library of Congress Prints and Photographs Division, US News & World Report Magazine Photograph Collection.*

Kennedy's secretary of defense Robert McNamara. In December 1962, McNamara's triumphant announcement that the Skybolt guided missile had at last passed a flight test, just days after the weapon was canceled, did not go down well in either Washington or London. *Photo from the Department of Defense, by Oscar Porter, US Army.*

President de Gaulle in his element. Macmillan's often-troubled relationship with the Frenchman once led him to confide to Kennedy, "I think this man has gone crazy—absolutely crazy." *Photo used by permission of the Mary Evans Picture Library.*

Macmillan's longtime colleague and rival in love Robert Boothby. *Portrait by Allan Warren.*

A US tank at the new front line of the Cold War, Berlin, in August 1961. The sign at the left bears Walter Ulbricht's words of two months earlier—"No one has any intention of building a wall." *Photo courtesy of the US Army.*

A more somber Kennedy signs the US blockade of Cuba into law, October 1962. *Photo from the Library of Congress Prints and Photographs Division, New York World-Telegram and the Sun Newspaper Photograph Collection.*

Nikita Khrushchev jokes with his client Fidel Castro. One of the few light moments in an otherwise increasingly strained relationship. *Photo used by permission of the Mary Evans Picture Library.*

Kennedy entertains President Sukarno of Indonesia on a state visit to Washington. He got a cooler reception later in London. *Photo by Abbie Rowe, White House Photographs. Courtesy of the John F. Kennedy Presidential Library and Museum, Boston.*

The special relationship at work—Kennedy and Macmillan meet in the White House Cabinet Room. David Ormsby-Gore, who is holding a paper, sits on the left of the PM. *Photo by Abbie Rowe, White House Photographs. Courtesy of the John F. Kennedy Presidential Library and Museum, Boston.*

The Cuban "quarantine" goes into effect. Macmillan was not alone in calling the missile crisis "one of the great turning points in history." Years later, it emerged that two officers on a submerged Soviet submarine had come to blows as they debated whether to launch their weapons. *Photo courtesy of the National Naval Aviation Museum.*

Macmillan welcomes Kennedy to Bermuda, December 1961, for their fourth meeting of the year. After the formal reception by the island's governor, Major-General Sir Julian Gascoigne (Home and Ormsby-Gore look on), the two principals got down to some hard talking. Macmillan was not happy with the Americans' plan to resume nuclear testing, while Kennedy, who was suffering from an acutely painful back, was thought by some to have taken the opportunity of the PM's lengthy recitation on global monetary reform to discreetly take a nap. *Photos by Robert Knudsen, White House Photographs. Courtesy of the John F. Kennedy Presidential Library and Museum, Boston.*

Proving that he has lost none of his popular appeal, the president arrives with the First Lady to greet members of the Cuban Invasion Brigade at the Orange Bowl in Miami. *Photo by Cecil Stoughton, White House Photographs. Courtesy of the John F. Kennedy Presidential Library and Museum, Boston.*

When Kennedy came to visit Macmillan at Birch Grove, his home in the English countryside, the PM thought it all "more like a play, or rather the mad rehearsal for a play, than a grave international conference." Kennedy's helicopter appearing out of the clouds was probably the village's major talking point, although the sight of the presidential motorcade threading its way through the narrow local streets also left a strong impression. *Photos by Harold Waters.*

Birch Grove. The sign at the front gate translates as "No one attacks me with impunity." *Photos by Andrew Baird.*

Kennedy and entourage with Dorothy Macmillan, with whom he shared a wisecracking sense of humor, a love of gossip, and a tendency to stray from their wedding vows. They were also related by marriage. *Photo by Antony Lewis.*

The president and prime minister shortly before parting on June 30, 1963. It was their last meeting. *Photo from the collection of Paul Elgood, author of* Kennedy at Birch Grove.

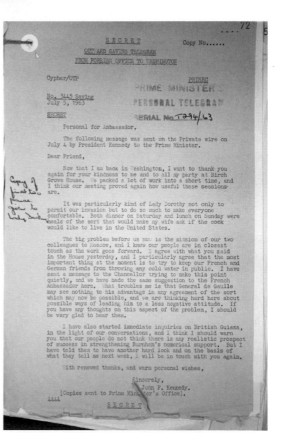

The president's thank-you cable to Macmillan, a mixture of the personal and the political. *Photo from the UK National Archives.*

Macmillan spent much of his last year in office engulfed in the sex-and-spy scandal that erupted around his minister for war, John Profumo—seen here at the height of the saga with his wife, actress Valerie Hobson. *Photo used by permission of the Mary Evans Picture Library.*

Macmillan with Jackie Kennedy. They kept up a long, effusive, and often deeply moving correspondence for more than twenty years following the president's death. *Photo used by permission of the Mary Evans Picture Library.*

In later life, Macmillan liked to circulate, like a modern-day King Lear, between his three daughters; he also enjoyed holding court in his London clubs. Here, Margaret Thatcher sits at his feet on his eighty-fifth birthday. *Photo used by permission of Corbis.*

tions to remove Cheddi Jagan from power. Among other steps, the agency made an $800,000 grant to the American Institute for Free Labor Development (AIFLD), which is said to have "maintained anti-Jagan labor leaders on its payroll, as well as an AIFLD-trained staff of eleven activists who were assigned to organize riots and destabilize the central government."[54] Following the February 1962 disturbances in Georgetown, with pictures of Kennedy being burned in the streets, Macmillan could only agree that perhaps Jagan "might be a second Castro. This naturally concerns the Americans."

Confirming this impression, David Ormsby-Gore later wrote that "from about the summer of '62, the President began to make it very clear to the British government that the granting of independence to Guiana, in circumstances where it could become a hotbed of Communism, was something that was really unacceptable to the United States."[55] Within only a few weeks, it appeared that the CIA could be reasonably confident of a successful outcome to its operations, as a series of labor- and race-related riots continued in the streets of Georgetown. By the late summer, some of the president's oldest and closest political allies were openly advising him on how best to secure the goodwill of a post-Jagan government. "Should our covert program succeed, we would wish to be in the position of being able to give the successor regime immediate aid," Arthur Schlesinger told Kennedy in September.[56]

By the middle of 1962, it seemed that the Special Relationship was often better at the personal level than in the minutiae of policy matters. Both Kennedy and Macmillan were inclined to be verbose and retreat into dense, self-justifying position statements—"hiding behind the jargon as behind a bomb-proof door," one British official privately remarked—on the likes of the Congo and Guiana. But the human factor continued to impress observers on both sides of the Atlantic, not only for its mutual empathy but also for the avuncular regard the PM clearly felt for the president—"almost a sort of love," David Ormsby-Gore thought, an emotion not normally associated with the upper echelons of Cold War diplomacy. Macmillan cabled on May 25:

> Dear Friend,
>   I write once again to send you my best wishes on your birthday. [He was four days early.] Looking back on the past year, you must, I think, feel considerable satisfaction. Both in the international field and, so far as I can judge, at home also, you have made a lot of progress in getting your policies accepted and respected.

Of course, nothing is ever perfect, particularly in the eyes of the newspaper col-
umnists. But from a rather long experience, I have found that when things are
really bad the newspapers shut up, and when the chorus gets going it is a very
good sign.

Anyway, I hope that for at least one day you will be able to forget the cares
of state and be with your family, to whom Dorothy and I send every good wish.[57]

The obvious warmth and charm of these sentiments did Macmillan proud. Alas,
though, presidential birthdays are rarely as tranquil as he might have wished. On May
29, Kennedy's schedule began with a working breakfast with members of Congress
and continued through a series of briefings at the Pentagon, followed by White House
meetings on Berlin and Taiwan, a reception for the foreign minister of Yugoslavia, and
finally a lengthy interview with the *Los Angeles Times*. Kennedy did at least have dinner
alone with his wife. Marilyn Monroe's sequined performance of "Happy Birthday, Mr.
President" had taken place at Madison Square Garden the week before.

Macmillan had clearly made up his mind that Kennedy's friendship should be
cultivated, and he enlisted a variety of distinguished Britons to join him in his charm
offensive. Senior cabinet ministers like Butler and Home were each reminded
to send the president their personal birthday greetings. Eighty-seven-year-old
Winston Churchill, still an MP, cabled his effusive best wishes for the occasion
and received a wire by return: "I am especially grateful for your birthday greetings, Sir, in view of the high admiration for you which I have in common with free
people everywhere. Sincerely, John F. Kennedy."[58] The president even merited a
two-page handwritten letter from the queen. "I have seen my Prime Minister who
has just returned from his visit to the United States," she observed, "and he has told
me how much he enjoyed being there, and particularly how much he valued this
chance to talk personally with you at this present difficult stage in the affairs of the
West. . . . It is a great comfort to me to know that you and he are so close, and that
you have confidence in each other's judgement and advice; I am sure that these
meetings and this personal trust and understanding are of the greatest importance
to both our peoples." The queen ignored any minor differences in specific Anglo-
American policy and instead wrote of her enthusiastic support for the personalities
involved. There was special praise for Gore and his wife. "David is, as you know,
very highly thought of here," she continued, "so it is excellent news that he and
Sissie are making their mark in Washington." After expressing pleasure in her recent

lunch with the First Lady, the queen even managed a tribute to the "enjoyable and interesting" Dean Rusk and concluded with the news that her husband would soon have the honor of visiting the World's Fair in Seattle, where His Highness would go on to narrowly miss Elvis Presley. "I envy him the chance of being in the United States again. We have had two such happy trips there," she concluded. "Your sincere Friend, Elizabeth R."[59]

"Dear Jack," Gore himself wrote the president in July, proving again that he enjoyed a level of intimacy with Kennedy unlike the generally more staid relations between other heads of government and foreign officers. "Thank you for the immensely enjoyable week-end at Hyannis Port. I do not know which was the more pleasurable, the brisk and invigorating Saturday or the warm lazy Sunday. There is no doubt that toying with the instinct of fear adds spice to life, and that is why one pretends [to be] smiling in a boat that may at any time tip over, [as] opposed to one that is relatively stable"——a metaphor, surely, for certain events that lay ahead. At times it almost seemed as if Gore was Kennedy's ambassador to Macmillan, rather than the other way around. After remarking that he was soon to visit London, he concluded his letter by telling the president, "It would be an immense help if I could come and have a talk with you sometime before I leave. The PM seems to be brooding over the world economic situation and may come up with some, I hope, bright ideas quite soon."[60]

Kennedy was able to engage in some similar clear-sky thinking of his own that month. In a keynote address in Philadelphia on the anniversary of the signing of the Declaration of Independence, he spoke of his hopes for the Common Market——"those nations of Western Europe [that] are today joining together, seeking as our forefathers sought, to find freedom in diversity, and in unity, strength. . . . We do not regard a strong and united Europe as a rival but as a partner," Kennedy announced, if so an advance from his remarks to Macmillan of just two months earlier. "To aid its progress has been the basic object of our foreign policy for seventeen years. We believe that a united Europe will be capable of playing a greater role in the common defense." He ended with a rhetorical flourish: "I say here and now, on this Day of Independence, that the United States will be ready for a Declaration of Interdependence, that we will be prepared to discuss with a United Europe the ways and means of forming a concrete Atlantic partnership, a mutually beneficial partnership between the new union now emerging in Europe and the old American Union founded here."[61]

That formula of a wise American superstate carrying Western Europe through its postwar reconstruction crisis has had an almost incalculable political effect on both sides of the Special Relationship ever since. The essential ingredients of the transatlantic role reversal, in which the New World colossus would seek to defend and sometimes dictate the interests of the fragile, ancient democracies, were now in place. Ironically, not all the intended beneficiaries of American largesse saw the matter of their salvation in quite the same sweeping, geopolitical terms. While Kennedy may have come to embrace the chimera of European political and economic unity, Macmillan had certain hardheaded doubts about the practical steps involved. Seen from up close, he remarked, the prospect of a "united Europe" was rather different.

Shortly after leaving Washington, Macmillan had gone on to talks with General de Gaulle at the Château de Champs, a moated, formally landscaped manor twenty miles outside Paris. These only partially succeeded in their aim of advancing Britain's case for membership in the European Community. De Gaulle remained deeply troubled by the Anglo-American alliance in general and its monopoly of Western nuclear technology in particular. "He several times repeated his determination to secure a small deterrent force for France," Macmillan reported to Kennedy on June 5. "I did ask him if he would feel, as I did, that a tripartite meeting with you and I might be useful. But he did not seem particularly attracted by the idea."[62] (This was mild compared to what Macmillan said of de Gaulle in his diary. "He *loathes* England," he wrote, "still more America—because of the War, because of France's shame, because of Churchill and Roosevelt, because of the nuclear weapon."[63]) De Gaulle later told a British diplomat that a closer alliance between France, the United States, and the United Kingdom in the early 1960s would have struck him as "a messy *ménage a trois*," a combination to which he was not partial.

No sooner was Macmillan back in London than Kennedy's secretary of defense Robert McNamara, never the Briton's favorite ally, announced in a major speech that all non-American nuclear weapons were "dangerous, expensive, prone to obsolescence, and lacking in credibility as a deterrent."[64] The PM went ballistic. McNamara's "foolish speech" had "enraged the French," he wrote. "In NATO, all the allies are angry with the American proposal that we should buy rockets to the tune of umpteen million dollars, the warheads to be under American control. . . . It is a racket." When Dean Rusk arrived in London a few days later, Macmillan told him:

"We have an independent deterrent, and the French are going to get one. These are facts which the Americans cannot alter. There is therefore no point in going on talking about them."[65]

A "tacit understanding" on the subject ensued, Rusk noted, though that did not prevent a more serious breach between the Allies just six months later. This again touched upon the independent UK nuclear deterrent, and more specifically on Britain's purchase from the United States of the Skybolt airborne missile as a vehicle to deliver her own, domestic-built warheads. Unfortunately, Skybolt proved to be a disappointment in advanced tests—demonstrating only a 45–50 percent chance of successfully reaching a target—with development costs up 35 percent on original estimates. McNamara went on to mention to his new British counterpart, Peter Thorneycroft, that the United States had already invested $300 million and that it would be necessary to spend another $200 million ($2.4 billion and $1.6 billion, respectively, at today's prices) before a single Skybolt was ready to be fired in anger. Macmillan was not pleased to learn that Britain might yet be left with an arsenal of sophisticated nuclear warheads and, failing the offer of an alternative American system, no means with which to actually launch them against an enemy.

"When I [forged] 'interdependence' with President Eisenhower," the premier told Thorneycroft, "I think he personally was sincere. But lower down the scale, his wishes were ignored. So it is with President Kennedy. Your predecessor stood up to McNamara well. But we still had hopes that the Americans would play fair. I fear that this is beyond their capacity. I think you should make clear to them that we are not 'soft', and are quite well aware of the facts. Americans respect strength, and rather admire a 'tough' attitude. If only we can 'get into Europe' we shall, of course, have a much stronger position."[66]

Meanwhile, Macmillan acknowledged the ambivalence of the British position when he told the House of Commons that, while the country retained her independent deterrent, "as a matter of practice" this was being constantly refined and tested in conjunction with the Americans, while a joint European defense strategy "remained a point for consideration in accordance with changing circumstances."[67] Privately, the PM was left with the bitter thought that "the failure of Skybolt might be welcomed, in some American quarters, as a means of forcing Britain out of the nuclear club." When David Ormsby-Gore went to the president to convey official concerns about where all this was leading, and to protest McNamara's "foolish speech," Kennedy proved more sympathetic than some of his advisers. An hour later, the ambassador left with a ringing presidential commitment to his "first ally's" independent deterrent, as well as an invitation to spend another weekend at Hyannis Port. Gore was effusive in his thanks: "I want to assure you I will heed your advice about arguing our nuclear [position] in terms of *our* interests, not yours, and fully appreciate the wisdom of this. . . . It [was] a great encouragement to learn something at first hand of how you see the greatest of our world problems. I am most grateful for the opportunity, and want to say how much my friends and I admire what you are doing—it has changed our concepts of the possible."[68]

As well as the simmering dispute over nuclear weapons, there was a range of other transatlantic quarrels during the summer. India, with some reason, had come to see itself as threatened with invasion by the Chinese and was urgently requesting a delivery of Allied fighter aircraft to protect its cities. Again Macmillan urged Kennedy to hold back, telling him, "I fear that if the Indians are assured of Western air defence, they may become more intransigent," and the crisis passed.[69] There were the familiar differences about nuclear testing ("I recognize your own feeling that we could get along with a simple abolition of tests," Kennedy cabled on August 3; "I wish I could agree with you") and competing commercial interests around the globe. Kennedy wanted Macmillan to join him in an embargo of civil trade with Cuba (although the president made a personal exception when it came to cigars), and Macmillan replied that "this would not be immediately possible," as the Cubans remained keen to buy a range of British goods, including a fleet of London double-decker buses. There was also the long-running matter of the Congo, where Home wearily told the cabinet on July 10, "A new crisis seemed to be developing. At a late stage in the contacts between Mr. Adoula and Mr. Tshombe, it has become apparent that they are not in agreement on some of the fundamental constitutional problems."[70]

Macmillan's temper may thus already have been up by the time he came to return from an August afternoon's grouse shooting at Bolton Abbey to find a telegram awaiting him from the US embassy in London. In what must have seemed to him further proof of American diplomatic chutzpah, it announced that the Pentagon was about to supply a consignment of "Hawk" surface-to-air missiles to Israel, so preempting a possible sale of Britain's own "Bloodhound" rocket. Macmillan's immediately cabled salvo to Kennedy was not notable for its restraint. There was no salutation. "I have just received the information [about the missiles]," it started, "and that the decision will be conveyed to the Israelis tomorrow. This follows two years of close co-operation during which we decided [the sale] would be unwise. . . . Dean Rusk gave a most categorical assurance to David Gore that your Government would consult us. . . . To be informed on Saturday afternoon that your Government are going to make an offer to supply on Sunday is really not consultation." It was all a long way from the PM's warm birthday greetings to Kennedy of just a few weeks earlier. Having established his position, Macmillan went on to get personal. "I cannot believe," he fumed, "that you were privy to this disgraceful piece of trickery. For myself I must say frankly that I can hardly find words to express my sense of disgust and despair. Nor do I see how you and I are to conduct the great affairs of the world on this basis."[71]

Of course, it was all a misunderstanding. Dean Rusk clarified the position overnight, pointing out that the United States was only considering its options on Israel, which would be pursued in the "closest accordance" with Britain, and Macmillan went back to his office on Monday morning suffering from an acute ideological hangover. "My Dear Friend," his contrite letter to Kennedy began. "Since I sent my indignant message to you, Lord Hood [Gore's deputy in Washington] has telegraphed to say that he has had a talk with Mr. Rusk, which puts a different complexion on this affair. . . . This is just to tell you how glad I am that my serious concern was all based upon a muddle. . . . With warm regard. As ever, Harold Macmillan."[72]

On August 27, the Atlantic allies put out a joint statement assuring the world of their policy of achieving "a guaranteed end to all nuclear testing in all environments." Once again, the main parties—now expanded to an eighteen-nation disarmament committee—met for talks in Geneva, but these soon bogged down on the familiar issue of inspections. As summer turned to fall, it seemed the Alliance was threatened by a steadily increasing series of altercations and scandals. Soon there was the case of John Vassall, the former cipher clerk at the British embassy in Moscow who had been "turned" by the KGB after being photographed enthusiastically participating in a male orgy (his shorts, a court later heard, worn around his head). After seven years' relatively low-level service to the Soviet Union, Vassall was arrested in London on September 12. It still remains debatable whether this "little spy who is a bugger," as the British director of public prosecutions called him, did any lasting damage to Western security. But he undeniably harmed relations between the Allies' main intelligence agencies. With its intoxicating mix of sex and espionage, the Vassall affair proved to be both a prelude—a cartoon trailer, as it were—to the wider Profumo scandal that erupted in March 1963 and, in retrospect, also marked the beginning of the end of the Macmillan administration. "The last year of my [term]," the PM later wrote, with detached understatement, "was over-shadowed by a series of difficulties, starting with some genuine apprehensions as to security, and spreading rapidly."[73] Compounding his problems with Kennedy, meanwhile, was the passage of the latter's Trade Expansion Act.[74] While the president saw this as good for both the United States and Europe—"a decisive point for the future of our economy, for our relations with our friends and allies, and for the prospects of free institutions and free societies everywhere," as he rather bombastically put it—the PM had a narrower focus. "Dear Friend," he wrote on September 24, "I believe that our concern about the purposes and consequences of your legislation has a more solid basis than [you] imply. My people disagree with yours about the facts. . . . This is no small matter for us. . . . One thing that worries me is that if the United States claims to control not only its own trade, but other countries' trade, your example may be followed."[75]

Six days later, Kennedy met with British Foreign Secretary Lord Home and their respective advisers in the White House. They were there to discuss a developing situation, which had assumed new urgency on September 21, when the CIA learned of "a first-hand sighting of a truck convoy of 20 objects, 65 to 70 feet long, which resembled large missiles" traveling toward the southwest coast of Cuba. In the days prior to this, Kennedy had announced that the Castro regime would "not be allowed to export its aggressive purposes by force or the threat of force. It will be prevented by whatever means may be necessary from taking action against any part of the Western Hemisphere."[76] He added that he was calling up 150,000 more army reserves to active duty with immediate effect. That week, the Senate voted by 86 to 1 to authorize the president "to prevent the creation, or use of, an externally supported offensive military capability endangering the security of the United States." Following that, Macmillan and Kennedy jointly announced that they were "agreed on the serious nature of developments in Cuba" and would seek "ways and means of containing further Communist expansion and subversion in the Caribbean."[77]

The outcome, Macmillan added, was destined to be a "rather alarming" one.

7

TO THE BRINK

Like the Berlin Crisis, the construction of offensive missile bases in Cuba failed to catch the West completely by surprise. The drama, which brought the world closer to thermonuclear warfare than ever before or since, did not begin with the US reconnaissance flight of Sunday October 14, which produced 928 photographs of the weapons, nor did it begin when the evidence itself was brought to President Kennedy's White House bedroom with his breakfast tray on the morning of the 16th. It had been building all summer, and the CIA had been fielding reports from operatives on the ground for several weeks before the first confirmed sighting of a missile convoy rumbling toward the coast of Cuba on September 21. On July 30, Khrushchev had asked Kennedy, "for the sake of better relations," to stop American U-2 flights over Soviet ships in the Caribbean, a request that the president's brother later noted had "raised several flags" within the administration. By the end of August, New York Republican senator Kenneth Keating was openly stating in speeches that he had evidence there were upward of two thousand Soviet troops in Cuba and that "concave metal structures supported by tubing" appeared to be for rocket installations. In remarks widely reported over the Labor Day weekend, Keating went on to complain that the administration was more concerned with the midterm elections in nine weeks' time than with preparing an "effective response to the construction of hostile bases" just ninety miles off the coast of Florida.[1]

During the late summer of 1962, the confirmed arrival in Cuba of Russian SA-2 antiaircraft weapons was another "cause for vigil," the CIA conceded in a situation file for the president. Although the agency noted that the Soviets had not yet fitted the weapons with live warheads, it added that "there is little reason to suppose that they would refuse to [do so] if the move could be controlled in their interest."[2] In mid-September, meanwhile, the sixty-year-old director of Central Intelligence, John McCone, was on his honeymoon at Cap Ferrat on the French Riviera, where he was accompanied not only by his young bride but also by a full CIA cipher team.

Commendably focused on events unfolding across the Atlantic, McCone asked first himself and then the president the question (obvious now, but not at the time) what the growing number of SA-2s had been sent to Cuba to defend. Could it be a full-scale nuclear missile battery? Added to the reports of his national-security officials, Kennedy was also receiving advance intelligence from Colonel Oleg Penkovsky, the deputy head of Soviet military planning who served as a double agent under the code name "Ironbark." Equipped with a Minox pocket camera and an apparently burning conviction that he must "tell people in the West what conditions in the USSR are really like," he would eventually hand over some ten thousand pages of classified material on Soviet rocket emplacements. A CIA station chief named Hugh Montgomery later recalled how he had arranged for Penkovsky to be one of the Russian officials invited to a July 4, 1962, party at the US ambassador's residence in Moscow. Penkovsky was told to visit the bathroom and to leave photos of top-secret Cuba documents in a sealed polythene bag inside the toilet cistern, where, with some difficulty, Montgomery later retrieved them. All the files circulated to President Kennedy and his advisers during the thirteen days of the active crisis bear the name Ironbark, indicating that they made use of that source. Penkovsky himself was arrested by the KGB on October 22, 1962, the day on which Kennedy publicly revealed the existence of the missiles in Cuba, and was executed by means of a bullet to the head the following May.[3]

Following McCone's honeymoon cable to Washington, other US security officials also chimed in with their own warnings about events in Cuba. Speaking in 1998, Sidney Graybeal of the CIA's Office of Strategic Research remembered that "there was a lot of human intelligence coming out of Cuba through Miami, and other sources, [and] a lot of these reports would talk about missiles being moved around. I looked over these reports in minute detail, and most of them could be explained away . . . but five of them really worried us, because there would be a description of a canvas-covered object going through a town at night—always late at night, these missiles would be moved—and this particular missile trailer could not turn a corner. It had to back up, and this source was describing this long, telephone pole–like object, he didn't call it a missile, and it couldn't get around the corner."[4]

In London, Cuba was the first order of business at the cabinet meeting of October 9, more than a week before Kennedy flashed Macmillan a cable to formally notify him of the crisis. Alec Home told his colleagues that "current Russian activities on the island had caused intense feeling in the United States. President Kennedy had been placed in a difficult personal position. . . . He seemed inclined to believe that the Soviet government were deliberately increasing the scale of Russian activities in Cuba [to] provoke a US intervention . . . the pretext for Russia's forcible occupation of West Berlin."[5] Although Kennedy could not be sure at this time if the Soviets were in fact deploying offensive weapons in Cuba, the photographs he reviewed over breakfast on Tuesday, October 16, finally settled the issue. After quickly issuing instructions for a White House meeting later that morning, the president placed a call to his brother, the attorney general. "We have some big trouble. I want you here," he told him.

More than fifty years later, Khrushchev's principal reasons for acting as he did are still open to debate. As Home recognized in his remarks of October 9, the Americans primarily saw the missiles as a device to blackmail them into withdrawing their troops four thousand miles away in Germany. "I realise fully that Khrushchev's main intention may be to increase his chances in Berlin," Kennedy told Macmillan on October 21. In that early flurry of messages on Cuba, barely a day passed without one or both of the Western leaders reverting to their default position that the Russians were really playing for stakes much closer to their own border. "I need not tell you," Kennedy remarked on the 22nd, "the possible relation of this secret and dangerous move on the part of Khrushchev to Berlin."[6]

This apparent Russian attempt to leverage its chances of finally annexing West Berlin was obviously incompatible with Khrushchev's promise that "nothing would be undertaken" to upset the international strategic balance before the US midterm elections. But, then again, neither Kennedy nor Macmillan could ever hope to match the Soviet leader's ability to simply abandon a stated position when it suited him to do so. Few could. When Khrushchev briefed Anatoly Dobrynin on the latter's departure to take up his duties as Soviet ambassador in Washington, "It was clear he regarded the problems of Germany and Berlin as the principal issue in Soviet-American relations, and he wanted them solved."[7] According to Dobrynin, "Khrushchev believed he had a chance to shift the status quo in his favor in Berlin."[8]

Linkage aside, Khrushchev seemed to have been motivated at least in part by sheer mathematics. In February 1962, Robert McNamara had told the Senate Committee on Foreign Relations that the United States had "a clear military superiority for major nuclear conflict." Although Kennedy had campaigned for president just fifteen months earlier with the warning that America was "fast losing the arms and satellite race with the Soviet Union," it soon transpired that the "missile gap" was the other way around. In December 1961, the US National Intelligence Estimate concluded that the Russians had no more than twenty-five intercontinental ballistic missiles (ICBMs), and possibly as few as ten, and that none would be added in the near future. Depending on how the figures were calculated, the United States had between twelve and fifteen times as many. Frustrated by the imbalance in long-range rockets, Khrushchev, the theory goes, devised a plan to place a small percentage of his medium and intermediate ones, of which he had several thousand, where they could better menace targets as far west as Dallas. This was presumably what the Soviet chairman had in mind when, in April 1962, he casually asked his defense minister, "Rodion Yakovlevich [Malinovsky], what if we throw a hedgehog down Uncle Sam's pants?"[9]

Other clues to Khrushchev's thinking lay in the presence of the newly installed squadron of US medium-range Jupiter missiles in Izmir, Turkey, aimed provocatively at the southern underbelly of the Soviet Union. Kennedy himself was quick to make this point when he sarcastically asked at a White House meeting, "Why does [Khrushchev] put these rockets in there [Cuba], though? It's just as if we suddenly began to put a *major* number of MRBMs [medium-range ballistic missiles] in Turkey. Now that'd be *goddamned dangerous*, I would think." After a pause, McGeorge Bundy, not known for his sense of humor, solemnly noted: "Well, we did it, Mr. President."

Khrushchev may also have had a more narrowly ideological motivation for ratcheting up the Cold War to the point where his revolutionary fervor outran his ability for rational thought. He appears to have been benevolently fond of Fidel Castro and his Bolshevik-like vanguard, a fellow feeling that only intensified following the Bay of Pigs affair. "The fate of Cuba and the maintenance of Soviet prestige in that part of the world preoccupied me," Khrushchev wrote in his memoirs. His paternalistic concerns had some basis in fact. Along with the trade embargo, the United States had soon put in place a full range of covert anti-Castro activities. Under the code name of "Operation Mongoose," these included the publication of suitably tailored news articles, the training and arming of militant opposition groups, and the establishment of necessarily clandestine guerilla camps on Cuba itself. Some critics later remembered that President Kennedy had recently listed the James Bond adventure *Dr. No*—a yarn in which Bond battles the maniacal dictator of a Caribbean island—as one of his ten favorite books. Perhaps it was coincidental, but soon the CIA was pursuing a more direct route toward effecting a regime change in Havana, including schemes to supply Castro with a box of poisoned cigars or to plant explosive seashells in his favorite swimming hole. One memo speaks apparently seriously of spraying a broadcast studio with hallucinogens shortly before Castro entered it, in the hope that his subsequent "addled and incoherent performance" would fatally undermine his credibility with the public. According to a CIA officer named Thomas Parrott, there was even a plan under discussion to convince the people of Cuba that the Second Coming of Christ was imminent, at the climax of which "an American submarine would surface off the coast and send up some star shells. And this would be the manifestation of the Second Coming, and Castro would be overthrown."[10]

On October 4, 1962, Attorney General Robert Kennedy opened a meeting in the Justice Department by "saying that higher authority is concerned about progress of the MONGOOSE program, and that more priority should be given to trying to mount sabotage operations. . . . He urged that 'massive activity' be mounted within the entire MONGOOSE framework. There was a good deal of discussion about this, and General Lansdale said that another attempt will be made against the major target which has been the object of three unsuccessful missions, and that approximately six new ones are in the planning stage."[11]

Although the CIA and others had made it clear that something was afoot in Cuba, the full enormity of Khrushchev's nuclear play took the US administration by surprise. "Oh shit! Shit! Shit! Those sons of bitches Russians," Bobby Kennedy exclaimed when his brother told him the news.[12] Some of the other members of the inner circle wondered if Khrushchev had lost his mind or if there had been a coup of some sort in the Kremlin, "and the hard-line boys have moved into the ascendancy," as Dean Rusk put it. The president remarked later, on the morning of October 16, that Khrushchev was "playing God" and asked in exasperation, "Can any Russian expert tell us—why they . . . ?" Speaking at the week's first White House crisis-management meeting, he added, "Well, it's a goddamn mystery to me."

Kennedy may have been shocked, but he recovered quickly. The author of *Why England Slept* didn't need to be reminded of the lessons of appeasement as they had applied twenty-four years earlier and might do again here. Convening a group of thirteen advisers who called themselves the Executive Committee, or ExComm, of the National Security Council, the discussions about an American response began within three hours of Kennedy first drowsily viewing the pictures of Soviet missiles. Although recently returned from his honeymoon, John McCone was now absent, attending a family funeral. The CIA's Sidney Graybeal briefed the group on the aerial photographs, which were propped up in front of them on an easel. Apparently recognizing the historic nature of the occasion, Kennedy surreptitiously triggered the tape recording system that he had installed the previous July. In the Oval Office, the microphones were hidden in the kneehole of the president's desk and under the nearby couch, while here in the Cabinet Room they were concealed in lighting fixtures on the wall and under the coffin-shaped table.

At that Tuesday-morning meeting, the president was, as usual, in his dark suit, but some of his hastily summoned team wore striped sports coats and white shoes. Bobby Kennedy bounded in in his shirtsleeves, with a facial expression that one observer said was "shark-like." The treasury secretary and former Eisenhower aide Douglas Dillon was present, forming a human link back to the Suez affair of almost exactly six years earlier. Although different in scale, and in the threat of an imminent nuclear holocaust, the two crises shared the not-insignificant fact that they erupted immediately before a major American election. On October 19, Kennedy went directly from an ExComm meeting where his Joint Chiefs of Staff argued for a swift, "surgical" air strike against the rocket installations in Cuba to campaigning on behalf of Democratic congressional candidates in Cleveland and Chicago. Although both crises had also blown up around the same basic theme of a troublemaking populist leader in cahoots with Nikita Khrushchev, one was a case where the British response had taken the Americans by surprise, and the other was one where the US administration initially chose not even to consult its main foreign ally. The first sure sign that this was 1962 and not 1956 was that Kennedy said nothing to Macmillan about the missiles in Cuba for five days after he had learned of them. Sidney Graybeal later remembered that the first ExComm meeting had been interrupted when the door of the Cabinet Room "suddenly burst open, and [four-year-old] Caroline Kennedy came in, and said, 'Daddy, Daddy, they won't let my friend in.' The President got up, went over, put his arm around her, took her out of the room, came back within a minute and said, 'Gentlemen, I think we should proceed.'" For that brief moment, Kennedy's young daughter had commanded more of ExComm's undivided attention than Macmillan or any of America's other allies had thus far.[13]

Even so, the president's eventual top-secret cable on Cuba failed to come as a total surprise to the British. On October 19, David Ormsby-Gore had reported to London that he expected "an impending crisis, probably about missiles in Cuba."[14] Jacqueline Kennedy later remembered learning of the crisis while entertaining the Maharajah of Jaipur at dinner in the White House, and finding "upstairs, David and Jack squatting on the floor, looking at the missile pictures."[15] It says something about the nature of the Special Relationship in 1962 that the president was apparently prepared to confide in the British ambassador before he either consulted Macmillan or advised a single other head of government. Bobby Kennedy's notes of the ExComm meeting of Sunday, October 21, lay out a timetable of action working back from a public statement by the president at 7:00 p.m. Washington time—"P hour"—on October 22. At "P hour minus 24," all US forces were to prepare to go to a DEFCON 3 state of alert. Strategic Air Command would then be instructed to prime all American nuclear assets, including the opening of designated missile silos, "as directed by military readiness requirements." ("With no publicity," the notes added, rather unnecessarily.) Other forces were then to begin to mobilize for a blockade of Cuba, and "to prepare for furnishing military riot control support to selected Latin American countries." Only then was "Notification to be made as follows to key NATO countries by US ambassadors," a list led by Britain at P hour minus 12; with France to follow at P minus 4; and Germany, Canada, Italy, and Turkey bringing up the rear at P minus two.[16] The first intimation most other nations had of the gathering storm was when Rusk started briefing a group of forty-six foreign ambassadors in the conference room of the State Department less than an hour before Kennedy addressed the world.

Macmillan was working alone in his study at Admiralty House at around ten o'clock on Sunday night, October 21, when the duty clerk appeared with an "eyes only" teletype from Kennedy. "Dear Prime Minister," it read, "I am sending you this most private message to give you advance notice of a most serious situation, and of my plan to meet it. I am arranging to have David Bruce report to you more fully tomorrow morning, but I want you to have this message tonight so that you may have as much time as possible to consider the dangers we will now have to face together."[17] After reading the clipped, 250-word account of the looming crisis in which "I have found it absolutely essential . . . to make my first decision on my own responsibility, but from now on I expect that we can and should be in the closest touch," Macmillan replied with a "Dear Friend" cable just an hour later. "I am most grateful for your private message," he told Kennedy. "Naturally I am thinking about you and all your problems at this difficult time." The PM's emollient tone slipped only when he came to record the scene in his diary on the morning of the 22nd. "The first day of the world crisis!" he wrote.[18]

After a fever of diplomatic activity, it was agreed that while Ambassador Bruce briefed Macmillan, the venerable ex–secretary of state Dean Acheson would fly to Paris to see de Gaulle. Acheson was summoned from his Maryland farm at eight o'clock on Sunday morning and told to be ready to take off two hours later. The banks were closed, and he had to borrow sixty dollars pocket money from his secretary. Acheson's air force jet touched down for a fueling stop at ten that night, local time, at Greenham Common, fifty miles west of London, where it was raining heavily. David Bruce went out to meet the plane. Acheson gave him a set of classified U-2 photographs to present to Macmillan, and Bruce in turn handed Acheson a hip flask of scotch that he had thoughtfully brought with him. Watching the two gray-suited diplomats silently conduct their exchange by the dim light of an airfield hut, a British MI5 officer was reminded of "one of those classic espionage swaps somewhere in the alleys of Berlin." The presence of several heavily armed US Marines and Secret Service personnel only added to the melodrama of the occasion. Before taking his leave, the normally staid, sixty-four-year-old ambassador whispered to Acheson: "Put your hand in my coat pocket." Acheson did so and found that it contained a revolver. Bruce explained that he had been issued it earlier in the evening by the security officer at the American embassy and told to keep it on him at all times for the foreseeable future. Some "uneasy laughter" had followed, Acheson remembered.[19] It is not known if Bruce was "packing heat" when he arrived at Admiralty House by appointment twelve hours later to confer with Macmillan.

That Monday-morning meeting, the premier wrote, was "the beginning of the week of most strain I can ever remember in my life." Macmillan saw Bruce alone in his study for a few minutes, and then each was joined by a small team of advisers. Chester Cooper of the National Security Council had accompanied Acheson on the flight to England and now found himself studying the workings of the Atlantic partnership at close quarters. "Macmillan's reaction when he saw the pictures was very interesting," he recalled. "He looked at them for a little while, and then said, more to himself than to us, pointing at the missile sites, 'Now the Americans will realise what we in England have lived through for the past many years.' Then he was concerned that this remark, which was quite spontaneous, would indicate that he was either unsympathetic or perhaps even chortling over our difficulties. He hastened to assure us that it was an instinctive reaction, and that he was terribly worried about the missiles, [and] would provide the United States with whatever assistance and support was necessary."[20]

Macmillan's first reaction when replying direct to Kennedy shortly afterward was to advise him to "seize Cuba and be done with it," thus avoiding drifting into the sort of quagmire the British had done at Suez.[21] But by the time he came to actually send his cable five hours later, he was more inclined to the long view. The main Soviet strategy, he now reflected, seemed to be to "move forward one pawn in order to exchange it for another," in other words, to trade Cuba for Berlin. Kennedy's blockade of one would, he believed, swiftly be answered by Khrushchev's blockade of the other. In that case, the PM continued, matters would escalate either to world war "or to the holding of a conference."[22] After ending his message to Kennedy by promising to support him in the UN Security Council, Macmillan called in his latest chancellor of the exchequer, Reginald Maudling, and put him in the picture. "His advice was sensible," the premier jotted in his diary, no doubt recalling what he still bitterly thought of as the Americans' financial blackmail of him six years earlier. "He would see Governor of Bank. There would be heavy buying of gold, and a general fall of all stocks and shares—but no general panic."[23]

In his cable of Sunday evening, Kennedy had promised Macmillan that he would soon be sending him the text of his public statement on the missile crisis. In fact, the draft arrived in London at 5:00 p.m. on Monday, just seven hours before the president went before the cameras. The PM had time only to skim through it before wiring his reply. It was a full day for officials on both sides of the Atlantic. At an ExComm meeting at 11:30 that morning, Kennedy had approved a range of proposals, including a naval blockade of Cuba, although on legal advice he agreed that this should be styled as a "defensive quarantine." The president finally informed the rest of his cabinet of the crisis at four that afternoon. Kennedy then briefed key congressional leaders, an experience that he later told his brother was "a tremendous strain."[24] After listening to the president, several lawmakers criticized the idea of a blockade as a feeble response to Khrushchev's action. Senator Richard Russell,

Democrat of Georgia, announced that the United States was "at a crossroads," and that "we're either a first-class power or we're not." Other legislators of both parties told Kennedy that a war with Russia was inevitable at some time in the future, and that it might as well be now as later.[25]

In London, Macmillan went from a series of meetings with European ambassadors—impressing on the French, for one, that there were "dangerous shoals to be navigated" ahead, and that they should all "support the American course" accordingly—to a closed-door briefing by Roger Hollis, the director general of MI5, on the implications of the United Kingdom's latest security scandal. This happened to be the day on which John Vassall was sentenced at the Old Bailey to eighteen years' imprisonment. Following that, Macmillan read a hastily prepared report by the British air staff, giving their conclusions on the American U-2 photographs. They saw evidence of a total of six offensive-missile sites, four of which they believed were ready or close to ready. Despite Kennedy's repeated assurances that the pictures were unchallengeable, the PM had thought it wise to seek independent corroboration, typical of the friendly but wary approach he generally took to Washington. By one of those coincidences shunned in fiction but quite prevalent in international affairs, Macmillan was also scheduled to host a dinner that night in honor of General Lauris Norstad, recently appointed as the Supreme Allied Commander in Europe— the "nuclear war man" who had consistently urged Kennedy that the best way to assert American rights in any territorial dispute was to bomb the nation's adversaries back to the Stone Age. In a quiet moment at the dinner, Norstad advised Macmillan to put British troops on a high state of alert, and Macmillan declined, pointing out the lesson of 1914 that "mobilisation sometimes causes war." Later in the evening, the PM briefed Hugh Gaitskell, the leader of the parliamentary Opposition, on the crisis. ("He did *not* take a very robust attitude," Macmillan sighed.)[26] Around one o'clock, the premier retired, alone as usual, and read Jane Austen in bed.

Like Macmillan, Kennedy was much too realistic to believe that he could successfully appeal to Khrushchev's basic good sense. In his televised address, the president reeled off a list of precautionary measures that he had already taken in response to the crisis, and he ended with a call to reason—the Russians, he said, should "abandon this course of world domination, and join in an historic effort to end the perilous arms race, and transform the history of man." But meanwhile, he was also putting his naval blockade in place and making preparations for an air strike, should the offensive missiles not be removed. Some members of ExComm had feared an immediate Soviet military reaction to the president's speech, which Khrushchev duly labeled a "serious threat to peace and security" that entailed "naked interference" in Cuban affairs.[27] That night, George Ball, the undersecretary of state, slept restively on the couch in his office. Around six on Tuesday morning, he was shaken awake by his boss, Dean Rusk, who bore a cup of coffee and a morbid joke. "We have won a considerable victory," Rusk told him. "You and I are still alive."[28]

Fifteen minutes after finishing his speech, Kennedy took the elevator down to the newly created Situation Room in the basement of the West Wing and picked up the hotline to Macmillan. It was the first of a dozen such calls he placed over the next week, which often took place late at night, London time. Kennedy was generally at his most alert as Macmillan was preparing to go to bed. (As the week progressed, both men would unsurprisingly become almost stupid with fatigue—ironically, it was the boyish president who seemed to flag more easily than the owlish prime minister.) Their first conversation reads almost like a continuation of Kennedy's scripted address to the public. He spoke torrentially, while Macmillan limited himself to the occasional soothing platitude. At one point, the president remarked that "we are attempting to begin [our response] in a way to prevent World War 3," and the PM agreed that this was prudent. Macmillan later wrote in his diary that Kennedy "seemed rather excited, but very clear. . . . He was grateful for my messages and for David Gore's help. He could not tell what Khrushchev would do. . . . He is building up his forces for a *coup de main* to seize Cuba, should that become necessary."[29] The transcript of the call makes it sound like one of those edgy, faintly comic exchanges beloved of the playwright Harold Pinter. Each party had to hold down a button on the apparatus in order to transmit and release it again to receive. The result was a series of self-contained statements, punctuated by a good deal of static, although Macmillan wrote that the calls, as a whole, "were a great comfort for me, since I felt all the time intimately informed of each changing aspect of these terrible days."[30]

In fact, from the British point of view, the situation was even more fraught with danger than it appeared in Washington. As Macmillan well knew, the Soviets had long had an arsenal of several dozen intermediate-range nuclear weapons pointed in his direction. In 1960, they had deployed missiles in East Germany, cutting the flight time to London in half. "We mean business," Khrushchev had impressed upon Senator Hubert H. Humphrey during the course of a free-ranging Kremlin conversation on the general state of the Cold War. Soviet troops in Eastern Europe were "not there to play cards," he added.[31] Perhaps it was this fact that had led Macmillan, on first hearing of the rockets in Cuba, to incautiously remark that now the Americans would realize what many in Europe already took to be a fact of life. He did not need to be reminded that the Russians were as likely to retaliate to the president's naval embargo by ordering a strike on key NATO targets as they were by raining missiles down on Washington. Three weeks earlier, Macmillan had written to Kennedy: "I know there are sometimes differences between us as to method, [but] never, I assure you, as to our singleness of purpose."[32] He was speaking about trade barriers, but it applied equally well to their attitudes on the missile crisis. For Kennedy, it was a lever to break the wider strategic deadlock with the Soviets. For Macmillan, it meant the threat of total national annihilation.

The president may not have consulted the premier for the first five days of the thirteen-day Cuban standoff—yet, in one sense, Kennedy was extraordinarily receptive to British counsel. Shortly before noon on Sunday, the 21st, the Ormsby-Gores arrived at the White House for a previously scheduled family lunch. After the meal, Kennedy took the ambassador aside and laid out his basic alternatives in Cuba as he saw them: "bomb the hell" out of the rocket sites, or impose a quarantine and appeal to the United Nations. It was the essential dilemma of all postwar-American foreign-policy crises. "What would *you* do?" Kennedy then asked.

It is worth remembering that, at this stage, the president still hadn't mentioned the matter of the missiles to his own cabinet, let alone to the American people. Although Gore had previously seen the aerial photographs, Kennedy's direct question forced him to improvise. Thinking well ahead of events, he replied that he saw "very serious drawbacks in the first course of action. . . . Very few people outside the United States would consider the provocation offered by the Cubans serious enough to merit an American air attack." Kennedy then revealed that he had reached the same conclusion. On that note, the two shook hands and agreed to go sailing at Hyannis Port when the circumstances allowed. Cabling the substance of their conversation to Macmillan, Gore added the detail that Kennedy "finally said that he could not help admiring the Soviet strategy. They offered this deliberate and provocative challenge to the United States in the knowledge that if the Americans reacted violently to it, the Russians would be given an ideal opportunity to move against West Berlin. If, on the other hand, he did nothing, the [Allies] would feel that the Americans had no real will to resist the encroachments of Communism. . . . The President impressed upon me how vital it was to keep all this information secret."[33]

Two days later, on the eve of the blockade going into effect, Gore was back at the White House for dinner. Afterward, he went upstairs into a little-used family office where he and both the Kennedy brothers spoke further over brandy and cigars. The president wanted to know what he could do to spin public opinion in Western Europe, and Gore advised him to release a selection of the U-2 photographs so that the evidence would be there for everyone to see in the newspapers. Apparently, nobody had previously considered this idea. "He quite understood," Gore wired Macmillan, "and after he had sent for a batch of photographs, he gave instructions as to which of them should be published, and he emphasised the importance of clear explanatory notes being attached to them." Gore then went on to suggest that, to give the Russians the maximum time to consider their position, the line of interception around Cuba should be reduced from eight hundred miles to five hundred miles—a concession the Kennedys immediately agreed to and that ExComm ratified at its meeting early the next morning.[34]

The informal exchanges between Kennedy in his large, dimly lit underground Situation Room, furnished with satellite maps and futuristic steel chairs, and Macmillan, in his modest, book-lined upstairs den in Admiralty House, with a view across the London rooftops to the dome of St. Paul's Cathedral, continued throughout that week, in which ordinary Americans and Britons braced themselves for the possibility of a thermonuclear war. The president may have been informing the premier rather than actively consulting him, but Kennedy clearly enjoyed the opportunity to unburden himself in this way to the man he had come to privately dub "Uncle Harold." Other than the attorney general, none of the other members of ExComm were aware of the regular transatlantic conversations, and Kennedy refrained from making any similar person-to-person calls to other Allied heads of government. There was almost something of an illicit romance about the late-night exchanges. Nor was it Macmillan's role merely to grunt affirmatively to each of the president's proposals. On October 23, the PM read a minute from his law officers urging him to "make it clear. . . . Exactly what our views are on the legality of the proposed blockade, and emphasise that, while in the present circumstances we will co-operate with [the United States] and not stand on our rights, we do not concede that they have any legal right to search or detain . . . ships on the high seas."[35] In his discussion with Kennedy that evening, Macmillan pointedly asked if he was now "going to occupy Cuba and have done with it, or is it going to just drag on?" The president admitted that "we are preparing a potential for that kind of action [if] necessary." Macmillan then wanted to know, "Is your blockade going to extend beyond the military and arms into things like oil and all the rest of it, in order to bring down the Castro Government?" Kennedy replied, "At the beginning we're going to confine ourselves to offensive weapons of war in order not to give him a complete justification for Berlin."[36] Macmillan's aim, despite the public assurances that paid generous tribute to Kennedy's tactical acumen, was, first, that NATO and the Commonwealth should separately make clear to Khrushchev their disinclination to see Cuba become an armed Soviet republic and, second, that the "two ugly sisters," as, at moments of profound stress, he referred to the United States and the Soviet Union, refrain from blowing up the world.

It now appears that outcome came considerably closer than even Macmillan knew. By the time the American quarantine went into effect on the morning of October 24, 1962, the United States had secretly mustered a task force of some thirty-five ships with seventeen thousand marines aboard, with six army-combat divisions in reserve, ready to set sail from ports in southern Florida, should the president decide to seize Cuba. A fleet of forty-seven further ships, with supporting air cover, was deployed to enforce the blockade. Meanwhile, the Soviet missiles already on Cuba were 90 percent operational, and Russian supply ships continued to steam westward toward the exclusion line. That same morning, Strategic Air Command was ordered, for the first time in its existence, to move to DEFCON 2—or "Code Red"—the last stage of alert before nuclear war. For the remainder of the week, B-52s armed with hydrogen bombs circled continually over the Norwegian Sea, ready to move on the commander in chief's order to their preassigned targets in the Soviet Union. Kennedy himself remained under intense political pressure to take the most direct response possible to events in Cuba. John McCone of the CIA wrote a memorandum for the file of the president's initial meeting with the members of ExComm and the congressional leadership:

> Secretary Rusk stated that he did not wish to underestimate the gravity of the situation; the Soviets were taking a very serious risk. . . . Sen. Russell questioned the Secretary as to whether things will get better in the future, whether we will have a more propitious time to act than now, the thrust of his questioning being, "Why wait?" Rusk answered that he saw no opportunity for improvement.

The president [said] we are taking all military preparations for either an air strike or an invasion.[37]

In turn, Khrushchev responded to Kennedy by a cable reaching Washington late on October 24, which suggested that the final crisis of US-Soviet relations had now arrived. Referring to an "American ultimatum" and "threats," the Soviet chairman went on to complain: "All this is due not only to hatred for the Cuban people and their government, but also for reasons having to do with the election campaign in the USA. . . . The actions of the US in relation to Cuba are outright piracy. This is the folly of a degenerate imperialism," Khrushchev added, before warning that "people of all nations, and not least the American people themselves, could suffer from madness such as this." The cable continued with a blanket refusal to accept "bandit actions" by "US ships in the open sea," stressed that the Soviet Union would "take those measures we deem necessary and sufficient to defend our rights," and concluded: "We have all the means necessary to do so. Respectfully, N. Khrushchev."[38]

At a politburo meeting on the 24th, Khrushchev told his colleagues that all the essential nuclear hardware and accompanying technical crews had successfully reached Cuba. Then he wondered aloud whether he should halt at least some of the twenty-five Soviet vessels still sailing at full speed toward the Caribbean. The CIA believed that fourteen of these carried fuel or parts destined for the missile sites. Earlier in the day, Robert Kennedy had called on Anatoly Dobrynin and told him, "I don't know how this is going to end," since the Americans were "fully determined" to prevent any further Soviet traffic to Cuba. Something about the attorney general's tone had prompted Dobrynin to urgently communicate these views to Moscow. With minutes to spare before the blockade went into effect, the first of the Russian ships in the line stopped in its tracks. After what seemed an agonizingly long delay to those waiting by the teletype machines in Washington and in London, it then turned around. Having beat a retreat, Khrushchev then publicly warned that if American ships interfered further, he would order his submarines to sink them. In several meetings that day, he seemed unable to decide whether President Kennedy was truly the evil mastermind behind American policy or merely the puppet of hard-liners in the Pentagon. "Who asked you to do this?" he demanded in one message, as if doubting what he called the "little rich kid's" freedom of action. Speaking to an American businessman in Moscow later that day, Khrushchev asked: "How can I deal with a man who is younger than my own son?"[39]

In London, Macmillan announced that the British government would back American action in the UN Security Council. He also sent off more strongly worded cables to Commonwealth leaders, urging them to issue their own statements of solidarity with Washington. Speaking in the Commons, Macmillan declared that this was "not the moment to go into the niceties of international law," leaving unsaid the opinion of his government's own legal team. His public commitment can be contrasted to the attitude of several other senior Allied ministers, notably in Canada, France, and Italy. Shortly after 11 o'clock that night, an hour at which Macmillan had been known to be turning in with a good book, Kennedy called once more. It's worth repeating again that the two principal leaders of the free world communicated by means of a contraption more like an antique field wireless, bolted to the table in front of them—in Macmillan's case, with the uncompromising label "PROPERTY OF HM GOVERNMENT" stamped on its base—than any more recent concept of a sophisticated "hotline." Not only was there an unwieldy "Transmit/Receive" button to press, but often several seconds' awkward delay then occurred between each transition. More than once, the exchange was punctuated by the comedy sound effect of either Kennedy or Macmillan barking the word *Over!* while struggling to coordinate the switch settings with the other party. As the PM conceded, the vagaries of the system "made conversation somewhat jerky, and, although at the moments of great danger it was invaluable, yet I much preferred written messages. Indeed I sometimes looked with horror at the records of our conversations, which seemed intolerably disconnected and often futile. However, since the President liked this method, it was not for me to discourage him."[40]

> *Macmillan:* Well, I'm all right. What's the news now?
> *Kennedy:* Well, we have no more word yet on what's going to happen out there. As you have probably heard, some of the ships, the ones we're particularly interested in, have turned around—others are going on . . .
> *Macmillan:* You don't really know whether they're going back, or whether they're going to try and make it, do you?
> *Kennedy:* Some of the ships that have turned back are the ones that we were the most interested in, and which we think would have given us some material. Others are continuing. . . . I don't know whether they are going to make us sink these, or whether we are going to be permitted to search them. That's still a question.

Also in doubt, Kennedy admitted, was what action he might take to remove the rockets that were already in Cuba:

> We're going to have to make the judgment as to whether we're going to invade Cuba, taking our chances, or whether we hold off and use Cuba as a sort of hostage in the matter of Berlin. Then any time he takes an action against Berlin, we take action against Cuba. That's really the choice we now have. What's your judgment?

Macmillan replied that, on the whole, he would like to think about it, and Kennedy then went on to speculate further on his options:

> If [the Russians] respect the quarantine, then we get the second stage of this problem, and work continues on the missiles. Do we then tell them that if they don't get the missiles out that we're going to invade Cuba? He will then say that if we invade Cuba that there's going to be a general nuclear assault, and he will in any case grab Berlin. Or do we just let the nuclear work go on, figuring he won't ever dare fire them, and when he tries to grab Berlin, we then go into Cuba? That's what I'd like to have you think about.

As the conversation wore on, the picture emerged both of two chess grand-masters plotting their moves and of two battle-hardened politicians calculating the odds. In the midst of the strategic theorizing, each man pointedly took the time to ask the other one how he was coping with his domestic opposition. Macmillan then expressed the view that this was all a "big issue" about which he felt "pretty sure we ought not to do anything in a hurry." Kennedy replied, "Right, prime minister," before reiterating his own basic fallback position on Cuba—"We are mobilizing our force, so if we decide to invade we will be in a position to do so within a few more days."

The discussion then turned to the United Nations, where Macmillan thought the new secretary-general, U Thant, was being "rather tiresome" in calling for a morato-rium of both missile shipments and the blockade. "It looks sensible, and yet it's very bad," Macmillan fretted. "Well, yes," Kennedy said. While the president then won-dered how precisely to respond to Thant, the premier was focused on the endgame. "Well now, how do you think we shall get out of this in the long run?" Macmillan asked.

"Do you think we ought to try and do a deal, have a meeting with [Khrushchev], or not? What initiative do you think ought to be taken, and by whom?" Kennedy told him that the next twenty-four hours would prove critical. By then they would know more about Soviet intentions toward the blockade. In one scenario, the president admitted, "We risk war . . . and equally important, at least of some importance, we risk the loss of Berlin." Pending that, Kennedy was doubtful about the value of a summit, and in the same vein he went on to politely sidestep Macmillan's proposal that he fly personally to Washington to meet him. It was another small reminder of who was the suitor and who was the elusive quarry. At close to midnight, having touched on the prospect of imminent global annihilation, their conversation ended on an almost comically banal note:

> *Macmillan:* We'll have a talk on Friday night. Is that the best we can do?
> *Kennedy:* That'll be fine, prime minister, unless you're going to be away on Friday night?
> *Macmillan:* I shall stay in London, but I think it very useful if we can have a brief chat each evening if it's not inconvenient to you, then we can just compare notes as to how things are going on.
> *Kennedy:* Good, I will call you then, tomorrow evening, prime minister, at 6:00 my time.
> *Macmillan:* That'll do me fine. Goodnight.
> *Kennedy:* Goodnight, prime minister. Thank you.[41]

Macmillan later wrote of "the frightful desire to do something" during that week. One possibility he raised with Home, his Foreign Secretary, was to continue to press ahead with plans for a tripartite summit meeting in London. Macmillan's enthusiasm for sitting around a conference table with his fellow world leaders amounted, even in normal circumstances, to something approaching a fetish. Hardly an hour passed during the second half of October without him reverting to the subject of "talks," which he mentioned almost as often as Kennedy did Berlin.

It transpired later that others were busy tunneling along their own individual routes to this same conclusion—among them the thirty-six-year-old Russian naval attaché in London, Captain Yevgeni Ivanov, who had lunch on October 24 with his friend, a forty-nine-year-old osteopathic physician and society portraitist—with a line in limited-edition satirical cartoons—named Stephen Ward. (It is said that one of his more imaginative caricatures, among many other female studies, showed Lady Macmillan in an unusually relaxed pose.) For once, Ward recalled, Ivanov appeared to want to talk not about their mutual obsession—young women—but about great "issues."

Ivanov told Ward that the Russians and the Americans were on a collision course, and that the British alone could save the day by convening an immediate peace conference. Leaning forward to fix his friend with his flashing gray eyes and repeatedly licking his tufted mustache—he's said to have looked like a Russian spy out of central casting, as interpreted by Groucho Marx—Ivanov whispered that he could "guarantee" Khrushchev's acceptance of a British invitation to talks. Indeed, the chairman had personally told him that he was prepared to turn back the ships headed to Cuba and to dismantle the missiles already installed there. All that was required, Ivanov insisted, was the fig leaf of a seat at a "grand international congress," at which all the questions that lay between the Soviet Union and the Anglo-American allies would be "finally resolved, to the benefit of all mankind."[42]

Whether Ivanov really was in the confidence of the Kremlin, or just another of those plausible fantasists who tend to accumulate on the fringes of a world crisis, remains unclear. But Ward was flattered by his friend's words, which seemed to take their relationship from "one based primarily around a mutual appreciation of sex, to one touching on the future survival of humanity," as he later put it with characteristic modesty. Following their lunch, Ward lost little time in communicating Ivanov's remarks to his contacts in the British government. Perhaps, he suggested, the conciliation process could be set in play by his good friend Jack Profumo, the minister for war, who in turn could take it to the PM? During that week of the missile crisis, "the strain was certainly very great," Macmillan later reflected in the House of Commons.

> Naturally, the same was true of the Soviet government, who were doing all they could to further their policy and weaken the resolution of the West. Part of this Soviet activity was public, some of it private. . . . Ivanov, with the assistance of Mr. Ward, was perhaps rather more persistent than most. On 24th October, Ward telephoned the resident clerk at the Foreign Office and gave him an account of a conversation he had just had with Ivanov, this to be passed on to me.[43]

In the febrile atmosphere of "Missiles Week"—when even the normally imperturbable Lord Home remarked, "Man is now at the point of choice, and the choice is this: whether we blow ourselves to bits, or whether we sit down around the table and negotiate, and negotiate again, however long that process lasts"—it seemed entirely possible that a Russian spy, an osteopath of doubtful personal reputation, and the British secretary of state for war could among them constitute the one apparent hope of a diplomatic solution to the crisis.[44] In the event, their services as international peacemakers would not be required, and instead Macmillan continued to pursue his own course with Kennedy and others. At the time, he had no way of knowing that the names Ivanov, Ward, and, more especially, Profumo would, within a few months, conspire to help bring about his own downfall.

=====

The next day, Thursday, October 25, Kennedy chaired the regular morning meeting of ExComm, telling the group, perhaps unnecessarily, that he didn't want "a sense of euphoria to get around."[45] During the afternoon, he watched a rare live television broadcast from the United Nations, where the US ambassador Adlai Stevenson, abandoning his habitual air of gentlemanly reserve, furiously clashed with his Soviet counterpart, Valerian Zorin. Stevenson pressed Zorin to say whether or not the Soviets had placed offensive missiles in Cuba. "You will have your answer in due course," the hatchet-faced Zorin replied. "I am prepared to wait for my answer until hell freezes over," Stevenson said, jogging the Russian's memory by propping up U-2 photographs of the rockets on an easel in front of the Security Council. This coup de théâtre was warmly received at the White House. "I never knew Adlai had it in him," Kennedy remarked to his watching advisers. "Too bad he didn't show some of this steam in the 1956 campaign."[46]

At about 3:00 p.m., the president briefly strolled out onto the north lawn and stood, apparently lost in thought, alone and fully visible to the crowds on Pennsylvania Avenue. Though there were some demonstrators present—signs declaring "The End Is Nigh" had gone up on the White House railings minutes after the public announcement of the crisis on the 22nd—there was also some applause for Kennedy. At five o'clock that evening, he chaired the day's second ExComm meeting. Doodling on a yellow pad while his staff gave him the latest intelligence estimates from Cuba, the president scratched the word *decision* or *decisions* seventeen times on a sheet of paper. An hour later, Kennedy went upstairs to the second-floor family quarters, where he found his wife, four-year-old Caroline, and some friends busy at work carving a pumpkin for the following week's Halloween party. Among the group was thirty-year-old Robin Douglas-Home, a jazz-playing Scottish aristocrat and an accumulator of a vast number of lovers (among them Princess Margaret), who went on to write an authorized biography of Frank Sinatra, be party to a spectacular divorce case, and then commit suicide at the age of thirty-six. As well as being the kind of raffish, double-barreled free spirit the president adored, he was also the nephew of Britain's Foreign Secretary. After joining in a relaxed family dinner, Douglas-Home remembered Kennedy, puffing on a Cuban cigar, chatting "about such diverse subjects as Lord Beaverbrook's way of running his newspapers, Sinatra's handling of women, and why *Queen* magazine had published a fashion picture of a model lying on a white bearskin rug sucking her thumb."[47] The president made no mention of the missile crisis, although at one point he compared negotiating with the Soviets in general as "like trying to talk to people who've spent all their lives in a cellar." After an evening of studied gaiety, Kennedy went to bed around 10:00 p.m., later returning in his bathrobe to wish Douglas-Home good night.

As the crisis first erupted, in the week of October 15, the First Lady and her two children had been at Glen Ora, their rented country retreat near Middleburg, Virginia, about an hour's drive from the White House. They quickly returned to Washington. David Ormsby-Gore remembered that the president "wanted them to be there when he was making these awful decisions."[48] Some discrepancy exists as to what might have happened to the First Family had the worst come to pass. According to Kennedy's aide Dave Powers, the president had asked his wife if she and their children wanted to be taken to an evacuation center outside Washington and she had refused, telling him that she preferred them all to be together. Gore gave a slightly different impression of events when he later spoke of the contingency arrangements in place for him to join the Kennedys and senior members of the US administration in the executive fallout bunker beneath the Appalachians. In any event, there can be no doubt the president himself displayed an impressive sangfroid during those terrible days. Some insiders believed Kennedy's air of remoteness was central to his ultimate success—by keeping his emotional distance, he was less affected by the hour-to-hour drama of events than were some in his inner circle, including the attorney general. At the height of the crisis, with an ExComm meeting awaiting his attention, Powers came upon the president unhurriedly reading a book to his young daughter and wondered whether "it would be the last one he would read to her."[49] In a similar vein, the First Lady calmly proceeded with plans later that week to appear in an NBC television program on the National Cultural Center while continuing to tend to her infant son John, who was ill with a fever of 104°.

For others, the seemingly imminent threat of the end of the world meant different things. For Robin Douglas-Home, it was excitement: being at the center of events in Washington was "sexually energising"—a time of "intense living [and] romantic abandon." Perhaps more prosaically, David Ormsby-Gore "always remember[ed] our children being at school, with orders to bring their rations and clothes, and prepare to take off for the shelters, if necessary. We dusted off the Embassy evacuation drill."[50] Secretary McNamara careered about the Pentagon, rapidly issuing orders and once falling into a noisy quarrel with the navy's representative on the Joint Chiefs of Staff, Admiral George Anderson, about which of them, precisely, was in charge of supervising the blockade. Many ordinary Americans could do no more than watch and wait as events unfolded. The author's father, a British naval officer, happened to be on secondment in the planning echelons of NATO at the Pentagon. During that week, he would sometimes appear in the evening looking pitifully tired, and we would ask him what he had done that day. "Nothing much," he said. Then later that night, you would hear a reporter on the radio speaking about how the United States was promising "to make certain critical decisions within the next 24 hours," followed by a public-service announcement advising us how to "duck and cover" in the event of an atomic blast.

In Britain, the crisis was experienced as a case of psychotically foolish American brinkmanship. Or at least that was the consensus among the headline writers in Fleet Street. Even the staunchly pro-establishment *Daily Mail* called the US quarantine "an act of war." Clearing its front page for a searing editorial, the paper went on to ask whether "in advancing to the brink, President Kennedy may have been led more by popular emotion than by calm statesmanship. . . . The perilous trend of events now set in motion must be halted before it is too late." The *Times*, the *Daily Telegraph*, and the *Express* all broadly followed in kind. Unsurprisingly, the reaction on the political left was even more hostile. The Labour leader Hugh Gaitskell questioned the legality of the blockade, and thirty-seven of his MPs signed a motion of solidarity with Cuba. Several trade unions declared a one-day strike as a gesture of defiance against American policy. There were noisy demonstrations at the front gate of the US embassy in Grosvenor Square, with cries of "Viva Fidel, Kennedy to Hell," although no one bothered to protest outside the equivalent Russian office. The debating unions of both Oxford and Cambridge Universities passed motions attacking American aggression and questioning whether there really were any rockets in Cuba. Taken as a whole, the British reaction was a close forerunner to the widely heard complaint against US overseas adventuring that would follow in the wake of the 9/11 attacks thirty-nine years later. You got a particular whiff of this when the ninety-year-old pacifist-philosopher Bertrand Russell sent a well-publicized message to Kennedy, whom he described as "much more wicked than Hitler," calling his recent behavior "a threat to human survival." On October 24, the president took time away from his ExComm duties to fire off a reply. "I am in receipt of your telegram," he told Russell. "While your messages are critical of the United States, they make no mention of your concern for the introduction of secret Soviet missiles into Cuba. I think your attention might well be directed to the burglars, rather than to those who caught the burglars."[51]

The moderates—or "wets"—in Macmillan's own party were cross, as usual, with America, and at one point the premier recorded in his diary that even his inner cabinet "seemed rather shaken" by Kennedy's actions. He would go on to remark disparagingly on the "weaker brethren, at home and abroad," who fell for Khrushchev's line, and summed up the general mood of appeasement: "It was like Munich." Through all this, the PM himself persisted with his support for his principal ally. "The American administration [proceeded] with remarkable skill and energy," he later wrote, adding that this was the event that turned Kennedy from a charming lightweight into a statesman. "It [was] a tribute to his calm wisdom . . . that, largely influenced by his brother, he was determined to find a method by which Khrushchev could, should he wish it, retreat without too much loss of face."[52] Historians may question Robert Kennedy's unfailingly restrained and dispassionate counsel, but Macmillan was well ahead of the political pack in consistently backing the president's own judgment on Cuba.

Macmillan's sense of moral certainty in the cause seeps through his official statements and private remarks on the crisis. Like Kennedy himself, he displayed a natural composure—almost a detachment—that sometimes made him seem more a bystander than a participant in events. As the full enormity of the Cuban drama unfolded on October 23, Macmillan still found time for a convivial lunch with political colleagues. "A merry party," he noted in his diary. "John [Wyndham] was very funny about the occasion when he was 'privately vetted' by MI5."[53] Macmillan also managed to get away during the crisis for a much-needed night's rest at Birch Grove. It was there, in the mists of the Sussex autumn, that he wrote up the notes of "two *long* telephone talks with the President," adding: "The situation is very obscure and dangerous. It is a trial of will." It's not entirely clear if Dorothy Macmillan remained at her husband's side throughout the week of October 22, or if, under the prevailing nervous strain, she again sought out Robert Boothby's company. Boothby, now sixty-two, had not lost any of his flair for public controversy over the years. In the days before the missile crisis, he was embroiled in a new dispute arising from his remarks on an edition of *Any Questions?*, a popular BBC radio show. Referring to a succession of Canadian-born British newspaper magnates, Boothby said: "I would keep them all out of this country. I have known them all. Keep them out. We have just passed an Immigration Bill to keep out the West Indians. My God, I would pass an Immigration Bill to keep out the Canadians. They have done nothing but damage to this country."[54] Boothby's glib badinage, of the kind to which he was all too addicted, not surprisingly brought him an immense amount of grief in the press, not to mention a writ for libel. Dorothy Macmillan was certainly at her husband's side in London during the climactic weekend of October 27–28. After she had congratulated him on the outcome and had been rewarded by a lingering kiss, a gesture no one even in their private office had ever seen before, Macmillan recorded that "on that Sunday afternoon, my colleagues and I were able to share the feeling, if not of triumph, yet of relief and gratitude. We had been on the brink, and almost over it."[55]

═══

On Thursday, October 25, Macmillan chaired a cabinet meeting with a "highly pressing" first order of business—not Cuba, but the government's (rightly apprehensive) assessment of likely trade-union reaction to the Beeching report, which would propose closing some 2,300 of Britain's train stations and 6,000 miles of track, with a resulting loss of 70,000 jobs. Only after this, and the many other recent trials of the "pay pause" had been debated, did Alec Home inform his colleagues "of the latest developments in the situation arising from the imposition by the United States Government of a partial defensive blockade in the Caribbean," as he put it in his most fruity style. After summarizing the "quite direct danger" of the situation, Home reported that he had received the Soviet chargé d'affaires in London, who had proposed that the British host an immediate peace conference. Home had told him that, "while the Government were ready and willing to do so, it would be necessary for the USSR to create a suitable opportunity by making it possible for President Kennedy to agree [to] negotiate." In other words, the missiles would have to be removed first. Macmillan concluded the cabinet by saying that he was "ready to take any opportunity of intervening if [he] felt that by doing so the prospect of a settlement could be advanced." But he would not be party to any compromise reached by "lowering the resistance of the free world to aggression." The situation remained "extremely serious," he added. "It was still developing rapidly, and it might be necessary to call a meeting of ministers at short notice."[56]

Soon after, Macmillan read a secret paper from David Ormsby-Gore, telling him that US intelligence agencies had now identified a total of nine medium-range missile sites and twenty-four ground-to-air (coastal-defense) sites, all of them fully operational, in Cuba.[57] At three o'clock that afternoon, the premier addressed a packed House of Commons. Speaking in a low, tired voice of "a situation that is without precedent," he defended the American quarantine and poured scorn on the continuing track record of Soviet lies and evasions. This part of his speech closely followed the current US position, which Kennedy had supplied him in the form of a list of talking points earlier in the day. "My government," Macmillan said, "will add their support to any measures which genuinely lead to peace. . . . Nevertheless, I think what has happened in the last few weeks must confirm our view that in these grave matters we cannot rest upon mere words and promises. These need, if they are to restore confidence, to be independently verified and confirmed."[58]

At 11:30 that night, London time, Kennedy called again. The first thing he said was: "Prime Minister, how did you do with your debate?"

"We did very well, actually very good, very good," Macmillan assured him. "I sent you the text of what I said, and I think it was very well accepted. I made all the points I could, and the reception was good, very well received . . ."

After that, the president spoke about the possible role of the UN, and more particularly its secretary-general, in brokering a truce between the two sides. "I have just seen your message to U Thant," Macmillan told him. "It seems to me extremely ingenious and very calm, because you are saying that the—as you say, the real point is that they ought to get rid of these weapons." Without pausing to acknowledge the compliment, Kennedy continued: "As I say, the fourteen ships that have turned back are obviously the ones that have the sensitive cargo that he doesn't want us to be able to produce. The ships that are continuing probably are ones that don't have anything important in them, but we cannot permit him to establish the principle that he determines which ships will go and which will not, but, as I say, I think we will—tomorrow night—we will know a lot better about the matter of the UN's actions, and Khrushchev's attitude about continuing the shipping . . ."

"That is very interesting about the ships," said Macmillan. "And we will . . . [*speech garbled*] the situation tomorrow night." "Yes," said Kennedy.

Macmillan then offered to take the initiative and call the president back the following day, but Kennedy apparently chose not to hear this, or not to respond to it, and instead continued with his narrative.

"That is correct," he said. "We will know tomorrow night whether Khrushchev will accept U Thant's proposal to cease all shipping going to Cuba during these talks, number one. Number two, if he doesn't do that, we will know what their reaction will be to our searching of a vessel, so I think that I could call you tomorrow night at the same time, unless this is too late for you."

"No, indeed," said Macmillan. "I am very much obliged to you. We will have a talk tomorrow night. Good night."

"Good night, prime minister. I'll send you Khrushchev's message of last evening. Good night."[59]

Always preferring the written word, Macmillan also sent an overnight cable with his response to "the $64,000 question which you posed on the telephone." What followed was an avuncular but surprisingly firm note of warning, and probably the most direct words that passed between them that week. "After much reflection, I think that events have gone too far," Macmillan began. He could no longer countenance any American plan for "taking out" Cuba. Instead, he wanted Kennedy to insist that, while the existing missile sites must go, "some system of inspection" should take the place of the naval blockade. The United Nations, or some other independent body, would then intervene to stop the work on major military installations in Cuba. "This would enable you to say that you have in fact obtained your objectives," Macmillan reasoned. "For if there are no ships arriving, then the purpose of the quarantine is served; and if there is no more construction, the purpose of largely immobilising this threat is also served. At the same time, you will no doubt continue with your military build-up for any emergency. This may be as important a factor for persuading the Cubans to accept inspection as in other directions."[60]

The immediacy of the crisis comes through in both the conversations and the messages. Kennedy frequently spoke of the "unofficial" or "unreliable" reports reaching him, noted that "we still don't know whether we're going to have an incident," told the PM he was "just informed" about developments in the United Nations, and at one point remarked that "we had a message from U Thant about a half hour ago."[61] For his part, Macmillan was sometimes absorbing the latest highly detailed briefing documents his secretary brought him while simultaneously offering advice to the president. He was much more than a mere accessory to American actions. In general, Kennedy was best at dealing with minute-to-minute events, and Macmillan preferred to put things in their broader context—it was all "rather like 1914," he commented more than once, privately concluding that, as then, "troop movements [and] harsh rhetoric" were unlikely to keep the peace.

At seven in the morning on Friday, October 26, the US destroyer *Joseph P. Kennedy, Jr.*, named after the president's late brother, stopped the Panamanian-owned freighter *Marcula* in the open sea some three hundred miles east of Miami. The *Marcula* was bound for Havana from the Soviet port of Riga. It was the first boarding and search operation carried out under the American quarantine, and it produced little evidence of missile running, with a cargo of half a dozen dilapidated trucks, some drums of detergent, and vast numbers of Russian toilet rolls, stacked on pallets, apparently destined for the people of Cuba. At the ExComm meeting three hours later in the White House, Kennedy announced that his main concern was no longer the blockade per se, but the continuing work on the missile sites already in place. "We can't screw around for two weeks and wait for [the Soviets] to finish these," he remarked. Despite Macmillan's warning, the president still saw only "two ways of removing the weapons. One is to negotiate them out. Or the other is to go in and take them out. I don't see any other way." Later, Kennedy told Macmillan in their nightly phone call that, unless the Russians stopped work on the bases within forty-eight hours, "We are going to be faced with some hard decisions."[62]

Even by the prevailing standards, October 26 was a day of extraordinary drama. In London, Macmillan noted, "a mass of messages kept coming backwards and forwards."[63] The PM was busy reading cables from Kennedy and sending ones out urging de Gaulle and the NATO leaders to stand by the United States. In Washington, the ABC television producer John Scali had a hastily scheduled working lunch with a Soviet consular attaché (and KGB station chief) named Aleksandr Fomin. This was in some ways the corresponding American tryst to the Ivanov-Ward one of two days earlier, but for considerably higher stakes. "The situation is very serious," Fomin announced as they sat down, looking furtively around the room. "Something must be done." As soon as their waiter had left them, Fomin leaned forward across the table, giving Scali's arm a comradely squeeze, and in a sudden, hushed burst of words told him that "high sources" in the Kremlin might now be amenable to removing the existing missile bases in Cuba in exchange for Kennedy's pledge not to invade the island. "The *highest* sources," he elaborated, in a conspiratorial tone.

A few minutes later, Scali found himself walking rapidly from the restaurant, his napkin still flapping around his shirt collar, to the State Department, where Secretary Rusk himself heard him out. Rusk told Scali to go back to his contact later that afternoon to let him know that the US government "sees real possibilities in this, and supposes that representatives of the two governments could work it out," although he added the rider that "Time is very urgent."[64] When Khrushchev got the message, he began composing an excitable letter to Kennedy, which betrayed the first hint of anxiety—if not panic—on the Soviet side. If "war should break out, then it would not be in our power to stop it," he wrote. Instead, the superpowers would "clash, like blind moles, and then mutual extermination will begin." If Kennedy promised not to attack Cuba and to call off the blockade, then "the presence of our military specialists [there] would disappear."[65] What specifically inspired Khrushchev to write the letter, which bore several handwritten corrections in vivid, purple ink, has never been made clear. As well as Fomin's report, there was also the disturbing news in the daily-intelligence folder awaiting the Soviet chairman on October 26 that the Kennedy administration had decided to "finish with Castro." The American invasion could begin "at any moment," the report continued, and special beds had already been prepared in US hospitals to deal with casualties. The Soviet deputy foreign minister, Vasily V. Kuznetsov, recalled that when the leader read this news, "he dropped a load in his pants."[66] Khrushchev spent that night sitting up in his Kremlin office with a few members of the politburo, though rumors that he was intoxicated are probably groundless. In general, Khrushchev, like Stalin before him, much preferred plying his colleagues with vodka until they became so drunk they made fools of themselves.

Off Cuba itself, meanwhile, the World War II–era destroyer USS *Beale* was tracking the Soviet Project 641 submarine *B-59* as it proceeded into the Straits of Florida. After trailing its quarry at a distance of about five miles, the *Beale* closed in at first light and dropped signaling depth charges in order to force the submarine to the surface. Nobody on the American side then knew that the *B-59* was armed with six fifteen-kiloton nuclear weapons. Years later, it transpired that an argument had broken out among the submarine's senior officers as to whether or not they were under a full-scale attack, and, if so, how best to retaliate. In a scene that could have come out of a Hollywood action movie, the *B-59*'s captain, Valentin Savitsky, and his deputy, Vasili Arkhipov, then came to blows as they debated the wisdom of making their torpedoes ready for launch. The latter eventually prevailed, after insisting that they would not go down in history as "the men who started World War III." The submarine then surfaced and accepted an American boarding party before reversing course back to the Bahamas. Speaking in 2002, on the fortieth anniversary of the incident, Thomas Blanton, director of the US National Security Archive, said that Commander Arkhipov had single-handedly saved the world from a certain nuclear exchange.[67]

The saga on the high seas also coincided with a fever of war preparations in Washington. On the morning of the 26th, US Army trucks hauling Skysweeper anti-aircraft guns began lumbering down Route 1 into Key West, six minutes away from Cuba by fighter jet. At the day's regular noon press briefing, the State Department spokesman reminded reporters of Kennedy's warning that, should the offending Soviet missiles not soon be removed, "further action will be justified [to] safeguard the hemisphere." At two o'clock that afternoon, orders went out to the Federal Information Agency to hurriedly print three million leaflets in Spanish, which were to be dropped over Havana as part of the "hearts and minds" component of an American invasion. They explained that the attack had been forced upon the United States and called on the people of Cuba to overthrow their warmongering leader. It was unlikely that this would happen just as Castro was rallying the masses in a stirring radio address. Later on the 26th, he also sent a private message to Khrushchev advising him that the moment had come to "eliminate" American threats to Cuba, "through an act of clear legitimate defense . . . however harsh and terrible the solution would be, for there is no other."[68]

The repeated use of the transatlantic hotline was a sure sign of the pace of events. Kennedy called Macmillan twice that Friday. In the second conversation, which began at close to midnight, London time, the PM again showed his affinity for the big picture:

> *Kennedy:* There are some reports around, some Russian conversations . . . they
>   might do something about withdrawing the weapons if they could get a ter-
>   ritorial guarantee of Cuba. But that is so unofficial that I'm not in a position
>   now to know whether there's anything to it or not. . . .
> *Macmillan:* The idea that you've just mentioned is that Cuba might be made
>   like Belgium was [pre-1914] by international guarantee—an inviolable
>   country, and all of us would guarantee its neutrality and inviolability. Is that
>   a possibility?
> *Kennedy:* Well, that is a matter which seems to me we ought to be thinking about,
>   and we will be thinking about that in the next 24 hours as to whether there
>   is any room for a settlement on that basis. That would leave Castro in power,
>   and it would leave the Russians perhaps free to ship in a good deal more
>   offensive equipment.[69]

Sitting up alone in his study an hour later, Macmillan was at pains to clarify what he had said about Belgium on the outbreak of the First World War. "I was wrong in making that analogy," he signaled Kennedy. "It is more nearly an analogy with Austria today, under the state treaty."[70] But if the PM's history was off for once, his conversation with the president had still produced some new ideas.

> *Macmillan:* There is just a third point that occurred to us. If we want to help
>   the Russians save face, would it be worthwhile our undertaking to immo-
>   bilise our Thor missiles which are here in England during the same period—
>   during [a] conference?
> *Kennedy:* Well, let me put that into the machinery, and then I'll be in touch with
>   you on that.
> *Macmillan:* I think it is just an idea that it might help the Russians to accept.
> *Kennedy:* Sure, prime minister, let me send that over to the Department.[71]

Kennedy's measured response fails to betray much enthusiasm for the temporary defusing of Britain's stockpile of sixty PGM-17 Thor missiles. They were scheduled to be decommissioned anyway about a year later. The rockets had a range of 1,800–2,000 miles, which would have allowed Moscow to be hit from a launch site in the United Kingdom. Macmillan had accepted the weapons in a deal struck with President Eisenhower at their first fence-mending session at Bermuda in 1957 following the Suez debacle. Even so, the idea of dismantling Allied rockets as a quid pro quo for Cuba clearly appealed to Khrushchev, too, because he made a similar proposal in a letter to Kennedy that Radio Moscow began broadcasting only a few hours later.

Meanwhile, having spoken of Belgium, the United Nations refugee camps in Nicaragua and Guatemala, the continued threat to Berlin, and all the other adjuncts to the main crisis, the principal Western leaders, still not knowing if a general war would start at any moment, brought their latest conversation to an end as gently as two old friends finalizing some social arrangements.

> *Kennedy:* Well, I will be in touch in [the usual] way with you tomorrow on that matter, and I'll send you tonight the memorandum on the U Thant conversation. Thank you. And I hope all goes well.
>
> *Macmillan:* Well, thank you very much, and of course Bundy can always ring up de Zulueta here. They can speak to each other, so it is quite easy to have a chat.
>
> *Kennedy:* Fine, prime minister. And I'll be in touch with you very shortly. Thank you and goodnight.
>
> *Macmillan:* Goodnight.

But before retiring, which he did just before two o'clock that morning, Macmillan also read a short report from among the pile of documents awaiting him in his red ministerial box. Prepared by the British Joint Intelligence Committee, it contained that group's assessment of the current balance of nuclear power and concluded: "Provided warheads are available, missile units in Cuba could be allocated certain strategic targets on the American Continent at present allocated to other Soviet forces. If all the known sites are completed, we estimate that the overall Soviet initial launch capability against the US will have increased significantly by the end of 1962."[72]

On that note, Macmillan finally turned in with his Jane Austen.

Given the mood the next day in Washington—where McNamara recalled that, under increasing pressure from the Joint Chiefs of Staff, "the air strike was ready to go in 48 hours"—Macmillan remained "happy to agree, and indeed to propose" decommissioning the Thors that had now become pawns in a nuclear chess game. "This was only an attempt to find some escape for Khrushchev," the premier later recorded in his memoirs. Meanwhile, Gore was writing to the president to tell him, "It [was] the view of Her Majesty's ambassador in Havana that the time is right for a major propaganda effort directed at the Cuban government and people." Specifically, Gore proposed that Kennedy might wish to improve the signal strength of the Voice of America radio transmission going out in the Caribbean.[73] In London, Macmillan spent an "agonising" weekend waiting on events. Philip de Zulueta phoned McGeorge Bundy five times on Saturday. Kennedy's ExComm group met for four hours in the afternoon and for two more hours that night. Not having heard directly from the president, the PM eventually cabled: "The trial of wills is now approaching a climax. . . . We must now wait to see what Khrushchev does." As ever, Macmillan was keen on the idea of a great conference but was also rightly wary of Captain Ivanov as an intermediary. "Some rather devious approaches had been made [by] a member of the Russian Mission," he later wrote. "Alec Home and I agreed to regard [these] as mere attempts to drive a wedge between London and Washington. . . . The appeal seemed to me likely to conceal a trap."[74]

But before anyone could meet and sign another piece of paper, the crisis itself took several more alarming turns. Khrushchev's rambling note of Friday night was followed by a more polished one on Saturday morning. Among other things, it agreed "to expel those weapons from Cuba which you regard as offensive," provided the United States in turn remove its "analogous" missiles in Turkey. This was a reference to the wing of fifteen PGM-19 Jupiter medium-range rockets stationed at Izmir, about four hundred miles (or two and a half minutes' flight time) from the southern coast of Russia. That afternoon's ExComm meeting was forced to consider how a Turkey-for-Cuba missile swap might be received by the NATO allies, and, for that matter, whether there was a hidden subtext to the Soviet proposals. Had Khrushchev been overruled, or even ousted, by his colleagues on the politburo? Which of the two messages bearing his signature warranted a formal reply? While Kennedy and his advisers were debating that, word came in that the Cubans had shot down an American U-2 on aerial reconnaissance, killing its pilot. The president vetoed his generals' demands for an immediate retaliation. In a public statement, Kennedy repeated that nothing could be negotiated until work stopped on the missile bases in Cuba. He then sent cables to Macmillan, de Gaulle, and Adenauer, telling them that, if "satisfactory responses" weren't received from Moscow, "the situation is likely to enter a progressively military phase." Kennedy didn't mention to the Allies that a second U-2 plane had narrowly escaped a confrontation with Soviet fighters. Khrushchev, proving he was still in control, cabled Kennedy: "What is this, a provocation? One of your planes violates our frontier. . . . Is it not a fact that an intruding American flight could be easily taken for a nuclear bomber, which might push us to a fateful step?"[75]

In this suspenseful and dangerous atmosphere, it was Robert Kennedy who proposed that the Americans simply ignore the Soviets' Saturday-morning message and instead reply to the one of Friday night. As a result, the president's own late-night cable to Khrushchev failed to specifically mention the missiles in Turkey. Rather, he again said, "The first thing that needs to be done is for work to cease on offensive bases in Cuba." Only then would it be possible to "mutually work toward a more general arrangement regarding 'other armaments.'" To emphasize that the Americans meant business, Robert Kennedy summoned Ambassador Dobrynin to his office at the Justice Department at nine that Saturday night and personally read him his brother's message. This was an unusual function for the US attorney general to perform, and it clearly signaled the urgency of the situation. In his subsequent cable to the Kremlin, Dobrynin remarked that Bobby was "extremely agitated, the first time I had ever seen him in such a condition." Kennedy had told him that there were "hotheads among the generals, and in other places as well, who were spoiling for a fight." He had concluded the interview by saying, "Time is running out" and that the president "hoped that the head of the Soviet government would understand what he meant."[76]

Khrushchev did understand. After a perfunctory meeting of the politburo at noon on Sunday, October 28, he cabled the president to say that he had "given a new order to disassemble the arms which you described as offensive, and to crate and return them to the USSR." There was no mention of the Turkish Jupiters, which would be quietly dismantled six months later. As it happened, Macmillan, still in an agony of suspense, had cabled Khrushchev about an hour earlier to tell him, "We *supported* the American demand that the missiles be taken out of Cuba. I appealed to [him] to do this, and then turn to more constructive work—disarmament and the like."[77]

It's impossible to say what part, if any, Macmillan's intervention had in influencing the final outcome. On the whole, it seems likely Khrushchev was more impressed both by Dobrynin's overnight wire and the report (which turned out to be false) that the president was again scheduled to speak on television to the American people. In general, Macmillan had given a master class in controlled realpolitik, making it clear he saw no course of action other than doing all he could to sustain the US cause. Kennedy himself was in bed with the morning papers when he heard that the crisis was over, just as he had been when it began. At noon on Sunday, he sent off a short wire acknowledging Khrushchev's "important contribution to peace." Macmillan had just finished a working lunch with ministers in Admiralty House when news came through, much like an old stock-market report, on the upstairs ticker tape. He immediately slumped down in an armchair, then remarked that it was like the end of a wedding, "when there is nothing to do but drink the champagne and go to sleep."[78]

Macmillan cabled Kennedy that afternoon to tell him, "Whatever dangers and difficulties we may have to face in the future, I am proud to feel that I have so resourceful and so firm a comrade." Perhaps the "comrade" was ironic. At the next morning's cabinet meeting, the PM paid a fulsome tribute to the president's "great skill" and "unwavering determination to attain his objective," while mentioning in what "very close consultation" he, personally, had been with Washington throughout.[79] Late on Sunday night, the 28th, the president cabled back:

> Dear Prime Minister,
>   I am grateful for your warm generous words. Your heartening support publicly expressed and our daily conversations have been of inestimable value in these past days.
>
>   Many thanks.
>   John F. Kennedy[80]

Despite such good cheer, the missile crisis did not end with Khrushchev's "disassemble . . . crate and return" order, which Kennedy read among his breakfast things on that unseasonably warm Sunday morning in Washington. Three weeks of hard negotiation followed about the continued presence of Russian IL-28 bombers in Cuba, which the Kremlin had failed to include in the original protocol. Only then did the United States formally lift the five-hundred-mile quarantine and return her troops to DEFCON 4. Although the missiles were duly dismantled and loaded onto departing ships, Castro—in some ways anticipating the Saddam Hussein role in the 1990s—rejected any international inspection of the sites both then and well into the future. Of the four principal players in the drama, he was the only one who remained in power two years later, and still with no end in sight. It could be said that neither Castro nor Kennedy won, but nor was there a reconciliation. The United States continued its policy of bringing down the Havana regime by covert subversion on and off for the next ten years.

For his part, Macmillan faced regular, and often hostile, questioning about Cuba during his remaining time in office. "Does not the Prime Minister recognise his [support of the United States] constituted a resort to force, in violation of the United Nations charter?" the Labour MP Konni Zilliacus (an unrepentant admirer of Khrushchev) asked him in the House on November 15, 1962. "Is not the Government supposed to support the UN? Why does he condone this act of aggression . . ."[81] On December 7, the Foreign Office drew up what it called an "interim balance sheet" on the situation in Cuba. It found "some grounds for short-term satisfaction"—mankind still existed—but worried that "Castro has stubbornly refused to allow neutral inspectors. . . . There were signs of considerable Cuban irritation with [the] Soviet Union. . . . The full Communist part of the bargain has not been carried out."[82]

President Kennedy certainly won a personal victory. The events of October 1962 settled for all time the question of whether he had the character, and the equilibrium, to face down an enemy many in the West were convinced was contemplating preemptive nuclear war. Kennedy's hard line, and in particular his military buildup in Florida, was apparently enough to satisfy the Soviet leadership that they were no longer dealing with the "rich kid" Khrushchev had mocked following their meeting in Vienna. At the same time, the president had outfaced those of his advisers—like his air force chief General Curtis LeMay—who wanted immediate military reaction. LeMay, surely the prototype for the cigar-chewing Jack D. Ripper in *Dr. Strangelove*, later told Kennedy he considered the resolution of the missile crisis the "greatest defeat in our history."[83] This was a minority opinion. Kennedy's Gallup poll rating rose from a solid 61 percent in the week of October 19 to an enviable 74 percent just a month later. In the US midterm elections, held on November 6, the Democrats added two seats in the Senate and retained control of both houses of Congress. Kennedy's thirty-year-old brother Ted easily won a special senatorial race in Massachusetts. Across the country, Richard Nixon was defeated in his campaign for governor of California and told the press, "You won't have Nixon to kick around anymore," announcing his retirement from politics. He was elected president six years later.

Of course, Kennedy had also contributed to bringing about the missile crisis in the first place. Without the Bay of Pigs escapade, Castro might have had an entirely different reaction to the Soviet delegation that had arrived in May 1962 to quietly discuss using his country as an advance rocket base. As it was, he had told his guests only that if they wanted to "buttress the defensive power of the entire socialist camp," then he had no particular objection.[84] Some of the details of the Kennedy administration's Operation Mongoose, the ill-fated attempt to sabotage Castro's revolution, read like a luridly melodramatic James Bond movie script, as executed by Woody Allen. Overall, these were not initiatives that conspicuously added to the reputation of American foreign policy for probity and high-minded principle. Without Kennedy's decision—or, more accurately, his endorsement of Eisenhower's decision—to install the Jupiter rockets in Turkey, it remains doubtful that Khrushchev would ever have thought of Cuba as anything but a small offshore subsidiary state where he and his fellow politburo members could occasionally repair for an agreeable winter holiday.

For all that, it's hard to fundamentally disagree with the verdict of David Ormsby-Gore, in an effusive handwritten letter to Kennedy on British embassy paper, of October 30, 1962:

Dear Jack,

I have an aversion to tempting fate by offering congratulations before one can be completely certain of the final outcome, but as I know that older and wiser men have been prepared to take the risk, on this occasion I now do the same.

I am lost in admiration for the superb manner in which you handled the tremendous events of the critical week we have just lived through. I know what a mass of conflicting advice you received, and I can only say that looking back at it you acted at each stage with perfect judgement. I mean it quite sincerely when I say that America and all of the world must feel a deep sense of gratitude that you were President of the United States at this moment in history. I and countless millions are deeply in your debt.

Well done. With best wishes as always. Yours ever

David[85]

Historians will argue whether Macmillan himself played an active role in the crisis as much as he served as a friendly sounding board for Kennedy's decisions. Summarizing events in the cabinet of October 29, the PM said: "Both the president and his advisers had shown themselves ready to ask for and consider advice. This had been done quite informally, and without commitment on either side." The whole thing had been like a war, he later wrote in his diary, "and we in Admiralty House felt as if we were in the battle HQ."[86] Referring to the late-night transatlantic phone calls, Macmillan told a BBC interviewer that he had perhaps "played our cards above their face value" and that, with the fate of the world in the balance, it had been no time for gentlemanly reticence.[87] Set against this, David Ormsby-Gore, uniquely qualified to make the judgment, wondered about the true extent of British influence. "I can't honestly think of anything said from London that changed the US action—it was chiefly reassurance to JFK."[88] Speaking with his usual candor where the British were concerned, McGeorge Bundy agreed, "I don't think [Macmillan's] advice on the Cuban Missile Crisis was very important," adding that the hotline talks had been more in the spirit of "'Let's see what Harold thinks, shall we call him up?' . . . more to touch base than because of a sense that [Kennedy] really wanted to know what Macmillan thought about a thing."[89]

That may have been true as far as it went, but it told only half the story. If Kennedy was necessarily at the forefront of events, Macmillan played a significant role behind the lines, keeping the NATO and Commonwealth leaders firmly on side. He had been in touch with the European allies throughout the crisis, he noted, adding in the privacy of his diary: "The French were contemptuous; the Germans *very* frightened, though pretending to want firmness; the Italians windy."[90] Robert Kennedy wrote in his account of the affair (later published by the Macmillan firm) that, but for this support, "our position would have been seriously undermined." Dean Rusk, also not one generally to overpraise the British, thought that, "in terms of mobilizing the unanimity of NATO," Macmillan's role had been "very important."[91] When the PM wrote to congratulate David Ormsby-Gore on his performance as a de facto member of Kennedy's cabinet, Gore wrote back:

> The President has, I know, already told you how much he appreciated your support and advice during that critical week. In this, he was being deeply sincere, and he has repeatedly said the same thing to his closest friends, adding that he has no similar contacts with any other ally. He is furious with newspaper commenta-

tors who suggest that recent events indicate that there is little value for the US in the special Anglo-American relationship.[92]

In the Commons debate on the crisis, the Labour leader Hugh Gaitskell made much of Macmillan's "passive" and "supine" role in events in a rather forlorn attempt to prove that Britain had become "a wholly-owned subsidiary [of] American interests." Gaitskell was not to know that the president himself had told Gore that, "with the exception of Bobby, the Prime Minister was [the] one I felt the most connection to" during the fateful week of October 22. Nor could he know, since it hadn't yet happened, of the call Kennedy placed to Admiralty House on November 14 to discuss the continued presence of Russian aircraft and other munitions in Cuba. "We might get the [planes] out," Kennedy began, "but they want us to withdraw the quarantine and the over-flights. . . . The question is whether we should do that, or take some other action. For example, we might say the whole deal is off and withdraw our no-invasion pledge, and harass them generally. I think what I will do, prime minister, is to send you a message about what we propose to do in Cuba. I should be grateful for your judgment. I will send you a message tomorrow, and we could perhaps have a telephone conversation on Friday."

Macmillan responded, "I would be grateful. You must not give in to him."[93]

The talks on removing the Soviet bombers continued another few days. Khrushchev then pulled them out, along with the missiles, although he ended up getting at least some of what he wanted. Kennedy officially undertook not to attack Cuba and more privately gave orders to dismantle the Turkish Jupiters. The American assurance has lasted for fifty-two years, surviving the collapse of the Soviet Union itself. On October 15, 1964, the politburo unanimously granted Khrushchev's "wish" for retirement, citing his "advanced age and deterioration of his health." In their final interview, the departing leader's colleagues had accused him of "unpredictable, arbitrary, and unrestrained" behavior, as well as "harebrained scheming, hasty conclusions, rash decisions, actions based on wishful thinking," and of "juggling the fate of the world" in Cuba.[94] It seems fair to say that he had overplayed his hand. It was exactly two years since the U-2 piloted by US Air Force Major Rudolf Anderson had first brought back conclusive proof of the Soviet missiles. This was the same Major Anderson who was then shot down over Cuba on October 27, 1962, making him the one human casualty of the crisis.[95]

Macmillan thought the whole affair "one of the great turning points in history," insisting it had brought the Allies closer together. Despite the barbs that the United States had treated Britain with contempt, dragging her into a near cataclysm, the premier was adamant that he had been a willing and responsive partner. Criticisms of the British role were a product of "ignorance, annoyance and shame," he wrote, as well as "a desire to injure and denigrate me personally."[96] Perhaps the truth was that, if Kennedy felt the interests of the United States required a certain course of action, then that course would be taken. He would always listen to his primary ally and try to accommodate him. But essentially American policy—in this case, that the missiles pointed north from Cuba had to go—would be unchanged.

In the end, Kennedy and Macmillan proved that they had the character and the experience to withstand the pressures on them for devastating military action. Still, it had been a close-run thing. In their remaining time in office, both men would increasingly turn to the question of arms control as the best hope for their countries' continued coexistence with the Soviets—only a partial solution to the Cold War, Kennedy admitted in a speech the following July, but still preferable to an action that could "wipe out more than 300 million Americans, Europeans, and Russians in less than sixty minutes."[97]

8

FAMILY FEUD

I t took only a month for the Western allies to plunge from their greatest col-
laborative triumph to their greatest mutual crisis of confidence. This was the
Skybolt affair: on the one hand, about the technical capabilities of an air-to-
ground missile system; on the other, about whether Britain could still maintain a
credible independent nuclear force or simply become a forward base for American
assets, much as Khrushchev had envisioned with Cuba. At one point, the strain was
enough for Kennedy to "fl[y] into a terrible rage," David Ormsby-Gore recalled.
"He went through the roof. . . . We were sitting by the pool at Palm Beach behind
[JFK's] house, ready to have a swim, when the crisis burst. He was having a mani-
cure, the manicurist sitting beside him. . . . This wonderfully sunny scene beside
the pool—and suddenly this vast explosion and this violent language going out
via telephone while the wretched manicurist went on cutting his nails."[1] Writing
to Macmillan in January 1964, Jacqueline Kennedy generally remembered the
warmth of Anglo-American relations over the previous three years, "even when
unforeseen disastrous things like Skybolt happened."[2] The PM himself wrote of
the "protracted and fiercely contested" discussions on the subject at a summit in
Nassau, adding: "I had to pull out all the stops—adjourn, re-consider; refuse one
draft and demand another, etc, etc."[3] It was more akin to dealing with the Soviets at
their most intransigent than a close ally. Looking back in his memoirs, Macmillan
almost seemed to be pulling rank on the Americans. "The arguments were fierce,
and often painful. . . . Both [Kennedy] and McNamara were sometimes strangely
ignorant of the immediate past. In this I, who had lived through it all for over
twenty years, had an advantage," he wrote.[4]

Clearly, Macmillan was frustrated by the American lack of perspective on a
strategic arrangement the administration had inherited from the previous regime.
It remained for him to remind Kennedy of the "solemn commitments" entered into
by his predecessor only two years earlier. Essentially, Skybolt was another product

of Macmillan's long and generally successful post–Suez reconciliation with President Eisenhower. The basic idea behind the weapon was to combine the flexibility of the manned bomber with the destructive firepower of the intercontinental ballistic missile (ICBM), making what was considered by many to be an attractive alternative to the ground-based nuclear missile. As Macmillan put it with exquisite courtesy in a letter from April 1960 to the queen:

> I am very anxious to get rid of these fixed rockets. This is a very small country, and to put these installations near the large centres of population—where they have to be—would cause increasing anxiety to Your Majesty's subjects.[5]

Although he failed to mention it to the queen, there were also, at least in theory, distinct technical advantages to Skybolt compared to Britain's existing arsenal of Thor missiles. The latter required a full thirty-minute procedure for fueling and counting down, making them vulnerable to a preemptive enemy strike and, once fired, could not be recalled or redirected. (The rockets had an autodestruct mechanism, but tests suggested it had only a 50 percent chance of working under flight conditions.) There was also the matter of the Thors needing a dual-key system: the British could unilaterally order a launch, but only an on-site American officer could authorize arming the missile's warhead, which offered the promise but not, some felt, the substance of a truly independent weapon. At a stroke, Skybolt seemed to dispense with these checks and perceived weaknesses. By contrast to the Thor system, the new weapon could be operated unilaterally by the Royal Air Force (RAF) and could be simply loaded onto a bomber that then "loitered" over a target while awaiting orders. Since the planes took to the air in shifts and could be refueled by flying tankers, a minimum number of missiles would be aloft and ready around the clock. During his visit to Camp David in March 1960, Macmillan duly agreed to purchase 144 Skybolts at what he called an "advantageous" price. Essentially, the British contribution would be limited to the cost of adapting her fleet of "V" (Vulcan) bombers to take the new weapon, as well as providing the Americans with a forward nuclear-submarine base at Holy Loch in Scotland. As part of the deal, Britain's Blue Streak surface-to-surface missile, on which some £62 million had been spent in research and development, was scrapped. Reporting these arrangements in cabinet, Macmillan noted that a "static ballistic weapon system was [now viewed as] excessively vulnerable. . . . Our contribution to the nuclear deterrent must in future be based on some mobile means of delivery." The Prime Minister added that, "during his recent visit to Washington, he had satisfied himself that we should be able in due course to obtain from the United States, on acceptable terms, supplies of [Skybolt], to be armed with a British warhead."[6]

As a result of the neighborly "Harold" and "Ike" exchange that followed this compact, Macmillan came away convinced that he had secured not only Britain's next generation of nuclear deterrent but also its possible successor. "President Eisenhower gave us a firm, although not legal, assurance that if by some mischance the development of Skybolt proved unsatisfactory, we would be able to obtain . . . the essential elements of Polaris, to be fitted to submarines of our construction," he wrote.[7]

Macmillan's statement in cabinet would later arouse some sardonic comment in British and American political circles, where it was evident that their two leaders had once again fallen prey to a high-level misunderstanding to rival the disastrous confusion between the same pair in the immediate buildup to the Suez Crisis. Early in the Kennedy administration, it was noted that Skybolt's development costs had risen by more than a third of their previous estimate, meaning that the Department of Defense was spending some $30 million a month just to get it operational. Nor were the weapon's initial tests encouraging—in its first six outings, the rocket either simply failed to launch or exploded prematurely.[8] Similar compatibility trials with the British Vulcan bomber were a disaster. The intimacy and mutual accord of previous Allied exchanges on their strategic-defense system were soon gone, to be replaced by a chilly formality. Some British commentators came to grow particularly disenchanted with the "robotic" figure of Secretary McNamara, with his oiled hair and that thin film of superiority between himself and the rest of the human race that apparently came from having a $65 billion annual budget (more than half of the total state expenditure) at his disposal. In time, the series of RAF test failures—once spectacularly causing a near midair crash of two Vulcans—aroused the British capacity for self-mocking humor. Writing of this period, journalist Bernard Levin thought the protracted series of glitches "a dreadful symbol of the country's erratic attempts to move into the future, a paradigm of national impotence as the rocket failed to go off, failed to achieve its intended climax, [or] blew up in mid course." Macmillan was to write of "disquieting rumours" of Skybolt's performance as early as October 1960, although it was to be another two years—during which the Americans "consistently assured me these [technical difficulties] would be over-come"[9]—before the long-simmering problem boiled over into a major crisis.

Characteristically, there had been a promise on Kennedy's part of "complete candor" and the "utmost harmony" toward the Western allies in general, and Britain in particular, on his assuming office. After the partial repeal of the McMahon Act in 1958, the United States had gone on to freely share the technical data that had allowed Macmillan and his scientists to develop first the Blue Steel and then the Blue Streak long-range missiles. In London, there were grounds for supposing that this happy state of affairs would continue apace in 1961. In an action memorandum of February 20th that year, just a month after his inauguration, Kennedy told his secretary of state: "I hope we can press on, as a matter of high priority, the develop-ment of formulas for fair sharing in both foreign aid and military partnership with our European allies. . . . We need to make rapid progress with these ideas. . . . I know that George Ball has been making good headway in this area, and all I am saying is that I hope he will keep it up as a matter of urgency."[10]

In the event, experience would soon come to modify some of the president's high hopes for ever-closer Allied convergence on strategic arms. Within a year, the pressure of events in Berlin and elsewhere had led Kennedy to adjust his initial enthusiasm in favor of a more guarded policy that recognized only the "mutual respect [that exists] between the United States and the different entities that make up the NATO alliance"—not quite the same thing. In another action memo, this one from April 10, 1962, he wrote: "Weapons being dispersed [to the Allies] are now subject to the same kind of reservation placed on provision of Pershing missiles to Germany, namely, subject to review in the light of continuing studies of NATO strategy."[11] In practice, this meant that neither Kennedy nor his secretary of defense thought to inform the British of their decision to revisit the Skybolt program until the order confirming its cancellation was already on the president's desk. Typically, Ambassador Gore was to learn of the latest twist to American policy before Mac-millan did. After being called in and told, in so many words, that the whole strategy of Britain's "independent nuclear deterrent" had at a stroke been made redundant, Gore returned to his office "in shock . . . a compatriot who saw him later in the day recalls that he 'was like a man who'd learned the Bomb was going to drop, the end of civilization, and he doubted he could stop it.'"[12]

Macmillan, in turn, had some grounds for warmth at what he called "this evidence of American disregard for our interests." Both Kennedy and McNamara had assured him as recently as the summer of 1962 that all was well with Skybolt, and Britain had formally placed her order for the weapon that July as a result. Once again, the subsequent crisis found the PM shooting on the grouse moors as the guest of his Foreign Secretary in Scotland. He was not pleased at this "new and embarrassing development vitally affecting the future of our strategic deterrent." It was true, he conceded, that until then Kennedy had lived up to his pledge to freely share the technology Britain needed to develop a nuclear warhead. But in return, Macmillan had been consistently called upon to defend his decision to provide a British home for the American Polaris submarines, a supposedly "craven" and "reckless" concession that had been fanned into a long-running controversy by both the popular press and the Labour opposition.

In fact, Polaris would be a constant political irritation for Macmillan, more than once forcing him to explain the seemingly paradoxical deal whereby Britain provided a physical shelter for the submarines, attracting the interest of the Soviet nuclear planners as a result, without then being allowed to buy, lease, or operate any of them herself. The row had erupted in parliament as early as November 1961, when, to a chorus of catcalls and boos, Macmillan announced: "I believe it to be in the interest of this country and of the free world that [the Polaris] agreement should be continued."

A year later, in the immediate aftermath of the Cuban missile crisis, Macmillan was asked in the House, "in view of the danger of Britain becoming involved in a nuclear war, as was recently revealed, if he will now request President Kennedy to remove the Polaris base from Britain?" "No, sir," he replied. Two weeks later, Labour MP Christopher Mayhew wanted to know if the government had learned the "primary lesson" of Cuba and "were prepared to put forward their proposals for the withdrawal of the [American] offensive weapons from our country?" Again, the PM demurred. On December 6, 1962, it was the turn of Labour's Tom Driberg, who reminded the House of "the events at a US base in Norfolk in 1958, when a mentally deranged master-sergeant threatened to explode an atom bomb," and wanted to know if the prime minister now "had plans to review the arrangements for American nuclear facilities in the United Kingdom" as a result.

"I do not," Macmillan replied. "The American serviceman referred to locked himself in a shed for eight hours. The anxiety was not that he might explode an atomic bomb—there were none there—but that he might do something foolish with a pistol. I did not think it necessary to consult the President of the United States about this. [*Laughter*]"[13]

Perhaps more ominously, General de Gaulle had seized upon the British "nuclear courtesy" to the Americans as further proof of an Anglo-Saxon conspiracy which "pitiably treated," "ignored," or even "humiliated" the French.[14] Neither Kennedy nor Macmillan probably would have put it in quite those terms, but de Gaulle's complaint had some merit. At a meeting with Macmillan at Rambouillet in late 1962, the French head of state had confidently predicted that, were Skybolt indeed to fail, then Britain and France would surely collaborate on a nuclear missile. After a pause, Macmillan had replied that this was not necessarily the case—instead, Britain would continue to persevere with the Americans, either to purchase Polaris outright or to develop a ballistic submarine system of her own. This was a heavy blow to de Gaulle. As a result, the French would be obliged to design and build, at immense cost, their own unilateral, six-vessel atomic fleet, or force de frappe, which entered service only in 1971. (De Gaulle himself had left office, and indeed died, prior to its eventual commission.) Macmillan was to painfully learn the political cost of his exclusive nuclear alliance with Kennedy when, just four weeks later, de Gaulle publicly announced that, were Britain permitted to enter the Common Market, it was certain that "a colossal Atlantic fraternity would develop under American dependence."[15] The following week, France formally vetoed Britain's application to join Europe. Macmillan had paid a heavy price for his persistence with the Atlantic "Special Relationship." "What happened yesterday was bad, bad for us, bad for Europe, and bad for the whole free world," he announced in a public broadcast. "A great opportunity has been missed. . . . Europe cannot stand alone. She must co-operate with the rest of the free world, with the Commonwealth, with the United States in an equal and honourable partnership. That is why we in Britain need to stand by the Atlantic Alliance."

There was an added irony to the situation, because exactly twenty years earlier, at the Casablanca conference in January 1943, Macmillan, in his role as viceroy, had been instrumental in securing recognition of de Gaulle's leadership of the Free French Forces, in the face of opposition from both Franklin Roosevelt and Winston Churchill, a mandate de Gaulle fully exploited. Perhaps also compounding the problem at their Rambouillet talks was the fact that Macmillan chose to speak to his host in French. Although he was more than proficient in the language, some of his more technical points on the merits of Skybolt and Polaris—and on the exact provisions of the McMahon Act, as amended by their old comrade General Eisenhower—were thought only to have confused de Gaulle further. It proved to be the last meeting between the two men.

Following his public announcement of regret about de Gaulle's European veto, Macmillan allowed himself some private comments on the subject. These were considerably more robust. "French duplicity has defeated us all," he wrote in his diary. De Gaulle's foreign minister, Couve de Murville, had "behaved with a rudeness which [was] unbelievable." Alluding to domestic reaction in Britain, Macmillan added: "There is the return of the old feeling, 'the French always betray you in the end'. There is a *great* and *grievous* disappointment at the end of a fine vision."[16]

Given these events, Macmillan might have been excused when he later complained of an apparent lack of American sensitivity to the political risks he had run for Skybolt. It all appeared to be "tactless . . . unhelpful . . . rather a blind spot," both for Kennedy and the senior members of his administration. On June 16, 1962, Robert McNamara gave his notorious Ann Arbor speech, which seemed to mock the whole concept of Britain's national deterrent as "dangerous, expensive, prone to obsolescence, and lacking in credibility." Furious backpedaling on McNamara's part quelled some of the firestorm that erupted in the UK press, but not surprisingly Macmillan continued to think it ill-judged—"equal [parts] vigour and clumsiness," as he put it in his memoirs.[17] Even then there was no clear warning that the Pentagon might be on the point of retreating from their commitment to provide long-range guided missiles for use by British aircraft. On September 20, Macmillan's defence minister, Peter Thorneycroft, met with McNamara in Washington. The official British record of the talks concludes with the words: "Their [American] plans assumed delivery of Skybolt."[18]

Following that, any technical differences between the Allies were momentarily swept aside by the urgent demands of the Cuban missile crisis. By the time the last of the Russian bombers returned home in late November 1962, McNamara had moved from "unsparing support" of Skybolt to a position close to canceling it. A further series of test failures had shaken the Pentagon's confidence in the weapon. "We were genuinely shocked when we found out how far off the beam the program was, how much it was going to cost, and the technical difficulties," the US undersecretary of defense, Ros Gilpatric, recalled.[19] McNamara himself, a former president of the Ford Motor Company, was not one to be swayed by woolly concepts of good-will toward a foreign ally when there were hard questions of business efficiency and basic cost control to be considered. By now, Thorneycroft, though still not officially advised of any Pentagon reappraisal of Skybolt, was sufficiently worried to inform his Foreign Secretary: "Cancellation . . . would have the most profound repercus-sions over the whole field of Anglo-American relations. . . . I should be grateful for your support, and the support of the ambassador in Washington, in making clear to the Americans the disastrous effects [it] would have. . . . It would certainly provoke a first-class political crisis in this country."[20]

These powerful tides of feeling account for the fact that Kennedy himself, nor-mally so attuned to British sensibilities, was so surprised by the force of Macmillan's stance on Skybolt when the two leaders later met in Nassau. According to the State Department adviser Walt Rostow, the PM "again commenced with his Edwardian Shakespearian drama for the missiles" once seated across the table from the presi-dent.[21] By then it had finally become clear that the Americans had no intention of persevering with Skybolt, but that they were prepared to offer the British the AGM-28—or "Hound Dog"—supersonic cruise missile as a substitute. The more you study the politics of Allied rocket technology in 1961–62, the more you find its distinguishing features (apart from the silly nicknames) to have been the tragi-comic misunderstanding between the American conviction on the one side that it was all a straightforward business proposition between a supplier and a customer, determined solely by market forces, and the deep British sense of unease on the other that they were being kicked out of the nuclear club by the perfidy of an ally who had good reason to be grateful to them. There was an added irony to the par-ticular timing of events: on December 22, just hours after the British and American delegations returned home from Nassau, the Pentagon triumphantly announced that Skybolt had at last passed a test, immediately after the executive decision had been made to scrap it. This was the news that caused Kennedy, back by his pool in Florida, to explode with anger. "Bob's normally so goddamned good at everything," he kept mumbling, in a mixture of astonishment and rage. It was perhaps as well for McNamara that by then he happened to be at a remote ski lodge in Colorado and thus not immediately available to take the president's call. Macmillan took a more measured view but still remarked, in pained terms, on this exquisite coincidence of events. "It was rather provoking that Skybolt should go off so well," he wrote to Kennedy on Christmas Eve. "It would have been better if it had been a failure. However, these are the chances of life."[22]

=====

It was against this backdrop that Dean Acheson, the svelte, sixty-nine-year-old doyen of American foreign policy, gave a speech at West Point with the seemingly unexceptional title, "Our Atlantic Alliance: The Political and Economic Strands." Most of what Acheson said that early-December afternoon was a routine tour d'horizon about the need for closer cooperation in the face of the continuing Soviet threat around the globe. It was the two relatively short sentences toward the end of his remarks that exploded across the Atlantic like a cruise missile. Great Britain had not only lost an empire, Acheson said, but her attempt "to play a separate power role—that is, a role apart from Europe, a role based on a 'special relationship' with the United States, a role based on being head of a 'commonwealth' which has no political structure, or unity, or strength—this role is about played out."[23]

In properly assessing what followed, it should be remembered both that Acheson had no official status in the Kennedy administration and that, even during his time as Truman's secretary of state, he had never been one to embrace the view that there was some mystical bond between Great Britain and the United States. In June 1950, he had called Britain's initial failure to join the European Community the "greatest blunder" since the war. Nor was Acheson (whose father was British) a martyr to false modesty, with Macmillan privately noting of him: "He was always a conceited ass." Some even thought of him as an unintentional figure of fun, striding about in his slightly over-florid ties, a macaw in the rookery of international diplomacy. In his diary, Macmillan called him "a kind of a caricature of an Englishman . . . always overstates his case. . . . Fortunately, the President dislikes him very much indeed."[24] It would be fair to say that the majority of the British press and political reaction to Acheson's West Point speech was unappreciative. The *Daily Express* editorialized about a "stab in the back" coming so soon after the "sterling British contribution" to defusing the Cuban crisis, while the *Telegraph* scoffed that the former secretary of state was "more immaculate in dress than in judgement." Macmillan, then in the thick of the Skybolt-Polaris debate, was sufficiently stung to remark in an open letter on Acheson's "denigrat[ion] of the British people," an error that had been made by several others, "including Philip of Spain, Louis XIV, Napoleon, the Kaiser and Hitler." This was much the same retort Macmillan had made a few months earlier to Khrushchev. Acheson's remarks, if tactless, were of course painfully close to home in assessing the continuing decline of British postwar influence. They stung as much as they did precisely because they touched on the transitional state of affairs for Britain in 1962, busy as she was in dissolving her empire but not yet accepted into the European free market. Acheson's speech may thus have been fair comment. It was not, however, the ideal prelude to a summit meeting that already marked the greatest single test of Anglo-American relations since the Suez Crisis.

On December 11, McNamara appeared briefly in London, where he informed the press that he now had "fundamental doubts" about Skybolt, before flying on to a NATO meeting in Paris. These latter talks were "wholly unsatisfactory," Macmillan recorded.[25] There seemed to be little question that the Americans meant to scrap Skybolt altogether. On a note of simulated moral outrage, a number of Labour MPs taunted Macmillan on his appearances in the House for Prime Minister's Questions on December 11 and 13. He then flew to Paris for his ill-fated meeting with de Gaulle, returned to London, collected his small ministerial team, and immediately flew on to Nassau. There is general agreement among historians that the Special Relationship of this time as it applied specifically to strategic arms was something of a disaster. But nobody could fault the aging premier for effort as he jetted around, struggling to deal with the technical intricacies of air-launched tactical nuclear weapons and the larger question of his working partnership with the president of the United States. Macmillan was to note laconically that the British delegation set off for the Bahamas "with heavy hearts." According to the historian Nigel Ashton, "It was as though the Greek who had thought himself to be quietly running the Roman empire had for the first time realised that the governing characteristic of his condition was slavery." Macmillan was sufficiently depressed about the prospect of reaching agreement with the Americans at Nassau that he came prepared with a draft communiqué in his pocket to be used in the event the bilateral talks ended in failure. It read: "The Prime Minister recognises with regret that the US decision inevitably marks the end of a period of close Anglo-American co-operation, in which he himself has always believed."

Kennedy's own preparations for the Nassau conference were notable for the fact that he was under increasingly heavy medication for his back, and other ailments, to the point where his physicians had begun to squabble among themselves about the best course of treatment. Recently added to the presidential retinue, Dr. Hans Kraus, a New York orthopedic surgeon, was moved to tell Kennedy "that if I ever heard he took another shot [from Max Jacobson], I'd make sure it was known. No president with his finger on the red button has any business taking stuff like that."[26] Between arbitrating these feuds and indulging his still-active libido, Kennedy found the time to place an eve-of-departure phone call to former president Eisenhower to ask if there was "anything in particular" he, Kennedy, needed to know about the history of Skybolt. According to the transcript, neither man believed that the British had ever been led to understand that, if the weapon failed, they could rely on obtaining Polaris instead. ("Of course," Kennedy allowed, "this places Prime Minister Macmillan in a difficult position.")[27] Some observers wondered if it was purely by chance that the welcoming band struck up a spirited version of an old English folk song, the chorus of which ran, "Oh, don't deceive me," when the American delegation touched down at Windsor Field, Nassau, on the morning of December 18.

Kennedy, even so, was in high spirits. Just the previous day, he had told two radio interviewers that he was generally encouraged by the outcome of the "Cuban matter." For the first time, both the Soviet Union and the Western allies could start to "think seriously about a limit to how many [nuclear weapons] we need," he now felt. Having come through the missile crisis, Kennedy had set himself the goal of beginning to rein in the arms race during the two years—six, in the likely event of his reelection—he had left in office. Earlier that week, *Pravda*'s editor Yuri Zhukov had conveyed Khrushchev's willingness to negotiate in a message to Pierre Salinger. The Soviet leader believed that "the socialist countries have gained [enough] in Berlin from the Wall," and that for the time being he saw no reason for "renewed difficulties" over that city or "any other material property" with his wartime allies, so he said.[28]

When Kennedy arrived in the Bahamas, bringing with him not only his foreign-affairs team but also David Ormsby-Gore, he had at last been fully apprised about just how much Skybolt meant to Macmillan. Gore had sat next to the president during the two-hour flight, "conversing as politicians," and patiently explained to him that, without the weapon, the British "independent deterrent" would simply no longer exist.[29] This apparently came as a news flash to Kennedy. The two men had then hurriedly agreed to a compromise that they thought might adequately cover

Macmillan's nakedness on the subject. According to their formula, jotted down on an Air Force One notepad, the Americans would forgo Skybolt for themselves but would continue to develop it for the British. The costs of the system would be split fifty-fifty. It was just the sort of sweeping, blue-sky initiative senior politicians can sometimes achieve when separated from their armies of advisers. Unfortunately, even while Kennedy and Gore were fixing the terms of the deal over their in-flight martinis, on the ground Macmillan had reached a quite different conclusion. After weeks of agonizing on the subject, he was now convinced that Skybolt was a dead duck—or that, "while the proposed British marriage with [the weapon] was not exactly a shotgun wedding, the virginity of the lady must now be regarded as doubtful," as he put it in his inimitable style.[30] Skybolt, in other words, had simply failed in its tests too often for the PM to retain any faith in its arcane technology. As he saw it, the only effective option now available to the British was Polaris.

None of this was known to Kennedy as he strode confidently across the tarmac at Nassau to embrace his "firm friend [and] comrade" Macmillan.[31] It was their first meeting in eight months, and they went out of their way to show the world their respect and affection for each other. Within only a few moments, they were plainly no longer the bickering old couple they had played in public for several weeks beforehand. Macmillan warmly welcomed Kennedy, and Kennedy replied by noting the two men's affinity for Christmastime meetings in the tropics. The British party, having escaped from what was already the worst winter in living memory, as one nodded their approval of this policy. More formally, Kennedy went on to say that he had "benefitted greatly from the counsel and friendship which you have shown to me, Prime Minister, to my predecessor, your old friend General Eisenhower, and also to the American people, who have a heavy claim laid upon you from earliest birth." It was one of those slightly prim public declarations that reminded Kennedy's audience that this emblematic figure of his times in some ways remained a conventional political product of the 1950s, or even earlier.

That night, Macmillan and Kennedy took a long walk together under the palm trees, without secretaries and advisers. Again pulling rank, the PM spoke of the whole history of Anglo-American relations during his six years in office. "At Camp David in 1960, Eisenhower discussed with me both Skybolt and Polaris," he reminisced. "We accepted Skybolt because it seemed the best way for us to prolong the life of our bomber air force. . . . But if Skybolt were definitely to fail us, Ike assured me we could rely on obtaining Polaris."[32] We've seen that this was not entirely Eisenhower's own memory of events. Although Kennedy had now met Macmillan six times, he must again have been put in mind of the biographical sketch of him included in his Nassau briefing folder. "Underneath his calm, relaxed manner, the PM hides a tenacious and self-reliant personality," the profile concluded. "He is a deft and astute politician, [and] exercises a decisive voice in all major areas of policy."[33]

The subsequent full-scale talks confirmed both that Macmillan was an exceptionally able and determined negotiator and that he enjoyed an unusual rapport with Kennedy. "If you were in that kind of trouble, you'd want a friend," the president later remarked of Nassau. One American observer wrote that it "was a case in point where JFK did overrule his subordinates in order to help the PM. It was a case of 'king to king', and it infuriated the court."[34] Although Kennedy privately called the whole concept of Britain's national deterrent "a political necessity but a piece of military foolishness," he was forced to acknowledge the sheer force of Macmillan's grand set-piece speech that invoked the horrors of both World Wars, touched upon the course of Anglo-American friendship over two hundred years, and concluded with a veiled threat that, should the current negotiations fail, the United States might soon find itself dealing with a xenophobic Labour regime whose foreign-affairs spokesman was an "anti-nuclear alcoholic."[35] According to Ros Gilpatric, a key reason for the swift American U-turn on Polaris "was that Macmillan had such an extraordinary power of influencing an audience. . . . The speech he made on how, you know, the destiny of England depended on a nuclear role, and his government and everything else, apparently almost spellbound everybody from the President on down. I guess the reaction was, 'We've got to do something for Harold.'"[36]

On December 20, Macmillan sent five telegrams: one to the queen conveying Kennedy's personal best wishes, and four to the cabinet with the fine print of the missile negotiations. Butler chaired the meeting in London and noted that "it was clear a great deal had been achieved by the Prime Minister and his colleagues in Nassau in persuading the President to move away from the original US positions." The key phrase lay in the fourth telegram. In it, Macmillan "had particularly directed attention to the new [arrangements], which had the effect of giving us the sole right of decision on the use of our strategic nuclear forces . . . and asked whether the Cabinet endorsed the view, which he shared with the Foreign Secretary, the Commonwealth Secretary and the Minister of Defence, that these words could be publicly defended as maintaining an independent United Kingdom contribution to the nuclear deterrent."[37]

In the end, Kennedy archly agreed that "Looking at it from the [British] point of view—which they do almost better than anybody—it might well be concluded that . . . we had an obligation to provide an alternative" to Skybolt.[38] Macmillan got his Polaris missiles, which were to be equipped with British warheads. The weapons would be formally under NATO control, "save where Her Majesty's Government may decide that the supreme national interests are at stake." It was widely recognized as a major coup for Macmillan, except among those who thought Britain had no business in the nuclear club in the first place. On the last day at Nassau, someone took a photograph of McNamara and his opposite number, Peter Thorneycroft, sitting across the table from one another, looking as grumpy as a couple in divorce court. Some days after the conference ended, the Pentagon mentioned for the first time that they expected Britain to contribute significantly to future research-and-development costs of Polaris. Macmillan wrote directly to Kennedy refusing to do so. "But," he noted in his diary, "I have offered, in lieu, to add five per cent to the retail cost. So, if we bought fifty million pounds' of missiles, we would pay fifty two-and-a-half million pounds. Not a bad bargain. But it has caused me some sleepless nights."[39] Kennedy accepted Macmillan's offer.

A significant subplot to the saving of the British deterrent at Nassau was the provocative effect the whole affair had on General de Gaulle. To him, it was but the latest example of an Anglo-Saxon cabal that took insultingly little account of French sensibilities. Macmillan had told Kennedy during the conference that only some "technical detail on agriculture" could now possibly keep Britain out of the Common Market. This was a case of wishful thinking, as de Gaulle issued his veto of Britain's application just a month later. He undoubtedly had his reasons other than Polaris for doing so. There were genuine concerns about such contentious points as temperate-zone foodstuffs and the broader issue of the Commonwealth's special trading position with Britain. But for all that, Macmillan thought de Gaulle "did not want us in for two main reasons: 1. It will alter the character of the Community. . . . Now it is a nice little club [under] French hegemony. 2. Apart from our loyalty to the Commonwealth, we shall always be too intimately tied up with the Americans."[40]

The problem was not only de Gaulle's sense of being the poor relation of the wartime Allies, Macmillan felt. There was a degree of personal rancor—even derangement—as well. It was almost a political equivalent of dealing with a spurned lover, someone capable of a *Fatal Attraction*–like act of erotomania. Calling Kennedy on the hotline on January 19, 1963, Macmillan sounded genuinely concerned for de Gaulle's mental health:

> *Macmillan:* Well, I think it's a very bad situation. I think this man has gone crazy— absolutely crazy.
>
> *Kennedy:* Well, what do you think it is that's made him crazy?
>
> *Macmillan:* He's simply inventing any means whatever to knock us out.[41]

No one could have sugared the pill of Britain's continuing global decline better than Macmillan did at Nassau. Thanks to his powers of persuasion, the nation's nuclear doomsday machine was preserved for another generation to come. But clearly it was also a pyrrhic victory. The Polaris agreement was bound to gall the French, and there were renewed tensions with other Western leaders. The Canadian prime minister, John Diefenbaker, was due to fly later to Nassau for bilateral talks with Macmillan, but by appearing early he managed to bump into Kennedy on his way out. It was another scene out of a Feydeau stage farce. Macmillan remarked that the men went inside for a hurriedly arranged lunch, and "sat there like three whores at a christening."[42] At home in Britain, meanwhile, the opposition was divided between those who thought the premier had surrendered cravenly to the Americans and others who attacked him for clinging stubbornly to his nuclear bombs. "Nineteen sixty-two is over," Macmillan wrote in his diary a week after Nassau. "It has been a *bad* year, both in home and foreign politics. The government's position is weak, and there is a general view that the socialists will win the general election."[43] They did—in October 1964—although by then Macmillan himself was no longer an MP.

Given what was at stake in Nassau, Arthur Schlesinger summed up a widespread American view that it had "set back the cause of [European] integration, [and] caused a good deal of Allied dislocation." Yet for all that, Kennedy and Macmillan's mutual admiration was unchanged. The PM wrote to the queen that it had "been a hard and at times almost desperate struggle to maintain the two concepts of interdependence and independence. But I must pay tribute to President Kennedy's sense of fairness and willingness to be persuaded by argument and over-rule those of his advisers who were not sympathetic to our views."[44]

Before the conference convened, the US consul general in Nassau had written to the president to mention that "if you have any time off for relaxing, my wife and I would be delighted to gather together some of the more festive members of the international set [for] anything you name at our establishment."[45] In the event, Kennedy did not attend his consul's Christmas wine-and-cheese party but did bring with him an attractive nineteen-year-old White House intern named Marion "Mimi" Beardsley. She was flown to Nassau on Air Force One and was later spotted crouching in the presidential limousine while Kennedy concluded his talks with Macmillan. Although officially described as a press-office secretary, Beardsley's employment conditions were not very demanding. She "had no skills," Salinger's assistant Barbara Gamarekian recalled. "She couldn't type."[46] While Jacqueline Kennedy remained in Washington, the president was attended by Beardsley and as many as three other young women during his eighty-four hours in Nassau. "It was like the Rolling Stones on tour," a British official later said.[47] Kennedy spent most of the time he wasn't actively negotiating with the British cloistered in his ocean-front villa with his latest partner while the other conference delegates, exhausted by the long speeches and technical data, just wanted to turn in early with a good book. The indefatigable young president showed no sign of these normal human frailties. Forty years later, Mimi Beardsley, by then a grandmother and a New York church worker, issued a curt statement: "From June 1962 to November 1963, I was involved in a sexual relationship with President Kennedy." According to Barbara Gamarekian, the press knew all about Kennedy's activities but said nothing. "This is the sort of thing that legitimate newspapers [didn't] write about, or even make any implications about. It was kind of a big joke."

On Christmas Eve, Macmillan wrote to thank Kennedy for the events of the previous week:

> My dear Friend,
>
> I am indeed grateful to you for giving me [Jackie's recently published guide-book] "The White House" in such a beautiful edition. It is a great rarity, and I shall treasure it most carefully in my library. I value it very much because of its personal character.
>
> I enjoyed our talks in the Bahamas. Although rather strenuous, I think they were very rewarding. . . . I am being violently attacked, especially by the Beaverbrook press, for having sold out British interests. The left wing press is rather

less certain as to just what line to take. However, I feel certain that the dust will soon begin to clear, and that our agreement will become a historic example of the nice balance between interdependence and independence which is necessary if Sovereign states are to work in partnership together for the defence of freedom.

If I may, I will send you some further thoughts on the question of money.[48]

Thus it was that Macmillan, opposed by the French but armed with Kennedy's all-important blessing, could portray Nassau as a brilliant success for British interests. It's true that several senior members of the US administration, thinking him an arch manipulator, would no longer show any great desire for Macmillan's company. It's also true that, behind the scenes, like any partners, he and Kennedy occasionally had harsh words for each other. The president later commissioned Columbia University professor Richard Neustadt to prepare a detailed report on Nassau and told him: "We really ought to find out what [the British] were up to—or not up to—and why they acted the way they did." (It was essentially a case of the Allies being at cross-purposes, and of a lack of communication between the highest echelons of the US government, Neustadt concluded.) Like the rocket itself, Kennedy went into orbit when he heard that McNamara had then approved a Skybolt test—and publicly announced the results—immediately after the weapon was canceled. For his part, Macmillan more than once came close to wondering if the Americans could always be relied upon to fulfill their basic overseas obligations. "I reminded Kennedy of [the] earlier history," he reported to the cabinet on January 3, 1963. "And of my own reopening of the issue with President Eisenhower, which resulted in amendment of the Macmahon [sic] Act and the renewal of the US-UK partnership. . . . Current anti-American sentiment in the UK [is] not unnatural," Macmillan noted. "But the US have not bilked us on Skybolt (properly regarded): nor is it likely that they will bilk us on Polaris. And, if we are to retain an independent deterrent, there was no practical alternative. It is unrealistic to try to 'go it alone' like the French."[49]

While Macmillan continued to think it nearly incredible that one American administration could apparently be so ignorant of the actions of the one before it, in the end he took a gracious view of the affair. "The arguments were fierce and sometimes painful," he wrote of Nassau. "But I was happy to feel that there was no change in the relations between Kennedy and myself."[50]

Sitting alone in front of the fireplace at Birch Grove on Christmas night, reading the *Maxims and Opinions* of the first Duke of Wellington, Macmillan was struck by the similarities between the victor of Waterloo and himself. "Poor Wellington!" he wrote in his diary. "He was even worse treated by his friends than I have been!"[51] Back again in Admiralty House—the latest builders' estimate was that the work on Downing Street might possibly be finished by the summer—the PM discoursed gloomily on a variety of topics ranging from the treachery of de Gaulle to the retirement of the "irreplaceable" Sir Norman Brook after sixteen years as cabinet secretary, or de facto chief of staff. ("I made a short speech about him, and he replied; I have sent him a nice piece of plate, as a mark of esteem," Macmillan recorded in his diary.[52]) Adding to the somber atmosphere at the start of 1963 was the fact that much of Britain was quite literally at a standstill. The weather that had been steadily deteriorating for some weeks reached a nadir by mid-January, when it came to overshadow almost everything else as a national obsession. By day, heavy fog descended, bringing a return of wartime-blackout conditions. At night, the sea froze solid. Much of the country's road and rail networks were immobilized by snow, and the cold caused milk—still delivered to many doorsteps by a horse and cart—to explode spontaneously in its bottles. Social revolution might be abroad in the form of the Beatles and the Stones and their ilk, but looking out on most British streets that winter was to be immersed in a scene of Dickensian antiquity.

This was a markedly different holiday season to the one enjoyed by President Kennedy. Prior to flying to Nassau, Kennedy had allowed himself an early Christmas treat in the form of a spectacular weekend bachelor party at Bing Crosby's estate near Palm Springs. According to Seymour Hersh's book *The Dark Side of Camelot*—later corroborated by Mimi Beardsley—"the shouts and whoops of the partygoers" at Crosby's poolside on the night of December 8 "had the California state police guarding the property assuming the sounds were actually the nocturnal calls of coyotes." But as the unearthly shrieks grew louder, the officers thought it best to contact the secret service detail inside the compound and check that everything was all right. According to the president's bodyguard Larry Newman, the scene that greeted them was one that might have raised eyebrows at an orgy held during the most hedonistic days of the Roman Empire. "[Kennedy's executive aide] Dave Powers was banging a girl on the edge of the pool," Newman recalled. "The President is sitting across the pool and talking to some broads. Everybody was buck naked."[53]

After attending Mass early the next morning at Palm Desert's Sacred Heart church, Kennedy flew back to Washington, where he put in a full day's work conferring with McNamara, Rusk, and Bundy on a range of foreign-policy issues and later reconvening a meeting of ExComm to review events in Cuba.

On December 29, 1962, with a radiant First Lady at his side, Kennedy addressed a crowd of some fifty thousand Cuban exiles at the Orange Bowl in Miami. They were primarily there to welcome back the 1,113 veterans of the Bay of Pigs landing who had just been released from prison by Fidel Castro. Many of them had suffered excruciating torture during their eighteen months in captivity. Looking out on the rows of men on crutches or in wheelchairs, the president announced: "I am here today not to be honored, but to pay honor. I know of no men in modern history who showed more courage under more difficult conditions than those before me today." As the sun gleamed down, several thousand fluttering banners were waved aloft, and the fists shaken overhead stretched back to the far reaches of the stadium. There was a prolonged standing ovation for the president's remarks. From the side of the stage, a ragged squad of men marched up to ceremonially present him with their battle standard. Kennedy reverently accepted it and then raised his voice as he announced, "Although Castro and his fellow dictators may rule nations, they do not rule people. They may imprison bodies, but they do not imprison spirits." Another roar of approval erupted. Kennedy plunged on, his right fist now pounding down to emphasize the emotion of the occasion. "I promise to return your flag to you in a free Havana," he assured the freedom fighters and their families looking up at him. The roar this time was truly deafening; he had clearly struck the most responsive possible chord.

"Cuba libre!" the crowd chanted for several minutes.[54] It was an extraordinary scene, part military parade, part religious rally, and Kennedy's peerless talent for feeling out an audience's mood until he hit upon the best way to reach it again showed him to be the master politician of his age. Macmillan, for all his dry powers of persuasion, could never hope for the same delirious response.

The American (or Anglo-American) victory in the Cuban missile crisis changed everything. Before it, Kennedy was broadly on the side of the Pentagon chiefs who had managed to fuel US defense spending to the point that it accounted for 47.2 percent of total government outlay by September 1962. After it, he came to increasingly share Macmillan's concern about finding some way out of the "fantastic and retrograde" arms race. Khrushchev, too, despite hailing the outcome in

Cuba as a triumph for the "forces of peace and socialism,"[55] seemed to be thinking seriously about at least the financial consequences of attempting to reach missile parity with the West. "Conditions are emerging now for finding an agreement on the prohibition of nuclear weapons, [and the] cessation of all types of weapons tests," he had cabled Kennedy on November 12, 1962.[56] Having tested each other's willingness to affirm and assert what they saw to be their vital strategic interests, the two superpowers would, in their own ways, now come to question the wisdom of arming themselves to the hilt and preparing for the likelihood of a nuclear war. It was a tentative outbreak of the kind of sanity Macmillan had been quietly advocating since coming to office in 1957.

For all that, the removal of the Soviet rockets failed to immediately end Cuba's role, alongside Berlin, as the crisis zone of international affairs. As we've seen, it took several more weeks of negotiation before Kennedy felt able to finally lift his quarantine and declare that the outcome "might open the door to the solution of other outstanding problems." Meanwhile, Moscow and Havana blamed one another for the perceived national humiliation. "Fidel Castro openly advised us to use nuclear weapons, but now he retreats and smears us," Khrushchev complained at a politburo meeting on December 3, 1962.[57] The Soviet ruler sent his deputy Anastas Mikoyan to confer with Castro once the decision had been taken to dismantle the missiles. During his three-week visit, Mikoyan was on the receiving end of several outbursts from the Cuban hierarchy. A formal dinner in Havana intended to celebrate the forty-fifth anniversary of the Bolshevik revolution went badly enough for Khrushchev to threaten to end any further aid to Cuba. "Inappropriate" toasts had been drunk, it was reported, and when a senior Soviet diplomat had requested a bread roll, a Cuban in combat fatigues had "air-lined this to [him], catching him a sharp blow on the ear." Meanwhile, Castro privately expressed his view of Khrushchev as "that son of a bitch . . . bastard . . . asshole. . . . No *cojones*. . . . *Maricon* [homosexual]."[58] This was the reality of the "fraternal relationship between the USSR and the government and people of the Republic of Cuba," as the Soviet politburo labeled it in their agenda. Even before the missiles were crated up, Macmillan wrote that the West "is going to find it quite difficult to deal with Castro. He is naturally making a lot of trouble for the Russians. . . . Cuba will remain as the base for Communist propaganda throughout Central and South America."[59] On November 27, 1962, Khrushchev wrote to the PM to assure him: "I fully share your view, as well as that of President Kennedy, that the Cuban crisis has led to a better under-standing of the need for a prompt settlement of acute international problems."[60]

It was, Macmillan wrote in his memoirs, "An admirable sentiment—but leaving quite a lot unsaid."[61] In his letter, Khrushchev went on to note, "You say that the normalization of the situation in the Caribbean area opens up for us all an oppor-tunity to work towards the solution of the disarmament problem. We welcome your statement on this score." Not long after that, in one of those abrupt changes of direction that were so characteristic of his foreign policy, Khrushchev indicated that he might accept a partial test-ban treaty and that this need not be linked to any further "readjustment of controls" in Berlin.

Macmillan had always realized that to remove the Russian missiles alone from Cuba wasn't enough. The Allies also had to work with Moscow to bring about an end to nuclear tests, if not to start the process of mutual disarmament. Part of his reasoning was moral and part strategic. "Khrushchev may be the best type of Russian leader we are likely to get," Macmillan noted in his diary on November 27. "There is a strong argument for trying now to negotiate either some limited agreements or over a wider field."[62] A critical moment would come on December 19, when Kennedy and Macmillan were together in Nassau. A letter arrived from Khrushchev, speaking about the need for "cooling down" the arms race in general, before adding that he might now be willing to allow two or three inspections of Soviet nuclear-test facili-ties each year. It was a substantial advance on his previous position that had called any international scrutiny of Russian bomb sites "an act of espionage."

Macmillan also knew that he could expect to take intense political flak from a number of quarters for Britain's continued marriage to American nuclear inter-ests and systems. The most obvious critic was a notional ally, France. In December 1962, de Gaulle privately denounced Britain as a "semi-detached US state," and thus clearly "not a proper European."[63] The week after he ensured this fact by vetoing Macmillan's application for membership of the European Economic Community, de Gaulle signed a treaty of Franco-German friendship. Seventeen years after the end of the Second World War, France found herself effectively estranged from her principal liberators and aligned with her old enemy across the Rhine. There was no place for sentiment—or sometimes even for memory—in de Gaulle's repeated insistence that "France cannot be France without glory." Macmillan would also be roundly mocked by much of the British press and the Labour opposition (as well

as by a vocal minority of his own party, often led by his brother-in-law, Lord Salisbury) for seeming to prefer his Atlantic ally to Britain's Commonwealth dependen-
cies or continental neighbors. A question put to him in the Commons on January
22, 1963, by the Labour MP Stephen Swingler amounted to a sort of greatest-hits
compendium of the post-Nassau attacks:

> Leaving aside the Skybolt and Polaris scandals, which we shall discuss separately, is
> the Prime Minister aware that [he] does not mention a single proposal which he put
> to President Kennedy, or agreed with the president, for the improvement of interna-
> tional relations? Can the right hon. Gentleman answer my question, which is whether
> he did agree with the president about disarmament? Or about a nuclear-free zone? Or
> about Berlin? Or about bringing China into the United Nations? Or any such proposal
> at all? What effective move was made to improve world relations?[64]

From Kennedy's point of view, Nassau had been a comedy of errors with some
serious consequences. He now knew the depth of feeling in senior British circles
about that island maintaining an independent nuclear arm. Under the terms of the
sales agreement signed on April 6, 1963, the United States supplied the Royal Navy
with an initial consignment of sixty-four UGM-27 Polaris rockets at a cost "crip-
plingly disadvantageous" to the seller. Kennedy then offered the French the same
deal, but they preferred to go their own way. The president set the sales discussions
in progress with the British in an action memorandum of January 30, 1963. Among
other things, he "emphasized that in the course of the talks, US should not become
engaged in such a way that failure to achieve agreement would seriously damage
US prestige."[65] Kennedy later spoke of the Nassau accord as his "roughest [foreign-
policy] fix since meet[ing] Khrushchev."[66] It's not sure if he deliberately omitted the
Cuban missile crisis when he made the comparison. Richard Neustadt submitted
his findings on the affair in the fall of 1963. President Kennedy read the full 130-
page analysis over the weekend of November 16–17, as he prepared to leave for
campaign trips in Florida and Texas. The First Lady recalled him saying ruefully of
the task, "If you want to know what my life is like, read this." It was the only government paper he ever gave her. An annotated copy of the report—suggesting it might
be sent on as a Christmas gift to his good friend Macmillan—was found on top of
the files in Kennedy's briefcase following his assassination.

At the same time as they were trying to limit the prospects of mutually assured destruction, the Allies were also embroiled in a series of regional flashpoints around the world. Macmillan had long had his eye on the Congo. By December 1962, the factional rift between Cyrille Adoula and Moise Tshombe had taken on some of the same insoluble characteristics of the nineteenth-century Schleswig-Holstein question. Since Khrushchev had declared the Congo to be a haven of "Western colonialists" whom the Soviet Union "would struggle against with all its means,"[67] it became another East-West ideological battleground.

Just as Macmillan prepared to fly to Nassau to meet Kennedy, the House of Commons began a spirited debate on which of the two rival Congolese chiefs—separated, and sometimes inflamed, by the UN troops in their midst—to back. On December 13, David Bruce cabled to the State Department that Macmillan had "badly misjudged the temper of backbench opinion" on the issue and could be expected to request American help in securing another ceasefire.[68] Kennedy was unmoved. The best he would offer was to temporarily stay his hand before endorsing any UN military action to remove Tshombe. Kennedy spoke of this in terms of a grand strategic imperative to prevent Khrushchev from moving in. Macmillan, in his cool and cynical way, detected a more narrowly commercial motive. On November 27, he recorded wearily that the Congolese saga was "boiling up again. . . . I suspect the American copper interests in all this. They are equally jealous of Union Miniere and of the Northern Rhodesian copper companies."[69] A little over a month later, Tshombe was finally driven into exile in Spain, where he continued to blame Kennedy and the CIA for his fall. Adoula remained in power until June 1964, when a US-sponsored coup in turn removed him. Macmillan would later recall that "Kennedy and I, we drove the Russians out [of the Congo]," but it would be wrong to portray the affair as a shining triumph of concerted Anglo-American policy.[70] A more measured conclusion is that the Allies had reached broadly the same desired end in the Congo—the exclusion of the Russians—by separate and, at times, diametrically opposite means. At one point, Kennedy had been moved to summon David Ormsby-Gore to "chew him out" over Macmillan's erratic conduct.[71] In later years, the Americans expressed their support for the single-party rule of Joseph Mobutu, which lasted for over three decades, and the Russians declared a complete lack of interest in the whole area.

But clearly the one part of the global chessboard where a knight's move could produce a decisive result in 1963 lay in some form of long-overdue check on the runaway arms race. Neither Kennedy nor Macmillan could have known that New Year's that they were both already entering the final months of their terms in office. But the Cuban crisis appears to have made each man think more deeply about his responsibility for leaving the world a marginally safer place for his successors. Kennedy was so determined to reach an arms-control agreement that in December 1962, without telling Macmillan, he sent Khrushchev a message to allay any fears the Russian might have had about the recent Polaris agreement. The US goal "in making these missiles available [is] to prevent, or at least delay, the development of national nuclear capabilities," he wrote. This might have surprised Macmillan. Kennedy went on to assure Khrushchev that any future arms-limitation treaty "would take priority over any such agreements" as he had made with the British.[72] It was another case of the Allies stumbling along their own separate routes to the same destination.

Macmillan reaffirmed his belief, really the bedrock of his whole foreign policy, that without a verifiable nuclear-weapons agreement there would be an escalated arms race, and that in that event mankind was doomed.[73] Ultimately, none of the compelling strategic arguments for a national deterrent could avail against that hard truth. Macmillan's lifelong instinct whenever a significant international issue arose was to convene another conference. In March 1963, he was again writing to Kennedy to propose that the two of them meet Khrushchev at a new summit in Geneva. "I am sorry to inflict so long a letter on you," he wrote at the end of a typically detailed critique of Western nuclear options, "but I feel this very deep personal obligation upon me."[74]

Kennedy shared Macmillan's long-term philosophy about the desirability of eliminating weapons of mass destruction. But he faced an uphill battle to sell any meaningful arms agreement in Congress. In particular, the president's advisers warned him that the Senate would be unlikely to ratify a test-ban treaty without a built-in minimum of seven or eight annual inspections, more than twice the number Khrushchev had offered. American faith in essential Soviet goodwill in the missile arena was not at an all-time high in early 1963. While Kennedy patiently sought both to build a consensus on the Hill and to make oblique promises to Moscow about inspections, Macmillan renewed—or never abandoned—his own dogged pursuit of a conference. McGeorge Bundy, generally an admirer of the premier's tactical acumen, later recalled that this particular initiative had been poorly received in the White House. "We always had a row with the British on that question," Bundy noted. "The PM said he would go to a summit either if we were making progress or if we weren't, and the President's view was we'd go only if we were. We had several messages back and forth, in which we made it clear to old Harold that we were not pinned to his view of when a summit would be helpful."[75]

The climax of the nuclear-arms negotiations, as well as the process itself, bears out the authentic stamp of Kennedy and Macmillan as politicians. For all his air of languid detachment, it was the Victorian-born Englishman who wore his heart on his sleeve more often than the brash young American. Perhaps he thought he had less time available to him. While Kennedy favored the covert exercise of power (with occasional un-presidential eruptions of temper), "old Harold," though capable of an impressive disdain, was always the more likely of the two to work himself up into a nervous state that found expression in outbursts of rage, recrimination, or even despair.[76] It would be hard to imagine Kennedy putting his name to the sort of near-hysterical telegram Macmillan fired off on the subject of Hawk missiles in August 1962, or denigrating a fellow ally like de Gaulle to quite the extent the supposedly "unflappable" PM did. Flying home from the Bermuda conference after discussing the prospect of renewed nuclear testing, Macmillan had lapsed into a state of acute nervous depression and taken to his bed for much of the next week. A political colleague who drove to see him at Birch Grove recalled that for most of the day he "padded mournfully around the house, looking as though his pet dog had just been run over." But there again, it was Macmillan who was playing for the higher stakes in the relationship. With Polaris, he had cloaked British nuclear vulnerability by aligning with American interests and inadvertently lost his place in Europe as a partial result. Kennedy, of course, was also committed to the Atlantic partnership for a variety of strategic, political, and even sentimental reasons. But it's difficult to believe that he invested quite the same degree of personal intensity in the alliance as Macmillan. On January 19, 1963, in the course of a hotline conversation, the two men had an exchange that established for all time their profound, long-running, and yet on occasion comically mismatched story.

> *Macmillan:* I say, did you enjoy Nassau? I loved it, didn't you? I thought it was awfully good.
> *Kennedy:* Oh, which is that?

Macmillan: The Nassau meeting.

Kennedy: Oh, yes—very good, very good.[77]

Once again, it was Macmillan metaphorically doing the kissing, and Kennedy offering his cheek.

9
THE MEN WHO SAVED THE WORLD

Macmillan did not conceal his anger about France's treatment of Britain over the Common Market. In public, he said: "What has happened has revealed a division. The French and their government are looking backwards. They seem to think that one nation can dominate Europe and, equally wrong, that Europe can or ought to stand alone."[1] When Labour MP David Ginsburg asked him in the Commons "if he will now take the initiative to convene a summit conference covering economic and political affairs between himself [and] President de Gaulle," the PM replied, "No, Sir."[2] In private, Macmillan dropped even the pretense of civility. There was a flaw in the French character, he told one senior naval visitor to Birch Grove. "Good at cooking and sex," they were otherwise not greatly gifted.[3] He wrote in his diary that France "is trying to *dominate* Europe," and he described Alain Peyrefitte, their information minister, as "the new Goebbels."[4] Time and again, Macmillan portrayed de Gaulle as a dangerous megalomaniac, actuated by a strange mixture of excessive pride and unspoken shame at France's wartime record. What was more, to the fastidious Englishman, he had highly suspect manners. In December 1962, at Rambouillet, Macmillan and the other Anglo-French delegates had begun their meeting with a pheasant shoot in the château grounds. De Gaulle himself did not participate but stood behind his guests, keeping up a sardonic commentary each time they missed their target. Macmillan was later presented with a bill from the French government for his cartridges. It was not the only such apparent breach of etiquette to rankle him. Macmillan's naval visitor remembered him speaking of de Gaulle's veto not so much in political terms but as an "appalling betrayal of hospitality, freely accepted." In stating—and restating—his views on the subject, the PM expressed only one fundamental judgment.

"The fellow's been to my house," he repeated. "To *my house*."[5]

Nor was Macmillan happy with the broader strategic results of de Gaulle's treacherous—or, at best, narrowly pragmatic—decision. Speaking in cabinet on January 29, 1963, the PM was worried about the consequences for the Western alliance. "The [General's] ambition to impose French domination on Europe to the exclusion of Anglo-Saxon influence might develop rapidly, and in a manner which would impose new strains on NATO," he said. "It would be necessary to give very careful consideration, in consultation with our allies, to the course we should adopt in such circumstances."[6] The new cabinet secretary's shorthand notes of an Admiralty House meeting later that afternoon record Macmillan saying of the French veto:

> [A] grave situation. Reveals de G's long-term intentions. Reversion to pre-war Europe, except that de G hasn't Hitler's strength. He may just try to extrude U.S. and U.K. from Europe, and to do a deal with Soviet Union. Therefore we must keep in touch with our friends in Europe and with U.S.[7]

At least for now, it was the end of Macmillan's "Grand Design" for a united Europe working hand in glove with the Americans to stem the communist tide. All was in disarray. Macmillan wrote disconsolately to Kennedy, "Dear Friend . . . It is clear to me that de Gaulle, whose people are now putting out a most contradictory and really malicious series of statements on every sort of issue, is determined to get his way if he possibly can."[8]

On January 30, the president wrote back for the record:

> Dear Prime Minister,
>
> I am sure that you realize how sorry I am about the great disappointment you have suffered in recent days. My regret is compounded by my realization that part of your difficulties resulted from your country's historic association with the United States, and your own strong support of this alliance. I count on working closely with you in the coming days.
>
> John F. Kennedy.[9]

Several of the president's men were as dismayed as Macmillan was at the outcome, precisely because it meant their having to attune American policy to a Great Britain that was semidetached from the rest of Europe. McNamara had satisfied himself that the idea of an independent British nuclear deterrent was an expensive farce, and Rusk had satisfied himself of the policy advantages of moving away from a "special relationship" and toward a monolithic "system of . . . strict non-favoritism" to America's NATO allies. Only Kennedy himself consistently saw the twin Atlantic partners as bound together by more powerful ties of shared history and friendship.

In a private message to Macmillan, Kennedy wrote:

> You will know without my saying so that we are with you, in feeling and in purpose, in this time of de Gaulle's great effort to test the chances for his dream world. Neither of us must forget for a moment that reality is what rules, and the central reality is that he is wrong. . . . We are doing everything we can at this end, as our people will be telling yours. And if this is an unmentionable special relationship, so much the better.[10]

Kennedy's words summarize his partnership with Macmillan, where the PM's main role was to provide the scholarly rationale for the exercise of blunt American power. There were mutual advantages to diplomacy at the very top level that were sometimes lost in the corridors of each man's civil service. On April 13, 1963, Macmillan wrote of the Allies' latest test-ban proposal: "We are so nearly agreed that I would like to [settle] it with the President while he is at Palm Beach for the Easter holiday, and before the rats get at it."[11] Kennedy always seemed to enjoy his allies' faint patrician air of bumbling and self-deprecation more than an unsentimental technocrat like McNamara did. The president wrote a long Christmas letter in 1962 to Macmillan's Foreign Secretary, the fourteenth Earl of Home, who even more than his fellow Old Etonian boss seemed to epitomize the kind of graceful, slightly sleepy British aristocrat as much taken with the gentlemanly pursuits of hunting, shooting, and fishing as with the vulgarities of policy, and who commanded a natural calm and authority without any apparent exertion on his part. This was Kennedy's kind of public official. "Thank you very much for sending us your [letter] and your nice picture of the White House," Lord Home wrote back on January 7, 1963. "I wish we were still at our meeting in the Bahamas, as we are snowed in. Ever your friend, Alec."[12]

In the House of Commons, Macmillan continued to raise the hackles of skeptical MPs worried about the various costs and risks of that same conference. On February 28, Philip Noel-Baker of the Labour Party, a former Nobel Peace Prize winner, asked him, "What scientific advice [have you] received about the heightened danger of accidental nuclear war?" Macmillan took the question in its broader sense and talked about the tragedy of August 1914—"I have always thought this might not have happened if there had been modern methods of communication and flight, and so on," he said. Pressed on the specific matter of Polaris, he "on the whole discounted" the threat of a chain reaction of events brought about "by some man who was mad, or through some mistake made by an officer. We have provided for the prevention of that by every human means possible." It was a case of life imitating art, because *Dr. Strangelove* was then being filmed just a few miles away at Shepperton. The MP and gossip columnist Tom Driberg was determined to pin Macmillan down on what he called the "great paradox" of the Atlantic alliance. "When the prime minister says that the existence of [Polaris] is itself a deterrent against accidental nuclear war, can he explain how nuclear war could happen, by accident or otherwise, if there were not any nuclear weapons?"[13] The accidental sinking in April of an American Polaris submarine in the North Atlantic gave rise to another round of parliamentary attacks on Western nuclear strategy.[14]

By early 1963, several Conservative MPs had begun to wonder about their party's election prospects as against those of Labour under their newly installed leader, forty-six-year-old Harold Wilson. For a few, this even meant the removal of Macmillan. As the economic situation went from bad to worse, the few increased in number. By February 17, Macmillan was complaining in his diary about the part played by his troublesome brother-in-law. "I hear that a new Tory group called the Monday Club, which has been founded by Lord Salisbury and others of the right wing, [is] now demanding my resignation." The opposition, he admitted, "is reaching quite formidable dimensions. 'Macmillan must go' is the cry. . . . Of course, there's something in it. We have had a run of bad luck. Once this starts, everything seems to go wrong."[15]

Right up to the end, none of the State Department profiles prepared for Kennedy, with the exception of those at the nadir of the Profumo affair, ever spoke of there being a serious leadership crisis in Britain. One of the last reports he read from David Bruce insisted that the general mood was "apathetic, rather than rebellious." Macmillan was an increasingly good example of something often unrecognized in America, that an elected leader apparently untainted by personal scandal can be abruptly sacked by his colleagues for tactical reasons. In late July 1963, Kennedy told Macmillan that he had made a "wonderfully successful" contribution to world peace, and the president added how much he looked forward to their continuing partnership. There's no evidence he was aware that there was anything more than muttered criticism of his old friend from behind his own party lines.

On January 23, 1963, another of Britain's cyclical security scandals erupted, placing further strain on the Atlantic alliance at a departmental level. This was the defection to Moscow (not actually confirmed until July 1) of Kim Philby, formerly head of the branch of MI6 charged with investigating communist activity in the West, and more recently a news correspondent in Beirut. Twelve years earlier, he had tipped off two British double agents, Guy Burgess and Donald Maclean, shortly before their intended arrest by the security forces. In November 1955, Macmillan, as Foreign Secretary, had in good conscience told the Commons, "I have no reason to conclude that Mr. Philby has at any time betrayed the interests of his country, or to identify him with the so-said 'Third Man', if indeed there was one."[16] American interest in the case was further stoked by the fact that Philby had served from 1949 to 1951 as first secretary at the British embassy in Washington, effectively making him his country's intelligence representative to the United States. This had been an era of almost-promiscuous Western trafficking of nuclear secrets to the Soviet Union. Kennedy received a full CIA briefing on Philby in March 1963, although he tactfully appears to have said nothing directly on the subject to Macmillan.

While Kennedy seems to have reacted with indifference, Macmillan was apoplectic. Apart from the "almost historic" treachery of Philby, the humiliation inflicted on Britain's secret world by the so-called Cambridge Spy Ring would continue when a "fourth" and a "fifth" man both emerged later. In fact there seemed to be no end to the peculiar British genius for security flaps, often with a sexual subplot. Late in 1962, a senior civil servant named Barbara Fell was sentenced to two years' imprisonment for passing information to her young Yugoslav lover, who was in the pay of the KGB. The following July, Macmillan wrote in his diary of "the warning we had of a possible traitor—'Peters'—at the top of MI5. He'd been spotted wandering round the loos in the park. . . . He seemed to be somewhat unhinged."[17] "Peters" was in fact no less than the agency's deputy director general, Graham Mitchell, who elected to take early retirement as a result of the investigation. Mitchell's superior at MI5, Roger Hollis, himself came under suspicion as a Soviet mole, although a subsequent cabinet inquiry conducted by Lord Trend could neither deny nor confirm the allegations.

But much more important than the vagaries of British security was the need
to reach some form of accommodation with the Russians on nuclear tests. Both
Macmillan and Kennedy became increasingly convinced that taking at least this
first step in curbing the arms race would stand as their one true legacy. "Dear
Friend," the PM cabled on March 8, "I have now had a talk with David Bruce on his
return. . . . I was very struck by his insistence that you had now come to feel even
more strongly than before that cooperation and consultation between us on [arms
talks] was essential. You know how much I share this view."[18]

As usual, Macmillan was propelled by a mixture of high-minded principle and
low political calculation. On the loftier level, he saw the need to "break the dark
clouds cast by nuclear armaments . . . which could prove the terrible prelude to
the Third World War."[19] More fundamentally, he worried about what sort of global
adventure Khrushchev might embark on next, comparing him in his diary to Hitler.
It was vital for the nuclear powers to move rapidly toward some form of mutual
arms limitation while they still could. He wired Kennedy again on March 16:

> Dear Friend,
>
> Mr. Khrushchev, like an old elephant, has a very tenacious memory. For
> example, in conversation in Moscow in 1959, when this matter was first under
> discussion, I casually mentioned various figures for annual inspections, from
> twelve down to three, as an illustration of my general argument in favour of a
> test agreement. Since then he has affected to regard this chance observation as a
> substantive proposal by the British government. . . .
>
> What, then, are we to do? Of course, there are very strong arguments for
> doing nothing. Strong logical arguments, strong political arguments. But this is
> not the spirit in which you, who carry the largest responsibility, before God and
> men, have faced your duty, nor that in which I have tried to do the same. I have
> a feeling that the test ban is the most important step that we can take towards
> unraveling this frightful tangle of fear and suspicion in East/West relations—
> important in itself and all the more important for what may flow from it.[20]

Kennedy replied with the pragmatic suggestion that the two of them send a
joint letter on the subject to Khrushchev. He attached a draft. The old editor in
Macmillan seized eagerly on the already busily detailed text with a whole series of
proposed cuts and amendments. "We have been considering leaving out the words

'Or information' in the fifth sentence of the fourth paragraph. . . . We suggest that that sentence should come out, and the word 'Power' should be substituted for the word 'Weapons' in the preceding line. . . . By using a non-technical term, we think we could avoid the difficulty which your proposed phrasing might we fear raise."[21] Kennedy gave as good as he got in the course of a cable on April 7, which evinced all the caution customary when dealing with Nikita Khrushchev in the realm of nuclear weapons. It was more than ever like some form of advanced college tutorial, or what one official termed an "intellectual ping-pong game." Four days later, Kennedy picked up the hotline, telling Macmillan he had read his latest draft and mentioning that "I've only really got one change, and that would be on page five on the last version you sent me, where the words go, 'If we could make progress here, we might be able to envisage a meeting.'"[22] Kennedy still retained his misgivings about being seen to reward Khrushchev with a great conference. The full 1,200-word text finally went off to the Kremlin on April 15. Khrushchev was in seclusion in his Lenin Hills dacha, and it was another nine days before the letter was delivered. After reviewing the annual military parade in Red Square, he replied on May 8—upset, once again, by the vexed issue of inspections.

Meanwhile, Macmillan continued to promote the benefits of a closer Western alliance, both as it applied to Moscow and to secondary theaters like the Congo. His aim was to achieve what he called "equivalence" of policy, not identical, but parallel, to that of Washington. "The more I think of it, the more constructive I believe our Nassau declaration was," he told Kennedy. "In whatever form our plans ultimately emerge, the spirit in which they were launched has undoubtedly been more and more understood as the weeks have passed."[23] Others, on both the right and the left, remained to be convinced. In the Commons, the Labour MP (and future defence secretary) Denis Healey wanted Macmillan to make a statement about the "unpublished minutes and secret pledges made at Nassau," which seemed unlikely to happen. Emrys Hughes was concerned about costs. "Will the prime minister tell us whether the US will make any contribution to the very large sum of £25 million which is to be spent on a Polaris base in Scotland, when the people of Scotland are not to be given enough money for education, for roads and for essential social services?"[24] "Bobbety" Salisbury threw a tantrum and said it was all a sellout to Washington.

Whether in dealing with the Kremlin or supplying him with long-range missiles, Macmillan knew he couldn't do without Kennedy in his life. As a result, there was sometimes a supplicant note under the professed regard and warmth. Macmillan's letters frequently use the words *Please*, *It would be of assistance*, and *I am much obliged to you*. Kennedy's tend more to the declarative statement. On May 29, Macmillan again sent profuse birthday greetings across the Atlantic, adding that he had made inquiries into the source of a leak to Henry Brandon of the *Sunday Times*. In the light of the recent security lapses, this evidently touched a nerve. "I am deeply distressed to find [the leak] comes from our end," he wrote. "I cannot understand how this can have happened. . . . I send you my deepest apologies."[25] Kennedy was his usual gracious self but by then may have already begun to contemplate the prospect of a post-Macmillan Britain. On March 27, David Bruce had cabled back his impressions of the new Labour front bench. "They are a lively lot," he wrote, "exuding confidence, contemptuous of the present government, convinced of their ability, if elected, to revive the British economy and perform other near miracles. . . . The thirst for power has already brought about cohesion in their ranks. Former opponents of Harold Wilson now proclaim him peerless. He will, I believe, pursue a generally pro-American line."[26] Without entering into a debate about the validity of psychohistory, it seems fair to say that Kennedy had the sort of mind that enabled him to remain commendably loyal to a person while still allowing the possibility (sometimes the reality) of entering into relations with a rival candidate for his affections. Again, it was essentially a case of the suitor and his quarry. When, in the Commons, Emrys Hughes accused Macmillan of "just acting as a postman" for Kennedy, the barb, though laughed off, must have stung.

Despite what the critics thought of him, in a whole range of other global arenas, Macmillan was the undoubted master of Western strategy. The long and apparently insoluble problem of Indo-Pakistani relations, for example, rumbled on through 1963. Macmillan, who was intimately familiar with the whole history of British colonial rule on the subcontinent, pursued the modest goal of achieving "a measure of mutual respect and confidence" by brokering talks between the rival states. Kennedy perhaps complicated these by announcing his own wish to provide fighter jets on an exclusive basis to India. Macmillan thought him "obsessed with [his] anxiety about the aggressive intentions of 'Red' China"[27] and suggested that arming only one of the neighboring parties in the affair might be poorly received by the other. There was also the perennial British concern about costs. "As you know," Macmillan cabled Kennedy on May 15, "we have already committed £21 million to Indian defence, [and] we have a heavy burden in Malaysia which so far we have had to bear on our own. Therefore any further [contribution] will have to be pretty limited."[28]

The latest talks between India and Pakistan broke down in acrimony the following day. Macmillan eventually agreed to a deal for Britain, the United States, and Australia to provide the Delhi government with a modest number of aircraft "for training purposes." (Similar thinking affected the now steadily growing pressure for more American "advisers" in Vietnam.) Bar the arms talks, no other single foreign-policy issue occupied as much of the Allies' executive time in mid-1963 as the security of this remote former outpost of the British Empire. Macmillan later gave the view that Kennedy was "more nervous" than he was about a possible Chinese incursion in the area. In his donnish way, he went on to compare "British scepticism with American alarm. . . . Chinese expansionist policies were believed to be responsible for all the troubles in South-east Asia. It was this fundamental mistake which later led the United States into so many years of trouble."[29] While never saying "I told you so," there was a clear note of reproach in Macmillan's analysis of how an essentially tribal conflict had disastrously come to be "Americanized" into the Vietnam War. "Subsequent events," he wrote in 1973, "have tragically confirmed [my] judgement."

Some of this same central focus on anticommunism, the Chinese peril in particular, also tinged Kennedy's policy on Laos. Following a lull in the late winter of 1963, the situation there had again deteriorated into a three-way internecine war between, broadly, the right wing, the Pathet Lao insurgents, and the neutrals. A peacekeeping control commission only added to the confusion when the Polish contingent began sniping, literally, at the Canadians. There were frequent bomb outrages and assassinations in Vientiane, the region's administrative capital. Here, Macmillan felt, it was a case of the United States holding Moscow rather than Beijing principally responsible for promoting civil war. At an Easter meeting in Admiralty House with Averell Harriman and other State Department officials, "the PM pointed out that we [the Allies] were apt to assume greater control by the Soviets of other communists than they actually had."[30] As usual, Macmillan wanted the rival factions to sit down around the conference table. Kennedy wanted to encourage the belief that America *might* intervene militarily. But not quite yet. He "wished to retain the element of reversibility in all actions," he told his National Security Council. "There [would be] no public announcement of landings until after he had ordered such landings."[31] Meanwhile, Macmillan asked Home to try and interest the Soviet government in cosponsoring a general ceasefire, which duly went into effect on April 21.

Doubtless having regard to the recent fragile state of relations in the area, and also to the fact that Khrushchev remained keen to exploit any opening he could, Macmillan had been pressing for, first, talks, and then the establishment of an eleven-state Malaysia federation as a bulwark against communist ambitions. Although this strategy had kept the peace, there were mounting problems with President Achmed Sukarno of Indonesia. A visit by Sukarno to London in early 1963 was not judged a success by his hosts. According to a cable David Bruce sent the State Department on January 15, "I do not think it exaggerated to say Sukarno is regarded here as a bombastic rabble-rouser, an over-heated jungle Hitler, whose greed for political power is as insatiable as his private appetites. The impression he created generally during his visit was that he was a strutting, arrogant brothel crawler, surrounded by pimps, panders [sic] and sycophants, ambivalent between democracy and communism, unstable in character . . . madly ambitious, fickle, vain."[32]

In a reversal of their normal roles, Macmillan now wanted Sukarno out of the picture, while Kennedy thought "a meeting . . . or territorial summit of some kind" would suffice. The PM gloomily saw Indonesia as an example of rank Soviet meddling, aided and abetted by a tin-pot dictator "whose dogs eat better than the vast number of his people do."[33] The president apparently believed that Sukarno, for all his foibles, still provided the best safeguard for American oil interests in the region. In September 1963, Macmillan was moved to cable Kennedy his concern that "there is . . . bound to be a most dangerous and unpleasant conflict, unless Sukarno can be stopped" and appealed for "our two countries to stand together at this moment, in all respects." Kennedy evidently failed to see it in such stark terms, because Macmillan recorded his reply as "not altogether satisfactory." For once, British anxieties perhaps better suited the needs of the situation than American restraint. Sukarno went on to take an ever more stridently anti-Western line while warmly welcoming in Soviet scientific and trade advisers. In time, Kennedy's successor in office withdrew American economic support to Indonesia. "Go to hell with your aid," Sukarno told him. As a result of printing money to finance its ambitious defense program, including research into a nuclear bomb, Indonesia suffered an inflation rate of 600 percent in 1963–64. Sukarno was overthrown by a coup in

March 1967. He died three years later—either of kidney failure or, some insist, of CIA-induced blood poisoning—aged sixty-nine.

In one other small but touching instance of Britain asserting itself in the Atlantic relationship, Macmillan's diary recorded:

> Another long talk [with Kennedy] on the telephone last night. The new machine is (*a*) better—you talk as on an ordinary phone; (*b*) safer—it would take ninety years to break the code; (*c*) British. A score for us![34]

It was against this backdrop that the Allies again turned to the chronic problem of British Guiana—like Macmillan's periodic attacks of melancholia, one of those endlessly recycled crises that seemed to be finally cured, only to recur with greater intensity. The ambivalence of Cheddi Jagan's regime toward the West had recently met with a fresh outbreak of civil disorder. "Here we are in a great mess," Macmillan glumly told Kennedy in May 1963. "The situation gets worse and worse. The strike continues. Industry is at a standstill, and food is running out. Yet the [government] is not overthrown." (He was referring to Georgetown, not to London.)[35] Among the PM's options was to "effect the necessary change" in the Guyanese regime, or, alternately, "We could make the wretched place independent and get rid of all our obligations. This would be fine from our point of view, but not so good from yours. It would be fine for us because colonialism is unpopular even in your country, but it would be bad from the larger point of view which we share."

In a switch of the normal American line on British imperial rule, here Kennedy wanted to let "London drift on in its present course." The likelihood of a Labour government under Harold Wilson granting immediate independence to Jagan and his crew seems to have concentrated minds in both the White House and the State Department. In late June, Dean Rusk announced in his inscrutable way that "it was not an interest in the future of the colony, per se, but the uncertainty surrounding British Guiana's direction [that] held potentially damaging ramifications for the broader imperative of maintaining a close and cordial Anglo-American relationship."[36] More prosaically, Macmillan was again worried about costs. "It would be no good our holding the baby for several years, and attracting all the criticism and hostility which the resumption of colonial rule would arouse," he told Kennedy, "unless there were a reasonable prospect of putting the country on its feet economically. The scale of financial aid involved would, frankly, be beyond our resources."[37]

If this was a hint, it fell on deaf ears. Kennedy responded by inviting David Ormsby-Gore to join him for a weekend at Hyannis Port, where, among other things, he told him he wanted "this shitstorm in Guiana" to be on the agenda in his forthcoming talks with Macmillan.[38] Clutching hard at the remnants of his bonhomie, the PM in turn sent a "Dear Friend" cable informing the president that he was under "a misunderstanding [about] the practicalities" of imposed British overseas rule.[39] On June 30, Kennedy would sit down across a table from Macmillan at Birch Grove and again exchange views on this eternally troubled colony and its apparently disturbing association to Cuba. The State Department note of the meeting concludes: "The President said he agreed with the analysis of all the difficulties, but that these still paled in comparison with the prospect of the establishment of a communist regime in Latin America."[40] At that, Macmillan adopted his fallback position and called for an international conference.

Meanwhile, Kennedy and Macmillan had patiently chipped away throughout the spring at Khrushchev's seemingly inexhaustible fund of objections on the subject to salvage the nuclear test-ban talks. On May 29, Philip de Zulueta cabled McGeorge Bundy with the PM's latest proposals for another joint message to the Kremlin. But even in the charged atmosphere of nearly daily high-level exchanges between London, Washington, and Moscow, Macmillan was still able to get away on a golfing holiday for his wife and himself in Scotland. "It may be difficult to agree further amendments," de Zulueta wired. "The PM leaves at 6.15 PM our time on May 30, and will thereafter be away for about ten days."[41]

In the end, Khrushchev gave Kennedy enough encouragement in order for him to deliver a landmark speech at the American University in Washington on June 10, which took the theme of mutual tolerance between East and West. The president's remarks contained some sharply turned phrases: "Peace need not be impracticable, and war need not be inevitable," he declared. But Kennedy moved beyond rhetoric, announcing that the United States would forgo any future over-ground tests as long as the Soviets did. The timing of what became known as the "peace speech" was governed less by a sudden outbreak of goodwill and more by a last-ditch Allied attempt to appeal to Khrushchev's better instincts just ahead of a Sino-Soviet meeting scheduled to begin on July 5. If the hope had been to preempt any fraternal agreement Beijing might make with Moscow, the Western leaders would have been gratified by the result. One Chinese delegate to the talks expressed outrage at the continuing denigration of Stalin by the current Soviet leadership—"'Murderer', 'criminal', 'bandit', 'fool', 'shit', 'idiot'—all these curses and swear words," he remarked, "came from the mouth of Comrade N. S. Khrushchev." How was it that so many Communists all round the world had for so long considered "some sort of shit" to be their leader? Was Khrushchev himself, he inquired, "completely clean"?[42]

By now, Macmillan was embroiled in a domestic political crisis that threatened his survival as PM, and one that had all the ingredients of a classic British scandal—sex, espionage, and a possible connection to the highest rungs of the ruling establishment. In miniature, it centered on the balding but puckish figure of forty-eight-year-old John Profumo, the British secretary of state for war. In July 1961, Profumo had attended a party given by the osteopath Stephen Ward—the would-be intermediary at the time of the Cuban missile crisis—at Cliveden, the country estate where Ward rented a summer cottage. At some point, they had walked out to the swimming pool and there encountered an aspiring actress named Christine Keeler, a striking brunette, and her equally free-spirited blonde friend, Mandy Rice-Davies, a dancer and showgirl. Both women were, as the jargon of the day had it, of doubtful reputation. Keeler, who emerged nude from the pool to demurely shake Profumo's hand, then happened to be in a relationship with Yevgeni Ivanov, the Soviet naval attaché who would also go on to offer his negotiating services at the time of the Cuban crisis. Somehow inevitably, Keeler had in turn begun an affair with Profumo, which meant that she was sleeping both with the British war minister and with an alleged Russian spy, thus bringing a national-security dimension to the proceedings.

Keeler herself (who has been sometimes known to exaggerate) later claimed that Ward, too, had wanted her to extract British nuclear secrets, which he would then pass to Moscow, although other well-qualified parties doubt whether his interests extended far beyond acting as a ringmaster to the various liaisons—or, as he put it, "the fuckfest breaking out on all sides" that heady summer.

In March 1963, the story took on a new layer of complexity when a Labour MP named George Wigg—one of those both sinister and faintly comic figures who lurks on the edges of the "intelligence community," with the hooded eyes and sagging jowls of a particularly dilapidated bloodhound—raised the matter in the Commons. Profumo, after first indignantly defending his honor, then admitted that perhaps he had slept with Keeler after all, and that he was resigning his ministerial portfolio with immediate effect. He got a "Dear Profumo" letter back from Macmillan, accepting his decision with alacrity.[43]

The British press was not slow to build the affair into a cause célèbre that linked not only the Tory government but also the ruling elite as a whole to an underworld of prostitutes, pimps, spies, topless go-go dancers, and exotic household practices. One widely circulated story was said to involve an eminent politician who had waited on a table at a fashionable London dinner party naked, masked, and wearing a placard that read, "If my services don't please you, whip me"—if true, a sorry lapse from the late-Victorian public etiquette Macmillan himself seemed to embody. ("Of course," the PM wrote in his diary, "all these people move in a raffish, theatrical, bohemian society where no one really knows anyone and everyone's 'darling'.")[44] The premier saw the outbreak of the worst British political scandal of the postwar era as no reason to interrupt his extended golfing and shooting holiday in Scotland, which divided commentators between those who applauded his sang-froid and others who thought it a show of detachment too far.

Although Macmillan's government survived Profumo, it never quite recovered its former aura of respectability. A judicial report (which, unusual for a Crown publication, boasted chapter titles such as "The Slashing and the Shooting," "The Headless Man," and "He's a Liar"), marked the official end of the affair, though its longer-term consequences included a steady erosion of the widespread social deference previously largely undisturbed since the age of Prime Minister Gladstone. As a result, certain newspapers were able to dispense with their former air of fusty servility and replace it with that unique blend of moral indignation, gossip, and bare breasts that remains the popular template today. It's thus been called the ignition point of the United Kingdom's "modernization crisis." At one point while he was simultaneously negotiating a test-ban treaty with Kennedy and Khrushchev, Macmillan's personal approval rating fell to a figure of minus seventeen before recovering to only minus five. A Gallup poll in June 1963 showed 71 percent of voters wanting either the PM's resignation or an immediate election. In late July, Stephen Ward—a scapegoat, some felt, for his more aristocratic friends—appeared on trial at the Old Bailey on a variety of morals charges. Following a harsh attack on his character in the prosecution's closing speech, Ward went home to his flat and took a fatal overdose of sleeping pills. His suicide note read, "I am sorry to disappoint the vultures."[45]

Although the Profumo scandal was a peculiarly British affair, there was a strong transatlantic dimension to it. As a senator, Kennedy had slept with one Suzy Chang, a New York prostitute who had moved to London and was part of the Ward vice— or "V-girl"—ring. In June 1963, Chang was said to be anxious to sell her story of nights with a "high-elected US official" to the *New York Journal-American*. According to the journalist Seymour Hersh, Robert Kennedy used his considerable influence with the Hearst family, who owned the *Journal-American*, to kill the story.[46]

Then there was the exotic figure of Thomas Corbally, a New Jersey businessman, private investigator, and socialite who was living in London in 1963. Said to be in his early thirties, but actually born in 1921, the medallion-wearing Corbally also moved in Stephen Ward's circle—the two of them "ran sex orgies" from a Mayfair hotel room, so the FBI director J. Edgar Hoover advised his agents. By January of that year, Macmillan had heard the rumors about Profumo and Keeler, although his own advisers (either because they were involved themselves or to avoid a scandal) added little of substance. For independent information, the PM turned to David Bruce, the American ambassador, to make discreet inquiries. Bruce went to Corbally, who arranged for the ambassador's secretary to meet Ward at lunch. Fortified by several bottles of wine, Ward gave them the whole story. On January 29, the US embassy drew up a note detailing the events of the nude swimming party and of Profumo's subsequent involvement with the mistress of an alleged Soviet agent. According to Corbally, the note was then passed to Macmillan, meaning that the PM would have known the essentials of the matter in early February, some three months earlier than he later claimed.[47]

Though Kennedy was silent in public, he lapped up the details of the scandal, apparently regarding it as an enjoyable romp in itself, and possibly also as a cautionary tale. "You've read about Profumo in the newspapers?" the president asked Martin Luther King Jr. at a White House meeting. "That's an example of friendship and loyalty carried too far. Macmillan is likely to lose his government because he has been loyal to his friend."[48] This was also the conclusion of many of the daily briefings Kennedy's national security team brought him during the height of the scandal. "[Macmillan's] days in office appear to be numbered; seems to have outlived his usefulness," the brief said on June 12, 1963. "Party expected to seek a new leader before summer is out" was the next day's verdict. "Atmosphere of tension and uncertainty as dynamic as Suez," Kennedy read on the 14th. "Several ministers on the point of resignation. Could start a landslide against Macmillan."[49] The president's friend Ben Bradlee wrote of him as having "devoured every word about the Profumo case; it combined so many of the things that interested him: low doings in high places, the British nobility, sex, and spying."[50] Kennedy may have enjoyed the more salacious aspects of the scandal, but he also insisted that a planned visit to Macmillan should go ahead as scheduled in late June—while asking that it take place at the PM's home in Sussex, rather than in London.

On June 20, the Labour MP Marcus Lipton[51] got up amid some uproar in the Commons and asked Macmillan: "Is the trip of the President still on? Doesn't the Prime Minister think that the President should be given the opportunity of exchanging views with a new Prime Minister, and not one under notice to quit?" At that, several members rose from their seats to wave their order papers at Macmillan and shout, "Out!"[52] When the vote of confidence came to be taken at the end of the Profumo debate, there were twenty-seven abstentions among the Conservative backbenchers. Worse was to come during the PM's irregular "meet the people" tours, where hecklers—hitherto unknown on such occasions—now shouted ribald remarks at him about call girls and spies. He seemed suddenly to be a wretched and visibly older figure.

Kennedy, too, was under intense domestic pressure. On the eve of the president's flight to Europe, David Ormsby-Gore cabled Macmillan: "He will be leaving behind a disquieting internal situation. . . . The Negro leaders are beginning to talk about large-scale civil disobedience on a nation-wide basis. . . . Moreover, the racial crisis is causing new difficulties for [Kennedy's] legislative program. . . . There has been a marked lack of Congressional enthusiasm for the President's journey."[53]

This was the atmosphere in which Kennedy set out for Europe on June 23, where he drew ecstatic (in Berlin, frenzied) crowds throughout Germany and Ireland before reaching the relative tranquility of Birch Grove on the drizzly Saturday evening of the 29th. The presidential helicopter was late in arriving; Kennedy had ordered a last-minute detour to Chatsworth House, Dorothy Macmillan's ancestral home, where he paid an impromptu visit to the grave of his sister Kathleen. He knelt and prayed there in the rain. Macmillan may have welcomed the delay, as he and his wife prepared for their guest amid the scenes of commotion (including that of Secret Service agents perched in trees) that marked the refurbishment of a large but ramshackle neo-Georgian English country home into suitable overnight lodgings for the leader of the free world and his entourage. The PM later wrote, with just a touch of hyperbole, of "Helicopters, great machines taking over the whole building. . . . Dean Rusk living in the lavatory . . . there were about 18 [presidential aides] there, twenty of them . . . and they did nothing. All we wanted to do was to have a talk."[54] Jacqueline Kennedy, who was pregnant, stayed behind in Washington, and local rumor insists that the president's advance men had thus arranged for him to be joined by a "typist" in his bedroom at Birch Grove. A source familiar with the domestic arrangements for the trip assured the author that he had come across Kennedy late that night dandling a young woman on his knee and giving renditions of his favorite Irish sea shanties, though this detail has proved impossible to corroborate.

The talks themselves were studiously informal—"more like a play than a grave conference," Macmillan felt—and largely successful, at least in agreeing to a joint Anglo-American position for test-ban negotiations with the Soviets. Having disposed of the set agenda in little over an hour together, Macmillan and Kennedy then called in their respective teams and went through the pantomime of pretending to have a detailed discussion on the future of NATO. This took place over the Birch Grove drawing-room table and, Macmillan thought, appealed to his guest's "puckish humour."[55] The president, who sat in a rocking chair, pretended to consider rival candidates to be the new supreme allied commander in Europe, and the PM in turn pretended that they should appoint a Russian to the post. A senior State Department official, not known for his light touch, helpfully observed that "that would require very considerable serious consideration, Prime Minister."

Unlike Kennedy's hosts elsewhere in Europe, Macmillan pulled out all the stops to give the impression of his staging a slightly eccentric house party rather than a great political rally—shuffling around in his ancient tweed suit, collar askew, and once inquiring of a blank-looking Dean Rusk and his team if they would like him to "be mother," by which it was explained he meant pouring their tea for them. It was later thought that in general the president entered more into the spirit of the visit than his senior officials did. There was a perpetual chorus of newspaper reporters, antinuclear demonstrators, and curious neighbors at the front gate. At one point, Dorothy Macmillan invited some local schoolboys into the house to meet the president, though a somewhat awkward moment ensued when Kennedy then genially asked them to sing him their school song. They had none. The president was driven to Mass early on Sunday morning and showed that he had not lost his acute feeling for the workings of British domestic politics. According to Philip de Zulueta, "He turned [to me] in the car, and enquired if a nuclear test-ban treaty would be of assistance to the Prime Minister. I said that it would . . . but that the fundamental point was the state of the economy. Kennedy quite agreed with this."[56]

Macmillan himself was far from insensitive to the potential political benefits of the trip, coming as it did in the immediate wake of Profumo. He showed the iron grip hidden beneath the dotty image when, at one point, he took Kennedy's scheduling secretary aside and advised him that it would be a poor idea for his chief to attempt to meet Harold Wilson. The PM's own Gallup poll rating rose gratifyingly in the first week of July, although the Conservatives as a whole remained 17 percent behind Labour. Macmillan thought it all a great success—"the reporters were admirably shepherded by Harold Evans on my side, and the President's Press Secretary, Pierre Salinger, equally efficient but operating upon somewhat cruder lines. . . . Far too soon, the visit drew to an end. Kennedy went, as he came, by helicopter"—to Macmillan, leaving an indelible image of his young friend ascending into a now-cloudless summer sky.[57] Having arrived at the exact moment his host had most needed a balm for his soul, the president's visit now struck Macmillan in quasi-spiritual terms. "He was gone," he wrote. "Alas, I was never to see him again. Before the leaves had turned and fallen, he was snatched by an assassin's bullet from the service of his own country and the whole world."[58]

On July 1, Kennedy wrote to say, "As I leave England I send you both my warmest thanks for your generous and open-hearted hospitality which made a memorable 24 hours at Birch Grove. I think we did good work together, and proved again the value of our informal meetings. Certainly we have never met in more agreeable or comfortable circumstances. I shall not forget. . . . With renewed thanks, JFK."[59]

Macmillan told the cabinet that day that it had been "an international meeting of a quite unique character because it could only have taken place between the British and American Governments. It is inconceivable that a series of agreements could have been reached on such a wide number of difficult topics, except by people who regarded themselves as partners and even as brothers."[60] He was equally effusive in his private note to Kennedy: "I felt [the talks] were a wonderful example of the way in which countries, and perhaps even more individuals, who trust each other can work rapidly and effectively together. . . . It has been a great pride to me to feel that in this we have been in part equal to the Churchill-Roosevelt relationship at the most critical moment of history."[61] Some of the gilt later flaked off the meeting when the two foreign ministers again clashed over British Guiana, and when McGeorge Bundy went on to make an unguarded remark to the effect that all the United States wanted out of Britain was "a government"—the cause of a hurried note from Kennedy to Macmillan. But these were more typical of the bureaucratic dealings between London and Washington than of the relationship at the top.

So happy was he with Kennedy's visit that Macmillan danced a little jig and triumphantly waved his stick in the air, much to the delight of the onlookers, when walking back to the house from seeing him off. With that one gesture, said a watching schoolboy, he "seemed to grow about ten years younger." Kennedy had very publicly demonstrated his commitment to his closest ally. What was more, he had pointedly avoided visiting France and de Gaulle. Jackie Kennedy had described her husband as "very depressed" at the prospect of Macmillan being brought down by the Profumo affair. "So Jack wanted to do something really nice—to [visit]," she said, "and also to give him a nice present, and to hell with the State Department budget."[62] Kennedy gave Dorothy Macmillan a gold dressing-table set, and he distributed signed photographs down the family. Perhaps relishing the symbolism of the gift, the prime minister in turn presented his guest with a pair of bone-china blue jays. The official catalog lists the birds as "perched on tree stumps, with backs glazed blue, breasts pink, staring fondly into each other's eyes." The owlish features of one of the pair subtly suggest Macmillan. The PM kept the president's rocking chair in his study for the rest of his life. On July 5, Macmillan wrote to the queen with much the same story—he and Kennedy understood each other, he told her. "We do not seek to take points against each other; we do not try to deceive each other, and if we disagree we do so openly and honourably. In other words, in our race against time both sides started on every issue at least three-quarters of the way down the course." Alluding to the "distasteful" Profumo saga, Macmillan concluded: "It has not been, as Your Majesty knows, an easy time for me, but I am hopeful that we shall end the summer in reasonably good condition, and that will give time for decisions to be taken calmly and sensibly in the autumn."[63] That same day, Kennedy cabled again from Washington to thank the Macmillans for their hospitality, and particularly to praise the quality of his three meals with them.[64] For the first time, he used the same "Dear Friend" prefix as Macmillan did.

=====

On July 15, an Anglo-American delegation arrived in Moscow to hold high-level talks on the test-ban problem. Averell Harriman led the US side; Lord Hailsham (the ex–Quintin Hogg), the British. The former was a seventy-one-year-old railroad heir and one-time secretary of commerce, whose negotiating skills had helped to broker the Lend-Lease exchanges of 1940–41. The latter was the fifty-five-year-old sometime–minister for science, currently with a roving brief in Britain's northeast, a stocky and pugnacious character perhaps chosen for the role less for his diplomatic finesse than in the hope that he might prove compatible with the more flamboyant of his Russian hosts. On July 23, Khrushchev himself unexpectedly appeared at the talks and ended up taking Hailsham and Harriman out to an extended dinner. After months of stonewalling about on-site inspections, the Soviet leader now not only wanted to conclude a comprehensive test ban, but he pressed his guests for a general "non-aggression pact" to be hammered out as well.[65] The British were willing enough, Macmillan signaled, but Kennedy preferred to take one step at a time. A certain tension crept in between the two Western delegations as a result. Hailsham cabled back that Harriman "seem[s] . . . tired and becoming a little deaf. The Americans [are] rather suspicious of me personally. At one moment they suspected I was in [cahoots] with the Russians!"[66] With his ebullient table manners, not unlike Khrushchev's, Hailsham was said to be the center of attention at the various official banquets, which were bedecked with portraits of Kennedy and Macmillan used in *Pravda*'s standard anti-Western editorials.

In general, the Moscow negotiations were notable for the fact that the host government was willing to push for an agreement, as well as for catching Khrushchev in one of his abrupt upswings of mood about the West. As the pace of events accelerated, so the Kennedy-Macmillan exchanges increased. As in the Cuban crisis, they were in constant touch, sometimes firing off as many as six cables each a day. Both men were deeply concerned that the chance to agree to a test ban not pass them by. Macmillan and Kennedy showed signs of genuine idealism, but they also worried that Khrushchev could be ousted at any time and replaced by an even less congenial figure.

On July 16, Macmillan wrote, "rather to my surprise, with that sudden change of direction which has been such a marked feature of US policy in recent years, the President started an altogether new hare."[67] Kennedy now wondered if, by sharing American nuclear technology with France, de Gaulle could yet be tempted to join in a test-ban treaty. "Dear Friend," the PM wrote back, with a very different take on affairs, on the 18th: "It seems to us that our immediate object is fairly simple. It is to stop de Gaulle from destroying the moral effect of any such treaty we may get with the Russians, by making some intemperate remarks. . . . The General is evidently in a difficult mood. . . . [He] shows no disposition to compromise. This is all the more reason for concentrating in the first instance on the limited objective."[68] What Macmillan called "rivers of telegrams" ensued.[69] On the 22nd, he wrote to Kennedy: "I expect that you like me are watching anxiously over the weekend the cables arriving from Moscow, as one watches the score in a game." Judging from Kennedy's wire that night, the Allies were once again on the same page when it came to de Gaulle. "I am concerned by mounting evidence of the General's unfriendliness," he wrote. "I think it quite possible that he will say some harsh things about us."[70]

After a £3 million refurbishment and fourteen labor strikes, 10 Downing Street was at last ready for occupation again. Evidently there were still teething issues with some of its equipment, because the text of one cable from Macmillan to Kennedy read:

> Dear Friend
>> I was very glad to get your message last night. We seem to BEK3 819 . . .
>> FOJZNNI
>> WG: WHAT IS WRONG ---?
>> I WILL BEGIN MESSAGE AGAIN . . .[71]

On July 23, Kennedy called in David Ormsby-Gore and spelled out "in full" his misgivings about the current state of the Moscow negotiations. In particular, there was the matter of the French. "The President has just heard," Gore cabled Macmillan, "that de Gaulle [may] try to do a deal with the Soviet Union to obtain nuclear information in order to rid himself of his hateful Atlantic links."[72] Kennedy went on to reiterate that he wanted a stand-alone test ban, without any further wishful talk about a so-called peace treaty. After some "frank" remarks on the subject, he concluded by genially inviting Gore to join him for another long weekend at the Cape before the ambassador took his summer holiday in England.[73] "Dear Friend," Kennedy then cabled Macmillan, "the one question which might prevent accord this week would appear to be the handling of the non-aggression pact issue. The communiqué language suggested by Hailsham in Moscow seems to me to go too far."[74] "*Bad* telegrams from

Moscow this morning," Macmillan wrote in his diary on the 24th. "I have told Gore to stay in Washington, postponing his leave. The Americans are being very stubborn."[75]

After intense three-way maneuvering, the breakthrough came about on July 25. The outcome was in doubt up to the last moment, with Hailsham cabling back that morning that he foresaw "a struggle and perhaps a breakdown." Four hours later, Kennedy himself was on the line to tell Macmillan that he had authorized Harriman to sign a limited test-ban agreement and that the deal was in fact being initialed as he spoke. The treaty, which barred tests underwater, in the atmosphere, and in space (but not underground) and allowed up to seven annual on-site inspections by each side, would be widely hailed as a significant thaw in East-West relations, if not the beginning of the end of the Cold War. In a televised address, Kennedy told the American people that "for the first time, a shaft of light [had] cut into the darkness" of the arms race. The US Senate would go on to ratify the treaty by a vote of eighty to nineteen. Macmillan wrote in his diary that, after initially speaking to Kennedy, he had "had to go out of the room. I went to tell D[orothy] and burst into tears. I had prayed hard for this, night after night."[76] At 11:00 p.m. on the 25th, he went into the chamber of the Commons to deliver the news. "The House was very full," he wrote. "The statement was well received, and the questions which followed were friendly and generous. . . . When I left, the whole of the Conservatives stood up and waved their order papers. Many of the Opposition stood up also. It was like the greatest of my Parliamentary successes."[77]

The following morning, Hailsham himself flew home to something of a hero's welcome, bearing Khrushchev's gift of caviar for Macmillan. It was thought wise for this to be x-rayed before its consumption. The PM in turn sent back a vase and a jar of "ripe" Stilton cheese. Years later, Hailsham wrote of the Moscow treaty as "the last time that Britain appeared in international negotiations as a great power."[78]

The two Western leaders exchanged mutual "Dear Friend" cables on July 25–26. Macmillan told Kennedy, "I found myself unable to express my real feelings on the telephone tonight. My task has been relatively easy, but I do understand the high degree of courage and faith which you have shown." Kennedy told Macmillan, "No one can doubt the importance in all this of your own persistent pursuit of a solution. You have never given up for a minute, and more than once your initiative is what has got things started again. I want you to know that this indispensable contribution is well understood and highly valued."[79] Arthur Schlesinger spoke for many in government when he wrote that the treaty "would not have come about without the intense personal commitment of Kennedy and Macmillan."[80] Perhaps with just a touch of color, Jacqueline Kennedy later called the agreement "the one thing that matters in this whole century." Both the principals involved saw it as their shining foreign-policy achievement, and as a critical step back from the brinkmanship that had nearly led to war over Cuba. As such, it may be the one truly imperishable event of their administrations. It was a great moment for the Kennedy-Macmillan dyad. Only twenty years later was the long-retired premier to reflect bitterly on how much better the deal might have been but for Kennedy's "weakness."

"I mean weakened by constantly having all those girls, every day," Macmillan told his biographer Alistair Horne. "He was weak in pressing the Russians for seven inspections instead of three. If we could have had that, it would have eventually led to no testing in the air at all. . . . I feel this is a great opportunity that we missed, and I do blame Kennedy's weakness."[81]

It's not known how, if at all, Kennedy's "girls" distracted him from the business of negotiating a test ban, but it may be remembered that Macmillan spoke at a time of widespread protests at the British government's decision to house American cruise missiles and of renewed East-West tensions in general. In old age, the terrible thought seems to have occurred to him that all his work to restrain the cold warriors and military establishments on both sides of the Atlantic had been in vain.

The Nuclear Test Ban Treaty was signed in Moscow on August 5, 1963. Macmillan cabled Kennedy on the 6th: "I got back last night from a short visit to Chatsworth. . . . I must take this opportunity to send best love from all there. You know how devoted Debo and Andrew are to you. Your short visit will long remain a source of great interest in all the estate and countryside."[82] Two days later, he wrote again to commiserate with the Kennedy family on the death of their infant son Patrick, after only thirty-nine hours of life. The First Lady later recalled being "moved beyond words" by Macmillan's handwritten letter, which remarked, "The burdens of public affairs are more or less tolerable, [but] private grief is poignant and cruel."[83]

The PM had finally begun to feel old, he told colleagues, before sometimes going on to complain of the way in which, after fifty years, his war wounds had come back to haunt him. Health problems compounded the burdens of office that would have been natural in any man approaching his seventieth birthday. In recent months, the pain in Macmillan's upper legs and back had become almost unbearable, and, like Kennedy, he now regularly wore a corset under his shirt. For once, his annual trip to the grouse moors failed to do much for his spirits, and there was further grief awaiting him when it came time to return to London in late August. While Macmillan gradually settled back in at Downing Street (still not ready for full occupation until October 1), Dorothy went north to Scotland and a rendezvous with Boothby.

Through all this, Macmillan and Kennedy continued to exchange views on a wide range of issues around the world. On August 3, the president signaled his renewed concern about events in Indonesia. "I am quite worried that hopefully successful Manila summit will be torpedoed unless August 31 date for Malaysia can be postponed briefly to give Sukarno a fig leaf. . . . I well realize that kowtowing to Sukarno is a risky business, but a little give now may be worth the risk, especially if the likely alternative is a further step-up of subversive pursuits. This is your show, but I feel we ought to place our worries frankly before you."[84]

Macmillan wrote back: "Dear Friend. Thank you for your message. . . . I share your concern about the outcome of this Malaysia meeting, but I do not believe that Sukarno can be bought off with a fig leaf. He would need something much bigger to cover him effectively."[85]

Macmillan, in turn, was surprised and shocked to only now discover that the number of American "advisers" in South Vietnam had risen from several hundred to nearly seventeen thousand, although in later years he always loyally insisted that Kennedy, had he lived, would never have allowed the United States to drift into the decade-long war of attrition that followed.

During September 1963, the pattern of exchanges continued: Kennedy's pragmatic approach to government meshed with the high and even utopian ambitions of Macmillan's vision of a world without nuclear bombs. "Dear Friend," the PM wrote in one of his last cables to Washington, "I have been pondering deeply on what is to be done next. . . . Unless the momentum is kept up we may not be able to act at all. Any new offers which we make may be thrown away, and the river of hope which you and I have guided into its present course will dribble away into the sand. . . . I would be most happy to come over to spend a day or so with you at any time," he went on, the supplicant side of the relationship thus preserved to the end.

"Of course I am in your hands. I am only desperately anxious that we should not lose that sense of urgency which alone can produce results."[86]

For Macmillan, grand strategy was the very essence of government. Even at the darkest hour of the Cuban missile crisis, he liked to expound on his dreams for a "general détente between the West and Communism, in which all the questions which seem insoluble by themselves might be subsumed into a new general approach,"[87] preferably hammered out at one of his beloved summits. To Kennedy, painting the big picture was more a hobby than the act of every day. One man was given to scholarly theorizing, which he combined with an impressive grip of fine detail. His work was never done. The other was less enamored with the abstract. Clearly, Kennedy did not enjoy late nights spent drafting lengthy economic and political blueprints for the world when there was no specific call for him to do so, especially with so many other pressing calls on his time.

On September 23, Macmillan was again appealing for Western solidarity to tackle the challenges of Southeast Asia. In particular, he wrote, Sukarno should not be allowed to threaten his neighboring states "without encountering united resistance" from the Allies, failing which there might be the "most dangerous and unpleasant" consequences.[88] Kennedy's reply, if perfectly civil, betrayed some of the lightly mocking tone with which he occasionally met Macmillan's soaring rhetoric on the fragility of man's tenure of the planet. "I have telegraphed our Indonesian friend," he said. "I told him that I could not believe he wanted to carry matters to the point where a showdown might become inevitable. . . . He has agreed, and is even willing to attend a summit meeting without preconceptions. This move suggests that he is quite loath to burn all his bridges."[89] Some advisers close to the president wondered if "the old boy," as one official referred to Macmillan, might be "just a touch loco" on the subject of Indonesia. A briefing paper to Kennedy on October 4 read: "The British regard Sukarno as their Castro. . . . They fear that the US is not going to press him hard enough to force him to behave."[90]

Meanwhile, the rapid sequence of events completed the *fin de régime* atmosphere for Macmillan at home in Britain. Tired and depressed, and again falling in the opinion polls, he told colleagues he would announce his resignation in mid-October, to take effect at the Christmas parliamentary recess. On September 21, Macmillan wrote in his diary that he had "reached the definite decision" to go before the end of the year. Many ordinary Britons simply saw their shuffling PM as an increasingly anachronistic figure in a fast-developing era of flares, miniskirts, and the flying pudding-bowl haircuts of the Beatles jubilantly hollering "She Loves You." On September 26, the official report into the Profumo affair went on sale, further adding to public skepticism about the ruling establishment. The following week, Macmillan, now rejoined by Dorothy, finally finished unpacking the last of the family china at 10 Downing Street. It would all be crated back up just sixteen days later. After further discussions with his colleagues, Macmillan again changed his mind about quitting, writing in his diary on October 7: "I have . . . decided to stay on and fight the General Election."[91]

Then events took a hand. That same week, Home was in the United States to address the UN Security Council before going on to meet Kennedy in the White House. In London, Macmillan chaired a scheduled cabinet meeting on October 8 but abruptly left the room halfway through the agenda, thus missing a discussion about how to respond to de Gaulle's recent proposal for the construction of a tunnel under the English Channel. After noting that there would be "political advantage in decid[ing] as soon as possible in favour"[92] of the plan, most ministers hurried away from Downing Street to catch a train to their party conference two hundred miles to the north in Blackpool. It turned out that their leader, who was in excruciating pain, was suffering from the not-uncommon condition of an enlarged prostate. It wasn't immediately known if cancer was involved. In the course of the next few days, Macmillan came to accept that it was the end of his career. Not far beneath the failing premier's public assurances that all was well, that after a "brief rest" he would be back on his feet again, lay resignation and even relief. He told one of his doctors that "the whole thing [had] come as manna from heaven—an act of God."[93] One of Macmillan's final acts in office was to publish the text of an exchange between Kennedy and himself on the recently signed test-ban treaty. The president's "Dear Friend" letter paid generous tribute to the PM's "steadfastness of commitment and determined perseverance," and Macmillan's reply spoke of "the duty of our two countries to work together for world peace" before concluding: "I have been very much sustained by the knowledge that you share this conviction, as you have demonstrated so signally by your actions."[94]

Macmillan's surgery duly took place in London on October 10, as his colleagues in Blackpool chaotically jockeyed for position to replace him. There was no cancer. Still in some pain, and woozy from the postoperative drugs, he consoled himself by reading the Book of Samuel, which speaks of a long-suffering people's oppression by the Philistines. Disconcertingly, a period that Macmillan had hoped would demonstrate the full force of his partnership with Kennedy on the world stage instead saw the United States take unilateral action on a range of issues—entering into yet more nuclear-arms talks with the French (which only confirmed de Gaulle's determination to go it alone), defusing a potentially explosive border-crossing dispute in West Berlin, and signing a major trade agreement with Moscow, among others. Without the personal connection, it was as though Kennedy had suddenly dropped his faithful Atlantic ally into oblivion. "The *public* events of these days are quite beyond me," Macmillan was left to ruefully note in his diary. The queen and the queen mother had called the hospital four times to inquire about him, he added, "but it has been a bad [time], and I can't understand what they are saying."[95]

When the Conservatives assembled at Blackpool on October 9, the leading contenders as Macmillan's successor were Richard Austen "Rab" Butler, his long-serving deputy; Lord Hailsham, fresh from antagonizing his US counterparts in the test-ban negotiations; and Reginald Maudling, the chancellor of the exchequer, at forty-six representing youth. Three days later, Maudling had been ruled out after delivering a monotonously flat speech to the party faithful, Hailsham was excluded by virtue of openly campaigning for himself in a manner widely thought vulgar, or, in the *Times*'s withering view, "indulging in those excesses more worthy of an American convention" (among them, bottle-feeding his infant daughter Kate in full view of the television cameras), and Butler, the heir apparent, once again self-destructed by going to the opposite extreme and seeming not to care one way or the other. Out of the vacuum emerged the diffident, patrician figure of Lord Home (soon to be plain Sir Alec Douglas-Home), the Atlanticist foreign minister. Discreet soundings were taken among Conservative MPs and reported to the convalescing Macmillan. On the morning of October 18, the queen took the unprecedented step of coming to her prime minister's hospital bed in order to accept his resignation. Macmillan received her wearing his pajama bottoms and a white silk shirt, which he partly covered with a well-darned, brown V-necked sweater. The effect, as one biographer writes, "was comic rather than dignified."[96] Macmillan advised his monarch to send for Home, which she duly did. His appointment was not noticeably a step in the direction of modernizing Britain. Having come to office in January 1957, following a series of Tory backroom maneuvers, Macmillan left it again in similar fashion nearly seven years later. Forty minutes after his resignation, a security officer appeared in the outgoing PM's hospital room to remove his special "scrambler" link to the White House—at once both a symbolic and a tangible end to the "Dear Friend" partnership.

Macmillan sometimes sardonically referred to the remaining time left to him following resignation as his "life after death." Once predicted to be a matter of months, or at best a few years, it lasted for nearly a quarter of a century. One of his first actions (and his last ever to use his government apparatus) was to exchange teletype messages with Kennedy. The president was relaxing at Hyannis Port on October 18, a Friday, and took the opportunity to send an eloquent but short note of farewell. "In nearly three years . . . we have never had a failure of understanding or mutual trust," he wrote, perhaps tactfully omitting the Skybolt affair, and added, "I believe that the world is a little more safe and the future of freedom more hopeful than when we began." Macmillan replied effusively, noting that the two of them "were influenced by the same feelings of trust and understanding, both for our countries and for the whole world." He concluded, "I rejoice that we have at least achieved something together."[97] A poignant sign that life went on without him was Home's swift calling of a new constitutional conference to determine the future of British Guiana. It opened in London on October 22, and Macmillan waited in vain throughout the week for a messenger to arrive bearing official papers for his comment. As Cheddi Jagan was preparing to fly home to Georgetown at the end of the meeting, he was asked if he might like to pay a courtesy call on the former PM but found that there was no time in his schedule to do so.[98]

In Washington, Vietnam pressures were producing more anxious moments. Kennedy, while promising to withdraw one thousand troops from the area by the end of 1963, had privately concluded that the Saigon regime of President Ngo Dinh Diem was incapable of defeating the communist incursion from the north. Some of Diem's generals felt the same and engineered a coup against him on November 1. The next day, the deposed president was placed in an armored car, told that there was no US plane available to fly him to safety, as he had asked, and then brutally shot and stabbed to death in an act of carnage that might have shocked the Manson family at its worst. Taping a statement for the record two days later, Kennedy was contrite. "I feel that we [at the White House] must bear a good deal of responsibility for it," he said, "beginning with our cable of early August in which we suggested the coup. In my judgment, that wire was badly drafted. It should never have been sent on a Saturday. I should not have given my consent to it."[99] Kennedy had real foreign-policy accomplishments to his name, including managing the now-receding crisis in Berlin, defying Khrushchev's nuclear ploy in Cuba, and most recently concluding the test-ban treaty with the Soviets and Britain. To these were now added his legacy in the generals' putsch in Vietnam, the butchering of Diem and his brother, and, as an unintended consequence, the final unraveling of that country into a decade of full-scale war.

A still-decrepit Macmillan could only watch these events in impotent regret. Preparing a summary of world affairs at the time of his resignation, he wrote of South-east Asia as a whole that: "In Thailand, there [is] relative quiet. In Laos, sporadic and inconclusive fighting. . . . In South Vietnam, owing to the weakness of [Diem's] government, the prospects look gloomy for the prosecution of any successful defence against the Communists from the North."[100] Historians are left to speculate whether a continued Kennedy presidency, with Macmillan's uninterrupted advice and support, might have approached the situation in a different way than that of their successors in office. We can never know, as just twenty days after Diem's murder, the echo of the assassin's rifle in Dallas reverberated around the world.

One of the more cruel torments of Macmillan's extended retirement was being witness to the deaths of so many colleagues, friends, and loved ones. His immediate family circle aside, none of these losses affected him more profoundly than Kennedy's assassination on November 22, 1963. In keeping with tens of millions of others, Macmillan would always remember precisely where he was that dark Friday evening—as it happened, dressing for dinner at the start of what was meant to be a relaxing shooting weekend at the country home of his old political assistant John Wyndham. It was "a staggering blow," Macmillan wrote in his diary that night. Merely hearing the newscaster's words on the radio was "overpowering, incredible," he added, telling Wyndham it felt as if he'd been struck an "actual blow—the breath literally went out of me."[101] Macmillan felt too shocked to make any public comment at all that weekend and physically not up to the challenge of flying to Washington for the funeral. For Douglas-Home, who did go, it was "almost beyond comprehension" to now find himself helping to bury a man who had been "so exuberant and vital" at their meeting just six weeks earlier.

The day after Kennedy's death, Macmillan left his house party and was driven back to Birch Grove. There was still no television to be found among the main home's thirty-odd rooms, so a small black-and-white set was borrowed from the cottage of an estate worker on the grounds. Macmillan spent the remainder of that miserably wet and blustery weekend "with unearthly howlings at the windows," sitting together with Dorothy in a small upstairs study, a blanket over their knees, watching the flickering images from across the Atlantic. On Sunday, he wrote to the president's young widow, who in a few short months had lost both her infant son and her husband. Jacqueline Kennedy later said that the letter had "made the deepest possible impression" on her and that nothing else she read on the subject affected her quite as much as it did.[102]

On November 25, at the same hour as Kennedy's funeral procession was leaving the White House, Macmillan unexpectedly appeared on the floor of the Commons. It was his first time there since his illness, and the chamber was uncharacteristically silent as he rose slowly to his feet. Macmillan's pale, drawn face and trembling hand testified to the emotion of the moment. Like many others present, he wore a plain, dark suit. His voice faltering, and struggling, he later confessed, to "get through without a breakdown," Macmillan nonetheless was at his most vivid—starting quietly, "like the rustling of a few leaves," one commentator thought, before "welling up with a power that was like an organ filling a church."[103]

Macmillan began:

My only purpose in rising is to add a few sentences as a friend and, in a true sense, a colleague. Every few months we met—sometimes on British, and sometimes on American, soil—and in between we interchanged frequent messages and telephone talks. Anyone who knew the President could not fail to realise that behind the captivating charm of manner lay an immense fund of deeply pondered knowledge on a wide range of subjects—political, economic, military. He was one of the best-informed statesmen whom it has ever been my lot to meet, but he was altogether without pedantry or any trace of intellectual arrogance. . . .

In this country we shall always remember him as a sincere and loyal friend of Britain. To the whole world without distinction his life and words and actions were a constant inspiration. He did not regard it as a statesman's duty to yield to public opinion, but to strive to lead it. Subjected to great pressures on many conflicting issues, he seemed sometimes to be almost a rather lonely figure, but always true to his own integrity and his own faith. What he said, he meant, and he did his best to accomplish. To him the words 'peace and progress' were not just a phrase for a peroration, but a living and burning faith.

So it was, as has been said already, that when that terrible news came on Friday, everyone in this country—and, I think, in every country—felt stunned by the shock of what seemed to us—to each one of us—a personal bereavement, and to the whole of humanity, struggling in this world of darkness, the sudden and cruel extinction of a shining light.

We mourn for him and for his bereaved family, to whom we offer our respectful sympathy, and for all the American people; and we mourn him—and this is perhaps the greatest tribute to Jack Kennedy's life and work—for ourselves, for what we and all the world have lost.[104]

After that, there was nothing more to be said, and the House adjourned. As Macmillan and his colleagues filed out into the fog and rain, in Washington the president's coffin was being borne away for burial.

10

AFTERMATH

Macmillan was in despair. In the space of just five weeks, he and Kennedy had both been removed from the world stage. The assassination was a political loss, Macmillan told the House, "cut[ting] short the life of one who will stand high even among the great names of American Presidents."[1] But it also came as a personal blow "painfully close to that of the death of a child." Macmillan's attitude toward Kennedy had always been ambivalent, compounded of exasperation and respect, of distrust and admiration. In private, he had sometimes spoken of the young president in terms he'd wisely chosen to avoid in public. The gap between how Kennedy was judged in his lifetime and how he was depicted in death would become increasingly wide over the years. But underlying it all, Macmillan had felt a very real and lasting affection for a man who had been of the same generation as his own son, Maurice. Kennedy's mixture of recklessness, calculation, idealism, exuberance, impetuosity, and courage had evoked a feeling of protectiveness among many of the elder statesmen of his day. Macmillan often appeared to watch him with that combination of nervousness and pride an accomplished actor might feel for a mercurial young protégé stepping up to take his first starring role in public. The subsequent performance had occasionally come to the brink of disaster, Macmillan admitted, but ultimately had shown a "vigour and vitality . . . a leadership to which all the peoples of the world, of whatever race, creed, or colour, looked with confidence and hope."[2] Kennedy's abrupt exit not only chimed with Macmillan's long-held fatalism about life in general, but it also finally extinguished any lingering political ambitions the Briton may have had. After negotiating the likes of the Cuban missile crisis, the prospect of a long and increasingly marginalized exile on the backbenches, debating provincial factory closures, would have taxed even his reserves of self-discipline and civic duty. Macmillan announced his retirement from parliament in September 1964, eleven months after leaving office. The Labour Party narrowly won the general election that followed in October, removing the Conservatives after thirteen years in power.

Meanwhile, under new management, the Atlantic allies continued to make progress, if slowly and painfully, toward peace. In December 1963, Douglas-Home inquired if President Johnson would "confirm the existing commitments, entered into by your predecessor, to consult with the UK before the use of nuclear weapons." The president did so with a single tick of his pen before moving on to other matters.[3] Cuba continued to preoccupy both the allies, and on December 12 of that year Robert Kennedy sent his colleague Rusk a lengthy memorandum about the "problem of student . . . and pacifist trips to Havana being organized over the Christmas holidays," before reminding him that "such travel is prohibited by law, and will result in criminal prosecution."[4] In West Germany, Konrad Adenauer finally stepped down twenty-four hours before Macmillan did in Britain, while Khrushchev and Douglas-Home were both summarily removed from office on the same day a year later. De Gaulle remained in power until April 1969, having survived long enough to see France move to the brink of civil war the previous spring. He died in November 1970, aged seventy-nine. His memorial service was attended by sixty-seven present or past heads of government, including Macmillan.

In time, an effusive and often deeply moving correspondence began between the retired British premier and America's canonized former First Lady. "Dear Prime Minister," Jacqueline Kennedy opened an eight-page letter, written on black-edged paper, on January 31, 1964. Admitting to feeling bitter and alone, the president's widow then spoke of her concept of the afterlife: "I used to think there was just nothing—or some great vague peace—but now I want to think as I did as a child—that when I die I will go to heaven and find Jack—and that he can see me now, and see all of us and how lost we are without him." "My dear friend," Macmillan replied to the woman thirty-five years his junior, before referring to his "strange relationship" with Kennedy and their vital ability to laugh "both at our advisers and at ourselves." Like war, an act such as the president's murder made one think, he admitted, "Can there really be a God, who created and guides the world?" Macmillan's conclusion was that there was. Over fifteen handwritten pages, he reflected on the mystery of human suffering and related the whole experience to the victim's natural inability to distinguish short-term grief from the promise of eternal happiness. "May god bless you, my dear child," he concluded. "You have shown the most wonderful courage to the *outer* world. The hard thing is really to feel it, *inside*."[5]

In December 1963, declining the invitation to become chairman of the

Kennedy Memorial Fund, Macmillan had written, "I still feel *low*." Five months later, in what would have been the week of the president's forty-seventh birthday, he was finally able to take part in a thirty-minute televised tribute that included members of Kennedy's family speaking live from Washington. Satellite technology was then in its infancy, and a series of screen blackouts, delays, and other technical issues resulted. But the central message—"Here was a staunch friend of Britain, and a courageous and unfaltering defender of peace and progress"—eclipsed all the problems. "I have written to you so many times," Jacqueline Kennedy cabled back, thanking Macmillan for his contribution. "Every time, I would at least have the sense to wait until morning, and read [the letter] over. Then I would decide I could never mail it. . . . But you did help me, more than you will ever know. . . . Just writing them was a release for so much that would have destroyed me had I kept it all inside. . . . I do thank you for having submitted to the ordeal, and for having done it so beautifully."[6]

"I wish I could have said more, but the [television] timetable stopped me," Macmillan wired back. Writing to the president's younger brother Ted, he added: "I thought in spite of all the technical difficulties, the broadcast went off well. I was deeply touched by Jackie's references to me. . . . The whole thing has made a deep impression here."[7]

Less agreeably, a large number of the curious or the obsessed about Kennedy's death would take the opportunity to write to Macmillan with their views and opinions, and sometimes their slightly wacky conspiracy theories, as to who was responsible for the tragedy. By mid-1964, there were so many alleged plots and subplots that Macmillan couldn't work out "whether it was Castro employing the mafia, or the mafia Castro." Not untypical was the stringer from *Fate* magazine, who wrote to Birch Grove to insist, "I warned the late President, suggesting that he should double his bodyguard. My reason for making this suggestion was based on an article I wrote for *Fate*. This was a clairvoyant survey of coming world events, and in it I included the forecast that he ran grave risk of assassination. . . . I have received neither acknowledgment nor reply to my letters," he was forced to admit.[8] It was as if the correspondents somehow seemed to feel themselves closer to Kennedy by communicating with his old comrade. Macmillan himself believed that a "lone malcontent" had fired the shots that killed his friend.[9]

In May 1965, Macmillan and his wife hosted several of the Kennedys when they came to England for the unveiling of a memorial stone to the president at Runny-mede. In a long thank-you note, Jackie wrote of her in-laws: "All that family, and all the confusion—you cannot travel with them without it." Speaking of her two young children, she added: "You have to have something that makes you want to live—and now I have them. . . . I don't know why I inflict you with all this—probably because I don't keep a diary or go to a psychiatrist—I pour it all out on you." For the first time, she now signed herself "With love." Macmillan wrote back fondly, if also more formally, expressing the view that "Jack and I ran the affairs of our two countries better than they are being managed now," and deploring the lack of "finesse" in their successors.[10] In September, another letter came from Jackie, extolling the recent joys of horseback riding and barbeques on the beach—it had all been a glorious summer, "except that Jack didn't come on weekends."[11] In time, Macmillan wrote back with "rather gloomy" news of his own: the drug-related death of his grandson Joshua, aged just twenty, followed by that of Macmillan's seventy-nine-year-old brother Dan, until lately chairman of the family publishing firm. "There were so many shared memories of childhood which can never be replaced," he told her.

By early 1968, the president's widow and children were living in a fifteenth-floor apartment on New York's Fifth Avenue. Approaching her fortieth birthday, and now stepping out with the Greek shipping tycoon Aristotle Onassis, Jacqueline Kennedy still retained some of her girlish and often coquettish charm. "My dear friend," she wrote Macmillan that January, reflecting on how, four years earlier, he had promised to stay in touch with her. That one assurance of his had often come crashing back to her, she said, thanking him for it in her slightly breathless manner. "I can still see the page it was written on as I did the first time—the color of the ink and paper. . . . If I write anymore I shall be embarrassed to ever look you in the eye again," she told her seventy-three-year-old pen friend.[12] Odd as their burgeoning relationship may sound on paper, in some ways nothing could have been more natural. Both of them were the bookish, submissive partners in mar-riages to energetic, headstrong spouses. Both had shown heroic forbearance in the face of their partner's infidelities. Above all, both had clearly been devoted to John Kennedy, and remained so throughout the rest of their lives. "Jack loved you," Jackie told Macmillan at one point.

Then, in June, by either the hand of another lone malcontent or a con-spiracy—some believed a combination of both—Robert Kennedy was fatally shot while campaigning for the Democratic presidential nomination in Los Angeles. Two nights later, Macmillan went on British television to speak movingly of the "essential goodness and charity" of the United States, notwithstanding its recent history of a "lunatic violence" that had also seen the assassination of Martin Luther King Jr.[13] "Tears on his cheeks and a lump in his throat," one paper reported, "Macmillan asked his fellow Britons to show 'a little understanding' for their American cousins. He said harsh, wrong things were being said about America and its people. . . . He told his countrymen they should show not only sympathy and sorrow, but determination to work together with them." On June 11, Macmillan wrote a long "Dear Friend" letter to Robert Kennedy's widow, reminiscing about a visit to their home and all the happy faces, "children and friends and dogs," he had encountered there. Typing a shorter letter to Jackie (his handwriting had begun to fail, he told her), he could express only respectful sympathy, as there was "nothing else that one can say, or do, that is of any use." Soon a New York literary agent was writing to ask Macmillan if some of his recent remarks could be included in a book to be called *Tribute to Robert Kennedy*. The altruistic friend of the family and the shrewd publishing professional both surfaced in his reply. "Yes," Macmillan wrote. "I want no fee, but I must retain copyright for my future use."[14]

At that stage, the focus of Macmillan's relationship with the Kennedys passed on to Edward, or "Ted," the youngest of the nine children. Born in 1932, the lubricious junior senator from Massachusetts was himself rapidly becoming a front-runner for the Democratic presidential nomination. Like many others, Macmillan privately saw the Kennedy siblings as "rather a case of the law of diminishing returns"—the virtues noticeably diluted, and the flaws magnified, in each successive brother.[15] When Ted wrote to ask if he would submit to an interview for the John F. Kennedy presidential library, the former PM replied that he would now prefer to keep his thoughts on his great friend the president for his memoirs. Macmillan did, however, agree to write a brief foreword to *Thirteen Days*, Robert Kennedy's posthumously published account of the Cuban missile crisis. "Dear Harold, thanks for sending me so promptly your preface," Ted cabled on September 20, 1968. Later that year, the publishing house of Macmillan agreed to bring out the book in Britain. In further correspondence, Ted Kennedy would go on to variously address the by-then octogenarian ex-premier as "Mr. McMillan," "Mac," and, again, "Harold." Even Jackie seemed to lose some of her precision on the subject. "Dear Mr. MacMillan," she wrote in November 1972.

"I have just finished watching you on television. . . . There is nothing in all these last long years that has moved me so much, or made me so proud." After expressing her delight that her eleven-year-old son had also been able to watch the broadcast, and apologizing for again "reaching out" to Macmillan, she ended: "Please be benevolent about this much too effusive letter—it comes with my love—and my respect and devotion always. . . . Jacqueline (Kennedy) Onassis." A family friend later asked Macmillan if he would care to become the patron of a "Kennedy Club" that she was opening in London. It was an outreach too many. "Turn it down," he scrawled across the letter, for a secretary's attention.[16]

Macmillan tempered his Christian beliefs with a deep-seated sense of the fundamental frustration and sorrow of human existence—"the abyss under every life," as he put it. He did not have to wait long for an event that, far more than any of his previous losses, served to confirm the fatalistic streak he once expressed by telling a cabinet colleague: "It is when things seem their darkest that they generally turn black."[17] On May 21, 1966, Dorothy Macmillan died, aged sixty-five. She had been putting on her walking boots downstairs at Birch Grove, complained of a suddenly violent backache, and a few moments later suffered a massive heart attack. Macmillan was in his upstairs room taking a nap and had to be woken up to be told the news. They had been married for forty-six years. There is no doubt that Macmillan was devastated, and that in the fullest sense he never recovered. Dorothy may have had her shortcomings as a wife and as a mother, but she had also been Macmillan's loyal and tireless supporter (not to mention his sometime cook, typist, and secretary) since the beginning of his career, with a natural exuberance on the campaign trail that rivaled Kennedy's. He had long relied on her for certain practical things in life, such as driving a car. It's no wonder that he described himself as "quite lost" in the weeks and months following her death. From now on, those closest to Macmillan would speak of a man who gave an overall impression of solitude, of remorse, of dejection, and, in the final analysis, of enormous vulnerability.

Macmillan's woes did not end there. In March 1970 his daughter Sarah died, the matter of her paternity never fully resolved, after a long struggle with alcoholism. This was the so-called Cavendish gene that seemed to be both especially cruel and rampant in that otherwise-privileged family. Macmillan's only son, Maurice, also a victim, finally achieved government office in the early 1970s but fell into chronic ill health and died following a heart operation in March 1984, aged only sixty-three. Maurice's younger sister Catherine married the Conservative MP Julian Amery, creating yet another political branch to the family tree, but also died in her early sixties. (The Macmillans' eldest daughter, Carol, said by a biographer to have herself "for a time almost succumb[ed] to the blight of alcohol,"[18] married an insurance broker, had five children—including the English professional cricketer Mark Faber, who died at forty—and, at this writing, is still alive and well, aged ninety-one.) Taken as a whole, this was not a dynasty in which an already-melancholic widower would necessarily find solace in his declining years. Following Dorothy's death, Macmillan moved into a small attic room at Birch Grove formerly occupied by the butler, sleeping in an iron cot and surrounded by sparsely dusted piles of books and sepia-tinged photographs of himself in the company of Kennedy and other past world leaders. "There was more than a touch of Miss Havisham about it," one visitor felt, recalling climbing a long, dark staircase to find the former prime minister sitting "alone there in his room, which was thoroughly cold, cluttered, and covered in cobwebs."[19] On occasion, Macmillan was seen out in the company of the Dublin-born Eileen O'Casey, a feisty, still-glamorous one-time singer and actress a few years younger than him, but despite wedding rumors in the early 1970s they remained as friends. "I know in my heart that he would have liked me to settle down with him," O'Casey later remarked, "as we got on so well together. . . . [But he] found it difficult to express affectionate feelings."[20]

Outside the immediate family circle, some of Macmillan's old colleagues and assistants fared less well than he did in their later days. We've seen that Douglas-Home lasted only a year in office. His successor as party leader and ultimately as prime minister, Edward Heath, was judged only a partial success, if later achieving the dubious honor of being voted by a panel of political writers "the rudest man ever to occupy 10 Downing Street." Meanwhile, David Ormsby-Gore retired as Britain's ambassador to the United States in the early days of the Johnson administration and returned home to a second career as a television executive and national film censor. His personal life did not always match his professional successes. Gore's wife of twenty-seven years, Sylvia—"Sissie"—died in a car accident in June 1967, leaving him to raise their five school- or college-age children. He would not be entirely alone in meeting the challenge. By the end of that year, *Women's Wear Daily* was reporting that Gore's widowhood would soon be ended by the announcement of his engagement—to Jackie Kennedy. In November, the couple went on a semiofficial trip to Cambodia and Thailand, adding considerably more fuel to the rumors. According to author Sarah Bradford, Gore later "admitted under pressure" that he and the former First Lady had slept together.[21] "But although we are close friends, there is no truth to the story of romance between us," he announced at the time. "I deny it flatly." Of course, they did soon get married, but not to each other. While Jacqueline Kennedy went down the aisle of a small, whitewashed chapel on a private Greek island with Aristotle Onassis, Gore—now Lord Harlech—married the former Pamela Colin, a New Yorker, at his family home in Wales. Like Macmillan's, his children would prove a source of both pride and exasperation—and occasional heartbreak—over the years. Gore's oldest son, Julian, who worked as a waiter and male model, died of a self-inflicted gunshot wound at his flat in London in November 1974 at the age of thirty-three. Julian's sister Jane had a long affair with Mick Jagger but ultimately survived the ordeal to become a happily married mother. Gore's youngest child, Alice, struck up a similar relationship in the 1960s with the rock guitarist Eric Clapton. After enduring heroin addiction together, the couple split in 1974, the beginning of a triumphant professional comeback for him and of a long personal decline for her. In April 1995, Alice was found dead in her rundown flat on the south coast of England, a half-empty syringe stuck in her arm. She was forty-two.[22] David Ormsby-Gore himself had died in January 1985 at age sixty-six, like both his elder brother and his first wife before him, the victim of a car crash.

In the United States, Gore's opposite number, David Bruce, also lost two children in tragic circumstances. Bruce's boss at the State Department, Dean Rusk, was caught in a political firestorm when, in 1967, his daughter, Peggy, married a college classmate who happened to be black. Rusk's subsequent appointment at the University of Georgia Law School only renewed the spirited miscegenation debate. Robert McNamara's son became a prominent critic of the war in Vietnam his father was instrumental in waging. A concern for the next generation had been a running theme for both Kennedy and Macmillan, as well as many of their senior advisers, during their time in office. While commendably focused on the communal future safety of mankind, that of their own children often proved sadly elusive. The president's only surviving son, John, died in July 1999 when the small plane he was piloting crashed into the Atlantic Ocean off Martha's Vineyard. He was thirty-eight; his wife and his sister-in-law perished with him. Some of the news media have referred to a "Kennedy curse" when describing the series of accidents, injuries, suicides, and other family misfortunes in the years since the president's assassination. Jacqueline Kennedy Onassis was widowed for a second time in March 1975. She worked as a book editor and a global celebrity-without-portfolio until succumbing to cancer in May 1994 at the age of sixty-four.

Early death is often seen as a kind of martyrdom. John Kennedy's brutal murder at the age of forty-six was widely portrayed that way, and in later years many well-placed commentators proved adept in advancing a canonized image of Kennedy that the man himself might not have endorsed quite as readily. In some critical circles, it was thought safe to assume that Macmillan's own stock would continue to plummet the longer he hung on, while Kennedy was now immortal.

In the same month that he turned seventy, Macmillan returned to become managing director of the family publishers. Much had changed in the forty-one years since he had last been gainfully employed there; a list once dominated by the likes of Hardy, Kipling, and Yeats had become the domain of Muriel Spark's post-Catholic satires and the Hebridean domestic romps of Lillian Beckwith. One of Macmillan's major undertakings following his return was to relaunch the truly magisterial *Grove's Musical Dictionary*. Retailing at some $3,000 a set, it contained 22,500 individual articles and 16,000 potted biographies. Two of its successive editors died during its thirteen years in preparation. Weighing in only slightly behind it were Macmillan's own six-volume memoirs, which between them ran to nearly two million words. In later years, he went on to write and publish three more autobiographical works, the last of which appeared on his ninetieth birthday. As a rule, Macmillan's books displayed the bleak humor of a man who knew that life could not possibly improve, and yet they also pulled off the feat of getting through the whole story without whining, blaming, or emoting. They were enormously successful.

Elected to the post in 1960, Macmillan was also chancellor of his beloved Oxford University for an incomparably long term of more than twenty-six years. Historian Alan Bullock admiringly remembered him holding his ground during the course of an angry demonstration in the streets of Oxford at a time of government student-grant cuts in 1973. "You see, it will be just like the First War, they'll catch us at the crossroads, at the King's Arms," remarked Macmillan, who was then approaching his eightieth birthday. At that, the chancellor had genially doffed his mortar board, bowing as he did so, a gesture that had immediately won over the crowd, which had then begun to laugh and applaud him.[23] It was exactly the sort of "unflappable" turn that had defined his long political career. Macmillan thought it "disgraceful" when in 1985 the university refused Margaret Thatcher an honorary degree, reportedly because of her government's attitude to higher-education funding, although he himself took issue with some of her broader economic policies. An unsolicited, eleven-page memo he prepared for her in the early 1980s agreed that while monetarism "might give a sense of exhilaration" to hard-core supporters, it would also lead to "unemployment, [and] a whole host of social ills."[24] (There is no evidence in the archives that Thatcher responded to this advice.) In both 1984 and early 1985 he publicly chastised the government's program of privatization, or "selling the family silver," as he put it. Referring to the coal miners' strike of that same winter, he said: "It breaks my heart to see what is happening in our country today. A terrible dispute . . . by the best men in the world. They beat the Kaiser's army, and they beat Hitler's army. We cannot afford action of this kind."

In November 1980, Macmillan made his last visit to North America, sixty-two years after his first. He gave a shamelessly sentimental and yet deeply moving speech at the British embassy in Washington, heaping praise on various past leaders of the Anglo-American alliance from the days of Roosevelt and Churchill through to Kennedy and himself. As Macmillan surveyed the scene, finally concluding that "I bring you nothing . . . I represent nothing . . . but only my affection and good wishes," many of the assembled guests pummeled their tables in applause, and even jaded political correspondents were seen to be misty-eyed with the emotion of it all.[25] As Macmillan then disappeared, holding the ambassador's hand for support, for a fleeting instant he was at the pinnacle again—"a living catalogue of the English-speaking political virtues at their best," one newspaper editorialized.[26] On his ninetieth birthday, he finally accepted the title the queen had originally offered him on his resignation and became the Earl of Stockton. His increasingly spare, ten-word-a-minute speaking style, a combination of whimsy, regret, and one-world Toryism, all tethered by a self-deprecating charm, more than once brought even the House of Lords to its feet. He still saw ministers privately and, in his final years, became almost an unofficial roving ambassador to China and the Middle East. Only at 10 Downing Street, it seemed, was his welcome sometimes muted. "No one knew whether to bow, shake his hand, or quietly slip out of the room when he arrived," one of Thatcher's cabinet members told the author.

If, for some, Macmillan had outstayed his welcome as prime minister, many of his old critics were inclined to be forgiving, as they, too, now basked in his various reminiscences and elegiac public appearances. The general tone of the ensuing coverage was respectful, and some of it was unashamedly nostalgic. Having listened to him "in complete awe," one veteran BBC correspondent was left to remark that it was like "visiting a magnificent Greek ruin." Macmillan also lived long enough to have the satisfaction of seeing some of the work he had started brought to fruition by others. In January 1973, Britain finally succeeded in joining the European Economic Community. It was exactly ten years since Macmillan's bid for membership had failed, and at the government's invitation he was present at the signing ceremony in Brussels—"a moving occasion for me," he remarked in the final volume of his memoirs. "The wheel had come full circle."[27]

Whether at Birch Grove, at Chatsworth, or on one of his regular Scottish tours, Macmillan would potter around like a figure out of P. G. Wodehouse, still able to enjoy a drink and a cigar, even if it was increasingly thought best to exclude him from the shooting parties. He suffered terribly when failing eyesight left his handwriting almost as bad as Kennedy's had been, thus ending much of his correspondence, and which in time meant he could no longer read the books that had sustained him throughout his life. From then on, it was as if Macmillan was waiting patiently for death. On December 29, 1986, in his own bed, surrounded by children, grandchildren, and great-grandchildren, and as the first snow fell outside, he slipped away just six weeks short of his ninety-third birthday. At the end, Macmillan looked at his family, said quietly, "I think I will go to sleep now," and peacefully died.

Macmillan's apparently stoical approach to the ups and downs of government, which could almost be taken for torpor, actually concealed, as the record of 1961–63 shows, great determination, a boldness that often took opponents and sometimes allies by surprise, a ruthlessness that at a stroke could see him sack a third of his cabinet (and give some of those retained a precisely timed five minutes to accept a new portfolio or else join the ranks of the departed), and, above all, an emotional, acutely sensitive, and occasionally fractious ("unstrung" was the word Dean Rusk once used) disposition that belied his image as everybody's genial uncle.

Despite this keyed-up side to his character, Macmillan remained seemingly immune to much of the normal cut-and-thrust of politics. The spirit of "Keep Calm and Carry On" pervaded. Just as a few examples: In November 1961, during a time of heated negotiations on nuclear testing, and in the course of preparing for a critical state visit by de Gaulle, Macmillan wrote in his diary of enjoying "wonderful sport" shooting at Birch Grove with a host of earls and generals, "as fine a team of guns as you [could] get together in this island." At the height of the sex-and-spy scandals of 1963, he was photographed unhurriedly trundling up to Scotland by train, a picnic hamper under his seat and a volume of Greek lyric poetry in his hand, apparently without a care in the world. Amid another "very hectic period" of world affairs, he was able nonetheless to slip away for yet more sport on the grouse moors—"One loves a holiday there," he later confided to the *Sunday Times*. "If you go to Venice or Florence or Assisi, you might as well be at Victoria Station—masses of tourists, chiefly Germans in shorts. If you go to Yorkshire or Scotland, the hills, the keepers, the farmers, the farmers' sons, the drivers, are the same. There is a sense of continuity."[28] In a way, that remark perfectly sums up the man. On the one hand, Macmillan, as a critic notes, "always seemed to be playing a character from some turn-of-the-century melodrama, shuffling and shambling around like a man of eighty," the epitome of Britain's ancien régime.[29] On the other, he had a highly charged and restless streak—one might very tentatively conclude, the result of his intensely close relationship with his mother, who by all accounts both pushed him to succeed and rather spoiled him. It could be said with truth that Macmillan later transformed himself into a public figure by an act of will rather than by being one of life's natural baby-kissers. No one who saw him in his early days as a diffident young publisher or as a provincial MP would have believed that one day he would glory in the title "Supermac" and meet as an equal with successive presidents of the United States. Macmillan reached the top only through an astonishing effort of will and all-consuming dedication. In that sense, he was more of a "made" politician like Richard Nixon rather than a congenital charmer like John Kennedy.

Time and again in the Macmillan-Kennedy partnership, it was the young American who proved to be the cool and phlegmatic one, and the avuncular Briton who habitually worked himself up into a nervous state to an extent that could make him physically ill before delivering a major speech. ("If only they knew," Macmillan once remarked when praised for his apparent coolness under political fire.) Engaging in excessive displays of emotion was not a part of Kennedy's makeup, by contrast. In July 1963, on hearing the news of a successful conclusion to the test-ban negotiations in Moscow, Macmillan, having waited anxiously by the phone all day, recorded in his memoirs: "I had to go out of the room. I went to tell Dorothy and burst into tears." Kennedy's own published schedule for the day in question notes only a meeting with Edwin Reischauer, his ambassador to Japan, a reception for some visiting Ethiopian dignitaries, and a leisurely family lunch.[30] None of those who saw him at around the time the flash came in from Moscow recall him being visibly moved, although it's thought he may have allowed himself a celebratory cigar following his late-afternoon swim.

Conversely, Macmillan could, and did, let the mask of impenetrable calm slip at moments of particular stress, giving way to petulant outbursts of temper. The cable he shot off to Kennedy in August 1962 raving about the Americans' "disgraceful piece of trickery" on missile sales may rank as the single most vitriolic high-level communication in the whole history of the Atlantic "Special Relationship" since Winston Churchill first coined the phrase in 1946. Kennedy certainly had his own moments of anger beneath the amiable, carefully controlled façade, but he generally reined himself in when it came time for him to speak as one head of government to another. "This is your show, but I feel we ought to place our worries frankly before you," or "I believe that on the historic evidence it is not likely that Mr. Khrushchev would make changes at a summit from [his previous] position as you suggest" were about as far as he ever went in expressing annoyance or impatience with his ally in London. Similarly, Macmillan was fussy about his health, if not something of a hypochondriac, in a way that rather jarred with his "unflappable" image. As PM he invariably traveled with his private doctor in tow, was fastidious about what he ate and drank, and frequently admitted to feeling exhausted or depressed. Kennedy, who had a whole series of truly debilitating illnesses, apparently thought it bad form to speak of such things in public. His aides were left to deduce from a scarcely perceptible grimace or a low sigh as he rocked to and fro in his chair that his back was giving him particular hell that day. In short, Kennedy was in some ways stereotypically "British," while Macmillan, both by birth and temperament, was nearly an American.

They were almost comically mismatched, and yet no other Atlantic partners since the days of Roosevelt and Churchill have given each other more practical cooperation on matters of mutual interest, particularly defense and security. (Since *cooperation* in this sense specifically involves the self-confidence to occasionally say "no" to an ally, we can exclude the years from 2002–2005.) One sign of the success of the Kennedy-Macmillan axis is the number of times they met, or spoke, and the relative speed with which they made their major decisions. These were two men who increasingly came to enjoy each other's company. As Macmillan said, their final encounter, at Birch Grove, was sufficiently relaxed and playful for the two principals to engage in a game of charades for the benefit of their unsuspecting aides. Another illustrative sign is to compare their relationship with that of their successors in office—from Lyndon Johnson's assessment of Harold Wilson as "a creep," through to Gordon Brown agonizing over the most politically correct gift to take Barack Obama, and receiving some hastily acquired DVDs in return. Even those ideological soul mates Ronald Reagan and Margaret Thatcher periodically ruffled one another's feathers on issues ranging from the Strategic Defense Initiative down to the US invasion of Grenada.

Perhaps the special quality of the period from January 1961 to October 1963 in Western foreign policy is simply that Macmillan acted with a healthy respect for his immeasurably stronger partner across the ocean, but rarely if ever stooped to fawning on him; and Kennedy responded with genuine warmth and affection for the one other friendly leader who had broadly the same perception as him of how the world worked, and in whom he may have recognized the endurance and wit of a master political operator much like himself.

Jacqueline Kennedy was the first, but not the last, to speak nostalgically of the whole match when she wrote to Macmillan in January 1964,[31] "You worked together for the finest things. . . . Later on, when a series of disastrous Presidents, and Prime Ministers who were not like you, will have botched up everything—people will say, 'Do you remember those days—how perfect they were?' The days of you and Jack . . ."

NOTES

The author relied on many primary documents, including quotations and transcripts from presidential and ministerial sources, among other government resources, which are thoroughly documented. Citing every individual direct quote would overburden the text and make reading cumbersome; therefore, in an attempt to balance accurate citation with ease of reading, the author has attempted to provide source information within the text where applicable.

CHAPTER 1. MENDING FENCES

1. Harold Macmillan, *At the End of the Day* (London: Macmillan, 1973), p. 472.
2. Ibid., pp. 472–73.
3. Ibid., p. 473.
4. Ibid.
5. Marcus Lipton, *Hansard* parliamentary report, June 20, 1963, UK National Archives (hereafter cited as "UKNA").
6. Macmillan, *At the End of the Day*, p. 486.
7. John F. Kennedy Personal Papers, John F. Kennedy Presidential Library and Museum (hereafter cited as "JFKL").
8. Kirk Lemoyne "Lem" Billings Personal Papers, JFKL.
9. Harold Macmillan, *The Macmillan Diaries: Volume II, 1957–1966* (hereafter cited as "*HMD*"), ed. Peter Catterall (London: Pan Books, 2012), passim.
10. Harold Macmillan, *Riding the Storm* (London: Macmillan, 1971), p. 157.
11. Harold Macmillan, *Tides of Fortune* (London: Macmillan, 1969), p. 622.
12. Nigel Fisher, *Harold Macmillan: A Biography* (London: Weidenfeld and Nicolson, 1982), p. 150.
13. Quoted in Winthrop W. Aldrich (1885–1974)—United States Ambassador; 1964; John Foster Dulles oral history collection, Public Policy Papers, Department of Rare Books and Special Collections, Princeton University Library.
14. Charles Williams, *Harold Macmillan* (London: Weidenfeld and Nicolson, 2009), p. 263.
15. Cabinet Papers, October 30, 1956, UKNA.
16. Ibid.
17. Selwyn Lloyd, *Suez 1956: A Personal Account* (London: Jonathan Cape, 1978), p. 209.
18. Dwight D. Eisenhower to Anthony Eden, memorandum of a telephone conversation,

November 7, 1956, in *Foreign Relations of the United States, 1955–1957, Suez Crisis, July 26–December 31, 1956, Volume XVI*, ed. Nina J. Noring (Washington, DC: US Government Printing Office, 1990), p. 1040.

19. Minutes of UK cabinet meeting, November 20, 1956, UKNA Cab 128/30.

20. As recalled by the author, who attended a speech by Macmillan at Oxford.

21. Humphrey, *Foreign Relations of the United States*, p. 1166.

22. Memorandum for the Record, John F. Dulles Papers, Dwight D. Eisenhower Presidential Library and Museum (hereafter cited as "DDEL").

23. Memorandum by the Marquess of Salisbury on the events of January 1957, in the Salisbury Papers at Hatfield House.

24. Victor Lasky, *JFK* (New York: Macmillan, 1963), p. 251.

25. Quoted in Kenneth P. O'Donnell and David F. Powers, *Johnny, We Hardly Knew Ye: Memories of John Fitzgerald Kennedy* (Boston: Little, Brown, 1970), p. 144.

26. Quoted in Robert Dallek, *An Unfinished Life: John F. Kennedy, 1917–1963* (New York: Little, Brown, 2003), p. 209.

27. Ibid., p. 193.

28. Quoted in Peter Collier and David Horowitz, *The Kennedys: An American Drama* (New York: Summit Books, 1984).

29. From the Harold Macmillan Archives (hereafter cited as "HMA"), as quoted in Alistair Horne, *Harold Macmillan: Volume II* (New York: Viking, 1989), p. 6.

30. Harold Macmillan, *Pointing the Way* (London: Macmillan, 1972), p. 334.

31. Williams, *Harold Macmillan*, p. 286.

32. *HMD*, entry for October 24, 1957.

33. Cabinet Papers, October 28, 1957, UKNA.

34. President Eisenhower to US ambassador to London, Department of State telegram, for delivery to Prime Minister Macmillan, April 30, 1958, State Dept. document 15830, declassified, US National Archives.

35. *HMD*, entry for June 7, 1958.

36. Dwight D. Eisenhower to John Dulles, John F. Dulles Papers, 1951–59, DDEL.

37. *HMD*, entry for January 22, 1959.

38. Quoted in Michael R. Beschloss, *Mayday: Eisenhower, Khrushchev, and the U-2 Affair* (New York: Harper and Row, 1986).

39. Horne, *Harold Macmillan: Volume II*, p. 280.

40. *HMD*, entry for November 28, 1960.

41. Harold Macmillan, *Winds of Change* (London: Macmillan, 1966), p. 87.

42. Fisher, *Harold Macmillan*, p. 146.

43. Macmillan, *Tides of Fortune*, p. 692.

44. Ferdinand Mount, "Too Obviously Cleverer," *London Review of Books* 33, no. 17 (September 8, 2011).

45. Williams, *Harold Macmillan*, chapter 5, passim.

46. William Manchester, *Portrait of a President* (Boston: Little, Brown, 1962), pp. 30–31.

47. Horne, *Harold Macmillan: Volume II*, p. 280.

48. Manchester, *Portrait of a President*, pp. 167, 30–31.

49. Selwyn Lloyd, MP, interview with the author, November 1972.

50. Conrad Black, *Richard M. Nixon: A Life in Full* (New York: Public Affairs, 2007), p. 431.

51. Herbert S. Parmet, *JFK: The Presidency of John F. Kennedy* (New York: Dial Press, 1983), p. 244.

52. See, for instance, Robert Dallek, *Unfinished Life*, pp. 475–76.

53. Cannon interview notes, April 5, 1963, box 1 of James M. Cannon Papers, JFKL.

54. See the David F. Powers Personal Papers, November 21, 1963, box 15, JFKL.

55. Harold Macmillan during a BBC 1 television transmission, April 23, 1971.

56. Horne, *Harold Macmillan: Volume II*, p. 98.

57. Quoted in ibid., p. 89.

58. Quoted in Robert Rhodes James, *Robert Boothby: A Portrait of Churchill's Ally* (New York, Viking, 1991), p. 118.

59. Horne, *Harold Macmillan: Volume II*, p. 90.

60. Ibid., p. 290. Among the many variants on this remark by Kennedy to Macmillan is the report of Bobby Baker to US Senate Democrats, attributing more direct words to the president: "I get a migraine headache if I don't get a strange piece of ass every day," as quoted in Seymour Hersh, *The Dark Side of Camelot* (Boston: Little, Brown, 1997), p. 389.

61. File PREM 11/3479, UKNA.

62. David Bruce, cable to State Department, December 1961, National Security Files, box 170, JFKL.

63. Manchester, *Portrait of a President*, p. 191.

64. Tip O'Neill, *Man of the House: The Life and Political Memoirs of Speaker Tip O'Neill* (New York: Random House, 1987), p. 45.

65. Quoted in Horne, *Harold Macmillan: Volume II*, p. 306.

66. Harold Macmillan in a radio and television broadcast to the British public in 1961.

CHAPTER 2. ANCIENT AND MODERN

1. William Taubman, *Khrushchev: The Man and His Era* (New York: W. W. Norton, 2003), p. 472.

2. Harold Macmillan, "Aftermath of Paris," in *Pointing the Way* (London: Macmillan, 1972), chapter 9, passim.

3. Ibid., pp. 277–78.

4. Ibid.

5. Macmillan, *Pointing the Way*, p. 279.

6. Ibid., p. 336.

7. Livingston T. Merchant, memorandum to the State Department, December 15, 1960, State Department Archives.

8. John Dulles, Subject Series, Memos of Conversations, box 12, John F. Dulles Papers, Dwight D. Eisenhower Presidential Library and Museum (hereafter cited as "DDEL").

9. Memorandum of conversations, box 12, John F. Dulles Papers, DDEL.

10. Macmillan, *Pointing the Way*, p. 208.

11. Alistair Horne, *Harold Macmillan: Volume II* (New York: Viking, 1989), p. 229.

12. Quoted in Harold Evans, *Downing Street Diary* (London: Hodder and Stoughton, 1981), p. 114.

13. Henry Brandon, *Special Relationships: A Foreign Correspondent's Memoirs from Roosevelt to Reagan* (New York: Atheneum, 1988), p. 156.

14. Harold Macmillan, *At the End of the Day* (London: Macmillan, 1973), p. 335.

15. Confidential source to the author.

16. Herbert Asquith, as quoted in J. R. Glorney Bolton, "Jowett of Balliol," *Spectator*, September 30 1943, p. 8.

17. Harold Macmillan, *The Middle Way* (London: Macmillan, 1938).

18. Harold Macmillan, *Tides of Fortune* (London: Macmillan, 1969), p. 17.

19. Quoted in "Nepotism on a Majestic Scale," *Times*, February 2, 2008.

20. Macmillan, *Pointing the Way*, p. 352.

21. Macmillan Deposit, box 553, Radcliffe Science Libraries, Bodleian Library, Oxford University, and as publicly quoted.

22. Robert Dallek, *An Unfinished Life: John F. Kennedy, 1917–1963* (New York: Little, Brown, 2003), p. 47.

23. See the Edwin Martin Personal Papers, "JFK Interview," John F. Kennedy Presidential Library and Museum (hereafter cited as "JFKL").

24. Taubman, *Khrushchev*, p. 379.

25. For the cable from John F. Kennedy to Harold Macmillan, see "UK: General, January–May 1961," box 127, JFKL.

26. Harold Macmillan, *The Macmillan Diaries: Volume II, 1957–1966* (hereafter cited as "*HMD*"), ed. Peter Catterall (London: Pan Books, 2012), entry for January 1, 1961.

27. Harold Macmillan, quoted in Nigel Fisher, *Harold Macmillan: A Biography* (London: Weidenfeld and Nicolson, 1982), p. 258.

28. Oral statement by Sir Alec Douglas-Home, March 17, 1965, JFKL.

29. "UK: General, January–May 1961," JFKL.

30. Quoted in Taubman, *Khrushchev*, p. 412.

31. Harold Macmillan, *Hansard* parliamentary report, January 31, 1961.

32. Desmond Donnelly, MP, in the House of Commons.

33. Woodrow Wyatt, MP, in the House of Commons.

34. Livingston T. Merchant, memorandum to the State Department, January 27, 1961, State Department Archives.

35. Presidential cable via the State Department, February 6, 1961, State Department Archives.

36. Cabinet Papers, February 7, 1961, UK National Archives (hereafter cited as "UKNA").

37. Macmillan, *Pointing the Way*, p. 327.

38. Macmillan, *Pointing the Way*, p. 328.

39. Questions by MPs in the House of Commons, primarily on February 16 and 17 1961.

40. *Hansard* parliamentary report, February 16, 1961.

41. Anthony Wedgwood Benn, letter to John F. Kennedy, from the correspondence files at JFKL.

42. US Information Agency Report to the President, March 3, 1961, "UK: Security, December 1960–March 1961," JFKL.

43. *Public Papers of the Presidents of the United States: 1961* (Washington, DC: US Government Printing Office, 1964), pp. 19–20.

44. John F. Kennedy, special message to Congress, February 2, 1961, in ibid., pp. 41–53; also quoted in Dallek, *Unfinished Life*, p. 333.

45. John F. Kennedy, speech at the Gridiron dinner, March 11, 1961, box 61, Theodore Sorensen Papers, JFKL.

46. A well-positioned anonymous source, interview with the author, April 2013.

47. Memorandum to the president, March 1, 1961, "Ghana: Security 1961: March 1–October 12," JFKL.

48. Memorandum to the president, March 29, 1961, "UK: Security, March–April 1961," JFKL.

49. Harold Macmillan, *Hansard* parliamentary report, March 7, 1961.

50. Dallek, *Unfinished Life*, pp. 351–52.

51. Macmillan, *Pointing the Way*, p. 308.

52. Macmillan later gave this perhaps comic account of his response to Kennedy to his Conservative Party colleague Selwyn Lloyd.

53. Macmillan, *Pointing the Way*, p. 335.

54. Ibid., p. 336.

55. Macmillan, quoting his own diary entry of March 26 1961, in *Pointing the Way*, p. 336.

56. Quoted in Horne, *Harold Macmillan: Volume II*, p. 293.

57. Earl Mazo oral history, Columbia University; also quoted in Dallek, *Unfinished Life*, p. 352.

58. See, for example, Fisher, *Harold Macmillan*, p. 288.

59. Henry Brandon diaries, June 9 1961, Henry Brandon Papers, US Library of Congress.

60. Digest of Acheson report to the president, April 4, 1961, "UK: Security, March–April 1961," JFKL.

61. State Department paper to the president, March 1961, State Department Archives.

62. McGeorge Bundy, undated note (probably April 1961), "State Department, Kennedy-Bundy Meeting, April 1961," JFKL.

63. Quoted in Victor Lasky, *JFK: The Man and the Myth*, pp. 6–7; and in Horne, *Harold Macmillan: Volume II*, p. 294.

64. *HMD*, entry for April 6, 1961.

65. John F. Kennedy, message to Harold Macmillan, "National Security Files: McGeorge Bundy Correspondence, May 6–May 15, 1961," JFKL; see also Macmillan, *Pointing the Way*, passim.

66. Quoted in Fisher, *Harold Macmillan*, p. 261; see also Sally Bedell Smith, preface to *Grace and Power* (New York: Random House, 2004).

67. Report to the cabinet, April 18, 1961, Cabinet Papers, UKNA.

68. Quoted in Macmillan, *Pointing the Way*, p. 350.

69. John F. Kennedy to Richard Nixon, April 1961; quoted, inter alia, by Professor Vernon Bogdanor in his lecture "The American Presidency: Transformation and Change 1961–63," London, May 27, 2008.

70. See Robert F. Kennedy oral history, John Bartlow Martin interview, JFKL.

71. Prime Minister Macmillan, letter to John F. Kennedy, April 25, 1961, "UK: Security, March–April 1961," JFKL.

72. Ormsby-Gore memorandum to the cabinet, May 3, 1961, Cabinet Papers, UKNA.

73. Prime Minister Macmillan, cable to John F. Kennedy, May 15, 1961, "UK: Security, May–September 1961," JFKL.

74. *Hansard* parliamentary report, May 16, 1961.

75. Ibid., May 30, 1961.

76. David Ormsby-Gore, letter to John F. Kennedy, May 18, 1961, "UK: General, January–May 1961," JFKL.

77. Quoted in Dallek, *Unfinished Life*, p. 397.

78. Cabinet minutes from June 6, 1961, CAB/128/35, Cabinet Papers, UKNA.

79. Ibid.

80. See Richard M. Nixon, *Leaders* (New York: Warner Books, 1982), p. 182.

81. Richard Nixon to Oxford-Cambridge university group, attended by the author.

82. Dallek, *Unfinished Life*, p. 408.

83. See *New York Times*, June 4, 1961.

84. See, for example, Dallek, *Unfinished Life*, p. 389.

85. Fisher, *Harold Macmillan*, p. 263.

86. Selwyn Lloyd, MP, oral interview with the author, November 1972.

87. John F. Kennedy, televised address, July 25, 1961.

88. Quoted in Henry Brandon, *Special Relationships: A Foreign Correspondent's Memoirs from Roosevelt to Reagan* (London: Arrow Books, 1989), p. 160.

CHAPTER 3. OPERATION ROSE

1. CIA/OCI to President Kennedy, DTG: 131317Z, "Cable to White House Hyannis," August 13, 1961, John F. Kennedy Presidential Library and Museum (hereafter cited as "JFKL").

2. Harold Macmillan, *Pointing the Way* (London: Macmillan, 1972), pp. 392–93.

3. US ambassador to London to the State Department, "UK: General, National Security Files, August–September 1961," box 170, JFKL.

4. See Robert Dallek, *An Unfinished Life: John F. Kennedy, 1917–1963* (New York: Little, Brown, 2003), p. 440, and chapters 12 and 16, passim.

5. National Intelligence Estimate, April 25, 1961, report no. 11-7-61, CIA Archives (hereafter cited as "CIAA").

6. Kissinger memorandum to the president, August 11, 1961, National Security File 81 (1961), JFKL.

7. Situation meeting of July 17, 1961, declassified, CIAA.

8. Prime minister's minute to the Cabinet, June 23, 1961, Cabinet Papers, PREM 11/3348, UK National Archives (hereafter cited as "UKNA").

9. Cabinet minutes from September 12, 1961, Cabinet Papers, PREM 11/3351, UKNA.

10. Quoted in Alistair Horne, *Harold Macmillan: Volume II* (New York: Viking, 1989), p. 312.

11. Quoted in Frederick Taylor, *The Berlin Wall: 13 August 1961–9 November 1989* (London: Bloomsbury, 2006), p. 343; see also Kenneth P. O'Donnell and David F. Powers, *Johnny, We Hardly Knew Ye: Memories of John Fitzgerald Kennedy* (Boston: Little, Brown, 1970).

12. Quoted in David Halberstam, *The Best and the Brightest* (New York: Random House, 1972).

13. Macmillan letter, September 15, 1961, quoted in Horne, *Harold Macmillan: Volume II*, p. 313.

14. *Hansard* parliamentary report, June 27, 1961.

15. Cabinet paper on East-West relations, July 19, 1961, Cabinet Papers, UKNA.

16. Macmillan, *Pointing the Way*, p. 393.

17. Quoted in Arthur Schlesinger Jr., *A Thousand Days* (Boston: Houghton Mifflin, 1975), as repeated in Schlesinger's speeches.

18. Quoted in Taylor, *Berlin Wall*, p. 224.

19. Quoted in Peter Merseburger, *Willy Brandt: 1913–1992; Visionär und Realist* (Munich, Ger.: Deutscher Taschenbuch Verlag, 2004), p. 393.

20. See *Pravda*, August 8, 1961, p. 2.

21. Dallek, *Unfinished Life*, p. 370.

22. McGeorge Bundy, memorandum to the president, *Nuclear Weapons and Berlin*, July 20, 1961, US National Archives, document E.O. 12958 SEC. 3.6.

23. Memorandum of decision, July 27, 1961, US National Archives, Security: 1961, file 600.00/2/7–2861.

24. Quoted in and by, inter alia, Professor Vernon Bogdanor in his address titled "From the European Coal and Steel Community to the Common Market," Gresham College, Museum of London, November 12, 2013.

25. Quoted in Honore M. Catudal, *Kennedy and the Berlin Wall Crisis: A Case Study in U. S. Decision Making* (Berlin: Berlin Verlag Arno Spitz, 1980), p. 182.

26. Cabinet memorandum, July 26, 1961, Cabinet Papers, UKNA.

27. See the correspondence in "UK: Security, 1961," JFKL.

28. William Taubman, *Khrushchev: The Man and His Era* (New York: W. W. Norton, 2003), p. 506.

29. Taylor, *Berlin Wall*, p. 335.

30. Harold Caccia, note to the Foreign Office permanent secretary, August 21, 1961, Cabinet Papers, PREM 11/3350, UKNA.

31. O'Donnell and Powers, *Johnny, We Hardly Knew Ye*, p. 343.

32. Allen W. Dulles, memorandum to the president, August 22, 1961, declassified, CIAA.

33. Harold Caccia, telegram to the Foreign Office, Cabinet Papers, PREM 11/3350, UKNA.

34. President Kennedy's letter to Gen. Lauris Norstad, July 21, 1961, US National Archives, Security: 1961, no. 6037279.

35. Harold Macmillan, *The Macmillan Diaries: Volume II, 1957–1966*, ed. Peter Catterall (London: Pan Books, 2012), entry for November 29, 1961; see also the note by Prime Minister Macmillan to the cabinet, November 27, 1961, Cabinet Papers, UKNA.

36. Arthur Schlesinger Jr., *Journals 1952–2000* (New York: Penguin Press, 2007), p. 140.

37. Harold Macmillan, *At the End of the Day* (London: Macmillan, 1973), pp. 146–47.

38. Ibid.

39. Harold Macmillan, letter to John F. Kennedy, January 5, 1962, in Macmillan, *At the End of the Day*, p. 155.

40. "Lord Harlech (David Ormsby-Gore) Oral History Project," JFKL; also quoted in Horne, *Harold Macmillan: Volume II*, p. 323.

41. See David C. Martin, *Wilderness of Mirrors* (Guilford, CT: Lyons Press, 2003), p. 124.

42. See Margarete Raabe, "Arbeitsgemeinschaft 13. August dokumentiert 57 weitere Todesopfer an der DDR-Grenze," *Die Welt*, August 13, 2004, and "Chronik der Mauer," http://www.chronik-der-mauer.de (accessed May 9, 2014).

43. Italics in the original.

44. BBC News report, August 12, 2007.

CHAPTER 4. SPECIAL RELATIONSHIPS

1. Elizabeth Carpenter oral history, Lyndon Baines Johnson Presidential Library and Museum.

2. Conversation with Arthur M. Schlesinger, quoted, passim, in Sally Bedell Smith , *Grace and Power: The Private World of the Kennedy White House* (New York: Random House, 2005).

3. Jacqueline Kennedy, interview in *Look*, November 17, 1964.

4. From the Harold Macmillan Archives, and as quoted in Alistair Horne, *Harold Macmillan: Volume II* (New York: Viking, 1989), p. 576.

5. Ibid.

6. John F. Kennedy, quoted in the *New York Times*, October 14, 1962.

7. Quoted in Timothy Naftali and Philip D. Zelikow, eds., *Presidential Recordings: John F. Kennedy: The Great Crises, Vol. II: September–October 21, 1962* (New York: W. W. Norton, 2001).

8. Quoted in Edward Klein, *All Too Human: The Love Story of Jack and Jackie Kennedy* (New York: Simon and Schuster, 1996), p. 230.

9. Quoted in Thomas C. Reeves, *A Question of Character: A Life of John F. Kennedy* (New York: Free Press, 1991), p. 318.

10. Harold Macmillan, letter to the queen, December 24, 1961, quoted in Harold Macmillan, *At the End of the Day* (London: Macmillan, 1973), p. 148.

11. See Richard Reeves, *President Kennedy: Profile of Power* (New York: Simon and Schuster, 1993).

12. See Reeves, *Question of Character*.

13. Robert Dallek, *An Unfinished Life: John F. Kennedy, 1917–1963* (New York: Little, Brown, 2003), p. 477.

14. Peter Collier and David Horowitz, *The Kennedys: An American Drama* (New York: Summit, 1984), p. 233.

15. Harold Macmillan, letter to Evelyn, Duchess of Devonshire, September 20, 1931, Devonshire MS Collection, Chatsworth House.

16. Quoted in Robert Rhodes James, *Robert Boothby: A Portrait of Churchill's Ally* (New York: Viking, 1991), p. 116.

17. Quoted in Hugh Dalton, *High Tide and After* (London: Frederick Muller, 1962), p. 327.

18. Quoted in Harold Evans, *Downing Street Diary* (London: Hodder and Stoughton, 1981), p. 2.

19. Alistair Horne, *Harold Macmillan: Volume I* (London: Macmillan, 1988), p. 148.

20. Horne, *Harold Macmillan: Volume II*, p. 583.

21. Quoted in Richard Davenport-Hines, *The Macmillans* (London: Heinemann, 1992), pp. 335–36.

22. Macmillan's war diary, October 1944, quoted in Horne, *Harold Macmillan: Volume I*, p. 228.

23. Harold Macmillan, *The Blast of War, 1939–1945* (London: Macmillan, 1967), p. 611.

24. Quoted in John Wyndham (Lord Egremont), *Wyndham and Children First* (London: Macmillan, 1968).

25. Horne, *Harold Macmillan: Volume II*, p. 155.

26. Ibid., p. 581.

27. Quoted in Nigel Fisher, *Harold Macmillan: A Biography* (London: Weidenfeld and Nicolson, 1982), p. 291.

28. Harold Macmillan, quoting from *Till the Clouds Roll By*, directed by Richard Whorf (Metro-Goldwyn-Mayer, 1946), in an address at the Conservative Party conference in Llandudno, Wales, October 1962.

29. Quoted in Norman Shrapnel, *The Performers* (London: Constable, 1978), pp. 29–32.

30. Emrys Hughes, *Macmillan: Portrait of a Politician* (London: Allen and Unwin, 1962), passim.

31. Fisher, *Harold Macmillan*, p. 125.

32. Quoted in Charles Williams, *Harold Macmillan* (London: Weidenfeld and Nicolson, 2009), p. 471.

33. Fisher, *Harold Macmillan*, p. 148.

34. For Macmillan's thoughts on his counterparts, see Horne, *Harold Macmillan: Volume II*, p. 368.

35. Quoted in William Manchester, *Portrait of a President* (Boston: Little, Brown, 1962), pp. 23–26.

36. Ibid., p. 39.

37. Horne, *Harold Macmillan: Volume II*, p. 158.

38. See, inter alia, public remarks by John F. Kennedy at Levittown, New Jersey, October 16, 1960, John F. Kennedy Presidential Library and Museum.

39. See Office of Management and Budget: Table 3.2, "Outlays by Function and Subfunction, 1789–2019, among other historical OMB historical tables. The figures cited for the record show defense spending of $64.2 billion in a total budget of $111.3 billion, or 57.68 percent, for fiscal year 1963.

40. Horne, *Harold Macmillan: Volume II*, p. 583.

41. Selwyn Lloyd, MP, to author, November 1972.

42. Horne, *Harold Macmillan: Volume II*, p. 165.

43. Quoted in Evans, *Downing Street Diary*, p. 172.

44. See the Department of State, Biographical Division, note to the president, March 20, 1961, "UK: Security, 1961," File JFKPOF-127-024, John F. Kennedy Presidential Library and Museum.

45. Report on the prime minister's Commonwealth Tour, circulated to the cabinet on June 4, 1958, Cabinet Papers, UK National Archives.

46. British political source, interview with the author, May 2013.

47. Quoted in James, *Robert Boothby*, p. 116.

48. Colin Brown, "Tape Reveals Macmillan's Agony over Destroying Wife's Love Letters," *Independent*, March 4, 1996.

CHAPTER 5. "THE PROBLEMS WHICH NOW CONFRONT US . . . ARE REALLY TERRIFYING"

1. Cabinet minutes from July 28, 1961, Cabinet Papers, UK National Archives (hereafter cited as "UKNA").

2. Harold Macmillan, *The Macmillan Diaries: Volume II, 1957–1966* (hereafter cited as "*HMD*"), ed. Peter Catterall (London: Pan Books, 2012), entry for July 22, 1961.

3. Ibid., entry for June 1, 1961.

4. Harold Macmillan, *Pointing the Way* (London: Macmillan, 1972), p. 397.

5. *HMD*, entry for June 25, 1961.

6. Macmillan, *Pointing the Way*, pp. 397–98.

7. Joint Atomic Energy Intelligence Committee statement, September 1, 1961, secret distribution to the secretary of state, declassified, US National Archives, Security.

8. Harold Macmillan, *At the End of the Day* (London: Macmillan, 1973), p. 154.

9. Arthur Schlesinger Jr., *A Thousand Days* (Boston: Houghton Mifflin, 1975), p. 456.

10. Macmillan, *At the End of the Day*, p. 174.

11. See Charles S. Sampson, ed., *Foreign Relations of the United States, 1961–1963, Volume VI, Kennedy-Khrushchev Exchanges* (Washington, DC: United States Government Printing Office, 1996), pp. 256–69.

12. Foreign Secretary's report to the cabinet, September 5, 1961, Cabinet Papers, UKNA.

13. John F. Kennedy, quoted in Glenn T. Seaborg, *Kennedy, Khrushchev, and the Test Ban* (Berkeley: University of California Press, 1981), pp. 126–27.

14. *HMD*, entry for October 24, 1961.

15. Cabinet minutes from September 19, 1961, Cabinet Papers, UKNA.

16. *Times* (London), leading article, July 13, 1961.

17. *HMD*, entry for December 23, 1961.

18. William Taubman, *Khrushchev: The Man and His Era* (New York: W. W. Norton, 2003), p. 503.

19. See the State Department memorandum, "The International Situation," September 8, 1961, US National Archives, 331.612.396.1-BF.

20. John F. Kennedy, quoted in Robert Dallek, *An Unfinished Life: John F. Kennedy, 1917–1963* (New York: Little, Brown, 2003), p. 463.

21. Macmillan, *At the End of the Day*, p. 151.

22. Draft message to President Kennedy, January 5, 1962, from the Harold Macmillan Archives, and quoted in ibid., pp. 154–63.

23. Ibid.

24. Ibid., p. 155.

25. Alistair Horne, *Harold Macmillan: Volume II* (New York: Viking, 1989), p. 283.

26. *IIMD*, entry for February 16, 1962.

27. Dallek, *Unfinished Life*, p. 613.

28. Ibid., p. 536.

29. White House press conference, October 11, 1961, quoted in *Public Papers of the Presidents of the United States: John F. Kennedy, 1961* (Washington, DC: US Government Printing Office, 1964), pp. 656, 660.

30. Dallek, *Unfinished Life*, p. 448; see also Ronald D. Landa and Charles S. Sampson, eds., *Foreign Relations of the United States, 1961–1963, Volume 1, Vietnam, 1961* (Washington, DC: US Government Printing Office, 1988), pp. 477–78.

31. Harold Macmillan, letter to John F. Kennedy, October 2, 1961, "UK: Security, October–December 1961," JFKPOF-127-014, John F. Kennedy Presidential Library and Museum (hereafter cited as "JFKL").

32. David Bruce, "eyes only" cable to John F. Kennedy, October 20, 1961, "UK: Security, October–December 1961," JFKPOF-127-014, JFKL.

33. Philip de Zulueta, note to Harold Macmillan, November 1, 1961, Cabinet Papers, PREM 11/3353, UKNA.

34. Harold Macmillan, cable to John F. Kennedy, November 9, 1961, "UK: Security, October–December 1961," JFKPOF-127-014, JFKL.

35. John F. Kennedy to Konrad Adenauer, September 4 1961, quoted in Charles S. Sampson, *Foreign Relations of the United States, 1961–1963, Volume XIV, Berlin Crisis, 1961–1962* (Washington, DC: US Government Printing Office, 1993), pp. 389–91; also quoted in Dallek, *Unfinished Life*, p. 429.

36. Harold Macmillan, cable to John F. Kennedy, November 23, 1961, "UK: Security, October–December 1961," JFKPOF-127-014, JFKL.

37. Macmillan, *Pointing the Way*, pp. 411–28.

38. John F. Kennedy, cable to Harold Macmillan, December 1, 1961, "UK: Security, October–December 1961," JFKPOF-127-014, JFKL.

39. Soviet Central Committees meeting, August 3–5, 1961, minutes in translation, from the Archive of the International Department of the Communist Party of the Soviet Union Central Committee; see also Taubman, *Khrushchev*, p. 502.

40. Taubman, *Khrushchev*, pp. 502–503.

41. "Roswell Gilpatric Oral History," quoted in Dallek, *Unfinished Life*, p. 345.

42. For details of the "Northwoods Plan," see the memorandum by the Joint Chiefs of Staff, March 13, 1962, declassified April 2001, US National Archives, Security.

43. "Restricted Data" memorandum by the US nuclear panel, October 25, 1961, declassified May 1994, US National Archives.

44. Colonial Office brief, file FO 371/15776, UKNA.

45. Duncan Sandy, letter to Harold Macmillan, January 11, 1962, Cabinet Papers, PREM 11/3666, UKNA.

46. Lord Home, note to Dean Rusk, February 26, 1962, Cabinet Papers, PREM 11/3666, UKNA.

47. "Hugh Fraser Oral History," JFKL, p. 10.

48. Quoted in Charles S. Sampson, *Foreign Relations of the United States, 1961–1963, Volume XIV, Berlin Crisis, 1961–1962* (Washington, DC: US Government Printing Office, 1993), p. 253.

49. Macmillan, *At the End of the Day*, p. 142.

50. "Cabinet Memorandum, Berlin—Note by PM," November 28, 1961, Cabinet Papers, UKNA.

51. See Louis J. Smith, *Foreign Relations of the United States, 1961–1963, Volume X, Cuba, January 1961–September 1962* (Washington, DC: US Government Printing Office, 1997), pp. 690–700.

52. Władysław Gomułka, quoted in Frederick Taylor, *The Berlin Wall: 13 August 1961–9 November 1989* (London: Bloomsbury, 2006), p. 426.

53. Cabinet minutes from November 9, 1961, Cabinet Papers, UKNA.

54. See, inter alia, Harry Thompson, *Peter Cook: A Biography* (London: Hodder and Stoughton, 1997), p. 77; see also William Cook, ed., *The Complete Peter Cook* (London: Century Books, 2002), p. 51.

55. Horne, *Harold Macmillan: Volume II*, p. 402.

56. Arthur Schlesinger Jr., *Robert Kennedy and His Times* (Boston: Houghton Mifflin, 1978), p. 326.

57. William Manchester, *Portrait of a President* (Boston: Little, Brown, 1962), p. 32.

58. John L. Helgerson, *Getting to Know the President: CIA Briefings of Presidential Candidates 1952–1992* (Washington, DC: Central Intelligence Agency, Center for the Study of Intelligence, 1996), chap. 3, "Into Politics with Kennedy and Johnson," passim.

59. 81 Cong. Rec., from April 20, 1950 (1950).

60. Arthur Schlesinger to John F. Kennedy, August 26, 1960, President's Office Files, box 32, JFKL.

61. Political source to the author, November 2012, quoting Arthur Schlesinger.

62. Surgeon Rear Admiral Cyril McClintock, RN, interview with the author, August 1974.

63. Macmillan, *At the End of the Day*, p. 145.

64. Ibid., p. 240.

65. *HMD*, entry for December 20, 1961.

66. Macmillan, *At the End of the Day*, p. 281.

67. Ibid., p. 146.

68. Ibid., p. 147.

69. Ibid., pp. 147–48.

70. John F. Kennedy, comment to Harold Macmillan, quoted in Horne, *Harold Macmillan: Volume II*, p. 290.

CHAPTER 6. AVOIDING THE ROGUE ELEPHANT

1. Surgeon Rear Admiral Cyril McClintock, RN, and a British political source, interviews with the author, May 1987.

2. Harold Macmillan, letter to John F. Kennedy, January 5, 1962, quoted in Harold Macmillan, *At the End of the Day* (London: Macmillan, 1973), pp. 157–63.

3. Quoted in Anatoly Dobrynin, *In Confidence: Moscow's Ambassador to America's Six Cold War Presidents (1962–1986)* (New York: Times Books, 1995), p. 52.

4. Quoted in Nikita S. Khrushchev, *Khrushchev Remembers* (Boston: Little, Brown, 1974), p. 494.

5. Dean Rusk to Foreign Secretary Alec Home, via the US embassy in London, August 11, 1961, "National Security Files: General," box 14A, John F. Kennedy Presidential Library and Museum (hereafter cited as "JFKL").

6. David Ormsby-Gore, cable to the Foreign Office in London, February 16, 1962, File FO 371/161947, UK National Archives (hereafter cited as "UKNA").

7. Harold Macmillan to Lord Home, February 21, 1962, Cabinet Papers, PREM 11/3666, UKNA.

8. Cabinet minutes from January 16, 1962, Cabinet Papers, UKNA.

9. David Shields, *Kennedy and Macmillan: Cold War Politics* (Lanham: University Press of America, 2006), p. 117.

10. Macmillan, *At the End of the Day*, p. 147.

11. Harold Macmillan, *The Macmillan Diaries: Volume II, 1957–1966* (hereafter cited as "*HMD*"), ed. Peter Catterall (London: Pan Books, 2012), entry for August 10, 1961.

12. Harold Macmillan, letter to John F. Kennedy, January 1962, quoted in Macmillan, *At the End of the Day*, pp. 154–63. The exact phrase reads: "the financial and administrative arrangements."

13. John F. Kennedy, letter to Harold Macmillan, in ibid., p. 164.

14. Cabinet minutes from January 18, 1962, Cabinet Papers, UKNA.

15. Cabinet minutes from February 6, 1962, Cabinet Papers, UKNA.

16. Memorandum by Foreign Secretary Alec Home to the cabinet, February 23, 1962, Cabinet Papers, UKNA.

17. Lord Home, note to the cabinet, January 16, 1962, Cabinet Papers, UKNA.

18. See "General Lucius Clay, Oral History Project," interview from July 1, 1964, JFKL.

19. Quoted in Marc Trachtenberg, *A Constructed Peace: The Making of the European Settlement, 1945–1963* (Princeton: Princeton University Press, 1999), pp. 348–49.

20. Charles S. Sampson, ed., *Foreign Relations of the United States, 1961–1963, Volume XV, Berlin Crisis, 1962–1963* (Washington, DC: US Government Printing Office, 1994), p. 309.

21. Aleksandr Fursenko and Timothy Naftali, *"One Hell of a Gamble": Khrushchev, Castro, and Kennedy, 1958–1964: The Secret History of the Cuban Missile Crisis* (New York: W. W. Norton, 1997), p. 194.

22. John F. Kennedy, letters to Nikita Khrushchev, February 21, 1962, and March 7, 1962, see the US Department of State Archive: Foreign Relations (Scientific Matters), document 388.

23. Foreign Office cable, October 22, 1961, File FO371/160559, UKNA.

24. Quoted in Alistair Horne, *Harold Macmillan: Volume II* (New York: Viking, 1989), p. 163.

25. David Ormsby-Gore, "Dear Mr. President" letter to John F. Kennedy, March 7, 1962, "United Kingdom: General, January–June 1962," JFKL.

26. *Hansard* parliamentary reports, January 23, 1962, and March 8, 1962.

27. Macmillan, *At the End of the Day*, p. 171.

28. Harold Macmillan, letter to John F. Kennedy, March 13, 1962, "UK: General, January–June 1962," JFKL.

29. Macmillan, *At the End of the Day*, p. 146.

30. Harold Macmillan, cable to John F. Kennedy, April 5, 1962, "UK: General, January–June 1962," JFKL.

31. Macmillan, *At the End of the Day*, p. 175.

32. Cabinet minutes from April 5, 1962, Cabinet Papers, UKNA.

33. Vyacheslav Molotov, letter to Nikita Khrushchev, quoted in William Taubman, *Khrushchev: The Man and His Era* (New York: W. W. Norton, 2003), p. 515.

34. US National Security Files, box 345, February 27, 1961; see also Robert Dallek, *An Unfinished Life: John F. Kennedy, 1917–1963* (New York: Little, Brown, 2003), p. 344.

35. *Hansard* parliamentary report, April 10, 1962.

36. See the Summary Record, C-R (62) 25, declassified 1997, National Intelligence Archives.

37. For the speech by John F. Kennedy at the University of California, Berkeley, on March 23, 1962, see *Public Papers of the Presidents of the United States: 1962* (Washington, DC: US Government Printing Office, 1964), p. 265.

38. Ibid., pp. 136–37.

39. Ibid., p. 322.

40. Macmillan, *At the End of the Day*, p. 177.

41. Ibid., p. 156.

42. Ibid., p. 61.

43. *HMD*, entry for May 6, 1962.

44. See "Papers of Arthur Schlesinger Jr., White House Files, box WH-36, Great Britain," JFKL.

45. *HMD*, entry for May 6, 1962.

46. Macmillan, *At the End of the Day*, p. 63.

47. Harold Macmillan, letter to John F. Kennedy, April 29, 1962, see "UK: General, January–June 1962, President's Office Files," JFKL.

48. John F. Kennedy, cable to Harold Macmillan, June 3, 1962, Cabinet Papers, PREM 11/3629, UKNA.

49. Ibid.

50. *HMD*, entry for April 26, 1961.

51. Quoted in Richard Mahoney, *JFK: Ordeal in Africa* (New York: Oxford University Press, 1983), p. 131.

52. De Zulueta minute, June 3, 1962, Cabinet Papers, PREM 11/3629, UKNA.

53. Harold Macmillan, letter to John F. Kennedy, May 30, 1962, "UK: General, January–June 1962, President's Office Files," JFKL.

54. See Fred Hirsch, *The Labour Movement: Penetration Point for US Intelligence and Transnationals* (Nottingham, UK: Spokesman Books, 1977).

55. "Lord Harlech (David Ormsby-Gore) Oral History Project," JFKL, pp. 46–47.

56. See Mark Curtis, *Unpeople: Victims of British Policy* (London: Vintage, 2004), passim.

57. Harold Macmillan, "Dear Friend" cable to John F. Kennedy, see "UK: General January–June 1962, President's Office Files," JFKL.

58. John F. Kennedy, cable to Winston Churchill, "UK: General January–June 1962, President's Office Files," JFKL.

59. For the queen's letter to John F. Kennedy, see "UK: General January–June 1962, President's Office Files," JFKL.

60. David Ormsby-Gore, letter to John F. Kennedy, July 24, 1962, "UK: General January–June 1962, President's Office Files," JFKL.

61. For John F. Kennedy's speech in Philadelphia on July 4, 1962, see *Public Papers of the Presidents, 1962*, item 278.

62. Harold Macmillan, letter to John F. Kennedy, June 5, 1962, quoted in Horne, *Harold Macmillan: Volume II*, p. 329.

63. *HMD*, entry for May 19, 1962; see also Charles Williams, *Harold Macmillan* (London: Weidenfeld and Nicolson, 2009), p. 408.

64. McNamara, commencement address at the University of Michigan, Ann Arbor, June 16, 1962, US Department of Defense Archives.

65. Harold Macmillan to Dean Rusk, quoted in Horne, *Harold Macmillan: Volume II*, p. 330.

66. Harold Macmillan to Peter Thorneycroft, September 23, 1962, Cabinet Papers, PREM 11/3779, UKNA.

67. *Hansard* parliamentary report, June 26, 1962.

68. David Ormsby-Gore, letter to John F. Kennedy, July 13, 1962, "UK: General, January–June 1962," JFKL.

69. Horne, *Harold Macmillan: Volume II*, p. 417.

70. Cabinet minutes from July 10, 1962, Cabinet Papers, UKNA.

71. For Harold Macmillan's outburst to John F. Kennedy from August 18, 1962, see Cabinet Papers, PREM 11/4052, UKNA.

72. For Harold Macmillan's retraction to John F. Kennedy on August 19, 1962, see ibid.

73. Horne, *Harold Macmillan: Volume II*, p. 460.

74. The Trade Expansion Act, enacted on October 11, 1962, gave the executive branch unprecedented authority to negotiate tariff reductions of up to 50 percent around the world.

75. Harold Macmillan, "Dear Friend" letter to John F. Kennedy, September 24, 1962, "UK: General, January–June 1962," JFKL.

76. See Louis J. Smith, *Foreign Relations of the United States, 1961–1963, Volume X, Cuba, January 1961–September 1962* (Washington, DC: US Government Printing Office, 1997), p. 1038.

77. For Macmillan and Kennedy's joint announcement, see "UK: General, January–June 1962, President's Office Files," JFKL.

CHAPTER 7. TO THE BRINK

1. Sen. Kenneth Keating went on to lose his bid for reelection in 1964 to former attorney general Robert Kennedy; President Kennedy always assumed that Keating had been briefed by "rogue elements" in the CIA. See, inter alia, *Memorial Addresses and Other Tributes in the Congress of the United States on the Life and Contributions of Kenneth B. Keating* (Washington, DC: US Government Printing Office, 1975), passim.

2. Louis J. Smith, *Foreign Relations of the United States, 1961–1963, Volume X, Cuba, January 1961–September 1962* (Washington, DC: US Government Printing Office, 1997), pp. 1004–1007.

3. See Christopher Andrew, "The Edge of Destruction," *Spectator*, December 1, 2012; see also Tom Bower, *The Perfect English Spy* (New York: St. Martin's Press, 1995), p. 286.

4. Sidney Graybeal, interview for US National Security Archives, titled *Cold War*, January 29, 1998.

5. Foreign Secretary Alec Home's remarks to the cabinet, October 9, 1962, Cabinet Papers, UK National Archives (hereafter cited as "UKNA").

6. Quoted in Tony Judt, *Postwar: A History of Europe since 1945* (New York: Penguin, 2005), p. 254.

7. See Anatoly Dobrynin, *In Confidence: Moscow's Ambassador to America's Six Cold War Presidents (1962–1986)* (New York: Times Books, 1995), pp. 51–52.

8. Ibid.

9. Quoted in Aleksandr Fursenko and Timothy Naftali, *"One Hell of a Gamble": Khrushchev, Castro, and Kennedy, 1958–1964: The Secret History of the Cuban Missile Crisis* (New York: W. W. Norton, 1997), p. 171.

10. See David C. Martin, *Wilderness of Mirrors: Intrigue, Deception, and the Secrets that Destroyed Two of the Cold War's Most Important Agents* (Guilford, CT: Lyons Press, 2003), p. 130.

11. For details of Operation Mongoose, see "Memorandum for the Record, Task Force Meeting of October 4, 1962," declassified February 23, 2006, National Security Archives.

12. Quoted in Ernest R. May and Philip Zelikow, eds., *The Kennedy Tapes: Inside the White House during the Cuban Missile Crisis* (Cambridge, MA: Harvard University Press, 1997), pp. 60, 88, 99.

13. See Graybeal, interview for US National Security Archives.

14. David Ormsby-Gore, report to London, October 19, 1962, quoted in Alistair Horne, *Harold Macmillan: Volume II* (New York: Viking, 1989), p. 363.

15. As quoted by Macmillan's biographer Alistair Horne, Jacqueline Kennedy seems to have mistaken the date of her entertaining the Maharajah to dinner, which the official White House record gives as October 23, as opposed to the 19th or 20th. It's possible that, speaking some twenty-five years after the fact, Mrs. Kennedy simply confused the sequence of affairs. If so, she was not the only person to be confounded by the fast-breaking events of that week.

16. Robert Kennedy's notes, see "Cuba, Executive Committee Meetings, RFK Notes and Memos," John F. Kennedy Presidential Library and Museum (hereafter cited as "JFKL").

17. For the Macmillan-Kennedy exchange on October 21, 1962, see Cabinet Papers, PREM 11/3689, UKNA.

18. Harold Macmillan, *The Macmillan Diaries: Volume II, 1957–1966* (hereafter cited as "*HMD*"), ed. Peter Catterall (London: Pan Books, 2012), entry for October 21, 1962; see also Horne, *Harold Macmillan: Volume II*, p. 364.

19. See "Dean Acheson Oral History, UK: General, 1962," JFKL.

20. For Harold Macmillan's remark over the photographs, see Chester L. Cooper, *The Lion's Last Roar: Suez 1956* (New York: HarperCollins, 1978), and as quoted in Horne, *Harold Macmillan: Volume II*, p. 365. Macmillan was also sometimes to refer to the situation in Britain as like "living on the edge of Vesuvius," in terms of facing the threat of a Soviet attack.

21. Harold Macmillan, *At the End of the Day* (London: Macmillan, 1973), p. 187.

22. Ibid.

23. Ibid., p. 189.

24. For John F. Kennedy's remark to his brother, see Robert F. Kennedy, *Thirteen Days: A Memoir of the Cuban Missile Crisis* (New York: W. W. Norton, 1969), p. 53.

25. Philip D. Zelikow and Ernest May, eds., *Presidential Recordings: John F. Kennedy: The Great Crises, Vol. III: October 22–28, 1962* (New York: W. W. Norton, 2001), pp. 68–88.

26. Macmillan, *At the End of the Day*, p. 190.

27. Quoted in Fursenko and Naftali, *"One Hell of a Gamble,"* pp. 240–44.

28. See Richard Reeves, *President Kennedy: Profile of Power* (New York: Simon and Schuster, 1993), p. 397.

29. Macmillan, *At the End of the Day*, p. 194.

30. Ibid.

31. For Nikita Khrushchev's remarks to Hubert H. Humphrey, see "Trip Files: Russia," Senatorial Files 1949–1964, box 703, Hubert H. Humphrey Papers, Minnesota Historical Society.

32. Harold Macmillan, letter to John F. Kennedy, October 5, 1962, "United Kingdom: Security 1962," JFKL.

33. David Ormsby-Gore, cable to Harold Macmillan, quoted in Macmillan, *At the End of the Day*, pp. 190–94.

34. Nigel Fisher, *Harold Macmillan: A Biography* (London: Weidenfeld and Nicolson, 1982), p. 297.

35. UK legal advice, October 23, 1962, see "Cuban Missile Crisis," daily chronology, UKNA.

36. Kennedy-Macmillan exchange, Cabinet Papers, PREM 11/3689, UKNA.

37. John McCone, "Memorandum for the File," October 24, 1962, declassified 2002, CIA Archives; see also "CIA Documents on the Cuban Missile Crisis, 1962," AllWorldWars .com, http://www.allworldwars.com/Cuban-Missile-Crisis-CIA-Documents.html (accessed May 19, 2014).

38. Quoted in Charles S. Sampson, ed., *Foreign Relations of the United States, 1961–1963, Volume VI, Kennedy-Khrushchev Exchanges* (Washington, DC: United States Government Printing Office, 1996), pp. 169–70.

39. Khrushchev's late son, Leonid, was actually born in November 1917, six months after Kennedy.

40. Harold Macmillan, *Pointing the Way* (London: Macmillan, 1972), p. 402.

41. Call between Harold Macmillan and John F. Kennedy, October 24, 1962, "Presidential Telephone Transcripts, October 1962," JFKL.

42. See Christopher Sandford, "Sex, Spies, and the 1960s," *American Conservative*, May–June 2013; see also Elie Abel, *The Missile Crisis* (New York: Lippincott, 1966), pp. 127–28.

43. *Hansard* parliamentary report, June 17, 1963.

44. Excerpted speech by Foreign Secretary Alec Home, included in "Foreign Office cable to H. M. Representatives, October 24, 1962," see "Cuban Missile Crisis," daily chronology, UKNA.

45. Quoted in Zelikow and May, *Presidential Recordings: John F. Kennedy*, 3:253.

46. See Kenneth P. O'Donnell and David F. Powers, *Johnny, We Hardly Knew Ye: Memories of John Fitzgerald Kennedy* (Boston: Little, Brown, 1970), p. 334.

47. See Robin Douglas-Home's article in the now-defunct magazine *Now*, March 1967.

48. Quoted in "Lord Harlech (David Ormsby-Gore) Oral History Project," JFKL.

49. Quoted in Thomas Maier, *The Kennedys: America's Emerald Kings* (New York: Basic Books, 2003), p. 383.

50. Horne, *Harold Macmillan: Volume II*, p. 368.

51. Al Seckel, *Bertrand Russell on Ethics, Sex, and Marriage* (Amherst, NY: Prometheus Books, 1987), p. 258.

52. Macmillan, *At the End of the Day*, p. 212 and passim.

53. *HMD*, entry for October 23, 1962.

54. Robert Rhodes James, *Robert Boothby: A Portrait of Churchill's Ally* (New York: Viking, 1991), p. 409.

55. Macmillan, *At the End of the Day*, pp. 214–15.

56. Cabinet meeting, October 25, 1962, Cabinet Papers, CAB/128/36, UKNA.

57. David Ormsby-Gore, message to Harold Macmillan, "Secret: From Washington to Foreign Office Cable No. 2684," see "Cuban Missile Crisis," daily chronology, UKNA.

58. *Hansard* parliamentary report, October 25, 1962.

59. See "UK: Security, 1962," File Ref. JFKPOF-127-018, JFKL.

60. Ibid.

61. Macmillan, *At the End of the Day*, pp. 195–211.

62. Quoted in Zelikow and May, *Presidential Recordings: John F. Kennedy*, 3:288–95 and 3:309–12.

63. Macmillan, *At the End of the Day*, p. 208.

64. See Abel, *Missile Crisis*, pp. 155–58.

65. May and Zelikow, *Kennedy Tapes*, pp. 485–91.

66. William Taubman, *Khrushchev: The Man and His Era* (New York: W. W. Norton, 2003), p. 568.

67. For the *B-59* incident, see Michael Dobbs, *One Minute to Midnight: Kennedy, Khrushchev, and Castro on the Brink of Nuclear War* (New York: Knopf, 2008), passim.

68. See James G. Blight and Bruce J. Allyn, *Cuba on the Brink: Castro, the Missile Crisis, and the Soviet Collapse* (New York: Rowman and Littlefield, 2001), p. 481.

69. Macmillan, *At the End of the Day*, pp. 209–12.

70. See "UK: Security, 1962," File JFKPOF-127-018, JFKL.

71. Macmillan, *At the End of the Day*, pp. 212–13.

72. "JIC (62) 93 (Final) Report—UK Eyes Only," Cabinet Papers, October 1962, UKNA.

73. "UK: Security, 1962," File JFKPOF-127-018, JFKL.

74. Macmillan, *At the End of the Day*, pp. 213–14.

75. Abel, *Missile Crisis*, p. 173.

76. Quoted in Fursenko and Naftali, *"One Hell of a Gamble,"* pp. 281–83.

77. *HMD*, entry for October 28, 1962; see also Horne, *Harold Macmillan: Volume II*, p. 377.

78. See Harold Evans, *Downing Street Diary* (London: Hodder and Stoughton, 1981), p. 224.

79. Cabinet meeting, October 29, 1962, Cabinet Papers, UKNA.

80. John F. Kennedy, cable to Harold Macmillan, "Presidential Transcripts," Files T524/62 and T525/62, JFKL.

81. *Hansard* parliamentary report, November 15, 1962.

82. Foreign Office, "Confidential Memorandum to Certain of H.M.'s Representatives," December 7, 1962, Cabinet Papers, UKNA.

83. See Alan Axelrod, *The Real History of the Cold War* (New York: Sterling, 2009), among many other corroborative quotes by the long-lived General LeMay.

84. See Taubman, *Khrushchev*, p. 545.

85. David Ormsby-Gore, letter to John F. Kennedy, October 30, 1962, "UK: General, 1962, President's Office Files," File JFKPOF-127-008, JFKL.

86. *HMD*, entry for November 4, 1962; also quoted in Macmillan, *At the End of the Day*, p. 220.

87. Harold Macmillan, interview for BBC 1 television broadcast, June 1, 1972.

88. Horne, *Harold Macmillan: Volume II*, p. 382.

89. See "McGeorge Bundy Interview, Nunnerley Papers," JFKL, pp. 2–3.

90. *HMD*, entry for November 4, 1962.

91. See "Oral Interviews, Secretary of State Dean Rusk," JFKL.

92. Horne, *Harold Macmillan: Volume II*, p. 384.

93. For the Kennedy-Macmillan exchange of November 14, 1962, see Macmillan, *At the End of the Day*, p. 215.

94. See Taubman, *Khrushchev*, pp. 10–13; see also "Roswell Gilpatric Oral History," JFKL; and Blight and Allyn, *Cuba on the Brink*, p. 251.

95. Major Anderson, a fourteen-year veteran of the air force, was aged thirty-five at the time of his death. The wreckage of his aircraft remains on public display in Cuba.

96. Macmillan, *At the End of the Day*, pp. 219–20.

97. For John F. Kennedy's speech on July 26, 1963, see "John F. Kennedy Personal Papers, 1963," JFKL, pp. 601–606.

CHAPTER 8. FAMILY FEUD

1. "Lord Harlech (David Ormsby-Gore) Oral History Project," John F. Kennedy Presidential Library and Museum (hereafter cited as "JFKL").

2. Quoted in Alistair Horne, *Harold Macmillan: Volume II* (New York: Viking, 1989), p. 576.

3. Harold Macmillan, *The Macmillan Diaries: Volume II, 1957–1966* (hereafter cited as "*HMD*"), ed. Peter Catterall (London: Pan Books, 2012), entry for December 23, 1962; see also Harold Macmillan, *At the End of the Day* (London: Macmillan, 1973), p. 360.

4. Macmillan, *At the End of the Day*, pp. 360–61.

5. See Horne, *Harold Macmillan: Volume II*, p. 276.

6. Cabinet minutes from April 13, 1960, Cabinet Papers, CAB/128/34, UK National Archives (hereafter cited as "UKNA").

7. Macmillan, *At the End of the Day*, p. 342.

8. "Harold Brown Oral History," recorded interview, July 9, 1964, JFKL.

9. Macmillan, *At the End of the Day*, pp. 342–43.

10. Kennedy note, February 20, 1961, "National Security Action Memorandum 22, UK: Security, Presidential Office Files 1961," JFKL.

11. Kennedy note ("Action Memorandum 143"), April 10, 1962, "UK: Security, 1962," JFKL.

12. See Richard Neustadt, *Report to JFK: The Skybolt Crisis in Perspective* (Ithaca, NY: Cornell University Press, 1999), p. 37.

13. *Hansard* parliamentary reports, November 7, 1961; November 15, 1962; November 29, 1962; and December 6, 1962.

14. Selwyn Lloyd, MP, quoting de Gaulle, interview with the author, November 1972.

15. See Don Cook, *Charles de Gaulle: A Biography* (London: Secker and Warburg, 1984), pp. 361–63.

16. Horne, *Harold Macmillan: Volume II*, pp. 447–48.

17. Macmillan, *At the End of the Day*, p. 334.

18. Cabinet Papers, PREM 11/3779, UKNA.

19. "Roswell Gilpatric Oral History," JFKL, p. 75.

20. Peter Thorneycroft, minute to the Foreign Secretary, November 8, 1962, Cabinet Papers, PREM 11/3716, UKNA.

21. "Walt Rostow Oral History," JFKL, p. 103.

22. Quoted in Horne, *Harold Macmillan: Volume II*, p. 441.

23. See David Dimbleby and David Reynolds, *An Ocean Apart: The Relationship between Britain and America in the Twentieth Century* (New York: Random House, 1988), pp. 254–55.

24. *HMD*, entry for December 7, 1962.

25. Macmillan, *At the End of the Day*, p. 343.

26. Hans Kraus, as quoted in the *New York Times*, December 4, 1972.

27. For the Kennedy-Eisenhower call from December 17, 1962, see "President's Papers, Telephone Transcripts 1962," JFKL.

28. Quoted in Charles S. Sampson, ed., *Foreign Relations of the United States, 1961–1963, Volume XV, Berlin Crisis, 1962–1963* (Washington, DC: US Government Printing Office, 1994), pp. 510–11.

29. Neustadt, *Report to JFK*, pp. 86–87.

30. Macmillan, *At the End of the Day*, p. 358.

31. See "UK: Security 1962, Nassau," JFKL, passim.

32. A very close approximation of these remarks, also privately reported to the author, appears in Macmillan, *At the End of the Day*, p. 357.

33. See "Department of State, Biographic Information Division Note, UK: Security," File JFKPOF-127-024, JFKL.

34. Richard Neustadt, as quoted in Horne, *Harold Macmillan: Volume II*, p. 439.

35. A reference to George Brown (1914–85), a trade-union agitator and maverick Labour politician (whom Kennedy knew and liked) with a well-publicized drink problem. In November 1963, Brown's slurred public tribute to the fallen president later led him to issue an apology for his "emotional" state.

36. "Roswell Gilpatric Oral History," JFKL, p. 88.

37. Cabinet minutes from December 21, 1962, Cabinet Papers, CAB/128/36, UKNA.

38. Quoted in Theodore C. Sorensen, *Kennedy* (New York: Bantam Books, 1966), p. 566.

39. *HMD*, entry for January 28, 1963; see also Macmillan, *At the End of the Day*, p. 363.

40. Macmillan, *At the End of the Day*, p. 120.

41. Quoted in Horne, *Harold Macmillan: Volume II*, p. 446.

42. See Richard Bothwell, *Alliance and Illusion: Canada and the World, 1945–1984* (Vancouver, Can.: University of British Columbia Press, 2007), passim; this is also noted in many Kennedy biographies.

43. *HMD*, entry for January 1, 1963; also quoted in Charles Williams, *Harold Macmillan* (London: Weidenfeld and Nicolson, 2009), p. 429.

44. Macmillan letter, December 21, 1962, quoted in Horne, *Harold Macmillan: Volume II*, p. 443.

45. See "UK: Security, 1962," File JFKPOF-127-024, JFKL.

46. Quoted in Robert Dallek, *An Unfinished Life: John F. Kennedy, 1917–1963* (New York: Little, Brown, 2003), p. 476; see also "'The World Knows What He Was Like,'" *The Age* (Melbourne, Australia), May 17, 2003.

47. Foreign and Commonwealth Office source, interview with the author, London, May 2013.

48. "UK: General," File JFKPOF-127-008, JFKL.

49. See cabinet minutes, oral, Cabinet Papers, CAB/195/22, UKNA.

50. Macmillan, *At the End of the Day*, p. 360.

51. *HMD*, entry for December 26, 1962.

52. Macmillan, *At the End of the Day*, p. 363.

53. See Seymour Hersh, *The Dark Side of Camelot* (Boston: Little, Brown, 1997); see also *American Thinker*, February 25, 2012.

54. Hersh, *Dark Side of Camelot*; see also "Presidential Daily Schedule, 1962," JFKL.

55. *Pravda*, December 13, 1962, p. 2.

56. See Charles S. Sampson, ed., *Foreign Relations of the United States, 1961–1963, Volume VI, Kennedy-Khrushchev Exchanges* (Washington, DC: United States Government Printing Office, 1996), pp. 205–206.

57. Quoted in Aleksandr Fursenko and Timothy Naftali, *"One Hell of a Gamble": Khrushchev, Castro, and Kennedy, 1958–1964: The Secret History of the Cuban Missile Crisis* (New York: W. W. Norton, 1997), pp. 324–25.

58. Castro on Khrushchev: see Michael R. Beschloss, *The Crisis Years: Kennedy and Khrushchev, 1960–1963* (New York: HarperCollins, 1991), p. 543.

59. Macmillan, *At the End of the Day*, p. 218.

60. Ibid., p. 220.

61. Ibid.

62. *HMD*, entry for November 27, 1962.

63. De Gaulle's comments were relayed by a senior military source in the UK embassy, Paris, to the author, April 2007.

64. Stephen Swingler, MP, in the *Hansard* parliamentary report, January 22, 1963.

65. See "Presidential Action Memorandum 218," January 30, 1963, "Papers of President Kennedy, National Security Files," JFKL.

66. Source familiar with Kennedy-Neustadt discussions, interview with the author, May 2013.

67. William Taubman, *Khrushchev: The Man and His Era* (New York: W. W. Norton, 2003), p. 488.

68. See "National Security Files, Congo Cables, Bruce, London to State, December 13, 1962," box 29, JFKL.

69. *HMD*, entry for November 27, 1962.

70. Ibid.; see also Horne, *Harold Macmillan: Volume II*, p. 406.

71. Quoted in Richard Mahoney, *JFK: Ordeal in Africa* (New York: Oxford University Press, 1983), p. 141.

72. Sampson, *Foreign Relations of the United States, 1961–1963, Volume VI, Kennedy-Khrushchev Exchanges*, pp. 231–37.

73. See Macmillan, *At the End of the Day*, p. 156, and passim.

74. Horne, *Harold Macmillan: Volume II*, p. 507.

75. "McGeorge Bundy Oral History," JFKL, p. 44.

76. Beginning with his apparent breakdown in 1931, Macmillan was always prone to a case of "nerves," while Kennedy rarely, if ever, let his mask of equanimity slip. Compare their reactions to the test-ban treaty of July 1963.

77. For the Macmillan-Kennedy exchange on January 19, 1963, see "Presidential Telephone Transcripts, 1963," File JFKPOF-127-022, JFKL.

CHAPTER 9. THE MEN WHO SAVED THE WORLD

1. Harold Macmillan, BBC broadcast, January 30, 1963; also quoted in Harold Macmillan, *At the End of the Day* (London: Macmillan, 1973), p. 369.

2. *Hansard* parliamentary report, February 26, 1963.

3. Private comment about Macmillan, made available by a senior political source to the author.

4. Harold Macmillan, *The Macmillan Diaries: Volume II, 1957–1966* (hereafter cited as "*HMD*"), ed. Peter Catterall (London: Pan Books, 2012), entry for January 28, 1963.

5. Senior political source to the author.

6. Cabinet minutes from January 29, 1963, Cabinet Papers, CAB/128/37/8, UK National Archives (hereafter cited as "UKNA").

7. Burke Trend's shorthand notes of the Common Market meeting on January 29, 1963, Cabinet Papers, CAB/195/22/8, UKNA.

8. Harold Macmillan, letter to John F. Kennedy, January 19, 1963, Cabinet Papers, UKNA.

9. John F. Kennedy, cable to Harold Macmillan, January 30, 1963, "UK: General, 1963," File JFKPOF-140-007, John F. Kennedy Presidential Library and Museum (hereafter cited as "JFKL").

10. John F. Kennedy, private letter to Harold Macmillan, quoted in "Kennedy-Macmillan Relations," *Euro-Atlantic Studies 2012*, p. 30.

11. Macmillan, *At the End of the Day*, p. 465.

12. For Foreign Secretary Home's letter from January 7, 1963, see Cabinet Papers, UKNA, and "UK: General, January 1963," JFKL.

13. *Hansard* parliamentary report, February 28, 1963.

14. The USS *Thresher* sank while conducting deep-sea diving tests some two hundred miles off the coast of Boston, with the loss of all 129 crewmembers. It remains the world's worst submarine disaster.

15. Macmillan, *At the End of the Day*, p. 396.

16. Quoted in John Fisher, *Burgess and Maclean: A New Look at the Foreign Office Spies* (London: Hale, 1977), p. 193.

17. Alistair Horne, *Harold Macmillan: Volume II* (New York: Viking, 1989), p. 466.

18. Harold Macmillan, letter to John F. Kennedy, March 8, 1963, Cabinet Papers, UKNA.

19. Macmillan, *At the End of the Day*, pp. 175–79.

20. Harold Macmillan, letter to John F. Kennedy, March 16, 1963, excerpted in ibid., pp. 456–57.

21. See "UK: Security, 1963," File JFKPOF-127-019, JFKL.

22. See "UK: Transcripts of President's Telephone Calls, 1963," File JFKPOF-127-022, JFKL.

23. See "UK: Security, 1963," JFKPOF-127-019, JFKL.

24. *Hansard* parliamentary report, April 25, 1963.

25. Macmillan, *At the End of the Day*, p. 470.

26. For the David Bruce cable from March 27, 1963, see "UK: Security, 1963," JFKPOF-127-019, JFKL.

27. Macmillan, *At the End of the Day*, p. 234.

28. Harold Macmillan, cable to John F. Kennedy, May 15, 1963, Cabinet Papers, UKNA.

29. Macmillan, *At the End of the Day*, p. 235.

30. See "Presidential Papers, W. Averell Harriman, April 1961–April 1963," File JFKPOF-030-006, JFKL.

31. Quoted in Edward C. Keefer, *Foreign Relations of the United States, 1961–1963, Volume XXIV, Laos Crisis* (Washington, DC: US Government Printing Office, 1994), pp. 758–61.

32. For the David Bruce cable from January 15, 1963, see "UK: Security, 1963," JFKPOF-127-019, JFKL. Added by an unknown hand to the ambassador's wire are the words: "Bundy . . . Did Sukarno get Bruce's watch, too?"

33. Harold Macmillan, speaking in retirement to a political source, made known to the author.

34. *HMD*, entry for November 16, 1962; also quoted in Macmillan, *At the End of the Day*, p. 244.

35. Harold Macmillan, note to John F. Kennedy, May 30, 1963, Cabinet Papers, PREM 11/4593, UKNA.

36. Cabinet Papers, PREM 11/4586, UKNA.

37. For Macmillan's note from June 15, 1963, see File PMPT 273/63, UKNA.

38. Kennedy's words as relayed by a political source to the author.

39. Cabinet minutes from June 15, 1963, Cabinet Papers, UKNA.

40. For the State Department note from June 30, 1963, see "Profile: Philip de Zulueta," HistoryCommons.org, http://historycommons.org/entity.jsp?entity=philip_de_zulueta (accessed May 24, 2014).

41. Philip de Zulueta, cable to McGeorge Bundy, May 29, 1963, "UK: Security, 1963," File JFKPOF-127-020, JFKL.

42. Quoted in Vladislav Zubok, "Deng Xiaoping," *Cold War International History Press Bulletin*, no. 10 (1998): 158.

43. John Profumo made his public admission on June 4, 1963. Since parliament wasn't sitting, and Macmillan himself was golfing in Scotland, the disgraced war minister came clean to Government Chief Whip John Redmayne. Profumo then disappeared from public life and spent some forty years working as a full-time volunteer at Toynbee Hall, a welfare center for down-and-outs in the East End of London. His award of the CBE (Commander of the Most Excellent Order of the British Empire) in 1975 for services to charity signaled a partial return to respectability. John Profumo died in March 2006 at the age of ninety-one.

44. *HMD*, entry for March 22, 1963.

45. See Christopher Sandford, "Sex, Spies, and the 1960s," *American Conservative*, May–June 2013.

46. Quoted in Seymour Hersh, *The Dark Side of Camelot* (Boston: Little, Brown, 1997), pp. 390–97.

47. FBI report to the president, "T. Corbally as Informant," June 18, 1963, declassified, FBI—Freedom of Information Division; see also Thomas Corbally's obituary in the *Daily Telegraph* (London), April 28, 2004.

48. Quoted in David J. Garrow, *The FBI and Martin Luther King Jr.: From "Solo" to Memphis* (New York: Penguin, 1983), pp. 61–63.

49. Daily reports prepared of UK press coverage, collated in "UK: General, 1963," File JFKPOF-127-009, JFKL.

50. Benjamin C. Bradlee, *Conversations with Kennedy* (New York: W. W. Norton, 1975), p. 230.

51. Marcus Lipton (1900–78) was one of those maverick public figures who combined left-wing rhetoric with a strong vein of British traditionalism. Scandalized by the scenes of young girls screaming deliriously at a 1970s concert by the bubblegum group the Bay City Rollers, Lipton announced in parliament, "If pop music is going to be used to destroy our established institutions, then it must be destroyed first." Earlier, in visiting a Brixton youth center where the future prime minister was in residence, he inspired the teenaged John Major to get into politics.

52. *Hansard* parliamentary report, June 20, 1963.

53. David Ormsby-Gore, cable to Harold Macmillan, June 19, 1963, Cabinet Papers, UKNA.

54. *HMD*, entry for July 7, 1963; see also Horne, *Harold Macmillan: Volume II*, p. 513.

55. Macmillan, *At the End of the Day*, p. 474.

56. De Zulueta memorandum, June 30, 1963, Cabinet Papers, UKNA; also quoted in Horne, *Harold Macmillan: Volume II*, pp. 516–17.

57. Macmillan, *At the End of the Day*, p. 473.

58. Ibid., p. 475.

59. "UK: General, 1963," File JFKPOF-127-009, JFKL.

60. Harold Macmillan to the cabinet, July 1, 1963, Cabinet Papers, PREM 11/4586, UKNA.

61. Harold Macmillan, private note to John F. Kennedy, July 4, 1963, in ibid.

62. Quoted in Sarah Bradford, *America's Queen: The Life of Jacqueline Kennedy Onassis* (New York: Viking, 2000), p. 259.

63. Harold Macmillan, letter to the queen, July 5, 1963, Cabinet Papers, UKNA; and as quoted at length by Macmillan in a speech at Oxford University, May 1979.

64. John F. Kennedy, cable to the Macmillans, July 5, 1963, "UK: General, President's Office Files, 1963," JFKL.

65. See Charles S. Sampson, ed., *Foreign Relations of the United States, 1961–1963, Volume VI, Kennedy-Khrushchev Exchanges* (Washington, DC: United States Government Printing Office, 1996), pp. 301–302.

66. Horne, *Harold Macmillan: Volume II*, p. 520.

67. Macmillan, *At the End of the Day*, p. 476.

68. Ibid., p. 477.

69. Ibid., pp. 479–80.

70. "UK: Security, 1963," File JFKPOF-127-021, JFKL.

71. Ibid.

72. David Ormsby-Gore, cable to Harold Macmillan, July 24, 1963, Cabinet Papers, UKNA; see also Horne, *Harold Macmillan: Volume II*, p. 521.

73. According to a Royal Navy source to the author.

74. John F. Kennedy, cable to Harold Macmillan, July 23, 1963, "UK: General, July–November 1963," JFKL.

75. *HMD*, entry for July 24, 1963.

76. See Horne, *Harold Macmillan: Volume II*, p. 522.

77. Macmillan, *At the End of the Day*, p. 484.

78. See Lord Hailsham (Quintin Hogg), *The Door Wherein I Went* (London: Collins, 1975), pp. 217–18.

79. "UK: General, July–November 1963," JFKL.

80. See Arthur Schlesinger Jr., *A Thousand Days* (Boston: Houghton Mifflin, 1975), p. 830.

81. Horne, *Harold Macmillan: Volume II*, p. 525.

82. "UK: Security, 1963," File JFKPOF-127-021, JFKL.

83. "UK: General, July–November 1963," File JFKPOF-127-010, JFKL.

84. John F. Kennedy, cable to Harold Macmillan, August 3, 1963, "UK: Security, 1963," JFKPOF-127-021, JFKL.

85. Harold Macmillan to John F. Kennedy, in ibid.

86. Harold Macmillan to John F. Kennedy, in ibid.

87. Macmillan, *At the End of the Day*, p. 151.

88. For Harold Macmillan's letter from September 23, 1963, see Cabinet Papers, UKNA; also quoted in Horne, *Harold Macmillan: Volume II*, p. 415.

89. John F. Kennedy, letter to Harold Macmillan, "UK: Security, 1963," JFKPOF-127-021, JFKL.

90. State Department paper, October 4, 1963, in ibid.

91. *HMD*, entry for October 7, 1963.

92. Cabinet minutes from October 8, 1963, Cabinet Papers, CAB 128/37/59, UKNA.

93. Memorandum of events by David Badenoch, son of Macmillan's specialist, as quoted in Charles Williams, *Harold Macmillan* (London: Weidenfeld and Nicolson, 2009), p. 447.

94. For the Kennedy-Macmillan exchange from October 9, 1963, see Cabinet Papers, CAB 129/114/80, UKNA.

95. *HMD*, entry for October 12, 1963.

96. See Williams, *Harold Macmillan*, p. 451.

97. Final Macmillan-Kennedy cable exchange, October 18, 1963, "UK: General 1963," JFKPOF-127-010, JFKL.

98. Royal Navy source to the author. In December 1964, Jagan began a period of twenty-eight years in parliamentary opposition before reemerging as president of Guyana from 1992 until his death in 1997.

99. See Edward C. Keefer, *Foreign Relations of the United States, 1961–1963 Volume IV, Vietnam, August–December 1963* (Washington, DC: US Government Printing Office, 1991), pp. 526–27; see also Robert Dallek, *An Unfinished Life: John F. Kennedy, 1917–1963* (New York: Little, Brown, 2003), pp. 683–84.

100. Macmillan, *At the End of the Day*, p. 245.

101. *HMD*, entry for November 22, 1963; see also Horne, *Harold Macmillan: Volume II*, p. 574.

102. Selwyn Lloyd, MP, conveying a paraphrase of this Jacqueline Kennedy–Harold Macmillan exchange, interview with the author, November 1972.

103. Ibid.

104. *Hansard* parliamentary report, November 25, 1963.

CHAPTER 10. AFTERMATH

1. *Hansard* parliamentary report, November 25, 1963.

2. Ibid.

3. Memorandum by William R. Tyler to the secretary of state, NARA: HR-M/DRP 2-7-00, December 9, 1963, declassified, State Department Archives.

4. Robert Kennedy memorandum, "Travel in Cuba," December 12, 1963, declassified, Office of the Attorney General (December 1963) Papers.

5. Jacqueline Kennedy and Harold Macmillan's exchange, quoted in Alistair Horne, *Harold Macmillan: Volume II* (New York: Viking, 1989), pp. 576–79.

6. Ibid.

7. Harold Macmillan, note to Senator Edward "Ted" Kennedy, June 2, 1964, quoted to the author by a source familiar with the Macmillan Deposit, box 553, Radcliffe Science Libraries, Bodleian Library, University of Oxford; see also "A Tribute," "Kennedy, Senator Edward M.," US National Archives.

8. *Fate* magazine letter, November 28, 1963; see also "UK: General, 1963," John F. Kennedy Presidential Library and Museum (hereafter cited as "JFKL").

9. Macmillan's view of the events of November 22, 1963, as conveyed by Selwyn Lloyd, MP, to the author, November 1972.

10. Quoted in Horne, *Harold Macmillan: Volume II*, p. 579.

11. Quoted in Sarah Bradford, *America's Queen: The Life of Jacqueline Kennedy Onassis* (New York: Viking, 2000), p. 310.

12. "UK: General, 1963," JFKL.

13. Harold Macmillan, BBC Television interview, June 8, 1968.

14. "UK: General, 1963," JFKL; see also Harold Macmillan, note to Senator Edward "Ted" Kennedy, June 2, 1964.

15. Selwyn Lloyd, MP, interview with the author.

16. See the oral histories, JFKL; also quoted by a senior political source to author.

17. Selwyn Lloyd, MP, interview with the author.

18. Quoted in Charles Williams, *Harold Macmillan* (London: Weidenfeld and Nicolson, 2009), p. 320.

19. Royal Navy source to the author, July 1994.

20. Quoted in Horne, *Harold Macmillan: Volume II*, p. 605.

21. Bradford, *America's Queen*, p. 324.

22. See numerous Clapton biographies, including that by author, *Clapton: Edge of Darkness* (London: Gollancz, 1995).

23. Horne, *Harold Macmillan: Volume II*, p. 599.

24. For Harold Macmillan's prepared memo to Margaret Thatcher, see Cabinet Papers, UKNA.

25. Horne, *Harold Macmillan: Volume II*, p. 596; also relayed by a political source to the author.

26. See the *Washington Star*, November 27, 1980.

27. Macmillan, *At the End of the Day*, p. 378.

28. Harold Macmillan, as reported in the *Sunday Times* (London), October 17, 1965.

29. *Sunday Times* (London), May 5, 2013.

30. See "President's Daily Schedule (Evelyn Lincoln Papers)," JFKL.

31. Horne, *Harold Macmillan: Volume II*, p. 577.

SELECTED BIBLIOGRAPHY

Abel, Elie. *The Missile Crisis*. New York: Lippincott, 1966.

Acheson, Dean. *Present at the Creation: My Years in the State Department*. New York: W. W. Norton, 1969.

Adler, Bill, ed. *The Eloquent Jacqueline Kennedy Onassis: A Portrait in Her Own Words*. New York: William Morrow, 2004.

Bradlee, Benjamin C. *Conversations with Kennedy*. New York: W. W. Norton, 1975.

Bundy, McGeorge. *Danger and Survival: Choices about the Bomb in the First Fifty Years*. New York: Random House, 1988.

Butler, R. A. *The Art of the Possible: The Memoirs of Lord Butler*. London: Hamish Hamilton, 1971.

Catterall, Peter, ed. *The Macmillan Diaries: Volume II, 1957–1966*. London: Pan Books, 2012.

Clifford, Clark. *Counsel to the President: A Memoir*. New York: Random House, 1991.

Colville, John. *Footprints in Time: Memories*. London: Collins, 1976.

Crankshaw, Edward. *Khrushchev: A Career*. New York: Viking, 1966.

Dallek, Robert. *An Unfinished Life: John F. Kennedy, 1917–1963*. New York: Little, Brown. 2003.

Denenberg, Barry. *John Fitzgerald Kennedy: America's 35th President*. New York: Scholastic, 1988.

Dulles, Allen W. *The Craft of Intelligence: America's Legendary Spy Master on the Fundamentals of Intelligence Gathering for a Free World*. New York: Harper and Row, 1963.

Eden, Anthony. *Full Circle: The Memoirs of Anthony Eden*. London: Cassell, 1960.

Evans, Harold. *Downing Street Diary*. London: Hodder and Stoughton, 1981.

Fisher, Nigel. *Harold Macmillan: A Biography*. London: Weidenfeld and Nicolson, 1982.

FitzSimons, Louise. *The Kennedy Doctrine*. New York: Random House, 1972.

Fursenko, Aleksandr, and Timothy Naftali. *"One Hell of a Gamble": Khrushchev, Castro, and Kennedy, 1958–1964: The Secret History of the Cuban Missile Crisis*. New York: W. W. Norton, 1997.

Gaddis, John Lewis. *The Cold War: A New History*. New York: Penguin, 2005.

Goodwin, Richard. *Remembering America: A Voice from the Sixties*. Boston: Little, Brown, 1988.

Hersh, Seymour. *The Dark Side of Camelot*. Boston: Little, Brown, 1997.

Hess, Stephen. *Organizing the Presidency*. Washington, DC: Brookings Institution, 1988.

Horne, Alistair. *Harold Macmillan: Volume I*. London: Macmillan, 1988.

———. *Harold Macmillan: Volume II*. New York: Viking, 1989.

Hughes, Emrys. *Macmillan: Portrait of a Politician*. London: Allen and Unwin, 1962.

Hunt, David. *On the Spot*. London: Peter Davies, 1975.

Hutchinson, George. *The Last Edwardian at Number 10: An Impression of Harold Macmillan*. London: Quartet, 1980.

James, Robert Rhodes. *Robert Boothby: A Portrait of Churchill's Ally*. New York: Viking, 1991.

Johnson, Haynes. *The Bay of Pigs: The Leaders' Story of Brigade 2506*. New York: W. W. Norton, 1964.

Judt, Tony. *Postwar: A History of Europe since 1945*. New York: Penguin, 2005.

Kennedy, John F. *Why England Slept*. New York: Wilfred Funk, 1940.

Khrushchev, Nikita S. *Khrushchev Remembers*. Boston: Little, Brown, 1974.

King, Anthony. *The British Prime Minister*. London: Macmillan, 1985.

Klein, Edward. *All Too Human: The Love Story of Jack and Jackie Kennedy*. New York: Simon and Schuster, 1996.

Koenig, Louis W. *The Chief Executive*. New York: Harcourt, Brace and World, 1964.

Lasky, Victor. *J.F.K.: The Man and the Myth*. New York: Macmillan, 1963.

Macmillan, Harold. *At the End of the Day*. London: Macmillan, 1973.

———. *Pointing the Way*. London: Macmillan, 1972.

———. *Riding the Storm*. London: Macmillan, 1971.

———. *Tides of Fortune*. London: Macmillan, 1969.

Maier, Thomas. *The Kennedys: America's Emerald Kings*. New York: Basic Books. 2003.

Manchester, William. *Portrait of a President*. Boston: Little, Brown. 1962.

Matthews, Christopher. *Kennedy and Nixon: The Rivalry That Shaped Postwar America*. New York: Simon and Schuster, 1996.

Morgan, Kenneth. *The People's Peace: British History 1945–1989*. Oxford: Oxford University Press, 1990.

Nathan, James, ed. *The Cuban Missile Crisis Revisited*. New York: St. Martin's, 1992.

Navias, Martin S. *Nuclear Weapons and British Strategic Planning, 1955–1958*. Oxford: Oxford University Press, 1991.

Neustadt, Richard. *Report to JFK: The Skybolt Crisis in Perspective*. Ithaca, NY: Cornell University Press, 1999.

Nunnerley, David. *President Kennedy and Britain*. London: Bodley Head, 1972.

Nutting, Anthony. *No End of a Lesson: The Story of Suez*. London: Constable, 1967.

Parmet, Herbert S. *JFK: The Presidency of John F. Kennedy*. New York: Dial Press, 1983.

Public Papers of the Presidents of the United States: John F. Kennedy. Washington, DC: US Government Printing Office, 1962–64.

Raison, Timothy. *Power and Parliament*. London: Blackwell, 1979.

Ranelagh, John. *The Agency: The Rise and Decline of the CIA*. New York: Simon and Schuster, 1987.

Reeves, Thomas C. *A Question of Character: A Life of John Kennedy*. New York: Free Press, 1991.

Rostow, Walt W. *The Diffusion of Power: An Essay in Recent History*. New York: Macmillan, 1972.

Rusk, Dean. *As I Saw It: A Secretary of State's Memoirs*. New York: W. W. Norton, 1990.

Sampson, Anthony. *Macmillan: A Study in Ambiguity*. London: Allen Lane, 1967.

Schlesinger, Arthur, Jr. *A Thousand Days*. Boston: Houghton Mifflin, 1965.

Schwarz, Urs. *John F. Kennedy, 1917–1963*. London: Paul Hamlyn, 1964.

Seitz, Raymond. *Over Here*. London: Weidenfeld and Nicolson, 1998.

Shields, David Brandon. *Kennedy and Macmillan: Cold War Politics*. Lanham, MD: University Press of America, 2006.

Sorensen, Theodore C. *Kennedy*. New York: Bantam Books, 1966.

Taubman, William. *Khrushchev: The Man and His Era*. New York: W. W. Norton, 2003.

Taylor, Frederick. *The Berlin Wall: 13 August 1961–9 November 1989*. London: Bloomsbury, 2006.

Thorpe, D. R. *Selwyn Lloyd*. London: Jonathan Cape, 1989.

Weiss, Richard. *The American Myth of Success: From Horatio Alger to Norman Vincent Peale*. Urbana: University of Illinois Press, 1988.

Williams, Charles. *Harold Macmillan*. London: Weidenfeld and Nicolson, 2009.

Wilson, Harold. *A Prime Minister on Prime Ministers*. London: Weidenfeld and Nicolson, 1977.

Wofford, Harris. *Of Kennedys and Kings: Making Sense of the Sixties*. New York: Farrar, Straus and Giroux, 1980.

Wright, Michael. *Disarm and Verify*. London: Chatto, 1964.

Younger, Kenneth. *Changing Perspectives in British Foreign Policy*. London: Collins, 1964.

IMAGE CREDITS

1. Macmillan birthplace. Photo by C. Sandford.

2. Kennedy birthplace. Photo courtesy of Patrick Dowdall.

3. Macmillans' wedding. Photo used by permission of the Mary Evans Picture Library.

4. Kennedy in car, waving in tickertape parade. Photo used by permission of the Mary Evans Picture Library.

5. Kennedy and Macmillan checking their watches. Photo by Don Pinder.

6. Kennedy pointing, standing next to Macmillan. Photo by Abbie Rowe, White House Photographs. Courtesy of the John F. Kennedy Presidential Library and Museum, Boston.

7. Group shot of US and UK officials. Photo by Abbie Rowe, White House Photographs. Courtesy of the John F. Kennedy Presidential Library and Museum, Boston.

8. The Kennedys and Macmillans together. Photo used by permission of the Mary Evans Picture Library.

9. Dean Acheson. Photo from the LBJ Presidential Library, by Yoichi Okamoto.

10. Robert Kennedy. Photo by Warren K. Leffler, Library of Congress Prints and Photographs Division, US News & World Report Magazine Photograph Collection.

11. Robert McNamara. Photo from the Department of Defense, by Oscar Porter, US Army.

12. President de Gaulle. Photo used by permission of the Mary Evans Picture Library.

13. Robert Boothby. Portrait by Allan Warren.

14. US tank in Berlin. Photo courtesy of the US Army.

15. Kennedy signing Cuban embargo proclamation. Photo from the Library of Congress Prints and Photographs Division, New York World-Telegram and the Sun Newspaper Photograph Collection.

16. Khrushchev with Castro. Photo used by permission of the Mary Evans Picture Library.

17. Kennedy with Sukarno. Photo by Abbie Rowe, White House Photographs. Courtesy of the John F. Kennedy Presidential Library and Museum, Boston.

18. White House Cabinet Room. Photo by Abbie Rowe, White House Photographs. Courtesy of the John F. Kennedy Presidential Library and Museum, Boston.

19. US blockade of Cuba on the high seas. Photo courtesy of the National Naval Aviation Museum.

20 and 21. Kennedy and Macmillan on arrival at Bermuda airport. Photos by Robert Knudsen, White House Photographs. Courtesy of the John F. Kennedy Presidential Library and Museum, Boston.

22. The Orange Bowl. Photo by Cecil Stoughton, White House Photographs. Courtesy of the John F. Kennedy Presidential Library and Museum, Boston.

23 and 24.   Kennedy motorcade at Birch Grove in England. Photos by Harold Waters.

25 and 26.   Macmillan's home at Birch Grove. Photos by Andrew Baird.

27.   Kennedy and Dorothy Macmillan at Birch Grove. Photo by Antony Lewis.

28.   Kennedy with Macmillan at Birch Grove. Photo from the collection of Paul Elgood, author of *Kennedy at Birch Grove*.

29.   Kennedy's telegram of July 1963. Photo from the UK National Archives.

30.   The Profumos in car. Photo used by permission of the Mary Evans Picture Library.

31.   Macmillan and Jackie Kennedy. Photo used by permission of the Mary Evans Picture Library.

32.   Macmillan and Margaret Thatcher. Photo used by permission of Corbis.

INDEX